Citizen-King

CITIZEN-KING

The Life of Louis-Philippe
King of the French

BY T. E. B. HOWARTH

LONDON
EYRE & SPOTTISWOODE

First published in 1961 by
Eyre & Spottiswoode (Publishers) Ltd
22 Henrietta Street, London WC2
© 1961 by T. E. B. Howarth
Printed in Great Britain by
Butler & Tanner Ltd, Frome & London
Catalogue No. 6/2439/1

To my wife

To my wife

Contents

Book One   *page* 13

Book Two   85

Book Three   153

Book Four   245

Appendix I   336

Appendix II   337

Select Bibliography   341

Index   345

Illustrations

1 Louis-Philippe at Reichenau — *facing page* 80

2 Louis-Philippe in 1835 — 80

3 The Duc de Chartres (Louis-Philippe's father) — 97

4 Queen Marie-Amélie in old age — 97

5 The Duchesse d'Orléans — 97

6 Mme de Genlis — 97

7 The Council of Ministers at the Tuileries, 1842 — 144

8 Thiers — 161

9 Molé — 161

10 Casimir-Périer — 161

11 Louis-Blanc — 161

12 Lamartine — 161

13 The July Revolution — 208

14 Queen Victoria's visit to the Château d'Eu, 1843 — 225

15 The Duc de Chartres — 272

16 A cartoon of Louis-Philippe — 272

17 The Letter of Abdication — 289

Acknowledgments

Acknowledgment is due to the Musée Condé, Chantilly, for plates 1, 2, 3, 4 and 5; to the Musée de Versailles for plates 7 and 10; and to the Gernsheim Collection for plate 14. Acknowledgment is also due to the Mansell Collection for photographs of plates 8, 9, 11 and 12; to Photographie Giraudon for photographs of plates 1, 2, 3, 4 and 5; and to Archives Photographiques for the photograph of plate 6.

Preface

This book attempts to demonstrate some of the difficulties of the political middle way and perhaps thereby to refurbish the portrait of its central figure, who remarked to an old friend, Cuvillier-Fleury, towards the end of his life: "They will never do me justice till after my death." Gladstone once declared that the Paris Revolution of 1848 was the greatest disaster in history. Without going so far as that, it is possible to argue that succeeding experiments in the difficult art of governing France have not always shown a notable advance on the eighteen years of constitutional monarchy under Louis-Philippe, which Mr P. E. Charvet in his recent book *France* describes as "a miracle of political skill and balance". Historians of extreme tendencies, to the Right and to the Left, will have none of this – the memory of Louis-Philippe and the July Monarchy is to them an object of hatred and contempt, as it was to their predecessors. But prejudice has a way of exposing itself by excess and if one scrapes away sufficient layers of it – if, for instance, one is prepared to see in the very word *bourgeois* something other than a mere term of abuse – Louis-Philippe emerges not perhaps as a hero, but as a man honourable as men go, and curiously likeable, as even his enemies were inclined to testify.

I am especially indebted to two historians, Mr E. E. Y. Hales, who was rash enough to challenge me to undertake this piece of work, and Mr C. W. Crawley, Vice-Master of Trinity Hall, who not only originally fired my interest in the period by his lectures twenty-five years ago but was kind enough to read my typescript and make a number of detailed suggestions for improving it. I also wish to record my gratitude to Her Majesty the Queen for gracious permission to consult the Archives of Windsor Castle; to the Warden and Fellows of Winchester College for granting me a sabbatical leave of absence which enabled me to work in the Bibliothèque Nationale, the Archives Nationales and the Musée de Condé; to Miss Winifred Towers for helping me to secure permission to work in the Bibliothèque de l'Institut; to Dr Peter Partner for much valuable criticism and encouragement; to Mr C. Callaghan of Twickenham; to Mr J. M. G. Blakiston for advice on the illustrations; to Mr J. H. Greenwood for making a map of the Valmy Campaign; and to Miss Judith Bazeley for her secretarial labours.

The abundance of printed material on this subject in French, some indication of which is to be found in the bibliography, has impelled me as a general rule to confine footnote attributions to comparatively out-of-the-way sources.

Book One

Damnosa hereditas – GAIUS

I

That the French Revolution began in 1789 used to be in the nature of an immutable historical truth. If we are now learning to look further back in time to a point where the discontent of the privileged classes – the so-called *révolte nobiliaire* – began to assume revolutionary proportions, it is arguable that the really decisive moment occurred on November 19th, 1787. On that day Louis XVI attended the Parlement of Paris with the intention of requiring it to register a loan of twelve million francs. This was a rather desperate expedient to put the royal finances into some semblance of order, so that the Court could continue the latest phase of its long-drawn-out struggle with the Parlements which, having raged intermittently from the early years of the previous reign, had erupted violently in the summer of 1787. After nine hours of heated discussion at the end of which the venerable Jansenist Robert de Saint-Vincent compared the monarchy to a well-bred young rake ruining himself at the hands of the money-lenders, the King at length emerged from his customary indecisive lethargy and delivered himself of the following words in as firm a tone as he was capable of achieving: "I command the edict to be transcribed on the register of my Parlement and to be executed in its due and proper form." This formula was not that appropriate to the time-honoured procedure of a *lit de justice*, whereby the Parlement could only register a royal edict and was expressly precluded from discussing it. Not unnaturally a frenzied hubbub ensued in which it was possible to hear words like "despotism . . . arbitrary power". The noise began to subside as a rather tall, heavily built red-faced man of forty with a high bald forehead rose from his seat and in an uncertain voice declared: "If the King is holding a session of Parlement, votes have to be counted; if it is a *lit de justice* he compels us to be silent". The

King said nothing, and the speaker, rushing his words as if fearful of forgetting his cue, ended: "This registration is illegal." In the ensuing heavily charged silence the King was heard to stammer angrily: "It *is* legal . . . it's legal because I wish it so." When at the end of the session the speaker emerged into the courtyard outside, the crowd unharnessed the horses from his coach and pulled him in triumph to his home in the Palais-Royal.

The popular hero was Louis-Philippe-Joseph, duc d'Orléans, and first prince of the blood. Less than six years later he was condemned to death as the citizen Louis-Philippe-Joseph Egalité by Fouquier-Tinville on March 6th, 1793, in this very same Grand' Chambre of the Palais de Justice, by then occupied by the Revolutionary Tribunal.

Strained relations between the kings of France and the dukes of Orléans were in no sense a novelty. The dukedom of Orléans had been united to the French crown between the accession of Louis XII in 1498 and the year 1626, when it was conferred on Jean-Baptiste-Gaston, brother of Louis XIII, whose intrigues against Richelieu in 1630 and Mazarin in 1650 typified the sort of activity with which the name of Orléans was to be persistently associated. He had no male heir and the dukedom passed to Philippe, second son of Louis XIII and Anne of Austria, who is a strange figure to find as the progenitor of a family, which was admittedly to display in the next two hundred years an unpredictable variety of character and talents. The soldiers who served under his command at the battle of Cassel in 1677 affirmed that he was more frightened of the April sun adversely affecting his complexion than he was of the powder and shot of William of Orange's forces. But his military prowess so outweighed his notorious effeminacy that he incurred the jealousy of his imperious brother Louis XIV and was never allowed after Cassel to take the field again. After his unhappy marriage to Charles II's sister, he was married to Elizabeth Charlotte of the Palatinate, daughter of the eldest son of Frederick Elector Palatine. Their son, again a

Philippe d'Orléans, before he became Regent of France during the minority of Louis XV, was equally the object of Louis XIV's jealousy, being suspected of poisoning the heir to the throne in 1712 and denied any proper outlet for his remarkable talents as long as Louis XIV was alive.

The son of the Regent Orléans in no sense resembled his brilliant and depraved father. A widower early in life, he severed all connection with court society and retired to the Abbey of Sainte-Geneviève, devoting his life to piety, good works and the study of Jansenist theology. He was the founder of a Chair at the Sorbonne for the exposition of the Hebrew text of the Old Testament, and himself left translations of Saint Paul and of the Psalms. His son, known as Louis-Philippe le Gros, reverted to type, displaying, as an Orléanist biographer elegantly puts it, "appreciably less severe morals". A fat, lazy, generous and affable man, with a decidedly Bourbon partiality for the world and the flesh, he was made early aware of the traditional family jealousy with which he was consistently viewed by Louis XV and did his best to avoid the political turmoil of that disturbed and difficult reign. As a young man Louis-Philippe le Gros wished to marry his cousin Henriette, Louis XV's second daughter, but despite the young lady's evident interest in the project, Louis XV refused his consent to a marriage which would have brought the House of Orléans in closer proximity to the throne. Louis the Pious, the recluse of Sainte-Geneviève, took no interest whatever in the perpetuation of the house of Orléans. Fortunately the widow of the Regent Orléans, the formidable daughter of Louis XIV and Madame de Montespan, described by Saint-Simon as "fille de France jusque sur sa chaise percée", who presided over the Palais-Royal in the absence of its austere master, took the matter forcibly in hand. In December 1743 Louis-Philippe le Gros, grandfather of the future King of the French, married Louise-Henriette de Bourbon-Conti. Painted by Nattier a few years later in the appropriate guise of a highly voluptuous Hebe, the young princess had just emerged from her convent, an extremely pretty girl of seventeen. The nuptial ardours of the young couple became immediately the leading subject of discussion both at court and among the officers of the French army during the War of the Austrian succession in Flanders, where the young Duchess joined her husband. Uxoriousness was not a fashionable habit at Versailles and the Duchesse de Tollard remarked that these young people had succeeded in rendering marriage indecent. The idyll did not, however, endure and by 1749 they were effectively separated, each going their own way, whither it is the concern of the moralist or the gossip-writer rather than the historian to pursue them. Their son Louis-Philippe-Joseph, the future Egalité, was born at St Cloud in April 1747. In 1750 there was a daughter who was to marry the Duc de Bourbon, the last of the Condé family, by whom she was the mother of the ill-fated Duc d'Enghien. The infant prince bore the title of Duc de Montpensier, his pious grandfather having still five years to live before the common people who venerated him as a saint fought over his garments as holy relics.

The education, or more properly the lack of education, of the French Royal family under the ancien régime is an important factor in the history of the last three kings of France before the Revolution. In one important respect the House of Orléans was more fortunate than the elder branch. The Regent Orléans had had a wide variety of intellectual interests as had Louis the Pious, though with a markedly different emphasis. Consequently there developed in the family a tradition of taste in pictures and furniture and an interest in science and new ideas. This was partly attributable to their need for some form of distraction to compensate for the inactivity imposed on them by the jealousy of Versailles. Louis-Philippe le Gros was no intellectual but enjoyed theatrical performances, in which he normally enacted with considerable acclamation the role of a fat peasant, and took a spasmodic interest in building and adding to the family collections. These interests attracted to him as they had to his forbears a private entourage of men of letters, actors, musicians, artists and *esprits forts*. In this way it would be possible indirectly for the young prince, who assumed the title of Duc de Chartres in 1752, to educate himself at a superficial level, despite the fact that he was by temperament at least as idle as his father. But the inadequacy of his formal education to some extent accounts for his subsequent defects of character and forms a remarkable contrast with the intensive upbringing to which he was to subject his own children. Spoilt early in life by his mother, who died aged thirty-two when he was twelve, Louis-Philippe-Joseph was placed in charge of the Comte de Pons-Saint-Maurice, a pompous and unimaginative personage who regarded it as his only real duty to ensure that the young prince was properly princely. The subordinate tutors, who included one member of the Academy and the charming draughts-man Carmontelle, were accordingly instructed in their pedagogic duties by some rather peculiar precepts. For example, Carmontelle was to instruct his pupil in mathematics "during the idle moments of the day . . . and without the unpleasantness which young people are almost always liable to associate with an air of studiousness". Or again, "he must never be allowed to fix his attention on low objects, as for instance servants or dogs". Three of his preceptors slept in his bedroom; at the age of fifteen his private household consisted of twenty-one retainers of one sort and another. Reasonably quick-witted, decidedly good-looking and, as his whole life was to show, incurably indolent, the young Duc de Chartres first emerged into the glare of publicity at the age of nine, when his father had him inoculated for smallpox by a famous Genevan doctor of the day at a time when the official attitude to the practice of inoculation condemned it as "perilous and detestable". He slept at Versailles for the first time on October 5th, 1759, preparatory to being presented to Louis XV the next day; exactly thirty years later to the day his name was to be associated with Versailles in a very different context. On this occasion, however, he was allowed to exercise some of the prerogatives of his rank, which included being granted permission to hand the King his shirt, the latter graciously accepting the proffered garment in a sitting posture to make things a little easier for the twelve-year-old. On November 18th in the same year he was baptized with Louis XV standing as godfather and his wife,

Maria Leczynska, as godmother. His first communion followed in the next spring; in July 1761 he attended his first Parlement; by the age of eighteen he was Colonel of the Chartres regiment of infantry and two cavalry regiments, was an expert rider and shot, and was deemed to have completed such education as had been considered necessary for him. One thing only remained to round off the upbringing of a prince of the blood under the ancien régime – a systematic course in amatory debauchery. Duly launched into this by his father, whose cynical deliberation in the matter recalls the attitude of Lord Holland to Charles James Fox in similar circumstances, the young man after a rather slow start took to this aspect of his education with a persistence and enthusiasm which ensured that he would at least be an expert in one field. A conscientious police agent had the somewhat depressing and monotonous function of recording for the information and delectation of Louis XV the nocturnal operations of the most prominent young man in the court society of the day. His reports are a model of precise documentation in respect of time, place, personnel and technique.[1] Occasionally he allows himself the luxury of something approaching a moral judgement and it would appear impossible to dissent from his magisterial summing-up of the Duc de Chartres in the phrase "tout annonce en lui un fond de libertinage crapuleux".

As the pace became hotter, the Duc d'Orléans, perhaps recalling the far-off splendours of his own protracted honeymoon, began to consider by 1768 the comparative advantages of directing his son's ardours into legitimized channels. There being no obvious German lady available, Louis-Philippe le Gros was eventually won over to considering the possibility of a marriage between his heir and the fifteen-year-old Louise-Marie-Adélaïde, daughter of the Duc de Bourbon-Penthièvre and Marie-Thérèse Félicité d'Este-Modena. The evident disadvantage of this match lay in the fact that for the second time in the history of the House of Orléans it would involve a union with the bastard offspring of Louis XIV. The Duc de Bourbon-Penthièvre, admiral of France and governor

[1] Bibliotheque Nationale MSS. fr. 11.360.

of Brittany, a veteran of Dettingen and Fontenoy, was the son of the Comte de Toulouse, offspring of Louis XIV and Madame de Montespan. On the other hand he was considerably the richest man in France being already the owner of Rambouillet, Dreux, Blois, Vernon, Chanteloup, Châteauneuf, Aumale, Armanvilliers, La Rivière, Gisors, Anet, Bisy and Lamballe (to which he was shortly to add Eu, Dombes and Sceaux). In character he was almost unique among the *grands seigneurs* of the period in leading an existence of the strictest rectitude, dispersing large sums of money to the poor and building hospitals and workshops. Already a widower, he had only two surviving children out of seven and his son was the great tragedy of his life. The same police officer whose meticulous observations enable us to understand all too well the propensities and pursuits of the young Duc de Chartres throws an even more lurid light on the character of the Prince de Lamballe, who had recently married an attractive princess of the House of Savoy, soon to be the close friend of the dauphine Marie-Antoinette. The early death of the Prince de Lamballe in 1768 left his younger sister an heiress with prospects of almost limitless wealth. The Duc de Bourbon-Penthièvre can hardly have regarded the Duc de Chartres as an ideal husband for his daughter, who was still under the tutelege of the nuns of Montmartre, but in the society of the day it would not altogether have been easy for him to find anywhere a young man of a congenially decorous moral outlook. A marriage with the House of Orléans would at any rate offset the stigma attached in the curiously inconsistent social hierarchy of the period to the legitimized descendants of Louis XIV's misdemeanours. Louis XV is reputed to have felt some repugnance at the idea of so much wealth eventually accruing to the Orléans family and events were to prove him unusually perspicacious. However, in the event, he gave his consent. A last-minute attempt on the part of the Condé family to repair their fortunes by putting forward the young Duc de Bourbon as a rival candidate for the young lady's hand was frustrated and the forthcoming marriage, which was to be of momentous consequence in the history of France, was announced by Louis XV on the 1st of

January 1769 as being fixed for the following April 5th at Versailles. It was a particularly magnificent ceremony attended by one present and three future Kings of France, who could not have anticipated that they were assisting at the nuptial celebrations of a future regicide.

II

What were in fact the foreseeable prospects of the young couple in the twenty years that were to pass before the collapse of the brilliant but febrile society of which they were such prominent members by the accident of birth? The proximity of the Orléans family to the throne of France in 1768 had recently become a subject of more than merely idle speculation. Louis XV was now a man of fifty-eight with, as it transpired, six years to live, but three years earlier the dauphin had died, leaving between the Orléans family and the succession to the crown his three sons now aged respectively fourteen, thirteen and eleven. There was no reason therefore to expect that the traditional attitude of wary suspicion with which the Orléans family was regarded by the elder branch would be appreciably modified. The consequences of this attitude proved disastrous for both the characters and the prospects of the Orléans princes. Deprived of all administrative and political functions, allowed to distinguish themselves in feats of arms only to the point where their public reputation could not represent a threat to the royal prestige, they were almost inevitably condemned to a life of frustrating boredom, only too likely to be relieved by viciousness and irresponsibility. In these circumstances certain attitudes and activities had become traditional in the family, some of which were in due course to play a large part in undermining the stability of the monarchy. Mention has already been made of their patronage of various artists and savants. Since the days of the Regent this had not amounted to anything very significant. But it was not long before the Palais-Royal became the headquarters of the most notoriously subversive writers and talkers in Paris. Again, it had long been a tradition in the family to be ostentatiously generous in works of charity and public relief, a means of acquiring popularity and prestige, which it would soon be possible to augment appreciably as a consequence of the gigantic increase in the family fortunes. This, in its turn, required the maintenance of a greatly increased administrative staff closely tied to the family interest. Conscious at once of their grandeur and their comparative impotence, both Orléans and Chartres, despite the easiness and affability of their manners and the looseness of their conduct, were almost obsessionally rigid on points of etiquette, *grands seigneurs* to a fault. Withal, their ambiguous but prominent position in the society of the day surrounded them with a great many far from disinterested adulators. They became natural figureheads for all the subversive elements in a society, which for all its apparent rigidity was about to disintegrate from above.

Four days after his wedding, Chartres and his young wife went to the Opera, where it was observed that a great many seats were occupied by beautiful, if not notably modest, young women dressed in widows' weeds, a concerted demonstration that the marriage was likely to cause temporary unemployment in a certain section of Parisian society. There followed the usual giddy round of summer entertainments as the young couple moved from château to château, Marie-Adélaïde being particularly captivated by the magnificence of Villers-Cotterets, where the entertainment included singing and dancing by a troupe of young ladies masquerading as shepherdesses in pink and blue, as was the fashion of the day, remotely inspired by M. Rousseau's belief in the virtues of the simple life. In all these festivities Chartres cut a dashing and popular figure. Throughout his life he always somehow succeeded in being a hero to his valets and it is possible to detect through all the scandal which accumulated around the record of his life certain redeeming qualities – generosity, physical courage and energy, gaiety and a capacity for making and keeping friends. But marital fidelity was inherently unlikely to be prominent among such virtues as he did possess, and the not very intelligent, lachrymose, sentimental and kind-hearted girl he had married soon lost such hold over him as she was able to acquire. In 1771 she gave birth to a stillborn daughter and it was two years later before a son and heir was born. In those two years certain events took place which were to prove of immense consequence for the future history of the family.

Old Louis-Philippe le Gros had for some time been living in uneventful concubinage with a Mlle le Marquis who had graduated to the Comédie Italienne from her original trade in oysters and had presented her patron with three children. But even extra-marital fidelity was not a leading characteristic in the family, and by 1769 the fat duke had fallen completely under the spell of the recently widowed Madame de Montesson, with whom he eventually contracted a morganatic marriage in 1773. This lady had originally been married at the age of sixteen to an even fatter retired general of seventy-eight, was intelligent, ambitious and strong-minded. Her intrusion on the family scene was to have two important consequences. She was closely linked with the leaders of the Paris Parlement, who were desirous of involving the Orléans princes in their struggle with Louis XV; and she was the aunt of Stéphanie-Félicité Ducrest de Saint-Aubin, Comtesse de Genlis.

In the year 1771 there was a head-on clash between Louis XV and the Parlements. Five years before the King had vented his impatience with the pretensions of that formidably obstinate corps of conservative lawyers in one of the most celebrated proclamations of autocracy in the history of the French monarchy. "It is in my person that sovereign power resides; the courts derive their power from me alone; to me alone belongs the legislative power. If the Parlements persist in offering the scandalous spectacle of a challenge to my sovereign power I shall feel compelled to employ the authority received from God in order to preserve my peoples from the tragic consequences of such enterprises." The Parlements, choosing to ignore observations of this sort, became more obstructive than ever and after the royal authority had been particularly flagrantly flouted in Brittany, Louis accepted the advice of his Chancellor, Maupeou, and abolished them. No doubt Louis-Philippe le Gros would personally have preferred not to become involved in the consequences of this coup d'état.

But it was naturally to the princes of the blood that the enraged *parlementaires*, exiled in mid-winter to the inhospitable provinces, turned for support in their opposition to the new courts set up to supplant them, the so-called Parlement Maupeou, in which among other scandalous innovations justice was to be free. An anonymous placard was posted on the Palais-Royal addressing the Duc d'Orléans in terms which were to presage the future fortunes of his house: "Show yourself, great prince, and we will put the crown on your head." In circumstances like these the family was never to be notable for immediate resolution, but the old duke on this occasion incurred Louis XV's wrath by summoning meetings of his very humble, very obedient and very faithful servants and subjects, Louis-Philippe d'Orléans, Louis-Philippe-Joseph d'Orléans and their cousins Condé and Conti, in which they suggested that "the acts of rigour which the King had been advised to perform were frightening all his subjects and tearing at the heartstrings of his true servants". The consequence was that much to their annoyance they were forbidden to attend at court. They were not forgiven until the end of 1772 and then only on the moderately punitive condition that both father and son paid formal calls on Madame du Barry. By that time Chartres had taken two steps which indicated that any rapprochement with the elder branch would be strictly temporary and superficial. In June 1771 he accepted the vacant Grand-Mastership of the Free-masons, an action of no political significance in itself, but one which was certainly not calculated to endear him to conservative circles at court; and secondly he incurred the suspicion, which would one day harden to implacable enmity, of the dauphine Marie-Antoinette by ostentatiously publishing the far from humble letter of submission which he and his father had written to Louis XV.

Although all this had given Chartres something of a taste for the heady pleasures of political popularity, his predominant interests for many years to come were of a different sort and the arrival at the Palais-Royal of Madame de Montesson's fascinating niece proved to be the point of origin in 1772 of one of the most decisive influences in his own life and in that of his eldest son, the future King of the French. Madame de Genlis was the last and finest flower of the system of petticoat government which flourished with such disastrous consequences almost throughout eighteenth-century Europe with the notable exceptions of Frederick the Great's Prussia and the England of Walpole[1] and the Pitts. She was in every sense of the word a dangerous woman, and even exercises posthumous powers of seduction at this distance of time over her twentieth-century biographers. When she entered the Palais-Royal, now occupied by Louis-Philippe-Joseph, at the age of twenty-six as lady-in-waiting to the young Duchesse de Chartres it was virtually inevitable that she would make very easy meat of the master of the household. The daughter of a bankrupt minor aristocrat, she had been brought up by her mother, as Lamartine put it, "for the dubious destiny of those women to whom nature has been prodigal in point of beauty and wit but to whom society has refused the necessary financial resources". Mother and daughter joined the sumptuous household of the financier La Popelinière at Passy. Here the young Félicité by dint of very hard work indeed acquired her mastery of the harp, whose strings she was to pluck to such effect, learnt a lot about dancing and acting and acquired a taste for learned conversation. She was also exceedingly pretty, and at seventeen married a young army officer, the Comte Charles-Alexis de Genlis, "tant bien que mal" as Talleyrand put it. She enjoyed a few months junketing at his château in Picardy in a whirl of peasant masquerades and milk-baths, but soon began to read voraciously to remedy the defects of a somewhat spasmodic education. By the time she was presented at Versailles in 1765 she had given birth to two daughters (a son was born two years later) and had developed into a mentally precocious and physically seductive young woman with no intention of restricting her range of activity to her conjugal duties. But at the heart of this unprincipled adventuress's character there lay a curious paradox. She had already developed what was to become the dominant

[1] Even Walpole was, of course, very dependent on Queen Caroline.

passion of her life—her rage for instructing and improving other people. She was always to evince a remarkable capacity in her own existence for separating precept from practice. Although her eye was no doubt fixed on the susceptible Duc de Chartres, she emphasized from the moment of her arrival in the Palais-Royal the more serious aspect of her variegated talents. She abandoned dancing. Her duties being the reverse of arduous, she employed her ample leisure in intensive study. She was to write one day a treatise entitled "Traité de l'emploi du Temps" in which she sententiously, if accurately, observed that "it is an important thing in life never to neglect the passing moment, the minutes and the seconds." At this period she was as good as her word, filling out her already considerable knowledge of literature and history with physics, chemistry and modern languages. Already an acquaintance of d'Alembert and of Rousseau, her circle now included Buffon, Gluck, Bailly and Hérault de Séchelles. Marie-Adélaïde's secular education among the nuns of Montmartre had been confined to what was known as *l'orthographe du cœur*, and she fell completely under the spell of her new lady-in-waiting, who gave her such entertaining lessons in spelling, mythology, history and painting. The Comte de Genlis, now Captain of the Guard of the Palais-Royal, being safely in garrison at Charleville, and showing a fatalistic lack of concern about his wife's worldly progress, it was only a question of time before Félicité yielded to the importunities of the Duc de Chartres. She thus at least avoided what Talleyrand called "le scandale de la coquetterie", an exhausting activity which would have interfered with her more serious studies. The effect on the duke was considerable in that he found himself genuinely in love for the first time with a lady who not only played the harp but was extremely learned and anxious to teach him painting. Meanwhile he still awaited an heir. After a miscarriage, Marie-Adélaïde decided to follow the example of Anne of Austria and take the waters at Forges in Normandy, which were supposed to provide a sovereign cure for sterility. Madame de Genlis had to accompany her and the letters between her and her lover, intercepted by Louis XV's postal intelligence service, do not make agreeable reading. Madame de Genlis having written in a long and passionate love-letter that the Duchesse d'Orléans had had some teeth removed, Chartres replied that he hoped to hear that her whole jaw had been removed and that he wouldn't mind if her tongue went with it. The following summer Madame de Genlis' dominance at the Palais-Royal is attested by the skill with which she finally overcame all objections to the marriage of her aunt, Madame de Montesson, with the father of her lover. Perhaps fortunately for family relations, the Duc de Chartres was able to avoid the embarrassment of visiting his step-mother until he became more used to the idea, because of the fact that his wife was enceinte. At half-past three on the morning of October 6th, 1773, she gave birth to a son who became King of the French fifty-seven years later.[1]

---

[1] See Appendix II.

III

Louis XV died of smallpox in May 1774 and few of his subjects regretted his passing. It is a travesty of the Enlightenment, by far the most significant development during his long reign, to interpret it as a sort of cosmic optimism, a belief in the possibilities of limitless progress, which was an attitude more typical of the social romanticism, which was to plague Louis-Philippe in the thirties and forties of the next century. Quite apart from that most cautionary of tales, *Candide*, it is a striking fact that many of the prophets of the Enlightenment were frequently inclined on the contrary to be prophets of woe, Rousseau for instance exclaiming in 1772: "I see all the states of Europe rushing to their ruin and all the people groaning." Nevertheless, the auspices of the new reign seemed initially favourable, despite the obvious personal limitations of the new ruler. A clean sweep of Louis XV's advisers and the appointment among a group of outstanding ministers as Controller-General of Turgot, one of the most self-confident of the political regenerators, held out promise of the fiscal and administrative overhaul, which seemed at this stage to be the necessary prelude to the modernization of French institutions. But the unpopularity of the Maupeou courts led Louis XVI to revive the Parlements as a concession to public opinion and within two years the incompatibility of these two gestures was demonstrated in the fall of Turgot and the reversal of his attempted onslaught on corporate privilege. "At last we shall have some money to spend," observed the King's younger brother, the Comte d'Artois. Vergennes, the Foreign Minister, displayed a similar optimism when he persuaded Louis XVI to recognize the new United States of America in 1778 as a prelude to a glorious but disastrously expensive war.

The relations between Versailles and the Palais-Royal at the outset of the reign looked like taking their usual course with the refusal of Orléans and Chartres to attend the obsequies of Louis XV, since this would involve them in meeting the Maupeou magistrates. Consequently they were ordered not to appear at Versailles, which immediately enhanced their popularity in Paris. Characteristically Louis XVI almost immediately changed his mind, and when he recalled the old Parlements his Orléans cousins were allowed to return to court. Louis XVI and Chartres disliked each other from the outset of their relationship, but for the moment Marie-Antoinette, like most other women, found Philippe amusing and persuaded her husband to allow him to undertake a period of service in the navy, a new enthusiasm of his which had as its object the reversion of the post of Grand-Admiral of France, at present held by his father-in-law, the Duc de Bourbon-Penthièvre. The latter was not fond of the sea and limited his interest in maritime warfare to observing mimic engagements in the Rambouillet canal from a comfortable seat on the shore. Philippe, being younger and more ambitious, was soon to find himself on active service against the English at the sea battle of Ouessant in July 1778, commanding a squadron from his flagship, the eighty-four-gun *Saint Esprit*. Although the French fleet under d'Orvilliers had the better of Keppel, Philippe, more probably through technical ignorance than lack of spirit, was singularly inactive at the moment of crisis and, although his supporters claimed that his conduct had been grossly misinterpreted, he was severely criticized at court. The collapse of his naval ambitions was signalized by his appointment to a sinecure command in the army. He quarrelled with Marie-Antoinette the following year, 1779, and frustrated in his ambitions and apparently condemned to a life of permanent inactivity in his early thirties, he drifted back into an existence of aimless and ostentatious hedonism which resembled that of the Prince of Wales, of whom he was to become a close friend. His tastes were expensive, involving frequent visits to England. He hired a town house at 35, Portland Place, and an establishment at Brighton, was painted by Reynolds and enjoyed watching his pink and black colours competing at Newmarket and Epsom. He visited the House of Commons, watched the Westminster election, hunted in Leicestershire and dined, wined and gambled with Fox and Sheridan. As the acknowledged leader of the Anglomania, which was then the rage in fashionable circles in France, he was prepared to gamble on anything, once laying a winning bet that he would ride naked from Versailles to Paris. Having exhausted the possibilities of the related follies of Anglomania and hippomania, he took to aeronautics, and in 1784 ordered the brothers Robert to construct him a private balloon. On July 5th of that year, before a vast concourse of fashionable carriages in the park of Saint-Cloud, Philippe and the brothers Robert, having proclaimed their intention of proceeding by balloon to Orléans, rose precipitately in the air, as the duke threw out the sandbags that acted as ballast. The balloon rapidly beat the previous altitude record of 3,000 metres and began to be blown about most alarmingly while the rudder and taffeta oars, with which the enterprising brothers had hoped to steer, proved completely useless. Showing very great courage, Philippe climbed the suspension ropes and gashed a hole in the balloon with his knife, whereupon the whole apparatus descended with terrifying rapidity, narrowly missing a pond and coming to rest in the adjacent park of Meudon. Like the battle of Ouessant, this somewhat grotesque adventure earned for Philippe innumerable savage witticisms from his enemies, who suggested falsely that he had crouched shivering in the hammock of the balloon, just as he had cowered below deck at the battle of Ouessant. In one way and another he seemed fated never to make his mark and he was increasingly tempted to concentrate on his own circle of clients and admirers at the Palais-Royal, which his father had made over to him in 1781.

By 1780 the income of Philippe and his wife equalled only the interest accumulated on their debts and bankruptcy stared them in the face, a situation from which it seemed they could only be rescued by the death of the virtuous old Duc de Bourbon-Penthièvre. Impressed by the amount of speculative building going on in Paris at the time, Madame de Genlis' brother, the

Marquis Ducrest, persuaded Philippe that the solution lay in the development and exploitation of the Palais-Royal itself, originally built for Richelieu in 1629 and rebuilt in 1763. The idea was to surround the garden with a rectangular block of buildings on three sides which would be let as shops looking on to covered arcades, to which the public would be given access. The opposition of the neighbouring householders and the initial cost of the enterprise were formidable difficulties to be overcome. However, after effecting economies which temporarily included reducing his household by a hundred valets and selling his racing stables to the Comte d'Artois, Philippe and his architect Victor Louis triumphantly carried out the enterprise in three years. The dazzling white arcades housed restaurants, cafés, billiard-saloons and shops of all sorts, while clubs, masonic lodges and gaming-houses flourished on the floor above. Into the same arcades, which are today filled for the most part with rather depressed looking shops selling foreign postage-stamps, thronged a huge crowd of Parisians, ranging from respectable citizens to money-changers and sellers of doves of every type and description. In Macaulay's view it was to become "the spot in all the earth in which the good and evil of civilization are most strikingly exhibited". The habitués of the Café Foy in arcades 56 to 62 were soon known to the police as a dangerous and seditious group and the underground Café du Caveau became the headquarters of the stock-exchange gamblers. The effect on Philippe's popularity among the Parisians was not unnaturally considerable. Meeting him frequently on their daily walks and noting the ease and familiarity of his manner, they contrasted him to his advantage with the King whom they practically never saw. When on the death of his father in 1785, Philippe became Duc d'Orléans, *Altesse Sérénissime* and first prince of the blood, he was already regarded as the most popular and generous benefactor of the common people.

In this first decade of Louis XVI's reign many changes had occurred in the life of the Orléans family, but as might have been expected Madame de Genlis had succeeded in consolidating and exploiting the position she had so dexterously acquired in 1772.

Her hold over the volatile emotions of Philippe had long been surrendered to a succession of *maîtresses en titre*, culminating in Madame de Buffon, the unhappily married daughter-in-law of the illustrious scientist, whose son was described by Rivarol as "the worst chapter in his father's natural history". But, although the Comte de Genlis, who became Marquis de Sillery, continued to be loosely attached to the Palais-Royal circle, he presented no obstacle to his wife's career. If her physical charms no longer captivated Philippe, Félicité had a good many other strings to her harp. Voyaging happily through Italy with Marie-Adélaïde, who for a long time remained naïvely besotted with the woman who had stolen her husband almost under her very eyes, she paid a ceremonial call on Voltaire at Ferney. Soon she was writing and producing "educational" comedies for her daughters, attended by audiences which included men of the calibre of La Harpe, the future mentor of Alexander I of Russia, d'Alembert and Diderot. But it was in 1777 that the first formal step was taken in the career of the most celebrated governess in history with the exception of Madame de Maintenon. In that year it was decided that she should be governess to the infant twin daughters, Adélaïde and Françoise, who had just been born into a family which now included, as well as Louis-Philippe, his second brother the Comte de Montpensier (born in 1775), and was to be rounded off by the birth of the Comte de Beaujolais in 1779. She decided, no doubt rightly, that the atmosphere of the Palais-Royal was not likely to be suitable for the intensive and high-minded education of the young princesses which she envisaged. So in the grounds of the convent of Belle-Chasse near the rue de Saint-Dominique was built a two-storeyed pavilion joined to the convent by a trellised corridor. It was to become the scene of perhaps the most remarkable educational experiment of the eighteenth century. If Madame de Genlis' educational responsibilities had been limited to the bringing up of the two princesses and her own daughters, Belle-Chasse would have excited less comment, although the governess's Saturday receptions attended occasionally by d'Alembert, Buffon and Madame du Deffand, and regularly by La Harpe, Bernardin de

Saint-Pierre and David were quite sufficient to keep it in the public eye. But in 1782 Philippe took the astonishing decision to entrust the education of his three sons to his former mistress. His reputation for eccentricity was already considerable but this seemed to be flouting convention a little too far. Madame de Genlis was greeted with hisses and hootings at a performance of *Les Femmes Savantes* at the Théâtre-Français and among much ribald verse, which the situation inspired, was the following:

> Le matin ma tête est sensée,
> Elle devient folle le soir.
> Je suis monsieur dans le lycée
> Et madame dans le boudoir.

It was commonly put about that the enormously fat Duc de Luynes was hoping to be employed as wet-nurse to the dauphin. However, for the future history of France the appointment of Madame de Genlis as the governess of Louis-Philippe was to prove no laughing matter because she was to make a brilliant success of her task. She had a philosophy of education based not altogether uncritically on *Émile*, and a practical technique far in advance of the standards of the day. At the base of it lay an absolute insistence on the virtues of industry and regularity, of which she herself was a shining example. Her own published works number over a hundred, and at the age of seventy-six she contemplated rewriting the whole *Encyclopédie* so as to inform it with a belief in revealed religion. "The fairy of the Encyclopaedia", as she was called in her early days at the Palais-Royal, evolved rapidly into a devout and severe opponent of the *philosophes* and she refused an offer of membership of the Academy from d'Alembert. Religious instruction at Belle-Chasse was originally, as was proper, in the hands of a certain abbé Guyot, who had once been to Russia, but Madame de Genlis, proclaiming that she had proved in her books how to teach religion so that it was a popular subject, soon got rid of him and it would seem probable that Louis-Philippe's slightly Voltairean brand of Catholicism can be traced to this unconventional method of instruction. For the rest much of Félicité's educational philosophy followed that of Rousseau – a close personal relationship between teacher and pupil, an emphasis on contact with nature and the desirability of illustrating for the pupil the practical utility of the subjects studied. Rigorous character-training and systematic physical culture (including even gymnastic exercises for the girls) completed a system which so impressed the great naturalist Buffon that he wrote to Félicité: "I am no longer the lover of nature, I leave her for you, Madame, who do more and deserve more. She only knows how to create bodies but you create souls."

IV

At its height Belle-Chasse numbered about a dozen pupils, including Louis-Philippe (created Duc de Chartres in 1785), his brothers Montpensier and Beaujolais and the surviving twin sister Adélaïde (Françoise having died of measles in 1782), Madame de Genlis' two daughters, her nephew César Ducrest, her niece Henriette de Sercey and that mysterious figure known to eighteenth-century history as *la belle Paméla*. The latter joined the circle from England in 1780, Philippe's agent there, Nathaniel Parker Forth, having been instructed to find a small, pretty, dark girl aged six who had to have a short nose and a total ignorance of the French language and would be brought up with the Orléans daughters. Forth discovered an illegitimate child called Nancy Syms whose mother was completely destitute and he recorded his success by writing to Philippe: "I have the honour of sending your serene Highness the prettiest mare and the prettiest little girl in England." When this ravishing creature arrived at Belle-Chasse the general, if uncharitable, conclusion was that she was the illegitimate daughter of Philippe and Madame de Genlis. Certainly both lavished an unusual amount of affection on the child whom they called Paméla and who was to have such a tragic destiny as the wife of Lord Edward Fitzgerald. Mrs Wyndham, Madame de Genlis' latest biographer, on the whole supports the story; the judicious M. Castelot and others discount it completely and there the mystery must be left except that one wonders whether even Philippe d'Orleans would have had the audacity to educate his bastards (another little English girl was drafted into the party a few years later) alongside his legitimate children under the tutelage of his former mistress. However, whatever the family affiliations of the various pupils at Belle-Chasse, they formed a very happy circle, united by their common adoration of their headmistress whom they all called "mon amie". There were recreations – music, plays and country expeditions – but work, especially for the princes, was very hard indeed. No minute, of course, could be wasted since Madame de Genlis considered that "holidays are more detrimental to education even than bad teachers".[1] Although she had ostentatiously abandoned rouge at the age of thirty-one, she was a great believer in other respects in what are today called visual aids. The rooms were decorated with the portraits of Roman emperors, the staircases with maps, the screens with the faces of the Kings of France. History was taught with the use of a magic lantern. Rousseau had a low opinion of the educational value of modern languages, but here Madame de Genlis felt differently. "I believe a knowledge of Latin to be very useful but not indispensable as it was a hundred and fifty years ago." She affirmed and she believed that if you knew French, English and Italian perfectly you would have the mastery of a literature equal or superior to what antiquity could offer.[2] But she borrowed a technique characteristic of Rousseau's theories by employing a German gardener to talk to the children on their morning walk and an English valet to talk to them in the afternoon. Supper was conducted in Italian and there was a period of Spanish. At twelve Louis-Philippe was extremely proficient in all four languages and his letters in after life were to be studded with foreign phrases used with a curious felicity and accuracy. The Belle-Chasse curriculum, giving pride of place to modern languages and literature, consisted also of history, geography, literary criticism (here Madame de Genlis ingeniously started with the worst authors and worked upwards), Bible study (omitting those sections of the Old Testament offensive to *la pudeur*), mathematics, physics, mechanics, chemistry, botany, mineralogy, anatomy, physiology, art, music, Latin, Greek, a little law, dancing, gymnastics, riding, fencing and swimming.

[1] A view also held by John Wesley, to judge by the curriculum he enjoined on Kingswood School, Bath.

[2] Sainte-Beuve criticized her educational system on the grounds that the children were not offered enough of the grandeur of antiquity.

Great emphasis was also laid on practical matters like carpentry, farming, metalwork, bookbinding, weaving and visits to factories.

It is not to be supposed that Madame de Genlis undertook all the teaching herself, although she certainly did a great deal of it. Among the subordinate tutors was an elderly mathematics master, M. Lebrun, one of whose jobs was to keep a day-to-day diary recording every detail of the princes' education, leaving in Madame de Genlis' words "a margin on each page for my observations". This document[1] in Lebrun's meticulous little handwriting, diversified by magisterial comments from the headmistress, gives an astonishing impression of the assiduity and regularity of the whole process. One entry, typical of innumerable others, will serve as an illustration. It is that of August 7th, 1788, the month in which the States-General was summoned for the following May.

> We rose at 6.30 the princes were properly dressed about quarter to eight, after having said prayers, completed the dumb-bell exercises and carried pitchers, all three showing the best possible will. We wished M. le Comte de Beaujolais many happy returns, as today he starts his tenth year. Breakfast as usual eaten with a hearty appetite and gay and intelligent conversation. At 8.30 Geometry, M. le duc de Chartres good, his brother very fair. At 9 writing, all three very good and showing plenty of application. At 9.45 dates, very good; then they were shown some patterns of material. At 10 Latin, M. le duc de Chartres very fair, M. le duc de Montpensier a very poor lesson. Arithmetic for M. le comte de Beaujolais, very good and showing great application. At 11 fencing – very good. Even M. le Comte de Beaujolais put his back into it. At quarter to twelve left for Belle-Chasse. . . .

It should be noted that all this took place regularly before the boys went to Belle-Chasse to continue the process under the eye of Madame de Genlis. They returned to the Palais-Royal each evening at 10. Breakfast as a rule consisted of bread and grapes or an apple, one of Madame de Genlis' severer marginal comments reading, "gluttony is the true avarice of children". The physical

[1] Journal de l'Éducation des Princes, in the Musée Condé at Chantilly.

exercises included not only dumb-bells and carrying heavy weights up and downstairs, but also walking about with large quantities of lead in one's boots and plenty of swimming, rowing and riding. The process of ten minutes' daily drill on dates was to make Louis-Philippe in later life a remarkable expert on historical chronology. No detail of the boys' development escaped Madame de Genlis' eagle eye. One of her comments on Louis-Philippe at a rather earlier period reads: "Pay the greatest possible attention to Monseigneur the Duc de Valois' manner of walking. He is very inclined to waddle. He bites his nails and picks them . . . He speaks without opening his mouth . . . he must learn to do this and articulate properly. He must also watch his tendency to forced and noisy laughter." On Louis-Philippe's own admission he was completely transformed as a result of these attentions, although he never quite lost a tendency to guffaw. Nine years old when he was removed from the care of his previous tutor, the indolent Monsieur de Bonnard, he was later to record just how much needed to be done with him. "She made a man of me. At eight I was a feeble, cowardly and effeminate boy. Vinegar made me faint. When I went for a walk two servants had to go ahead of me to drive away the dogs of which I was absolutely petrified. On this subject Madame de Genlis lectured me at great length. She must have carried conviction, because at the end of the conversation I asked her to give me a dog." He was even taught how to make vinegar, as well as mustard, artificial flowers and wigs. As late as December 1787 he was put on a diet of dried bread for failing to achieve the required standard.

The only person who suffered from the triumphant success of Belle-Chasse was the hapless Marie-Adélaïde who had to witness progressively the transference of her children's affections to the enchantress who had already alienated her husband's. Gradually as the revolution grew nearer, there developed an ultimately irreconcilable cleavage between husband and wife. The Duchesse d'Orléans, like her father, remained loyal to the throne, while Philippe and Madame de Genlis became more and more deeply implicated with the leaders of the opposition. Soon Philippe and his wife communicated only by letter. She writes, 'You have resolved to alienate my children even further from me than ever." He replies, "I will take care to bring them up in my principles and not in yours." And she concludes despairingly: "You seem to fear that I am passing on my opinions to my children. You are quite wrong. I love them too much for that. I feel it would be doing them harm to make them hostile to the spirit of the day in which they are destined to live." Louis-Philippe retained a certain devotion to his mother and respected the gentle distinction of her character at this period, but there is little doubt that at sixteen he was passionately in love with Madame de Genlis, on his own subsequent avowal more deeply in love than ever again.[1] It was some years before the scales fell from his eyes.

Meanwhile the long-standing feud between Versailles and the Palais-Royal had taken a dramatic turn amidst the death-throes of the ancien régime. The fall of Turgot was followed by that of Necker in 1781. The ingenious Calonne's attempts to solve the perennial problem of state bankruptcy fell foul of the Council of Notables, which was summoned in February 1787 to bypass the inevitable opposition of the Parlements. Philippe, although summoned to the meeting, preferred not to miss his hunting. But in the crisis that followed the fall of Calonne and the dismissal of the Notables after the Marquis de Lafayette had demanded the convocation of a States-General, it was impossible for him to sustain an attitude of political indifference, surrounded as he was by a circle of intimate friends who were the ringleaders of the opposition to the throne. Many of them were discontented or progressively-minded aristocrats, often boon companions of Philippe's, heavily indebted as a result of their expensive habits, and ready to make common cause with the Parlements in resisting any royal encroachment on their financial privileges. His own personal staff comprised a number of restless and ambitious intriguers, many of them relatives of Madame de Genlis, and she herself had attracted to her *salon bleu* despite her pious attitudinizing a group

[1] One of his letters to her includes the phrase: "What I love most in the world is the new Constitution and you."

· 41 ·

of the most advanced middle class revolutionaries of the day, most of whom would be future members of the Convention. Among the aristocrats, the most celebrated of the Palais-Royal habitués were the Duc de Liancourt, who as Louis XVI's Master of the Wardrobe was to inform him that the fall of the Bastille presaged a revolution not a revolt; the Duc d'Aiguillon and the Vicomte de Noailles, Lafayette's brother-in-law, who between them were responsible for launching the radical social reforms of August 4th, 1789, rather over-optimistically described as "the Saint-Bartholomew of privilege"; the Duc de Biron, who was to command one of Danton's armies, the Comte de la Marck and finally Talleyrand, all three of whom were old and valued friends of Mirabeau, whose hour was about to strike. Philippe's own household officers included Sillery, Madame de Genlis' husband, a future member of the Convention, and the Comte de Valence, her son-in-law, who was at this time in charge of Louis-Philippe's military education and would one day command a division both under Dumouriez and under the Empire. There was also a highly romantic journalist who had done well for the thirteenth child of a Chartres restaurant proprietor, and had the very special cachet of two months' imprisonment in the Bastille. His name was Jacques Pierre Brissot and in the winter of 1791-2 he was to be more responsible than anybody else for initiating a global war, which was to last with one short intermission for twenty-three years. Amongst Madame de Genlis' particular circle at Belle-Chasse were to be found Mirabeau and Pétion (with both of whom her relationship appears to have gone further than an interchange of views about the advantages of constitutional monarchy), Camille Desmoulins, Siéyès, Barnave, and that genius in the art of survival, Bertrand de Barère. Sillery associated with Danton, whom he described as "non pas un coquin ordinaire", and at a party at which Madame de Genlis played the harp, and Desmoulins was reminded of Herodias by Paméla's performance of a Russian dance, the guests included not only Pétion but Maximilien Robespierre.

A group of associates of this sort stretching in its ramifications from the majestic Duc de Liancourt to penniless and ambitious young visionaries, whether vicious like Pétion or virtuous like Robespierre, was a potent influence on the creation of public opinion, and public opinion in Necker's view was becoming more and more decisive. "Most foreigners have difficulty in conceiving the authority exercised in France today by public opinion; they have difficulty in understanding what this invisible power is, that is supreme even in the palace of the King. The fact is however so." There is, all the same, even in France, a gap to be bridged between opinion and action. For this to be achieved favourable circumstances and some form of leadership are necessary. The favourable circumstances were forthcoming in the two years between the dismissal of the Notables and the opening of the States-General; and the Orléans faction was to acquire a leader in the person of Choderlos de Laclos.

V

Calonne's successor as finance minister, Loménie de Brienne, although a member of the Academy and the least clerical of archbishops, hardly inspired confidence as a man capable of liquidating a deficit of 140 millions together with accumulated debts of twice that amount, and the failure of the experiment with the Notables made a constitutional conflict with the Parlements now unavoidable. Although certain reforming edicts were registered piecemeal in the early summer of 1787, the Parlement of Paris was demanding by July virtually complete financial control and the summoning of a States-General and was becoming increasingly fractious under the leadership of one of Philippe's cronies, Duval d'Espremesnil, who with his squeaky voice proclaimed that it was necessary to *"débourbonailler la France"*. By the end of July the land-tax and a stamp-tax were rejected and an attempt to pursue Calonne, reminiscent of the hunt for Buckingham in 1628, resulted in the Parlement being "exiled" to the provinces, a fate which had befallen it five times between 1750 and 1770. A crisis in foreign policy necessitated its recall in September for the session which ended with the Duc d'Orléans' notorious if rather shaky, emergence as a national political figure of the first importance on November 19th. The triumphal plaudits of the crowd which carried him back to the Palais-Royal contrasted rather sharply with a royal command the following day "exiling" the duke to his estate at Villers-Cotteret and imprisoning the abbé Sabatier de Cabre who had coached him specially for the occasion. Philippe's main motive for his outburst had undoubtedly been dislike of his royal cousins but it was consoling to read the protest of the Parlement of Paris: "if exile is the price of the fidelity of the princes of your blood we ask ourselves, with dismay and sadness, what is to become of the law and public liberty..."

"Public liberty" in their interpretation meant little more than control of the government by hereditary and venal magistrates but they were opening a path to something much bigger than themselves. They survived an attempt on the part of Lamoignon, the Minister of Justice, the following spring to proceed against them almost as vigorously as Maupeou had done, and this was followed by serious revolts in the provinces, and in the late summer of 1788 the recall of Necker and the promise of a States-General for the following May. But a States-General voting by orders with a majority of two to one for the privileged classes over the Third Estate, which was the constitutional solution of the Parlements, was by now no solution at all for the liberal aristocrats and the young middle-class lawyers and journalists who frequented the Palais-Royal. Their opposition to the court and especially their hatred of Marie-Antoinette had led many of them to become by degrees, and for good, bad or mixed reasons, champions of the common people. Prices had been rising steadily for some time and a series of natural disasters culminated in the appalling winter of 1788-9. It is more than doubtful if the Duc d'Orléans, sulking through his five months' "exile", cared overmuch about these things – according to Brissot, he was inclined to express his utter contempt for the common people. But he added to his household in October 1788 a recently retired captain of artillery, Choderlos de Laclos, who chose to dedicate his considerable ability to the task of projecting the Duc d'Orléans almost against his will into a position of pre-eminence, for which he had neither the talents nor the energy, in the revolutionary turmoil which was about to break out in France. In so doing he was to predetermine the future fortunes of Louis-Philippe, the young Duc de Chartres, who in this same year 1788 revealed his adolescent sympathy with the cause of liberal reform by symbolically (and effectively) breaking down with an axe the door of the most fearsome cell in the prison of Mont Saint-Michel on a visit there with Madame de Genlis.

Choderlos de Laclos was a characteristic representative of the restless and ambitious middle classes who chafed under the restrictions of a society which denied them what they considered to be the appropriate outlets for their talents. A conscientious officer, he had twice incurred reprimands from his superiors, once for the publication of *Les Liaisons Dangereuses* and once for a work criticizing the technical skill in fortification of the immortal Vauban. Like the young Napoleon he wanted to be posted to the military mission at Constantinople. When this was refused him, he became secretary at the Palais-Royal. Laclos and Madame de Genlis disliked each other at sight – *Les Liaisons Dangereuses* is a singularly unsuitable work *pour les jeunes filles* – but it was Laclos and not the governess who dominated Philippe in the decisive period between October 1788 and October 1789 and it was through his influence that the Palais-Royal became a rather better organized centre of revolutionary activity. The elements that lay to hand for Laclos to work on were the physical constitution of the palace itself, ideally designed for the propagation of rumour and intrigue; Philippe's wealth; and the number of Palais-Royal habitués who saw themselves as pre-ordained members of the forthcoming States-General. Philippe's good nature lent itself easily to the idea of showering largesse on the starving inhabitants of Paris that terrible winter and he was pleased to be called "the Protector of the People" and to be elected deputy for the noblesse by the *bailliages* of Villers-Cotteret and Crêpy-en-Valois, which he preferred to represent rather than Paris, which also elected him. Mirabeau had of course no illusions about his character – "relying on him is like building on mud. But he has been popularly acclaimed, he has an impressive name, he detests the King, he detests the Queen even more and if he lacks courage we will give him some." It was beyond even Laclos' organizing ability to create round such a figure a coherent conspiracy but in certain respects the activities of the Palais-Royal in the winter and summer of 1789 fomented and precipitated the revolutionary situation and launched Philippe on a career of inept political intrigue which was to culminate in regicide, which in its turn was to involve his family in long years of misery and exile.

During the winter of 1788 what Professor Cobban has called "the revolt of the drones" was nearing its term and the active middle classes were everywhere pushing forward their claims for recognition and their plans for a radical reassessment of the structure of French society. Much of the debate centred round the so-called *cahiers de doléances*, in which every electoral assembly was entitled to draw up an address to the crown setting forth its complaints and demands. The extent of Philippe's estates, covering more than three modern departments, naturally gave him a great stake in this process, and Laclos issued a hundred thousand copies of an Instruction in seventeen articles, which was widely copied, especially in the Loire valley. Certain simple peasant localities even forwarded their cahiers with the observation "drawn up in accordance with the instructions of Monseigneur le duc d'Orléans". The Instruction, in common with other cahiers throughout the kingdom, emphasized the need for personal liberty, respect for property and equality in taxation "which ought to be borne by princes as well as peasants". Siéyès, whose pamphlet *Qu'est-ce que le tiers état?* was so enormously influential, was, as we have seen, a familiar of the Palais-Royal and Pétion composed the cahier of Chartres. It is less easy to determine the complicity of the so-called Orléans faction in the first outbreak of blood-letting in 1789, the Réveillon riots of April, in which the workers of the Faubourg Saint-Antoine sacked the house of the wallpaper manufacturer Réveillon, something of a model employer who had however inadvisedly made a speech deploring the effect of high wages on productivity. If there was any one single reason for this affair it was probably the high cost of bread, but it was widely attributed, as were subsequent outbreaks of mob violence, to "bribery by the agents of the Duc d'Orléans".

Shortly afterwards there met at Versailles the long-heralded States-General, of which such millennial hopes were entertained. During the preliminary procession Philippe, dressed as a deputy of the noblesse, placed himself with the Third Estate near Mirabeau. When requested to take his proper place with the princes of the blood, he merely moved over to join the noblesse and proceeded with them amid loud acclamations from the crowd. But as a deputy he cut a very poor figure and refused the Presidency offered him, though there were delirious scenes on June 27th when at the climax of the procedural crisis he took his place with other liberal nobles alongside the Third Estate. Rumour continued to associate him with the most sinister machinations to which the frenzied daily tumult in the Arcades of the Palais-Royal gave every warrant. On June 30th crowds starting from the Palais-Royal forcibly released from the Abbaye prison some soldiers who had been incarcerated for refusing to fire on the people at Versailles, and it was noted that in the general holocaust of the Paris customs posts which began on July 10th two posts belonging to the Duc d'Orléans were spared.

It was during this fateful week-end that the influence of the Palais-Royal as a focus of insurrectionary activity came to a climax. On Saturday, July 11th, Necker was dismissed and he left for Basle that evening. He was replaced as head of the ministry by Breteuil, a notorious opponent of the pretensions of the National Assembly. By this time Maréchal de Broglie had turned the gardens of Versailles into an armed camp and the palace into the headquarters of an army of 50,000, stationed between Versailles and Paris, with a strong detachment under Besenval holding the Champs de Mars and the Champs Elysées. As the news of Necker's dismissal leaked through to Paris it provoked a fury of anger and resentment among the citizens parading their Sunday finery in the Palais-Royal. In the middle of the afternoon Camille Desmoulins, who after a completely unsuccessful career of eight years at the bar now felt that he at last had a truly gigantic brief, was hoisted on to a café table in the Palais-Royal and started his celebrated harangue, which was to launch the insurrection culminating in the fall of the Bastille. The chestnut leaves in the gardens provided cockades "the colour of hope" and it was convenient that in one of the arcades was M. Curtius' gallery, from which it was possible to extract wax busts of Philippe and of Necker, which could be carried triumphantly through the streets. Medals were also struck with Philippe's face on them and the superscription *Père du Peuple*. Across the river the next day at the Cordeliers, another briefless barrister with a much more powerful voice and compelling presence, Georges-Jacques Danton, could be heard inciting his audience to repulse "15,000 brigands mobilized at Montmartre and an army of 30,000 ready to pour into Paris, loot it and massacre its citizens".

Philippe must have heard from his windows the daily shindy in the arcades and gardens of his palace with mixed feelings. Events were moving more quickly than he could have envisaged and in a direction altogether unfamiliar to someone brought up in a tradition of aimless palace intrigue. To be the idol of the people, *le bon duc*, had been an agreeable and flattering experience, but he now seemed in imminent danger of having to mount his horse and do something decisive. When on July 12th Laclos circulated a statement that the Duc d'Orléans was about to issue a general subscription for the relief of the poor with himself at the head of the list, Philippe characteristically spent the day fishing at his house at Le Raincy in the suburbs with Mrs Elliott. She records that when on returning to Paris in the evening he heard what was afoot "he appeared surprised and upset; he told me that he hoped it would come to nothing". He spent the Sunday night not at the Palais-Royal but at Monceau, then just outside the walls, with Madame de Buffon. The next day he went early to Versailles and exercised his prerogative of handing Louis XVI his shirt in the royal bedchamber. He told the King he had come to take his orders. "Orders?" said the King curtly, "I have nothing to say to you. Go back where you came from." On the 14th itself he gave lunch to Lafayette and Bailly at Monceau where after hearing shouting they were told the news of the fall of the Bastille about two o'clock. Lafayette and Bailly left hastily for the scene of the events from which they were both to derive immediate profit, but Philippe stayed at Monceau. Madame de Genlis and her charges were safely off the scene at the country château of Saint-Leu. The following day Philippe went back to Versailles and so far from demanding the lieutenant-generalcy[1] of the kingdom or even making the slightest constructive suggestion confined

[1] A favourite plan of Laclos', based on the historical parallels of the Duc de Mayence and Gaston d'Orléans.

himself to asking timidly for permission to go to England. It becomes easy in the light of this to understand Mirabeau's assessment of Philippe's political capacity: "if we need some sort of a puppet it might as well be that b – as anyone else".

In the event Philippe did manage to escape to his beloved England but only after the night of August 4th had cost him 15,000 livres of income and his name had been particularly closely, if quite inaccurately, associated with the great march of the Paris mob on Versailles. It was on October 7th that Lafayette who was probably responsible for the decision, came to tell him that the King had determined to send him on a diplomatic mission to London to sound the British Government about the setting up of an independent kingdom in the revolted Austrian Netherlands. On October 14th he left Paris with Madame de Buffon and Laclos and established himself at 3, Chapel Street, near Park Lane. It was July 1790 before he returned. In London he achieved nothing because there was nothing for him to achieve. When he eventually returned to Paris it was only to be insulted even more ostentatiously than at Versailles by the courtiers at the Tuileries. As de Retz had said of his ancestor Gaston d'Orléans, "his weakness undermined all his other qualities".

VI

Louis-Philippe was in his seventeenth year during the summer of 1789 when it was notoriously bliss for a young man of advanced opinions to be alive. It seemed especially an exciting summer in which to be the heir to the Orléans tradition. Had not Charles James Fox written to Fitzpatrick, as the latter was leaving for Paris shortly after July 14th: "How much the greatest event it is that ever happened in the world! and how much the best! If you go without my seeing you, pray say something civil from me to the Duke of Orléans, whose conduct seems to have been perfect." Louis-Philippe himself summed up later the political orientation of his education as follows: "Madame de Genlis made honest and virtuous republicans of us but nevertheless her vanity made her desire that we should continue to be princes. It was difficult to reconcile all that!" All his life his problem would be how to come to terms with this paradox. But for the moment it was intoxicating for the young princes to listen to the perennially attractive governess commenting on Rousseau and persuading them of the virtue of renouncing their princely privileges in the name of humanity, that extraordinary abstraction which so hopelessly confused eighteenth-century thought. It is not difficult to poke fun at Madame de Genlis, as did Carlyle.[1] But she had made a great deal of Louis-Philippe, even if he had to pay the price of being enslaved to her body and soul. Her report on him in 1789 reads:

> The Duc de Chartres has greatly improved in disposition during the last year; he was born with good inclinations; he has now become

[1] "Pretentious, frothy; a puritan yet creedless; darkening counsel by words without wisdom! Sincere cant of many forms, ending in the devotional form. For the present on a neck still of moderate whiteness she wears as jewel a miniature Bastille, cut on mere sandstone, but then actual Bastille sandstone."

intelligent and virtuous. He has none of the frivolity of his age; he sincerely disdains the puerilities which so many young men pursue – such as fashions, trinkets, trifles of all kinds and the rage for novelties. He has no passion for money; he is disinterested, despises notoriety and is consequently truly noble; lastly he has an excellent heart which is common to his brothers and sister and which joined to reflection is capable of producing all other good qualities.

It was something of a phenomenon in the House of Orléans for the rising star of the new generation to be almost painfully virtuous, extremely intelligent and well read, industrious and high-minded. No European prince had ever been so deeply and deliberately imbued by his upbringing with the principles of the Enlightenment. He was already, as he was always to remain, a rationalist to the core, a believer in the sovereign power of rationally analysed and clearly expounded ideas. Although an enthusiast he was in no sense a romantic. He was not one to feed his imagination like Napoleon, four years his senior, on Ossian and Werther. What excited him above all in 1789 was to attend with his younger brother Montpensier the debates in the National Assembly and listen to the eloquence of Mirabeau and Barnave. Shortly after Philippe returned to France in the summer of 1790 he gave permission for his eldest son to become a member of the Jacobin Club. Louis-Philippe's own diary suggests that he himself took the initiative in what was the first decisive step in his career and one which he was to regret bitterly for many long years. He was received into the club on November 2nd on the same day as the National Assembly decreed the nationalization of Church property and in the same week as it blasted the political hopes of Mirabeau by decreeing that deputies should be excluded from the ministry, thus setting an example to so many subsequent French assemblies by fatally weakening the executive power through its distrust of the strong man in its midst. At first it all seemed very exciting and in the highest degree significant to a young man of seventeen who could now sign a letter "Louis-Philippe, a French prince by way of expiation for his sins and a Jacobin down to his finger-nails". True, it precipitated a violent quarrel between his parents, finally opening the eyes of Marie-Adélaïde to the effect on her children of the Belle-Chasse education. She demanded the dismissal of Madame de Genlis, at the prospect of which the young princess Adélaïde was overcome with convulsions and fainting fits. Forced at last, after some atrocious scenes, to choose between the two women, Philippe turned his wife out of the Palais-Royal early in 1791 with nothing but the clothes she was wearing. She took refuge with her father and established herself at the Château d'Eu in Normandy. They never saw each other again. Before she left she had the galling experience of seeing Louis-Philippe and his brothers dressed as officers of the National Guard of the district of Saint-Roch.

It was characteristic of the spirit of reflection with which Madame de Genlis had imbued her pupil that he should keep at this stage a day-to-day diary of his existence, full of naïf if generous sentiments. It is an intensely serious document, as befitted a young man who was beginning to see himself as destined to play an important part in the supreme crisis of his nation's history, and it is altogether devoid of the slightly disillusioned witticisms which inform much of his later writing. Of his assiduous attendance at the former Dominican convent in the Rue Saint-Honoré where the Jacobins nightly debated the issues of the day, he writes: "8 January 1791: To the Jacobins at 6. M. de Noailles presented a copy of a work on the Revolution by M. Joseph Tower,[1] in reply to that of M. Burke. He praised it highly and proposed I should translate it. This proposal was met with great applause. I accepted like a dolt, showing I was afraid I couldn't come up to their expectations." He sat on the committee for electing new members and on a commission to examine projects for a public educational system. On more intimate matters he confesses:

For about a year now my youth has caused me almost continuous struggles. I suffer greatly. But there is nothing bitter about this pain. On the contrary it makes me envisage a happy future. I think of the happiness I will enjoy when I have a kind and pretty wife who

[1] Dr. Joseph Towers was a Presbyterian minister, "forenoon preacher at Stoke Newington Green" (D.N.B.).

will afford me the legitimate means of satisfying these ardent desires by which I am devoured. I know all too well that the moment is far off, but it will come one day and that is what sustains me. Without it I would succumb and I would give myself over to all the dissipations of young men of my age. Oh, my mother, how I bless you for having preserved me from all these evils by inspiring in me the religious feelings which give me strength! If I didn't believe in an after-life and if I didn't know that if I were to do anything wrong in this respect it would be like a dagger in my heart . . .

His father would have found all this rather difficult to understand.

The question now was how to win his spurs and serve the glorious revolution. He could look for little guidance or leadership from his family. The Belle-Chasse circle had broken up in the autumn of 1791. The Princess Adélaïde's health being bad (and particularly bad whenever Madame de Genlis left her for a moment), it had been decided she must take the waters of Bath, and so Madame de Genlis, Adélaïde, Pamela and, somewhat incongruously, the dashing Pétion left for England in October 1790, where Madame de Genlis was able to renew some of the acquaintanceships she had made in 1785. Philippe's political fortunes continued, despite all Laclos' vigilance, to founder in the morass of his own idleness and turpitude. The flight to Varennes in June 1791 afforded him a last chance to come forward as the representative of some principle of popularly-based monarchy. Louis XVI was hopelessly discredited[1] but comparatively few of the political leaders were as yet ready to accept the logic of the republican solution. Outside the Tuileries on June 21st the morning after the flight of the royal family, Montpensier, aged sixteen, stood proudly on guard with sword and musket, while Pétion was preparing to escort the prisoners back from Champagne. Philippe drove up and down the Carrousel that day, was received with some acclamation as a Jacobin on the 24th and announced that the Palais-Royal would henceforth be the Palais-Orléans. The

[1] "L'individu royal ne peut plus régner dès qu'il est imbécile," observed Danton in the Jacobins. And Gouverneur Morris wrote, "It would not be surprising if such a dolt should lose his throne."

· 54 ·

idea of a Regency was very much in the air – at all costs the new Constitution about to be finalized must be given a chance to operate – and Laclos worked feverishly in the Jacobins. But by now few people believed in Philippe and above all he did not believe in himself. On the 29th he issued the following statement:

> I am ready to serve my country on land, on sea, in diplomacy, in a word in any post which demands only zeal and a limitless devotion to the public good; but if the question of a regency arises I renounce that right which the constitution gives me now and for ever. I go so far as to say that after having made so many sacrifices in the interests of the people and for the cause of liberty, I cannot now emerge from the position of simple citizenship which I have adopted with the firm resolution of never abandoning . . .[1]

Orléanism seemed to all intents and purposes a lost cause.

Ten days before the flight to Varennes, Louis-Philippe at last had the opportunity of starting his career. In 1785 when he became Duc de Chartres he had been granted the hereditary appointment of Colonel of the 14th regiment of dragoons (Chartres-Dragons) at the age of twelve. This gave him a dark green uniform with pink facings and silver buttons and epaulettes and something of a raison d'être for military instruction under the Comte de Valence. By the spring of 1791 war seemed possible and orders were issued for proprietary colonels to join their regiments. So on June 11th the young Duc de Chartres left Paris for Vendôme to take up his command. He proved himself from the outset a quite model young officer. His diary glows with his pride at finding himself at last on his own, in a position of command and responsibility. Belle-Chasse had taught him the value of early rising and he enjoyed inspecting the stables at six o'clock, wet or fine, while the other officers were still in bed; he was assiduous in his personal presence on parade; he put the regimental accounts in order; and he protested to the municipality about the ubiquity of undesirable female camp-followers. "Nothing stops me in the execution of my duty," he replied in a

[1] It seems possible that Madame de Genlis inspired the declaration out of jealousy of Laclos.

tone which would have delighted Madame de Genlis to one of his officers who suggested that as a prince of the blood he should not be seen quite so frequently with the soldiers in the stables. All this was astonishing enough in a proprietary colonel not yet eighteen, but Louis-Philippe was also fortunate in having the opportunity of diversifying the routine of garrison life by two acts of personal bravery, thoroughly well attested, of the sort that young men of his temperament dream about but seldom have the opportunity of achieving. Three days after the flight to Varennes two local priests, who had refused to take the constitutional oath insulted the "constitutional" vicar who was carrying the Sacrament in a Corpus Christi procession. A crowd assembled round the inn demanding their blood. The young colonel of the Chartres-Dragons broke into the crowd and by main force extricated the two priests and with the assistance of some unarmed dragoons led them away. About a mile off they reached a bridge where another crowd collected with every apparent intention of throwing them into the river. With the mob shouting bloodthirsty imprecations, Louis-Philippe, with the appropriate histrionic gesture which the crisis demanded, placed himself between the priests and a peasant who was aiming a carbine at them and so saved the situation. A few days later he dived into the river to save a local engineer from drowning and was awarded a civic crown by the municipality. After this triumph he wrote: "I think with pleasure on the effect which the news will produce at Belle-Chasse. I was born under a lucky star; opportunities offer and I have only to profit by them."

The opportunities were not long delayed. The declaration of Pillnitz in August 1791 suggested in a vaguely menacing way that in certain circumstances Leopold II of Austria and Frederick William II of Prussia might intervene to restore Louis XVI to his rightful position. That same month Louis-Philippe wrote in his diary: "A lovely day. Long live the dragoons! There's no regiment like them in France; with such men we'll give a fine reception to any beggars who have the audacity to set foot on French soil and the country will be free or we will perish with her.

Today we did an exercise and the dragoons showed incredible ardour, I was captured among the first." Twenty out of twenty-eight officers of the regiment refused to take the civic oath imposed by the Girondins of the Legislative Assembly and the Chartres-Dragons rode up to Flanders at the end of 1791, a stoutly Jacobinical force with a handful of career officers under their enthusiastic young colonel who found himself that winter officer commanding troops in Valenciennes.

VII

Madame Jullien, commenting on the elections to the Legislative Assembly in the autumn of 1791, observed that "everybody thinks there will come from the provinces Aristides, Fabricius, Cato and Cincinnatus". Instead, the destinies of France and Europe were now in the hands of the group of young fanatics initially calling themselves "Jacobin patriots", but soon acquiring notoriety as the Girondins. Doctrinaire intellectuals with an emotional desire for change for change's sake, they were impelled by their political hostility to the Feuillants of the Right to fill a totally inexperienced Assembly with the clamour of their revolutionary patriotism. Article VI of the Constitution was a renunciation of aggressive war and the National Assembly had decreed in 1790 "il faut déclarer que la France renonce aux conquêtes". But the Girondin leaders felt differently. Brissot, for instance, informed the Assembly that "the force of reason and of facts has persuaded me that a people who after a thousand years of slavery has achieved liberty needs war". And thus, competitive rhetoric in the Assembly, combined with the murky intrigues of the court, the pressure of the émigrés and divided counsels in the Ministry brought about a rapid drift towards war, which was finally declared against Austria on March 20th, 1792, with only seven dissentients. 80,000 men were stretched thinly along the frontier from Basle to Dunkirk with the remaining 50,000 in garrison, and two-thirds of the officers of the old régime had joined the émigrés. Nor with one exception was the Ministry of Girondin clients which Louis accepted on March 10th, calculated to inspire confidence. The Foreign Minister, Charles-François Dumouriez, who met Louis-Philippe for the first time this winter, was however a man of immense experience, ambition and energy, now in his early fifties. He claimed to have received twenty-two wounds[1] in the Seven Years War, had served in the Prussian army and had been for a time a prisoner in the Bastille. An admirer and follower of Mirabeau, he was at heart a supporter of constitutional monarchy and, as is evinced by a letter he wrote to Louis XVI in March 1791, initially opposed to war as a solution of the nation's difficulties. He now found himself in the spring of 1792 directing such strategy as the parlous situation of the nation admitted – defence of the frontiers combined with an attack on the Austrian Netherlands. Disaster followed disaster. The ill-prepared advance from Lille to Tournai developed into a panic-stricken retreat, leading to the resignation of one of the two heroes of the American War, Rochambeau, while the other, Lafayette, was plotting to salvage the principle of constitutional monarchy, of which he saw himself the preordained saviour, by marching his troops on Paris. In June the King, whose continued use of his power of veto exacerbated the hatred inspired by the Queen's Austrian connections, dismissed the Girondin ministry and Dumouriez was free to take up a command in the field. In an atmosphere enflamed by food shortages, inflation and fear of the Austrians, the Parisian populace was an easy prey for agitators of the calibre of Marat and Hébert and on June 10th the mob, armed with pikes and scythes, poured into the Legislative Assembly and thence into the Tuileries, Louis being compelled in his own palace to wear a red cap and drink to the health of the nation. From then on the Girondins were to pay the price for playing with fire. All citizens possessing pikes became eligible for the National Guard, hitherto a middle-class organization; all Frenchmen capable of bearing arms were called upon to serve "la patrie en danger"; on August 1st the Assembly authorized a general distribution of pikes; and about midnight on August 9th the tocsin was rung at the Cordeliers as the prelude to the attack on the Tuileries, the massacre of the Swiss Guard and the imprisonment of the royal family in the Temple.

Meanwhile, in the Army of the North the young Duc de

[1] Including one which would have been fatal but for a copy of *Les Lettres Provinciales* protecting his heart from a bullet.

Chartres was preparing himself with characteristic thoroughness for his first great trial of manhood. Just over a fortnight before the Assembly declared war on Austria he wrote to his mother on April 3rd:

> For a long time I have wanted to tell you about my morals, as I particularly want you to know how I am behaving. I can say without hesitation that they are in every respect as pure as they possibly could be, in fact completely intact. My dear mamma has perhaps been imagining that I have been getting into bad habits which are all too common. She can rest assured that nothing could be more untrue, because after all I have been inspired with too many religious principles for that and they are too deeply written in my heart for me to forget them. However, I won't conceal from you that I have not succeeded in keeping myself pure without struggles and suffering and even my health has sometimes been affected. But no matter, I will suffer patiently all the pains God can inflict on me, however great the temptations that surround me and mamma can be sure that I will win through for I would rather die than let myself down. I have opened my heart to you and hidden nothing. If my grandfather had any doubts on the purity of my morals I should be very sorry and ask you, mamma, to get rid of them. I ask your pardon for all these details, into which I've only entered because I know you will be glad to hear of them.[1]

A touching letter from a young man about to go to war at any time, but from a prince of the House of Orléans at the end of the eighteenth century little short of astonishing. With Montpensier he found himself serving under his father's crony, the Duc de Biron, another veteran of the American War. Biron, with a force of 15,000 men, had a staff which included the thirty-nine-year-old Colonel Berthier and Lieutenant-Colonel Alexandre de Beauharnais (future husband of the Empress Josephine) as Adjutants-General and as A.D.C.'s Chartres and Montpensier. Opposing them was the Austrian general Beaulieu, who was to be defeated by Napoleon at Lodi. Louis-Philippe was present at the very first

[1] Bibliothèque de l'Institut, Fonds d'Orléans, 2048.

exchanges of fire at Boussu and Quaragnon. On April 30th there was a more serious encounter at Quiévrain near Jemappes, preceded by a panic flight of several units in Biron's army. In the ensuing engagement Captain Mortier had a horse shot under him and Louis-Philippe was instrumental in ralleying some of the runaways. Biron wrote to de Grave, the War Minister: "Messieurs Chartres and Montpensier have accompanied me as volunteers and being exposed, for the first time, to a brisk fire from the enemy, behaved with the utmost heroism and intrepidity." Mention in dispatches was rapidly followed by promotion. In May the eighteen-year-old Louis-Philippe was appointed a brigadier on the same day as the vastly more experienced Berthier, who had served in America, studied the Prussian army at close quarters and was Chief of Staff to Besenval on July 14th, 1789. His brigade consisted of two regiments of dragoons in the Army of the North, which was now commanded by Lückner, a personally formidable if mentally limited septuagenarian of Bavarian-origin, who could only speak bad French, although the Marseillaise was dedicated to him, and who astonished Dumouriez by summarizing his tactical repertoire in the words: "Moi tourne par la droite, tourne par la gauche et marcher vite." It was a strange army, the blue-coated volunteer battalions serving alongside the white-coated regular units and the undisciplined *fédérés*, the first fruits of conscription, beginning to swell their numbers. But it already included among its serving officers, as well as Berthier, four future Marshals of the Empire – Lieutenant Macdonald, Captain Mortier, and Lieutenant-Colonels Davout and Oudinot, as also Moreau and Jourdan. Lückner managed to advance as far as Courtrai, Louis-Philippe's brigade being in the advance guard, but nervelessly abandoned it in face of an Austrian reaction and fell back on Lille. Dumouriez, relieved of his ministry, now betook himself to the Army of the North but was cold-shouldered by Lückner. At a conference in July with Lafayette, the commander of the Army of the Centre, Lückner recommended the King to make peace and proposed that he and Lafayette should swap armies, ostensibly so that Lückner, the senior, could command on the

Rhine – where the Austrian and Prussian army of Brunswick was expected – but in reality so that Lafayette might be nearer Paris and in a better position to rescue the King. While this extraordinary movement (which involved the two armies as well as their commanders) was afoot, Dumouriez was left temporarily in charge of the North and proceeded to make the most of his opportunities. By August 17th Lafayette was ordered to hand the Army of the North over to Dumouriez and two days later he crossed over to the Prussians and was to remain a prisoner for the next five years during which he can hardly have anticipated he would one day have the opportunity to create one of his younger military subordinates King of the French.

The Army of the Centre with headquarters at Metz was given to the Alsatian Kellermann, who had forty years' service behind him, and Louis-Philippe was ordered to join it. The very slim, fair-haired, blue-eyed young officer was ushered into Kellermann's command-post to be greeted by a large and alarmingly bony general, who, leaning against the mantelpiece, observed, "*Diable!* I've never seen so young a general officer! What have you done, citizen, to be already a general?" However the interview ended on a much more friendly note for the young brigadier's reputation as a brave man had already preceded him. On September 11th he was promoted lieutenant-general and appointed military governor of Strasbourg. This post he refused, pleading that at his age he preferred to remain active in the field. It was nine days before the battle of Valmy.

The capture against an almost total lack of resistance of the frontier fortresses of Longwy and Verdun by September 2nd seemed to many of the panic-stricken inhabitants of Paris to open the way to the capital to the mixed army of Prussians, Austrians and Hessians which the Duke of Brunswick had now interposed between Kellermann at Metz and Dumouriez at Sedan. Brunswick himself, cautious by temperament and as a man of liberal opinions convinced of the unlikelihood after August 10th of an effective counter-revolution, was opposed to any such plan but was overborne by Frederick William and the French émigrés. On

September 5th the allied armies with their supplies based on Verdun crossed the Meuse. The forty-mile wooded plateau of the Argonne separating the Meuse and the Aisne, traversed by the main road from Verdun to Châlons, seemed the only serious obstacle to their advance. Old Lückner was still technically generalissimo at Châlons with Laclos, no longer employed at the Palais-Royal, as his chief of staff, but he was effectively in command of nothing more than a very disorganized staging-camp of volunteers. Behind lay Paris. It was Dumouriez, diverted just in time by the force of events from his preoccupation with an invasion of Belgium, who alone had the energy and genius to control the situation and ultimately to save it. Appreciating that he must somehow block the enemy's advance and effect a junction with Kellermann moving north from Metz, he marched south on September 4th and occupied Grand-Pré, the centre of the three main defiles through the Argonne, and pushed detachments South to secure Les Islettes, the southernmost pass which commanded the Verdun-Châlons road. Dumouriez proclaimed Grand-Pré as the Thermopylæ of France, but by September 12th Clerfayt's Austrians, coming round the French northern or left flank, manœuvred him out of it and were thus athwart his line of communications to the rear. It was behind the position at Les Islettes in the vicinity of the village of Sainte-Ménéhould on the river Aisne, already famous in French history, that the decisive battle was to take place. Before effectively regrouping his forces, Dumouriez had to spend twenty hours in the saddle and inspire some courage into a division which had broken and run before a handful of Prussian hussars. But the position was desperate. In pouring rain with a partially demoralized force he had to await attack not only from the East, the direction of the original threat, but also from an enemy in his rear between him and Paris, and there was as yet no sign of Kellermann advancing from the South to his assistance. Everybody except Dumouriez was in favour of a withdrawal on Châlons, where Lückner was trying to organize his rabble of *sans-culotte* recruits. But Dumouriez stood firm, convinced that Brunswick dare not march on Paris with an

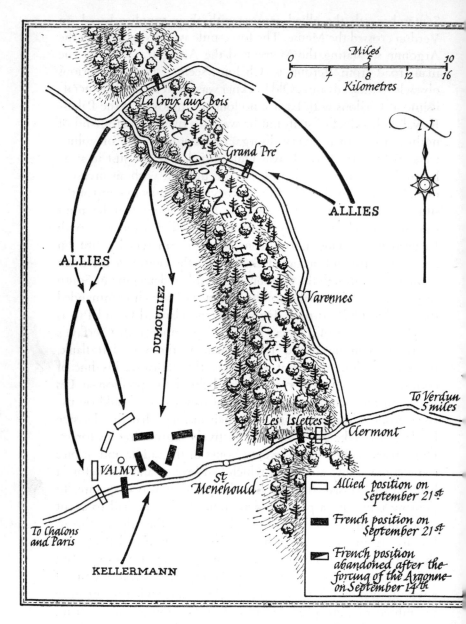

Miles
0   5   10
0   4   8   12   16
Kilometres

N

La Croix aux Bois

Grand Pré

ALLIES

ARGONNE HILL FOREST

ALLIES

Varennes

DUMOURIEZ

To Verdun
5 miles

Les Islettes

Clermont

VALMY

St
Menehould

To Chalons
and Paris

KELLERMANN

Allied position on
September 21st

French position on
September 21st

French position
abandoned after the
forcing of the Argonne
on September 14th

THE CAMPAIGN OF VALMY

undefeated French army across his line of communications. On the 18th some reinforcements from the North brought his force up to 35,000. And on the 19th Kellermann arrived with 16,000 of the best soldiers the French had in the field. As he arrived he divided his force into two lines, one under the Comte de Valence and the other under the Duc de Chartres. Louis-Philippe in the early morning of the 20th was ordered to establish a strong battery position on the crest of the hill of Valmy. His soldiers were so keen to follow him that he could persuade no-one to look after the baggage. He arrived on the feature at eight o'clock. By ten o'clock the cannonade, already aimed on a mill before his arrival there, became intense. There were a number of casualties, including Kellermann's horse, but only one dangerous moment when a shell exploded ammunition caissons in two battalions of Louis-Philippe's division. By eleven the early morning mist cleared and the Prussian military machine was seen, some 34,000 strong, assembling for the attack in parade-ground order. By two o'clock they had slowly shaken themselves out into columns of assault, but somehow the attack never came in. Nothing further happened except for a steady cannonade which probably in all amounted to 40,000 shots fired by the two armies, which nearly depleted Kellermann's stock of artillery ammunition and accounted for a few hundred casualties, the total losses on both sides in this strange but decisive battle. *Hier schlagen wir nicht* ordered Brunswick as he observed the steadiness of the French musketry under fire on the hill and the efficiency of their gunnery. Furthermore, his rations coming from Verdun, via Grand-Pré, were four days in arrears and his soldiers, living off muddy water, grapes and a rough concoction of wheat, were suffering increasingly from dysentery. Early in October the allies recrossed the Meuse on their way to the Rhine, Dumouriez could turn his thoughts again to Belgium and the French Revolution was saved.

At nine o'clock on the evening of September 21st, the day after the battle, Kellermann sent a despatch which was to appear in the *Moniteur* to the following effect:

Du Q-G de Dampierre-sur-Aube, le 21 Septembre 1792,
à neuf heures du soir.

Embarrassed in my choice, I will only cite, amongst those who have shown great courage, Monsieur le Duc de Chartres and his A.D.C. Monsieur le Duc de Montpensier, whose extreme youth makes their courage under one of the most sustained fires ever seen altogether remarkable.

Kellermann[1]

September 1792 was not a month in which hard-bitten military commanders thought it necessary to commend the services of young aristocrats for purposes of mere social propriety.

[1] Cf. Carlyle writing in 1837: "Egalité fils, Egalité junior, a gallant Field-Officer, distinguished himself by intrepidity; – it is the same intrepid individual who now, as Louis-Philippe, without the Equality, struggles, under sad circumstances, to be called King of the French for a season."

VIII

Not much more than a month later Louis-Philippe was to be afforded an even greater opportunity to distinguish himself in the field. But before that he was chosen to return to Paris with the official account of Valmy. Since he had last been home much had happened in the capital with inevitable repercussions on the fortunes of his family. His father had made one final, vain attempt on New Year's Day 1792 to ingratiate himself at the Tuileries when, according to the Minister of Marine, Bertrand de Molleville, he was not only insulted by the courtiers but even spat on while descending the queen's staircase. When war broke out, he tried to secure first of all some sort of naval appointment and then got permission to join the Army of the North, leaving for Flanders in May, accompanied by Madame de Buffon in the family tradition. But unemployed and frustrated, he was back in Paris for the final crisis of the monarchy on August 10th and on September 2nd he and Madame de Buffon from a balcony of the Palais-Royal saw the ghastly spectacle of the sadistic prison murderers parading the remnants of the Princesse de Lamballe's severed and mutilated body on the end of their pikes. She was his sister-in-law and had been his mistress. This revolting carnage made Philippe understandably sombre, but he was too deeply implicated by his past to do anything but drift with the tide. The young Beaujolais, a revolutionary patriot aged twelve, wrote to his brothers at the front: "They say four or five thousand people have been killed.[1] Oh! ça ira, ça ira, ça ira!" The Legislative Assembly, having destroyed the monarchy and with it the constitution, and plunged France into an apparently losing war, now expired. Philippe, who had been ineligible for the Legislative as a member of the National Assembly, sought election to the

[1] A considerable exaggeration, at any rate as far as Paris was concerned.

Convention and asked the Commune to help him solve an awkward problem by giving him a name which he could submit to the electors, since titles had been abolished and his family name of Bourbon was hardly an electoral asset. The lawyer Manuel selected the name Egalité, in consequence of which Louis-Philippe became Général Egalité, Montpensier Antoine Egalité and Beaujolais Léodgard Egalité.

The Convention met on September 20th, the day of Valmy, and the following day proclaimed the Republic. On the 22nd Louis-Philippe called on the War Minister, Servan, with the twofold object of rendering his report on the battle of Valmy and trying to avoid being posted as military governor of Strasbourg. He found this rather undistinguished personage in bed with his head wrapped in a cotton bonnet, ornamented with a yellow ribbon, and in a very bad temper. His report was listened to but the moment he protested about Strasbourg, Servan snapped irritably at him: "Impossible! Your job's been given to somebody else!" As he withdrew a man who had been looking out of the window with his back turned to the discussion come up to him and said: "Servan is an imbecile. Come and see me tomorrow and I will arrange it all for you." Louis-Philippe asked: "Who are you then who can treat ministers like this?" The stranger replied: "Danton, minister of Justice."

Louis-Philippe in later life loved to recount to his sons the interview that took place next day in a first-storey room in the Place Vendôme. Danton told him that he would not be able to stay with Kellermann's army, because the lieutenant-generals' posts had all been allotted. Instead he would go with Montpensier, deservedly promoted lieutenant-colonel after Valmy, to Dumouriez's army. Louis-Philippe agreed, though sadly, since Kellermann's army had many more regulars and better discipline. Thanking Danton, he was about to leave, when Danton called him back:

"You have finished with me, but I haven't finished with you. You are very young, although a lieutenant-general."

"I am about to be nineteen."

"Are you a patriot?"

"Yes, indeed I am, and that sentiment dominates my heart."

"Let me give you some advice before you go. You are talented and will make a success of things, but get rid of a fault: you talk too much. You've been in Paris for twenty-four yours and already, several times, you have made critical comments about September. I know, I've been told."

"But it was a massacre! One can't help feeling it was horrible!"

"Ah, there we are. I know you don't hide your feelings and can't help regaling your listeners with them. Watch out both for yourself and for them. Don't you realize these people were enemies of all of us who have taken part in the Revolution, of your father and your family? You've seen like me the abominable list drawn up at Coblentz. Hung, drawn and quartered. . . . I'm on that list, so is your father."

"That list is apocryphal as everyone knows," and Louis-Philippe continued to protest volubly against the killing of unarmed civilians.

Danton let him go on for a little and then said: "Do you know who was responsible for the September massacres? You are trembling. Tremble as much as you like but sit down and listen quietly." He then launched into a lengthy justification of the necessity of preventing conspiracy in Paris while all the able-bodied were on their way to the front and of ensuring the fidelity of the young volunteers to the principles of the Revolution by "putting between them and the émigrés a river of blood".

The interview ended with Danton saying: "Go back to the army, it's the only place to-day for a man like you coming from a family like yours. Your role is not to mix yourself up in politics, which is our job, but to fight bravely for your country as I admit you've done so far. I know only too well that this Republic we have just proclaimed won't last. Much more blood will be shed. However France will be brought back by her vices, and perhaps also by her virtues, to the monarchy; but not to that of the old régime, which is finished. There will be no going backwards and no fear of forfeiting the triumphs of the revolution. A democratic monarchy will be established. France will never put up with the elder branch of your family, while you, who have fought under the tricolour, you will have a great chance of reigning. Therefore your duty is to preserve yourself. . . . Now go away, general, and join Dumouriez's army and beat the Austrians." [1]

But however dark Danton's forebodings might be, for the moment the indecisive cannonade at Valmy served as a miraculous stimulant for the armies of the infant Republic. Dumouriez, primarily interested in settling old accounts with the Austrians in the Netherlands, allowed Brunswick's Prussians to retire unmolested after abortive negotiations, but in September Montesquieu's army conquered the Sardinian territories of Savoy and Nice and in October Custine overran the left bank of the Rhine, captured Mainz and was across the Rhine. Dumouriez's Army of the North was on the move when it was joined by Lieutenant-General Egalité with his brother as his A.D.C. Louis-Philippe would be able in the heat of battle to banish for the moment some of the disquieting impressions he had acquired during his short stay in Paris.

During the French preoccupation with the Argonne the Austrians had made a half-hearted attack on Lille but had now fallen back beyond the frontier. On October 27th Dumouriez issued an appeal to the Belgians to rise against their oppressors and, while forcing the Austrians to deploy widely by a series of feints, he proceeded to make his main thrust in the direction of the

---

[1] Cf. Revue des deux Mondes, December 15th, 1917. M. Denis Cochon had this story direct from the Duc d'Aumale. In the light of what is now known of Danton there would seem no reason to discredit its essential veracity. Danton was always more a patriotic empiricist than a doctrinaire republican. His venality is notorious and it seems unlikely that some of the flood of Orleans gold released from the Palais-Royal in 1791 did not stick to his fingers, especially since after the flight to Varennes he was instrumental with Brissot in preparing the Champs de Mars petition demanding Louis' replacement by constitutional means, a proposal which exactly suited Laclos' plans that summer. Furthermore in September 1792 he was very closely linked to Dumouriez who already had a high regard for Louis-Philippe. As to his complicity in the September massacres the very best that can be said for him is that he did nothing to stop them.

dismantled fortress of Mons. On November 2nd Louis-Philippe commanding the right wing of the advance guard captured an Austrian battery at the mill of Boussu, where he had first been under fire in the spring. An engraving of this action shows a good many dead horses and a line of French infantry keeping admirable dressing. On the 5th Dumouriez was confronted by an Austrian army only half as strong as his own in men and guns but in a formidable position on the heights of Cuesmes and Jemappes to the west of Mons. The Austrians were commanded by Clerfayt, who had turned Dumouriez's left flank in the Argonne, and was an impressive figure in his stars and gold lace. Dumouriez ordered d'Harville's corps to march to the right in an attempt to cut off the Austrian line of withdrawal from Mons, but in the event the latter was unable to get his raw volunteer battalions moving quickly enough and the battle of Jemappes on November 6th became essentially a frontal assault by the French. Clerfayt's right wing was entrenched in the large village of Jemappes; in the centre was a hill giving excellent artillery observation over the wood and marshy ground in front of it; and on his left were field-works constructed on more high ground in front of the village of Cuesmes. Dumouriez's first attack was repulsed all along the line. While fierce fighting went on in Jemappes and the French right made little headway in front of Cuesmes, the situation in the centre where the French were trying to cross the marshy ground in face of the plunging Austrian fire became critical. Louis-Philippe, commanding in this sector, had formed his division into battalion columns and marched on the wood to his front, leaving in rear a reserve of six battalions. He overcame the enemy light infantry in front of the wood and forced his way through it towards the slopes of the hill beyond. But as the heads of the columns emerged from the wood they were met with a withering fire from the Austrian guns from the redoubt above. They started streaming back into the wood in very bad order and with a good many officer casualties. Fortunately the Austrian infantry did not move and the handful of cavalry sent into the wood in pursuit of the French could achieve little.

Louis-Philippe rapidly formed a chain of cavalry picquets on the near side of the wood to check the fugitives as they broke out of the wood. He then regrouped such units and individuals as he could lay his hands on, christened them "the battalion of Mons" and put them in charge of General Desforest, who had collected five flags abandoned by runaways and despite their weight was carrying them like a fascis. Riding at the head of his men, the young general Egalité finally overran the Austrian centre, now feeling the pressure from Jemappes on the right, and his troops captured some Austrian guns at the point of the bayonet, Macdonald leading a dragoon regiment at the gallop on to the heights. Dumouriez himself rallied the French right, hitherto repulsed at Cuesmes, and by nightfall the victory was complete. Louis-Philippe entered Mons the next day. Dumouriez was now determined to exploit the victory and capture Brussels. On November 13th, 6,000 Austrians barred the route on high ground above Anderlecht and Louis-Philippe with the advanced guard dislodged them after six hours' fighting. On November 14th the army entered Brussels in triumph. Liège fell on the 28th, Antwerp the next day and Namur on December 2nd. By December Louis-Philippe had earned the right to a short spell of leave in Paris which would enable him to see his father in the Palais-Egalité. But before he left the front to which he was to return before the New Year, 1793, he must have realized that there were elements in the situation, both in Belgium and Paris, which were gravely disquieting, despite the speed and brilliance with which the Republican armies had conquered Belgium.

IX

"We must never rest till the whole of Europe is ablaze" was the manner in which Brissot epitomized the war-fever in the first days of the Republic, but the conduct of total war, in itself a new concept quite alien to the eighteenth-century tradition in military matters, required at the centre standards of industry and integrity, which France never found till the days of Carnot and the Committee of Public Safety. While the generals advanced the politicians were engaged in fighting each other to the death. The Girondins in the Convention were at grips with the extremist deputies of the Mountain (among whom Philippe Egalité took his seat), and were continually outflanked by the Paris Commune, now in the hands of violent and criminal demagogues like Hébert. Although the country as a whole still favoured moderate policies, the Girondins lacked the strength of character to provide them. In a hungry capital, fed on rumours of treachery and full of armed men, the phrase-makers and the men of blood were carrying the day. Among the worst mistakes of the Girondins was the appointment as War Minister of the Swiss, Jean-Nicolas Pache, who not only double-crossed his patrons by telling all their secrets to their enemies of the Mountain but regarded his tenure of the War Office as a splendid opportunity for enriching himself and his friends. While urging Dumouriez to attack Cologne or Maestricht he virtually denuded him of supplies. At Jemappes there were no doctors and no field-ambulances and on November 30th Dumouriez wrote to Pache to the effect that his army was melting away and that he was short of money, forage and bread. Huge numbers of the volunteers who had responded to the call of *"la patrie en danger"* now began to desert, so that most battalions dropped to about three hundred men. Dumouriez saw all too clearly the dangers of a further extension of the war. He wrote to

Pache: "I am altogether opposed to every external and aggressive war, especially one which takes us beyond our natural frontiers, that is, on the South the Pyrenees and the Alps, and the Rhine on the East and North-East." He was against the spoliation of the Netherlands and wished to make them independent rather than annex them to France. Other counsels prevailed in Paris. On December 15th the Convention issued its famous decree on the republicanization of conquered territories, irrespective of their constitutional or religious traditions. "Wherever the French armies shall come, all taxes, tithes and privileges of rank are to be abolished, all existing authorities annulled.... Commissioners of the Convention are to be sent into the country to fraternize with the people and emissaries from the government to provide for the maintenance of the French armies." Although Dumouriez succeeded in getting rid of Pache, he could achieve nothing else. Danton voiced the spirit of the day when in the debate on the King's death he bellowed: "Let us fling down to kings the head of a king as a gage of battle." War was declared on Great Britain, the United Provinces and Spain. With a little over 60,000 men, thoroughly badly supplied, Dumouriez knew what he was up against. "Let us perform incredible, nay, impossible feats," he wrote; "we must astonish the enemy, and deal blows with the courage of despair."

Louis-Philippe was in these circumstances beginning to learn before the end of 1792 that neither war nor politics are to be seen exclusively in the light of romantic idealism. Years afterwards he told Montalivet that it was in the moment of triumph at Jemappes that he swore: "to save the world if it were ever in my power the horror of these cruel sports". On returning to Paris he found his father lonely and in low spirits. Elected twentieth and last of the Paris deputies to the Convention, Robespierre being first and Marat seventh, he had been too long an enemy of the Girondins to do anything but take his place among the extremists. As one of his associates remarked rather unkindly: "When one has an income of 400,000 livres one must either be at Coblentz or at the top of the Mountain." Louis-Philippe in September had urged him to go to America instead of sitting in the Convention, but Philippe had merely replied: "Live with black men? Oh no . . . at least here, one has the Opera." His main anxiety was for his daughter whose name now appeared on the list of émigrés. Madame de Genlis was enjoying life in London, Bath and Bury Saint Edmunds and, finding Sheridan's company consoled her for the return to Paris of Pétion, she showed no inclination to bring back her charges despite Philippe's protests. When they finally returned in November they were met at Calais by a message from Philippe warning them not to proceed to Paris. The dauntless Félicité ignored this, but Paris was in fact no place for returned émigrés and soon Louis-Philippe, whose leave coincided with his sister's return, found himself conducting Madame de Genlis, Adélaïde and Pamela to the frontier, it having been decided that they should take refuge at Tournai where he would be able to look after them.[1]

Everything in Paris now centred on the trial of the King, an issue which was ideally calculated from the point of view of the Jacobins to divide and discredit the Gironde. The deputy Egalité's association with the Mountain involved him in an agonizing dilemma. He was present at the session on December 11th when Louis was questioned for three hours at the bar of the Convention. That evening when he returned home he found Louise-Philippe and Montpensier awaiting him anxiously. "What will you do if you have to judge him, father?" asked Louis-Philippe. "I will decline to give an opinion," was the answer. Louis-Philippe, possibly a little reassured, returned to Dumouriez's headquarters at Tournai but left Montpensier behind to watch a situation of mounting peril for the whole family. The crisis was not long delayed. On the 16th the idiotically romantic Girondin Buzot, who always tended to see every issue of the day in terms of classical antiquity, proposed a decree banishing all members of the Bourbon family "in accordance with that adopted by the Romans after the expulsion of the Tarquins". His fellow Girondin Louvet seized the tribune and exclaimed: "I demand that Philippe-

[1] On December 28th Pamela was married there to Lord Edward Fitzgerald, who was to die of wounds received in the Irish rebellion in 1798.

Egalité and his sons carry the burden of having been born near the throne outside the confines of the Republic." The Montagnards, sensing that all this was a Girondin device for complicating what was for them the simple issue of life or death for the King, sprang to the defence of Philippe. After a violent and confused debate and a strong speech by Marat at the Jacobins in favour of Philippe[1] it was eventually agreed two days later on the motion of Pétion to adjourn the discussion "till after the judgement of Capet". It seems at first sight curious that Philippe should not have wished to seize the opportunity of escaping from the impossible situation in which he found himself—certainly Louis-Philippe was by now sadly reconciled in his mind to the idea of exile. But all the evidence suggests that the wretched man was so paralysed with fear that the inertia and fatalism which had always been dominant in his character led him to hope that it would somehow be possible for him to sink into insignificance and be allowed to go on living his life of pleasure. To do anything at all seemed likely to be fatal and meanwhile there was always Madame de Buffon and the Opera. If so, events were to disillusion him rapidly. He dared not absent himself from the Convention on the 26th when de Sèze conducted the King's defence. There then followed a long delay while Buzot made his unsuccessful attempt to refer the whole question to a national plebiscite. But it was a hopeless gesture. Nothing could now save the Bourbon dynasty.

It was some consolation to Louis-Philippe at Tournai to be reunited with his sister and Madame de Genlis after such a long separation. More than a year ago he had written to Beaujolais from Valenciennes: "We must be patient and await the happy moment when *tout ce pauvre* Belle-Chasse will be reunited." Now at last, though the background was full of shadows and the future incalculable they were for the most part reunited and spirits were high. Montpensier went backwards and forwards to Paris and Pamela had gone to England with her husband. Beaujolais, the citizen Léodgard-Egalité, as he delighted to call himself, now aged

[1] Marat may well have been paid for his services.

fourteen, was still in Paris. Louis-Philippe sent him a New Year's Present with a mock-pompous letter informing him that

> today there left from the town and suburbs of Tournai-sur-Escaut
> . . . a parcel duly folded, tied with string and placed in charge of the
> carriage, called a diligence, which is in the habit of transporting,
> to the town and suburbs of Paris-sur-Seine all the men, women, dogs,
> cats and rabbits who intend to see and admire that immense con-
> glomeration of stones and human flesh. This parcel contains two
> waistcoats of striped cotton, destined, after being measured, cut,
> sewn, fitted and lined according to the fashions of that vast capital
> of the French republic, to cover, hide and preserve your belly from
> cold and damp . . . I kiss all your ears.

Montpensier used to tease Adélaïde by starting his letters "my dear little sister" and ending "I kiss your huge hands".[1] But it would not now be long before the former pupils of Belle-Chasse, united again for a moment, would be even more widely scattered.

On January 13th, 1793, as the moment approached when the decisive vote on the King's death must be taken, Montpensier and Madame de Buffon tried to ensure that there would be no weakness on Philippe's part and were told: "Rest assured, I wouldn't do that. I am incapable of any such action." The next day he told Mrs Elliott and Biron that he would not go to the Convention when the vote was taken. But on the 15th two deputies, Treilhard (one day to be a member of the Directory) and Merlin, had no difficulty in persuading him to go along – after all if his absence were noted it would not be helpful when the vote was taken on the banishment of the Orléans family which was hanging over his head. He proceeded to vote that the King was guilty and to vote against the judgement being ratified by an appeal to the people. On the 16th he arrived at the Convention at seven in the morning and sat there all day until the final voting began at eight in the evening. His turn did not come till after dawn. His nineteen fellow-deputies for Paris voted one after another for death. Finally his turn came. Without looking up, awkward as he always had been in a crowded assembly, he took

[1] Bibliothèque de l'Institut, Fonds d'Orléans, 2048 218/246, 247/306.

a crumpled piece of paper from his pocket and read aloud the words: "Uniquely concerned to do my duty and convinced that all those who have conspired or will in future conspire against the sovereignty of the people deserve death I vote for death," and mounted slowly back to his bench. 28 of the 749 members were absent and out of the 721 who voted 361 voted for death without any qualification or delay,[1] an absolute majority of one. Montpensier found his father later at the Palais-Royal sitting in front of his desk weeping. When the young man tried to embrace him he was repulsed with the words: "No . . . I am too miserable. I don't understand how they made me do what I've done." Philippe, as well as a good many of his fellow deputies, would have been wiser to have pondered Rousseau's dictum that "nothing here below is worth buying at the price of human blood".

At Tournai there were no illusions. Dumouriez wrote two days after the King's execution, "the catastrophe of January 21st without any doubt makes everyone in Europe our enemy", and Louis-Philippe wrote harshly to his father who angrily burnt the letter in Mrs Elliott's presence and proceeded to justify every word of it by descending to the ultimate in degradation on February 10th when he testified before the Convention, to the manifest disgust of Danton, that he was not the son of the late Duc d'Orléans, but of the latter's coachman Lefranc. Even his mistresses deserted him. But although Dumouriez had no respect whatever for the Convention, he was still at the head of an army, as was Monck in 1659. On February 7th he learnt that France was at war with the United Provinces and he hastily set his small forces in motion to conquer the Dutch if possible before the Austrians, Prussians and English came to their rescue. His colleague, the Venezuelan Miranda, and Louis-Philippe bombarded Maestricht while he himself advanced as far as Dordrecht. But the Austrians

---

[1] Condorcet, the last of the *philosophes*, voted for Louis to be condemned to the galleys – hardly a more merciful fate, considering that Louis was now a rather decrepit man of thirty-nine. Tom Paine's suggestion of detention in the United States was rather more humane.

under Coburg, Mack and the Archduke Charles, defeated Valence on the Roer and early in March the whole army was back on the defensive near Louvain. From there Dumouriez sent the Convention a letter in which he blamed their commissioners roundly for causing disaffection among the Belgians through the plundering activities of their agents. He then attacked the Austrians at Neerwinden[1] his troops having to cross a stream and advance up open slopes to close with the enemy. Miranda attacked on the left, Valence on the right; and Louis-Philippe, commanding 9,000 men in the centre, led his column with tremendous dash, had a horse shot under him and captured the village of Neerwinden itself three times only to lose it as, time and again, the Austrians poured in fresh troops covered by concentric fire from the high ground.[2] Valence on the right, himself receiving ten sabre-cuts, made little progress and on the left the great Archduke completely routed Miranda. Louis-Philippe's troops lay out all night and the following morning he withdrew them successfully in the face of a victorious enemy. As the beaten French withdrew through Brussels on March 24th, the crowd burnt the tree of Liberty in the Grande Place and Dumouriez was now placed between a victorious enemy army and his implacable enemies in the Convention. Louis-Philippe wrote sadly to his father: "Where I formerly saw through rose-coloured spectacles, everything now seems as black as pitch. I see liberty lost; I see the Convention totally destroying France through its neglect of all principle; I see civil war blazing; I see foreign armies descending from all sides on our unhappy country and I see no army of our own to oppose them."

Even before writing his offensive letter to the Convention, Dumouriez had had a stormy interview with three of their Commissioners – Camus, Merlin and Treilhard. They accused him of treachery and Camus, who knew rather more about ecclesiastical politics and pensions than he did about war, said "if

[1] The site of Luxembourg's victory over William of Orange almost exactly a hundred years before. The future Regent Orléans distinguished himself on that occasion.
[2] General Desforests of the five flags was wounded in the head.

I were sure of that I would become Brutus and stab you", to be met by the disconcerting reply: "My dear Camus, the threat of being killed by you assures me of immortality." After Neerwinden Dumouriez negotiated with the cautious Coburg for a safe withdrawal at the cost of abandoning Brussels. And on March 25th at Ath, where he had taken up a defensive position behind the River Dender, he conferred in the presence of Generals de Chartres and de Valence with the Austrian Chief of Staff, Baron Mack de Leiberich, who would one day find himself in a less favourable position to negotiate with the French at Ulm. Dumouriez had already secretly revealed the subject-matter of his conference with the enemy to Louis-Philippe. It was proposed that while the Austrians prolonged the informal armistice, Dumouriez should march his army to Paris, seize the members of the Convention and restore the Constitution of 1791, destroyed by mob violence on the previous August 10th. It would be useful to have 20,000 gold louis for distribution in Paris and there the Austrians might help.

A secret meeting between Dumouriez and Louis-Philippe had taken place by candlelight on March 22nd in the Convent of Saint Gertrude at Louvain. After unfolding his plans, Dumouriez urged his lieutenant not to get mixed up in the conspiracy, but to be discreet and confine himself to carrying out his duties as a soldier. As Louis-Philippe listened he must have recalled some identical advice he had received from Danton after Valmy. Years later he told his son, the Duc d'Aumale: "Disillusioned as I was by the laws and theories of government about which I had been so enthusiastic earlier, I had already decided to confine myself exclusively to the accomplishment of my military duties as he was asking me to do. I thanked him for the confidence he was showing me and I promised to guard the secret. There was never any other pact between General Dumouriez and me."

At Tournai on March 26th Dumouriez was extremely rude to three emissaries of the Jacobin Club, Debuisson, Proly (an illegitimate son of Kaunitz) and the Portuguese Jew Pereira, whom he interviewed in the presence of Louis-Philippe and Valence in

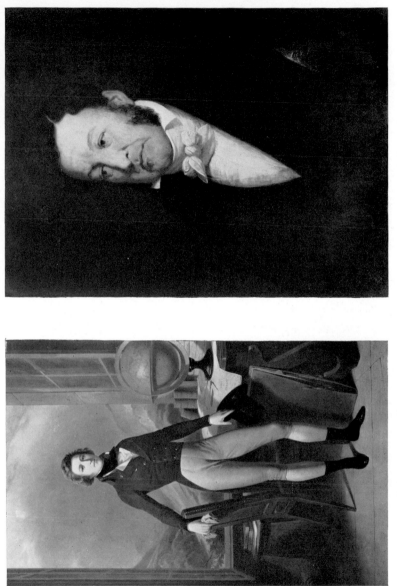

2. Louis-Philippe in 1835
by Scheffer

1. Louis-Philippe at Reichenau
by Winterhalter

Madame de Genlis' house. "I alone can make peace with Coburg and if I don't do so the Austrians will be in the Tuileries in three weeks." He talked of restoring the constitution of '91 and horrified the Jacobins, who hoped for his help in getting rid of the Girondins, by making it quite clear that he envisaged the dissolution of the Convention and the restoration of royalty, without however being precise about what king he had in mind.

Dubuisson's report to an outraged Convention resulted in the dispatch to the Army of the North of the War Minister, Beurnonville, a nominee of Dumouriez, who had fought at Valmy and Jemappes, together with four commissioners of the Convention, including Camus. At 4 o'clock on April 2nd the five delegates arrived at the house which Dumouriez was using as a headquarters in the small village of Boues-de-Saint-Amand near Tournai. Camus gave Dumouriez a copy of the Convention's decree ordering him back to Paris to explain his conduct. Dumouriez replied that the condition of the army prevented him going back to Paris, but with a note of irony offered to resign his command. After further sharp interchanges in which Dumouriez left them in no doubt about his attitude to the Convention, the delegates asked leave to withdraw for consultation. They came back shortly afterwards and Camus addressed Dumouriez as follows: "Citizen general, I suspend you from your functions. I forbid anybody to obey your orders and your person will be seized." Dumouriez snapped out an order in German and forty Austrian hussars entered the room and proceeded to escort the Minister of War and the four deputies to the enemy camp on their way to prison.[1] Louis-Philippe, present on this occasion, was by now implicated to the hilt.

For a few days the issue seemed uncertain, as Dumouriez issued proclamations against Jacobin anarchy and planned to occupy strongpoints on the road to Paris. One of these was, of

---

[1] Beurnonville tried to escape and was hustled back into a carriage with sabre blows. The prisoners were exchanged for Louis XVI's daughter, the future Duchesse d'Angoulême, at the end of 1795. Beurnonville later commanded the Army of the North.

course, Lille, and there the Republican cause had been for weeks in the very capable hands of Carnot. A letter addressed to Beurnonville from the *Comité de Défense Générale* which fell into Dumouriez's hand informed him of orders for the arrest of Louis-Philippe. By the morning of April 4th it was clear that the bulk of the army would remain loyal to the Republic.

Madame de Genlis had been enjoying frequent dinner parties with Dumouriez but her previous training had not exactly conditioned her to the life of a camp-follower of this Provençal Coriolanus and she had by now not unnaturally lost her nerve. When the news of the arrest of Beurnonville reached her at midnight on April 2nd, she decided she had had enough. She succeeded in convincing herself that the fifteen-year-old Princesse Adélaïde, suffering from fever, would be better left on her own. Her brother thought otherwise and just as Madame de Genlis was about to drive off to safety the following morning, he thrust Adélaïde, shivering with fever and dressed only in her night-dress and a muslin shawl, into the arms of the absconding governess. He was not to see his sister again until 1808 and the incident very much altered his subsequent attitude to *"mon amie"*.

On the morning of April 4th Dumouriez, accompanied by Louis-Philippe and a weak escort, left Saint-Amand for Condé where the Austrian generals awaited them for the discussion of armistice terms. On the way the party encountered a volunteer battalion commanded by a prematurely bald and bespectacled officer, who had served in the centre of the French line under Louis-Philippe at Neerwinden, Lieutenant-Colonel Davout, later Duc d'Auerstadt and Prince d'Eckmühl. As Dumouriez was ordering him back to camp some of the soldiers cried out: "Down with Dumouriez, the traitor!" There was nothing for it but to fly. As the cavalcade rode away at top speed in the direction of the Austrian camp, they were pursued by bullets. Dumouriez's horse refused to jump a ditch and he hastily mounted another offered him by Louis-Philippe's valet-de-chambre, Baudoin, who pretending to be wounded, sat down on the roadside and succeeded in giving wrong directions to the pursuers.

Dumouriez made one last dispairing effort the following day. Relying on his reputation with the regular troops of the line, he harangued detachments of them with some success in the camp at Maulde, accompanied by an Austrian escort. But while he was doing so the news arrived that the artillery had declared for the Republic and there seemed nothing for it but to go over to the enemy, as Lafayette had done before him. In his small entourage were three lieutenant-generals, Valence, Manassé and Louis-Philippe.

It would be twenty-one years before Louis-Philippe was to set foot on French soil again. By the age of twenty few young men had ever acquired such a varied experience of life. Born on the steps of a throne, he had known and talked in his adolescence with most of the important leaders of the revolution; in under two years' military service he had played a prominent and responsible role in three great battles, and knew himself to be a leader of men; he had seen the high hopes for the regeneration of his country, induced in him by a particularly intensive liberal education, at first gloriously realized and then subsequently frustrated and overthrown. And now, penniless, proscribed and a prey to cruel anxiety for the members of his family left in France, he set out on an exile the duration of which it was impossible to foretell.

Book Two

All places that the eye of heaven visits
Are to a wise man ports and happy havens.
Teach thy necessity to reason thus;
There is no virtue like necessity.

RICHARD II (I. iii)

I

The interaction between Louis-Philippe's complicity in the treason of Dumouriez and the fortunes of his family was inevitable, swift and deadly. When the news reached Paris, Philippe rose in the Convention to say that if his son was guilty he would not spare him any more than Brutus of old spared his son. One of the deputies quickly commented that it would not in that case be the first family sacrifice he had made in the cause of liberty. Unfortunately Louis-Philippe's letter, in which he informed his father that he no longer saw things through rose-coloured spectacles and denigrated the Convention, had been seized and was read out. Philippe and Sillery were put under continuous surveillance and Marie-Adélaïde in preventive detention at her father's Château of Bizey, where she was in mourning for the old Duc de Bourbon-Penthièvre, who had died in the previous month. This was swiftly followed as the Girondins closed in on their prey, by a decree arresting Philippe, Beaujolais, Montpensier, now serving with Biron's Army of the Alps, and Laclos. On April 8th the Convention consigned Philippe and Beaujolais to imprisonment at Marseilles, and on April 11th father and son set out on a long and agonizing journey which ended ten days later, when they found Montpensier, arrested at Nice, awaiting them in the prison of Notre-Dame de Garde. A month later they were transferred to the grim fortress of Saint-Jean where Philippe was confined in a dark, stinking cell with only a small grilled aperture to let in light and air. He was to stay there till he was removed on November 1st to be tried by the Revolutionary Tribunal. Montpensier and Beaujolais remained in Fort Saint-Jean for three more years.

Meanwhile, the Convention having put a price on his head and the émigrés in the Austrian armies regarding him as a Jacobin and the son of a regicide, Louis-Philippe had to seek refuge in Switzerland, travelling under assumed names with the faithful Baudoin.[1] At Frankfurt he learnt of the arrest of his father and brothers. At Baden he received news of his sister from the Comte Gustave de Montjoie who had escorted Madame de Genlis and Adélaïde (who had developed measles) throughout a highly hazardous carriage-journey to temporary safety at Schaffhausen. Here Louis-Philippe rejoined them. Thence they journeyed to Zürich, only to be told after a few days by the magistrates, who displayed the traditional Swiss concern for neutrality, that the presence in their midst of members of the House of Orléans was an embarrassment with which the civic authorities preferred to dispense. The same thing happened at Zug where some émigrés recognized Louis-Philippe. If there was ever to be any repose for the women of the party, living largely on the sale of one of Madame de Genlis' manuscripts, it would obviously be necessary for them to separate from the too easily recognized Duc de Chartres. Fortunately Montjoie had encountered the émigré Marquis de Montesquiou, a friend of Philippe's who after commanding the Armée du Midi with distinction in 1792 had fled to Switzerland, a country where he had long-standing connections. He arranged a retreat in a convent at Bremgarten for Madame de Genlis, still in possession of her harp, and the two girls, whose English enabled them to pass themselves off as Irish.[2] As to Louis-Philippe, Montesquiou could only advise him to wander incognito in the mountains to throw pursuers off the scent. Accordingly he went to Basle, sold his remaining horses, except one, for sixty louis and set out accompanied only by Baudoin. It must have seemed to him at times that he had neither friends nor hope. Dumouriez, it is true, still believed in him. At Düsseldorf he told Fersen that he thought very highly of the Duc de Chartres "who does not resemble his father in any way" and in a letter to Montesquiou he said:

[1] Service in the Austrian army, even if his sense of patriotism could have stomached it, would have involved reprisals against his family.

[2] Madame Lenox and her nieces the Mlles Stuart. Madame de Genlis doubtless found Scottish history romantic and perhaps not easily distinguishable from Irish.

"*embrassez pour moi notre bon jeune homme*" and went on to urge Louis-Philippe to keep a diary of his adventures, as "it would be pleasant to read the diary of a Bourbon concerned with matters other than hunting, women and eating". The letter ends "it is better for princes to write odysseys than pastorals".

The odyssey began with Louis-Philippe trudging on foot with a stout stick while Baudoin, being ill, rode the horse. They passed through Neuchâtel, Morat, Uri, Unterwald, Telemblat, Grindel-wald. The monks of Saint Gothard one night in August 1793 refused to grant hospitality to two such apparently broken-down young vagabonds and they had to spend the night in a dilapidated stable where muleteers were eating goat's cheese. Shortly afterwards, refused a bed for the same reason in the only inn at Gordona, Louis-Philippe woke up in the barn in the small hours to find himself confronted by a very large young man at the end of a musket, who explained that his aunt who kept the inn had given him orders to shoot if the travellers turned out to be thieves. They never dared stay more than forty-eight hours in one place for fear of being recognized.

All this was tolerable in summer, perhaps, for a young prince with strong legs and a campaign-hardened constitution, but already the summer was passing – the summer of butchery in the Vendée and at Lyon and raids by Coburg's hussars in the Somme valley – and Louis-Philippe was fortunate to be rescued by an ingenious plan devised by Montesquiou. In October 1795 the Duc de Chartres was appointed to the post of geography-master (with, as subsidiary subjects, history, mathematics, and modern languages) at a salary of 1,400 francs in the boys' boarding school owned by M. Jost at Reichenau, a village of the Grisons at the head-waters of the Rhine. The worthy Jost combined a veneration for the principles of 1789 with devout Catholicism and a belief in the virtues of economical administration and he would have flourished admirably under the July Monarchy. He had a great respect for Montesquiou, under whom he had formerly served. The latter had persuaded him to employ as a master an émigré in straitened circumstances called Chabaud-Latour, who had in the end not accepted the post. Louis-Philippe was substituted under the pseudonym of M. Chabos, only M. Jost, one of his friends and the headmaster (described by M. Jost as "a second Socrates") being in the secret.

Louis-Philippe's eight months as an assistant schoolmaster were to form a never-failing topic of after-dinner conversation in the Tuileries in the 1830's and to inspire a superb Winterhalter portrait, depicting a slim and handsome Prince Charming in tight-fitting breeches and a swallow-tail coat, carrying a slightly incongruous pair of gloves and standing by a school table loaded with a globe, a ruler, compasses and a folio of maps by an open window affording a glorious background of Alpine scenery. The reality was perhaps a little more sombre. Fortunately Louis-Philippe had good reason to believe in the virtues of education and he was assiduous in the performance of duties which might well have seemed unbearably trivial to a prematurely retired corps commander. The academic standards fell a good deal short of those prevailing at Belle-Chasse, the library consisting of an incomplete edition of Rousseau, a German copy of Raynal and some classical textbooks. There was also, as is usually the case in boys' boarding schools, trouble about the food, though M. Jost so far relaxed his parsimony in this field as to bring M. Chabos grapes and pears to his room. But because he was incapable ever of being unconscientious and perhaps also because there was in his character a strong streak of the didactic, Louis-Philippe made a good teacher. M. Jost was loud in his praises, criticizing his young assistant on three counts only – his tendency to refer in conversation with his pupils to important people he had met; his extraordinary mania for wearing a clean shirt every day; and his attitude to the food. However, he was treated with sympathy and understanding at the tragic moment when he heard on November 13th that his constant fears for the safety of his father were all too justified.

It was on November 1st that Philippe was brought in a carriage to the Palais de Justice, the day after twenty-two of the Girondins, including Sillery, Madame de Genlis' husband, had been guillotined. On the 6th he appeared before Fouquier-Tinville in the same room where he had defied the King at the meeting of the Parlement of Paris almost exactly six years before. His trial was a travesty, Fouquier-Tinville hardly bothering to refer to the defence arguments in his instruction to the jury. Throughout his trial and on the scaffold Philippe behaved with exemplary courage, profoundly impressing his confessor, the abbé Lothringer, with the genuineness of his penitence and his desire to expiate his sins. His last words, uttered in a calm voice were: *"Ecoutez les prières d'un mourant – dépêchez-moi vite!"* Philippe's children as well as his servants and many of his friends loved him despite all the defects of his character and for a time the new Duc d'Orléans was inconsolable, wandering half the night in the grounds of the Château of Reichenau in an agony of despair.[1] His father was dead and he felt himself in part responsible;[2] his beloved brothers were in prison; his sister was in the grip of a woman he now depised as much as he had formerly worshipped her. As to his mother he had little or no news. In fact, during the previous month, Marie-Adélaïde in very enfeebled health was consigned to the Luxembourg prison where she was to stay for eighteen months. Day by day news filtered through of the Revolution devouring its children. Brissot, Vergniaud, Bailly, Barnave, Biron and Lückner were guillotined; Pétion and Buzot later committed suicide in the woods and their faces were eaten by dogs. Only Laclos, with his genius for keeping in the shadows, managed somehow to avoid either execution or exile and after a short period in prison resumed not unsuccessfully his old military career.

It is not surprising that Louis-Philippe developed in these circumstances a bitter contempt and hatred for much of his

[1] A more common reaction was that of Miss Elizabeth Wynne whose diary, written in Switzerland, records on November 15th: "We heared today that the Duke of Orleans notwithstanding the foul and vile manner in which he behaved to gain the Jacobites [*sic*] friendship has been guillotined and died, as cowardly as he had lived. Hated by all mankind."

[2] It was true that at Philippe's trial the principal indictment was complicity in Dumouriez' treason.

Jacobinical past, although as a patriot he marvelled at the miraculous resistance of the Republican armies. He wrote to Montesquiou: "My blood boils in my veins when I see all these atrocities while I am condemned to inactivity. As you say, dishonour is at its height and the name of France would be dragged in the mud, if, by the side of all these horrors, one didn't find also the brilliant courage which has always distinguished it. But who are these unhappy soldiers fighting for?" When there were rumours of revolutionary activity in Switzerland he wrote: "One begins to see what one didn't see at the beginning that the people are everywhere the same and everywhere a wild beast hungry for wealth." He could do nothing active to repudiate his past except dissociate himself from the name Egalité and quarrel with Madame de Genlis who was claiming large sums of money for her services. The naïf and malleable young man who had once felt himself born under a lucky star was learning in a hard school of tragedy and disillusionment and learning above all that nothing in life is quite what it seems.

Lonely and dispirited, he felt above all the need for love and companionship, as a result of which his carefully preserved virginity capitulated to the charms of the college cook, Marianne Banzori. The researches of M. Raymond Recouly have documented this episode in great detail from a vigorous correspondence which developed between Montesquiou and Jost in the later stages of the proceedings and five letters written in German by Louis-Philippe to Marianne in the summer of 1794 after his departure from Reichenau. Just before Louis-Philippe decided to end his academic career the worthy Jost discovered that his invaluable cook was *enceinte*. Two and two were all too easily put together. Jost was very upset and wrote to Montesquiou: "I am not angry with M. Chabos for having fathered a child but I *am* angry with him for fathering it on my cook." The college of Reichenau had to find a new cook and Marianne was packed off to Milan where the child, born in December 1794, was consigned to the *Enfants Trouvés*, the expenses being borne by the providential Montesquiou.

This episode – the only one of its sort in a career which has been subjected to more muck-raking than any other in modern history – is no more creditable than, for instance, the liaison between Wordsworth and Annette in the previous year, but it is easy to see how it happened. What emerges from Louis-Philippe's letters written in German in rather incompetent Gothic script is that it was, while it lasted, a sentimental love-affair of a slightly ridiculous but genuinely romantic sort.

> You see, my dearest treasure, that your Chabosli loses no time in writing to you. I can't talk of what I've been through since I had to leave you. Ma petite, ma bonne petite, you can only judge it by what you have been through yourself. After being dragged so quickly from your beloved arms, near that fatal bridge, I wanted to go back to you, my darling. I half turned round but you were already far off . . . I got into the boat with death in my soul. The boatman said you were a charming little thing and that pleased me. So you see I'm not the only one who finds you pretty. I was so sad that I couldn't say a word and I had to pass the night there, first because of the lake and then because of my torn shoes and also because I couldn't reach my destination the same evening. I couldn't stay in the lounge of the inn. You were always present in my sight. I couldn't speak or think of anything else. I took some tea[1] and went to bed . . . Adieu, ma chère petite . . . Your Chabosli kisses you and loves you with all his heart.

But this and subsequent letters were intercepted by the outraged Jost and returned to Montesquiou and the idyll faded out in the way such things do. But one sees that the hero of Jemappes and Neerwinden was still emotionally very much an adolescent.

Before his departure from Reichenau (armed, one is glad to learn, with a certificate of competence as a teacher)[2] Louis-Philippe managed to remove Adélaïde, now sixteen and a half from the care of Madame de Genlis after an acrimonious triangular correspondence in which Montesquiou served as intermediary.

[1] Perhaps a straitened purse precluded a more fortifying cordial.
[2] Jost had made him pass examinations.

She went to live with her great-aunt the Princesse de Conti at Fribourg, whence they were compelled to move first to Bavaria and then to Hungary, Adélaïde finally joining her mother in Spain in 1802.

II

Between 1794 and 1800 when he settled in England, Louis-
Philippe was to wander over the face of the earth in so strange a
variety of places on both sides of the Atlantic that he seems to be
a sort of incarnation of Rasselas or Gulliver. The news of Thermidor afforded him a faint ray of hope, but while he was staying
with Montesquiou at Bremgarten rumours again began to circu-
late about him and beginning to despair of finding a safe resting-
place anywhere in Europe he conceived the idea of going to
America. That this idea eventually became a reality was due to the
intervention of another exile, the Comtesse de Flahaut, mistress of
Talleyrand and grandmother of Morny. She wrote to her old
acquaintance, Gouverneur Morris, a great admirer of Louis-
Philippe's mother, as follows: "I have seen the young Duke of
Orléans in Switzerland . . . he is melancholy, but gentle and
modest. His great ambition is to go to America and forget the
greatness and suffering which have been part and parcel of his
youth, but he has no money at all." A few days later he received
from Morris a letter encouraging him to go to America whenever he liked and a draft for a hundred louis on a Basle bank.
Accordingly, he left Bremgarten for Hamburg in March 1798
with de Montjoie and Madame de Flahaut, threading his way
gingerly past known émigré centres in Austria and Germany.
Hamburg being a hornet's nest of émigrés was no place to stay
in, but amidst a hectic society of French exiles living off the sale
of jewellery and complaining bitterly about German eiderdowns
there were two old acquaintances anxious to see him again –
Dumouriez and Madame de Genlis. The latter under the assumed
name of Miss Clarke was busily engaged in repulsing the matrimonial advances of an Altona baker and Louis-Philippe succeeded
in dodging her. Dumouriez, with whom he stayed for a week,
found him "resigned and courageous" and would have liked him

to stay longer but significantly observed "if we had been discovered it would have been said that I was grooming him for
royalty" – a comment reflecting Dumouriez's tendency to over-
rate his own importance. In any case it soon transpired that
Morris' plans were governed by considerations of speculative
investment rather than disinterested philanthropy. He began to
talk of mortgages on the Orléans estates but soon found, as did
many after him, that he was up against a very shrewd businessman
with a passion for casting accounts to the last farthing and a very
clear idea of what constituted a good bargain or the reverse. So
Morris' plan to establish Louis-Philippe as a landed proprietor of
62,000 acres on the right bank of the Saint Lawrence fell through
and, pending better times and prospects and probably on the
advice of Dumouriez, Louis-Philippe set out on an extensive tour
of the Scandinavian countries in May 1795, accompanied only
by Baudoin and de Montjoie.

This voyage which lasted a year and which is copiously documented in his letters to Montesquiou reveals in Louis-Philippe
qualities of curiosity, enterprise and tenacity. The travellers went
from Copenhagen to Oslo and thence to Trondheim and thereafter up the west coast of Norway in launches to Lapland. Doctor
Johnson, it will be recalled, observed that Lapland was "remarkable for prodigious noble wild prospects", but went on to imply
that Scotland was bad enough for most people. When Louis-
Philippe and his companions, taking in the Lofoten Islands on the
way, reached the North Cape on August 24th, 1795, their only
precursors had been the philosopher and mathematician Mauper-
tuis and the poet Régnard. The latter part of the journey was
conducted by reindeer-sledge, involving three weeks of camping
out in the Lapland night (which Wordsworth used as a simile for
serene old age), on a diet of milk and reindeer meat. An understandable fear of Catherine the Great, now grown notably irascible,
prevented the travellers going to Russia, as they would have
wished, and instead they journeyed south to Torneo on the gulf
of Bothnia, and finally, making a wide détour through Finland,
returned to Stockholm in October 1795. Hitherto Louis-Philippe

3. The Duc de Chartres
(Louis-Philippe's father)
by Reynolds

4. Queen Marie-Amélie
in old age
by Jalabert

5. The Duchesse d'Orléans
by an unknown French artist

6. Mme de Genlis
by Vestier

had managed to maintain his incognito but he was recognized by the French envoy at a state ball he imprudently attended and although well treated by the Swedish royal family he left for Holstein early in 1796.

In the political confusion of the first year of the Directory the fortunes of the head of the House of Orléans had become a matter of considerable interest to the different groups of exiles manœuvring to overthrow the bankrupt and apparently unstable government in Paris. Dumouriez had written to the Vendéen leader Charette just before the Quibéron expedition: "The young Duc d'Orléans is the only possible means of bringing together the republic and the monarchy . . . the people are tired and would readily put themselves under a king of whom they could be proud, who took part in the revolution and who would not be for them a living reproach . . . it would be a triumph for your constitutional ideas, cemented equally by the triumph of your monarchical principles, it is the Vendée giving the Revolution a King." Charette's reply was concise and obscene, but on the other hand it seemed to some of Louis XVIII's advisers that it would be wiser to win over this young man, who was known to be in the habit of frequently denouncing his own Jacobin antecedents, to the cause of legitimacy, recently proclaimed in terms of the most rigid conservatism from Verona. In February 1795 the future Charles X asked Mallet du Pan, the only able publicist the émigrés possessed, to tell him "where the Duc d'Orléans usually resides and where he may be at the moment, who are the chiefs of his party and the principal agents whom he employs". Mallet answered accurately: "He has partisans and no party: these things are confused every day", and proceeded to discuss the instructive historical analogy of 1688. When, therefore, Louis-Philippe found himself confronted by a peculiarly tactless emissary of his cousin in the person of the Baron de Roll he was peremptorily ordered to make his submissions in person to Louis XVIII and to join the émigré army then under Austrian command.

This was the first great crisis of decision that had confronted Louis-Philippe since the spring of Neerwinden. Its solution was curious and fortuitous in the extreme and its ultimate consequences of incalculable significance for the history of France. Explaining to de Roll that on returning from Scandinavia his first impulse had been to offer his services to Louis XVIII but that the reactionary language of the Verona proclamation had completely disillusioned him, he stated his intention of keeping himself entirely aloof as long as Louis XVIII refused to offer France a limited constitutional monarchy on the English pattern and that in any case his mother and brothers were in the hands of the Directory and he could not imperil their future. Not only that, but after angry altercations with de Roll, he wrote a letter on June 8th, 1795, for transmission to Louis XVIII in which he committed himself to the proposition: "that he had always recognized the right of the French nation to give itself a constitution and that he felt it his duty to recognize any government which would guarantee in France security of the person and of property and a reasonable degree of liberty."

There is no reason to doubt either that Louis-Philippe had by now ceased in every sense to be a Jacobin or that he was not now and subsequently a genuine advocate of the British system of constitutional monarchy, provided always it is recognized that that system reserved for the monarch a wide area of executive power. But if this letter had reached its destination the subsequent rather precarious reconciliation between the elder and younger branches of the Bourbon family would have been completely impossible and there would have been no place in France for Louis-Philippe at the Restoration and consequently little or no likelihood of a July Monarchy. That Louis XVIII never read the letter was due to the intervention of one of the more honest and least bigoted of his advisers, the Comte d'Avaray, who, realizing that the Royalist cause would not at this juncture be served by an open rupture on the issue of constitutional liberty between the two branches of the royal family, simply suppressed it.

Even if proceedings of this sort had not already alarmed the

Directory, that somewhat paranoiac institution had certainly been alerted by a characteristic démarche on the part of the irrepressible Madame de Genlis. Finding life at Hamburg and Altona understandably unsatisfactory, with only Beaumarchais to amuse her, she suddenly concocted in March 1795 an open letter to Louis-Philippe which she circulated as widely as possible. It is rather a revolting document whose sole object was to broadcast the lady's loyalty to the Directory and her repudiation of any association with an Orléanist faction in order that she might be allowed to return to France. It starts with some digs at Madame de Flahaut, goes on to remind the world of her intimate relations with her former pupils and then warns Louis-Philippe not to harbour secret ambitions. "You! Pretender to Royalty! Become a usurper, to abolish a Republic you have recognized, that you have cherished, and for which you have fought valiantly! And at what a moment! When France is organizing itself. When the government is established on a solid basis of morality and justice . . . Consecrate yourself to happy and sweet obscurity . . ." [1] Whatever that pillar of morality and justice, the Vicomte Paul de Barras, thought of this effusion he neither welcomed the idea of allowing Madame de Genlis to return to her native country[2] nor wished to hear the name of the Duc d'Orléans being bandied about Europe as a potential pretender to the throne. The Directory consequently hit on the device of utilizing the hostages they possessed in the persons of the Duchesse d'Orléans and Montpensier and Beaujolais.

Louis-Philippe's mother had been released in the summer of Thermidor and had begged the Directory to release her younger sons from Fort Saint-Jean. It had been for them a long, grim incarceration from which on one occasion they had escaped, only for Montpensier to fall and break his arm, whereupon Beaujolais, who could have got away, returned to look after him. Now the Directory proposed to the duchess the removal of the sequestration order on her property and the release of her

---

[1] As Talleyrand observed of her epigrammatically "the stability of complicated natures comes from their flexibility".

[2] She returned to France in 1800.

sons provided they went to America, whither Louis-Philippe was to precede them. The French minister to the Hanseatic towns after two months' search eventually tracked down Louis-Philippe at Friedrichstadt with a letter from his mother, urging him to accept the Directory's offer and enclosing a substantial credit from her admirer Morris. Louis-Philippe accepted the proposal with alacrity and on September 24th, 1796, as General Bonaparte was besieging Marshal Wurmser in Mantua before the battle of Arcola, he set sail from Hamburg with a Danish passport aboard the *America* (Captain Ewing) bound for Philadelphia.

After a pleasant voyage of twenty-seven days, during which Louis-Philippe maintained his incognito to the great advantage of an irascible San Domingo planter with no teeth and an understandable aversion to ships' biscuit who used him ruthlessly as an interpreter, the *America* arrived at Philadelphia. Louis-Philippe's first residence was a basement storey of a house belonging to the Rev. Mr Marshal in Walnut Street, where he anxiously awaited the arrival of his brothers, now aged twenty-one and seventeen respectively. When Montpensier and Beaujolais emerged into the free air like the prisoners in *Fidelio* they were both already stricken with the tuberculosis which was to consign them to an early death, but eager to renew the life of adventure and excitement which had been so harshly interrupted three years before. Eventually, after a dreary voyage of three months, they were able to rejoin their elder brother, whose modesty and good manners allied to his romantic background and present misfortunes had already made a favourable impression on some of the leading citizens of the United States. Not only did the Duc d'Orléans make the acquaintance of Governor Clinton, Judge Jay and Colonel Hamilton but he and his brothers were invited to visit George Washington for four days at Mount Vernon. The great man received them kindly and it would be pleasant to believe the story of the negro servant who introduced them with the words: "Your Excellency, there are three Equalities at the door." The month before they had already listened to Washington delivering his farewell address and been present at Adams' inaugural.

Washington's measured words on liberty – "it is, indeed, little else than a name, where the government is too feeble to withstand the exercise of faction, to confine each member of the society within the limits prescribed by the laws, and to maintain all in the secure and tranquil enjoyment of the rights of person and property" – must have echoed convincingly the thoughts of the ex-Jacobin and perhaps recurred to his mind more than once during the troubled days of the July Monarchy.[1]

During the greater part of 1797 the three brothers and Baudoin made an exhaustive and occasionally highly adventurous tour of what was for them a very new world. In three separate voyages they went South as far as Nashville, Tennessee, and then North via Pittsburg to Buffalo and Niagara; they then toured New York, Massachusetts and Maine; and finally early in 1798 descended the Ohio and Mississippi valleys to New Orleans, this last voyage involving forty days river transport in mid-winter. They experienced privations and dangers in plenty such as the navigation of rapids, shortage of rations and an enforced stay in Philadelphia during a plague of yellow fever. On one occasion Louis-Philippe's skill with his lancet earned him the highest honour a Red Indian tribe could bestow – the right to sleep in a tent between the two leading ladies of the society, the chief's grandmother and his great-aunt, the following day being given over to a ball-game of three hundred a side involving the consumption of six kegs of brandy.

It was in Boston that Louis-Philippe read of Augereau's coup d'état of 18 Fructidor and he learnt soon afterwards that his mother had been exiled to Spain on a small pension. It was this news that impelled the brothers to make the long journey from Philadelphia to New Orleans, then still in Spanish territory, since they hoped to cross thence to Havana and so on to Spain to rejoin their mother. With England and Spain at war it would be no easy passage. At New Orleans they were once again treated as princes

[1] Louis-Philippe wrote to Guisot in December 1839: "My three years' residence in America have had a great influence on my political opinions and on my judgement of the course of human affairs."

of the blood. After five weeks of Hispanic procrastination and visits to sugar plantations, they set sail for Cuba in an American corvette which in the middle of the Gulf of Mexico was caught by an English frigate under the command of the redoubtable sailor who would one day be Admiral Sir Thomas Cochrane, Earl of Dundonald. Louis-Philippe in later life was more than a little concerned with the British exercise of maritime rights of which this episode was to give him first-hand experience. As the three princes were discussing what to do in a cabin below deck, they were informed without ceremony by a midshipman that they would have to come aboard the British vessel. Once their identity was revealed they were escorted with all civility to Havana by Cochrane, but not before Louis-Philippe had fallen into the Gulf of Mexico owing to the inept handling of a rope used as a method of transit between the two ships.

By this time (March 1798) all three had one way and another learnt the gift of patience, but they were not consoled for over a year's total inactivity in Havana even by the agreeable nature of their environment. Eventually in May 1799 they heard from the Spanish government not that they would be allowed to visit their mother now established near Barcelona, but that they were to be expelled from Cuba instantly. Rather than accept an offer to return to Louisiana, they sailed to the Bahamas and thence to Nova Scotia, where they were received with great affability by the young Commander-in-Chief, Edward Augustus, Duke of Kent, the father of Queen Victoria, with whom Louis-Philippe struck up a close and lasting friendship. Although unpopular in the army because of his insistence on rigid discipline, he was a man of surprisingly liberal views in other matters and was unexpectedly respectable for one of George III's offspring. Continually harassed by the government, he dared not give the Orléans princes the use of a British ship, so eventually they sailed in a three-masted schooner to New York and thence to Falmouth, where they landed in the first month of the new century to begin a period of exile in England, from which Montpensier would never return.

III

Louis-Philippe was to spend the first fourteen years of the nineteenth century in exile before returning to France as a man of forty. Although as King of the French some of his more solid virtues seem perfectly well attuned to the outlook and ethos of the eighteen-forties, his character and thinking were indelibly moulded by what we tend to consider essentially eighteenth-century attitudes, so that the bourgeois monarch of July is not so much a new nineteenth-century political portent as the last of the enlightened despots. By education, by experience, by reading,[1] he belonged to the civilization which Burke extolled and Paine despised, a civilization of the élite, aristocratic and intellectual, an élite from whom and by whom all reform and progress must flow, gradually, rationally and *de haut en bas*. These years of exile spent largely in the graceful, aristocratic seclusion of Twickenham under George III and at the grotesquely anachronistic court of Palermo, in no sense modified his inherent and acquired tastes and aptitudes and he remained blind to much, if not all, of what was involved in the transition from the era of Speenhamland to that of New Lanark. Circumstances and the need for self-preservation virtually forced him into an uneasy submission to the elder branch of his family and a dynastic marriage completed a process whereby too much of his great natural ability was frittered away in the exasperating and often petty frustration of the outer fringe of legitimist politics.

The year 1800 represented, of course, something much more precise in the course of French history than a moment of transition in the highly theoretical study of the history of thought.

---

[1] As a young officer at Vendôme after a hard day's exercise with the Chartres Dragons we find him reading "some Président Hénault, some Caesar . . . some Mably . . . after dinner . . . Metastasio, Héloïse, Pope . . . some Emile".

Under the Directory, a monarchical restoration, Bourbon or Orléanist, did not seem beyond the bounds of possibility. But now Bonaparte was established as First Consul and Marengo in June consolidated his triumph. Louis-Philippe's first encounter in England was with Dumouriez who counselled him without further ado to make a full submission to Artois who, as a pensioner of Pitt, held court at 46 Baker Street on behalf of Louis XVIII, now at Mittau in Courland. The arguments in favour of doing so were compulsive. The triumphant ascendancy of Napoleon and the new spirit it had infused into France meant that the émigrés could no longer afford the luxury of divided loyalties and divided counsels; in any case there was no longer any semblance whatever of an Orléanist faction, even Dumouriez having thrown in his lot with the Legitimists; and as the British government had recognized Louis XVIII, Louis-Philippe would be cut off, if he did not submit, from any contact with his compatriots and could not hope for a single penny to live on by way of pension, an important consideration as Montpensier's health was now giving him much anxiety.

Legitimist biographers of Louis-Philippe naturally fall gleefully on his reconciliation with the future Charles X in February 1800, pointing pharisaical fingers of scorn at the events of July 1830. What in fact happened was that Louis-Philippe behaved with dignity, and Artois with the affability and charm which, with all his failings, were characteristic of him. What was put about by his deplorable entourage was something very different. The *Annual Register*, for instance, records Louis-Philippe as saying at the private interview: "that he had come to ask forgiveness for all his faults which he hoped would be forgotten. They were the effect of error, and were chiefly to be attributed to the evil counsels of an intriguing woman who had been entrusted with the care of his education." Louis-Philippe's own version in a letter to Morris is rather different: "We have read in the papers many fairy-tales on this subject. I'm sure you haven't paid any attention to them and that you know me well enough to be convinced without my having to say it that I didn't fail to show a proper frankness and dignity." But the vital testimony is in a letter from Mallet du Pan.

The Duke said nothing about repentance and pardon, as his royal Majesty's valets took care to spread about; he spoke of his faults and his devotedness, but with a proper nobleness and reserve. I shall not dilate upon the very favourable impression made here by the Prince, on both the English and the French. It would be difficult to have a better-formed, more enlightened and more cultivated mind, or to have greater power over language, to show more good sense, to possess more knowledge, or more simple and winning manners. He, at least, has learned to profit by adversity.

The Bourbons had learnt and forgotten nothing in the art of humiliating their close relatives.

This rather unsatisfactory reconciliation, which was followed by a formal letter of submission to Louis XVIII at Mittau, at least had the effect of opening the doors of London society to the three princes. They already had a close friend in the Duke of Kent. They were now received with great kindness by George III and his curious consort, were introduced to Pitt, and dined within the space of a few weeks with the Prince of Wales (at Carlton House), Grenville, Lady Salisbury and the Duke of Clarence. They were also allowed to sail in a frigate to Minorca to look for their mother and a Spanish ship took them to Barcelona harbour. Louis-Philippe was invariably unfortunate all his life in his relations with the Spaniards, and on this occasion he was curtly refused permission to land. Whether the long-anticipated reunion with his mother would have been all that might have been hoped at this stage is open to doubt, in that continuous misfortune had had a curious effect on Egalité's virtuous widow. When she crossed the frontier to Spain after Fructidor, the Spanish customs officials were astonished to find hidden in the luggage at the back of her berline a certain ex-Girondin deputy, M. Rouzet, who had attached himself to the Duchesse (as also, perhaps, to the prospects of her considerable fortune) with a leech-like fidelity which lasted for the rest of her life.[1]

[1] In 1801 Marie-Amélie installed herself at Figuieras with a household of

On his return to England from this frustrating episode, Louis-Philippe wisely decided to keep aloof from émigré society, contact with which tended to be humiliating, expensive and useless. The pension the brothers were now receiving from His Majesty's Government was modest, and a good deal of Louis-Philippe's time was taken up in the task of scraping together what remained of the prodigal Egalité's possessions in England.[1] He secured a substantial villa called Highshot House, with ten or twelve rooms, on the east side of Twickenham, then a village of some 3,000 inhabitants, nearly opposite the Crown Hotel. The establishment of the three brothers consisted of their old tutor of Belle-Chasse days, the Chevalier de Broval, later joined by de Montjoie, four manservants, a cook and a maidservant. Richmond and Twickenham at this period presented an almost perfect conjunction of art and nature and Louis-Philippe became deeply attached to what was to be his home on and off for the next fourteen years. Memorials of his existence during this long period of voluntary self-effacement at the height of the Consulate and Empire are scanty and unsatisfactory in that although it is possible to piece together how much of his time was spent we learn little about the develop-

some twenty persons presided over by Rouzet, who assumed the title of Comte de Folmont. Adélaïde joined them there that year. They all lived there quietly until 1808.

[1] The pension-list of the French royal family from Secret Service Funds in 1809 is nicely graduated as follows:

	£
The Comte de Lille (the future Louis XVIII)	16,000
Monsieur (the future Charles X)	6,000
The Duchesse d'Angoulême (Louis XVI's daughter)	4,000
The Duc d'Angoulême	3,600
The Duc de Berri	3,600
The Prince de Condé	6,000
The Princesse Louise	3,300
The Duc de Bourbon	2,400
The Duc d'Orléans	4,800
	£49,700

(Brit. Mus. Add. MSS. 37295.)
The three brothers started in 1800 with only £2,000 between them.

ment of his mind and character in his early thirties. He took up gardening and with a characteristic regard for economy he ordered on one occasion manure to be gathered from the road to be put in "the *platebandes* along the Serpentine walk". He made a study of the new and exciting science of political economy, he read Clarendon in the library at Donnington Park. He visited farms and factories and made short trips to Scotland and Ireland. We catch a glimpse of him through the eyes of Madame Vigée-Lebrun "sitting at a long table covered with books of which one was in front of him". Two of his own letters do, however, lift a corner of the curtain and tell us something of his aspirations and frustrations, as well as revealing how rapidly this rather untypical Frenchman became anglicized in exile. The first is dated July 28th, 1804, shortly after the murder of Louis-Philippe's cousin, the Duc d'Enghien, and was written in English to that remarkable prelate, Richard Watson, Bishop of Llandaff:[1]

I am extremely obliged to your lordship for your kind letter. I regretted that I had not the pleasure of seeing you whilst you were in town. The moment I heard you were there I went to Great George Street very early to be certain of finding you at home but I was informed you had removed and I could get no other direction, but it was somewhere in Albemarl [*sic*] Street or Conduit Street, they knew not which and as to number that was not to be thought of. Still had I been resident in town I had certainly found you out, but I had been very little in town last winter and never had a house or even apartments; I remained here in great retirement of which I grow more fond every day of my life.

I was certain your Lordship's elevated soul had resented with becoming indignation the foul murder of my unfortunate cousin. His mother being my aunt, he was, next to my brother, the nearest relation I had and as he was only a year older than me, we had been playfellows during our younger years. You must feel it was a sad blow to me. His fate is an awful warning to everyone of us that the Corsican usurper will never rest until he has erased the whole of our family from the list of the living. It makes me feel still more

[1] This letter was salvaged from the sack of Guizot's papers at the Ministry of Foreign Affairs in 1848.

forcibly than I did before (though it is scarcely possible) the blessing of the generous protection and support granted unto us by your magnanimous country. I have left my native country at so early a period, that I have not much the habits of a Frenchman, and I may say with perfect candour that I am attached to England not only by gratitude, but by inclination and habit. It is in the sincerity of my heart that I say: may I never leave that hospitable land.

But it is not only on account of my own feelings that I am so strongly interested in the welfare, prosperity and successes of England, it is also as a man. The safety of Europe, that of the world and the future happiness and independence of mankind rests upon the preservation and independence of England, and this is the noble cause of Buonaparte's rage against you and that of his gang. May you defeat his wicked plans and maintain this country in its present glorious and happy situation is the true wish of my heart and of my most fervent prayer. Your Lordship must be equally well acquainted with my opinion respecting religious differences among Christians and in other words amongst men who profess the same religion. I believe every man must remain true to the principles in which he has been brought up, but I equally believe that it is not in such times as these we live in that such differences can be a real cause of differences among Christians; the question is not whether one is a Christian of this or that sect but whether he is a Christian or not.[1]

This is in my humble opinion the only question at the time when the vital parts of religion and morality are attacked with such force and where the melancholy experience of the latter years show with what rapidity irreligion and immorality are spreading their baneful dominion over mankind.

From the knowledge I have acquired of your Lordship's great mind, I thought your opinion would be what I am very glad to find it is. I hope you will allow me to say that I congratulate you upon sentiments as worthy at once of an Englishman, a Prelate and a true Christian.

My dear Lord,

Ever your affectionate,

L.-P. P. Orléans

[1] Cf. one of Madame de Genlis' reports on her pupil: "Sous le rapport religieux il sera mauvais élève." Eighteenth-century English Latitudinarianism suited him perfectly.

The second letter looks back on his period of exile in England during a similar period of frustrating inactivity in Sicily in 1808. He writes to d'Antraigues:

It makes me doubly mad to see myself condemned to the humiliation of useless inactivity when I see all the things I could do if people didn't always appear to keep me under lock and key at Hampton Court or at Twickenham. My odd position certainly has advantages which I can exaggerate to myself, but which I think I could put to good account. I am a French prince and however also an Englishman, this of necessity because nobody knows better than I do that England is the only power which can protect me; but I am also an Englishman in terms of my principles, my opinions and all my habits . . . I may be harbouring illusions when I say I believe I could be very useful to them in their alliances on the Continent but I am quite sure I am *not* harbouring any illusions when I say that I am quite useless and merely a burden when I'm ordered to do nothing but drive a curricle from Hampton Court to London and from London to Hampton Court.

His appreciation of the charms of "that hospitable land" was real enough whether he was dining in magnificence at Stowe,[1] or teaching Tom Moore French songs at Lord Moira's house at Donnington Park, or dining in a Bucklersbury eating-house for 9*d*.,[2] and the ease and familiarity of his English relationships contrasted sharply with the humiliation to which he was subjected on his first visit to Louis XVIII at Hartwell. He arrived a little early after Mass one Sunday morning to be met in the hall by the

[1] "The French cook did not shine, and tho' he had the assistance of three more French cooks of his own choosing and that no expense was spared the dinner was neither good nor bien choisi. Gunter was more successful in his desert. . . ." (Wynne Diaries, entry for January 9th, 1808).

[2] At any rate according to Disraeli: "In the King's time there never was a dinner given at the Tuileries – no matter how stately; I have seen it in the Gallery of Diana with a hundred guests – without a large smoking ham being placed, at a certain time, before the King. Upon this he operated like a conjuror. The rapidity and precision with which he carved it was a marvellous feat; the slices were vast, but wafer-thin. It was his great delight to carve this ham, and indeed it was a wonderful performance. He told me one day that he had learnt the trick from a waiter at Bucklersbury, where he used to dine once at an eating-house for 9*d*. per head."

Duchesse d'Angoulême, Louis XVI's daughter who had married her cousin, the eldest son of the Comte d'Artois. At the sight, in no sense unexpected, of the son of Philippe Egalité, the lady became extremely pale and her legs gave way. As Louis-Philippe went forward to her assistance, she repulsed him and had to be led off to her apartments. She managed eventually to come down to luncheon and even engaged in a little conversation with the ex-Jacobin on the subject of her purely imaginary palpitations.[1] Whatever mental reservations about the reconciliation there may have been on Louis-Philippe's side, all was certainly not forgotten nor forgiven on the other.

Two major preoccupations increasingly disturbed Louis-Philippe's secluded cultivation of his Thames-side retreat – the state of his brothers' health and the insistent and natural desire, so clearly set out in his letter to d'Antraigues, to be of some service to the allied cause or at any rate to seek some outlet and employment for his own talents. His only positive achievement during these years – and one for which he received no thanks – was the decisive part he played in bringing Louis XVIII to England. In 1804 Louis XVIII endeavoured to convene a meeting of all the exiled princes in Calmar to discuss the new situation created by the proclamation of the Empire. The British government allowed Artois to go but Louis-Philippe was refused permission, having to content himself with writing a shrewd and perceptive letter on the subject of Napoleon's new honours, in which occurs the phrase "the imperial government is only one more phase of the revolution". However he busied himself in negotiating successively with Grenville, Fox and the Prince of Wales in an endeavour to secure asylum for Louis XVIII in England. Unable to secure their assent, he urged Louis not to wait for an invitation but to arrive and see what happened, a plan which succeeded admirably when Louis XVIII landed at Yarmouth in the autumn of 1807. The year before, Dumouriez approached Fox and Windham (whose gratitude Louis-Philippe had earned in 1804

[1] It would be interesting to know exactly when in the nineteenth century palpitations ceased to be a recognized weapon in the feminine armoury.

by drawing up for him a lengthy memorandum on the French armies)[1] with the suggestion that the Duke of Orléans would make an ideal king for the rebellious Spanish colonists in South America. This came to nothing as did an even more chimerical prospect whereby he was to become King of the Ionian Islands. The deadlock was in the event broken by tragic developments inside his own family circle.

Ever since their arrival in England, Montpensier's great personal charm and considerable artistic talents, had made him a universal favourite. He soon fell desperately in love with Lord Moira's sister, Lady Charlotte Rawdon, whom he proposed to marry, a project frustrated by the dynastic rigidity of both Louis-Philippe and Artois. But in 1807 his health began to fail and he died to the great grief of his brothers at Salthill near Slough in May of that year at the age of thirty-two and was accorded a state funeral.[2] Beaujolais at first appeared robuster and led a very much more vigorous social life, in some respects reminiscent of his father's, but he too was fated never to see his native land again apart from a distant view of the camp at Boulogne from aboard a British reconnoitring frigate. By 1808 the doctors considered it vital that he should live in a gentler climate and so in the spring of that year Louis-Philippe with a heavy heart set sail with him for Malta and in so doing opened a new and eventful chapter in his strange existence.

[1] Brit. Mus. Add. MSS. 37870.
[2] And eventually in 1829 a splendid epitaph in Westminster Abbey which rightly described him as "a tenera juventute in armis strenuus, in vinculis indomitus, in adversis rebus non fractus".

IV

The Comte de Beaujolais died at Malta in May 1808, aged twenty-eight, a few days after their arrival at Malta. For Louis-Philippe, exile was now combined with the spectre of loneliness, for at thirty-five he was still unmarried. He had lost his early grace and was becoming somewhat portly both in face and figure, although physically still hard and resilient. It seems that before leaving England he had thought hard about the possibility of marriage and a family and he was in correspondence with Ferdinand IV of the two Sicilies about the possibility of hiring a villa near Mount Etna at the time his brother died. It was unthinkable for an Orléans prince (even the unhappy Montpensier) to marry beneath his rank, but the available princesses in Bonaparte's Europe were few and far between. The most evidently eligible was Marie-Amélie, the only unmarried daughter of the eighteen children born to the King of the Two Sicilies, Ferdinand IV, brother of Charles IV of Spain (and a direct descendant of Louis XIV). The young lady (she was aged at this time twenty-six) was known to be virtuous and amiable, but as a prospective mother-in-law Queen Marie-Caroline, a sister of Marie-Antoinette, was the most daunting possible prospect. Masterful women were not uncommon in the Habsburg family, but Marie-Caroline was more than masterful – she was a witch. When Collingwood heard Louis-Philippe was going to Palermo he exclaimed: "God protect you from Queen Caroline. She is the wickedest woman He ever created"; and Napoleon, who had reason to know a great deal about her, warned his brother in 1806, "You have to do with a woman who is crime personified." It was in that year that Ferdinand and Marie-Caroline had to abandon their mainland possessions and since then they had been living under the protection of the British fleet in Sicily, where Ferdinand consoled himself by fishing and Marie-Caroline by hectic intrigue tempered by opium. It says a good deal, therefore, for Louis-Philippe's tact and Marie-Caroline's match-making proclivities that the sister of Marie-Antoinette rapidly overcame her repugnance to the idea of accepting the son of Philippe Egalité as a prospective husband for her daughter.

As to the princess in question, Marie-Amélie, the future Queen of the French, we are in the fortunate position of being able to analyse the progress of the courtship in the pages of her private diary. "He is of medium height," she writes, "rather stout, neither ugly nor handsome. He has Bourbon features,[1] is polite and very learned." He for his part knew of her reputed sweetness of temperament ("a harsh woman is an absolute scourge in a household" he told her mother) and was immediately impressed by her great natural dignity, which would one day lead Talleyrand to describe her as "the last great lady in Europe". Her own description of herself, accounted to be substantially accurate, runs as follows:

> I am tall and well-built, my face is rather long, my eyes are blue, neither particularly large nor small, but lively; my forehead is very high; I have no great quantity of hair but it is golden; my nose is aquiline, my mouth of moderate size, my lips red, my teeth not beautiful but well set;[2] a round chin with a pretty dimple; a long neck and good shoulders and a small bosom; my hands and arms rather ugly, a good leg, but rather long feet. Dans l'ensemble I have an air of modest but imposing nobility which makes people realize who I am.

As the advantages of the proposed match were increasingly borne in on Louis-Philippe, he was able to convince his future mother-in law of his unswerving allegiance to the principles of throne and altar (to a point somewhat in advance of his genuine convictions) and Marie-Caroline for her part wrote that she found he grew on acquaintance. Louis-Philippe, shortly after the deaths of his

[1] He bore in fact a striking resemblance to Louis XIV, later somewhat masked by the favoris and dewlaps, prominent in the Scheffer portrait.
[2] Not according to the Duchesse de Boigne.

two beloved brothers, was about to effect a wonderfully happy marriage, strong in love and mutual esteem, which was to survive domestic grief and public disaster alike.[1]

But before the marriage took place he was drawn into an ill-conceived political adventure the long-term consequences of which were to have a serious effect on his fortunes and reputation. 1808 was the summer of Dupont's surrender to the Spaniards at Baylen. Insurrectional Juntas had sprung up all over Spain and Palafox's heroic defence of Saragossa, amongst other feats of arms, suggested that here in the Peninsula allied intervention might at long last have decisive effects. Even before Sir Arthur Wellesley landed his fifteen thousand red-coats at Mondego Bay on August 3rd, Louis-Philippe set out for Spain from Palermo in a British ship, *Thunderer*. His prospective father-in-law was the brother of Charles IV of Spain, now languishing with his heir, the Prince of the Asturias, in Talleyrand's château of Valençay, and as such saw himself as the appropriate person to be Regent of Spain at the head of the insurrectionary Juntas. He decided to dispatch his second son, an ignorant and obese young man called Leopold, Prince of Salerno, to stake out his claims with his prospective son-in-law, the experienced Duc d'Orléans, as mentor. Here, surely, was the outlet for his military talents for which Louis-Philippe had been vainly hoping during fifteen long years of inactivity. Obviously excited by the prospect, he wrote to Marie-Caroline before setting off for Cadiz on July 28th, "the career of arms is the only one which suits my taste and my birth".

The upshot was disastrous. The British authorities at Palermo in letting them sail acted entirely on their own initiative, but by the time the *Thunderer* reached Gibraltar, then governed by that cautious dug-out, Sir Hew Dalrymple (soon to be the signatory of the Convention of Cintra), His Majesty's Government's wishes in the matter had become completely explicit. Under no circumstances were they to proceed further. Admiral Collingwood

---

[1] There is a curious Anglo-Saxon prejudice against the *mariage de convenance*. The superiority of the love-match is perhaps scarcely borne out by twentieth-century evidence.

advised strongly against the project, in legitimist circles it was put about that Louis-Philippe was aiming at the throne for himself, and the prevalent view in Downing Street was that nothing should be done in Spain which could possibly be construed as an attempt to impose conditions in return for British aid in the Peninsula. And in any case what was this French prince up to with his somewhat dubious antecedents? The Foreign Secretary, George Canning, was quite clear that Spanish affairs were complicated enough as it was and his letters whenever the Duc d'Orléans' name cropped up in the course of the succeeding year are distinctly sharp in tone.[1] A life of quiet retirement at Twickenham was one thing, involvement in Mediterranean politics quite another. And it would not be long before further events in Spain would appear to justify the Foreign Office view that this was a dangerous man who had to be watched.

So in the event Louis-Philippe was even refused a passage back to Palermo by the orders of the British Admiral, Sir Alexander Ball, a veteran of Les Saintes and Aboukir. He was in no position to antagonize his British paymasters and so headed for Twickenham, anxious to clear up the misunderstandings which threatened to undermine the confidence he had so laboriously built up during the years of exile between himself and the British ruling classes. The process was complicated by the fact that in addition to his own pension it was urgently necessary for him to do something for his mother and sister, whose house at Figuieras had been bombarded early in the year during fighting between the invading French armies and the Spaniards. At first he could get no response to his plea that they should be added to the pension list; nor would the government seem willing to give him facilities to return to the Mediterranean. Hawkesbury was polite, Canning decidedly less so. It was only by employing the good services of the Duke of Kent that eventually he obtained a grudging consent to both requests.[2] It seemed to Louis-Philippe not only humiliating to

[1] They are to be found in the Public Record Office – FO 27.78.
[2] In November 1808 Louis-Philippe wrote from Kensington Palace to the Duke of Portland pointing out that when he had gone to Minorca and

have to beg but unjust to be treated with such evident suspicion by the Foreign Office. It would not be for the last time; a new-comer joined the reconstituted government in 1809 as Secretary at War in the person of Viscount Palmerston.

Arriving at Portsmouth with permission to proceed to Malta, Louis-Philippe found awaiting him there his sister, Adélaïde, from whom he had been parted for fifteen years. She had found the company of M. Rouzet de Folmont increasingly disagreeable and her mother's infatuation for him ultimately unendurable and so had set out to seek her brother whom she had finally tracked down. Henceforth they would hardly ever be separated. He found Adélaïde much changed since the desperate occasion in 1793 when he had bundled her unceremoniously into Madame de Genlis' coach. Life for her since Belle-Chasse days had been consistently dreary and unrewarding and her plain features and the coarse complexion[1] she had inherited from her father denied her at thirty-one any emotional outlet other than the unstinting devotion which she lavished on the person and destiny of the brother, who must have seemed the one fixed point in a world which had so little fulfilled the optimistic expectations of her girlhood. She was a strong character – a woman of courage and decision, definite in her likes and dislikes, much less sensitive to other people's opinions than Louis-Philippe and with a wit and intelligence that enabled her to converse on public affairs to the admiration of men of the mental calibre of Talleyrand and Benjamin Constant.

In the spring of 1809, as the French armies were closing on the Danube, Louis-Philippe and Adélaïde were back in the Mediterranean with the twofold object of persuading their mother (now in Minorca) to join them and completing the marriage negotiations in Palermo. During Louis-Philippe's absence, Marie-Caroline's qualified enthusiasm for the match had cooled considerably, partly because of allegations emanating from émigré

Barcelona in 1800 the government had given him at that time unlimited credit (Royal Archives Add. MSS. Geo. 21/11/39).
[1] To say nothing of a deplorable taste in dress.

circles in London and transmitted by the Sicilian ambassador that Louis-Philippe was in Sicily merely as an English agent with orders to foment a constitutional revolution. Eventually after the last hesitations of Ferdinand had been overcome by a threat on the part of Marie-Amélie that she would take the veil if she were not allowed to marry Louis-Philippe,[1] the marriage took place in the presence of Louis-Philippe's mother and sister on November 25th, initially in the bedroom of Ferdinand IV (who had held up the proceedings by falling downstairs in his palace) and then in the exquisite Palatinate Chapel. Wife and sister took to each other immediately and henceforth Louis-Philippe would be surrounded by two adulatory women, whose existence was entirely devoted to his happiness. As to the bride and bridegroom, Marie-Caroline's verdict on them was: "Naughty Amélie has married the Duc d'Orléans; they have nothing to live on, are poor but happy, and love each other infinitely." [2]

1809 was a year of bitter disappointment for the enemies of Napoleon. The high hopes of the spring, during which Louis-Philippe sounded Metternich about the possibility of a command in the Austrian army, were shattered by the news of Wagram in July and the failure of the Walcheren expedition. Louis-Philippe's letters from Palermo show clearly that he was still restlessly hoping to be of some service to the allied cause that summer. But he would probably have resigned himself to the pleasures of domesticity in 1810,[3] but for a curious development in his affairs which led him to undertake another most imprudent adventure in Spain. The Chevalier de Broval, the leading (and at one time the

[1] Marie-Caroline's views were expressed in a letter at the end of October: "To add to all my sorrows, my daughter who is twenty-eight years old and despairs of not getting married, has become engaged to the Duc d'Orléans (dreadful name). I must put a good face on a matter that pains and humiliates me to excess, but my daughter is twenty-eight, knows everything and regards him as a hero, a god."

[2] The Sicilian background to Louis-Philippe's marriage is best studied in Harold Acton, *The Bourbons of Naples*.

[3] He seems to have made a start at overcoming his father-in-law's Anglophobia by asking the Duke of Kent to send to Palermo not only horses, but pedigree Scotch terriers (Brit. Mus. Add. MSS. 37290/109).

only) member of his household had gone to Catalonia in search of the Duchesse d'Orléans and while there had become much embroiled in Spanish politics. Perhaps as a result, early in 1810, the junta at Seville sent a secret emissary, Don Mariano Carnereiro, to Palermo with a letter from the Supreme Council of Regency of Spain and the Indies to S.A.R. the Duc d'Orléans which included the phrase: "the remembrance of the triumphs obtained by the ancestors of Your Highness still lives in Catalonia; it is the duty of your Highness to give new life to those laurels" and ends with the stirring appeal "may Your Highness raising your voice on the summit of the Pyrenees at the head of our victorious armies promise liberty to oppressed France and rescue the throne of your ancestors, restore order to Europe and proclaim the triumph of virtue over the ruins of tyranny and immorality".[1] This was altogether too much for Louis-Philippe to resist. It seemed quite suddenly after years of frustration as if Danton and Dumouriez were right after all and that he was being called by destiny to great things.[2] On May 21st he set sail in *La Venganza*, Don Mariano's ship, accompanied by de Broval, and landed at Tarragona just as Lerida had surrendered and O'Donnel's Catalan army was in retreat. Although he was greeted with something of an ovation, Louis-Philippe was offered not a Catalan army to command but a handful of French deserters. He decided to try his luck in the Southern sector and sailed to Cadiz (at that time beseiged by his future Prime Minister Soult[3]), arriving on June 20th.

On June 24th he despatched three letters[4] – one to Louis XVIII emphasizing that his actions were designed to further the cause of legitimacy; one to d'Antraigues, in which, after congratulating

[1] Brit. Mus. Add. MSS. 37290/163.

[2] Cf. a letter from his agent de Guilherny in London to de Broval written on April 7: "il est possible que les Cortes d'Espagne ouvrent à Monseigneur une grande et magnifique carrière politique" (Add. MSS. 37290/187). De Guilherny sent off three maps of Spain.

[3] Sébastiani, a future Foreign Minister of Louis-Philippe's, was commanding the French force at Granada.

[4] Add. MSS. 37290/169, 173, 177.

himself on remembering his Spanish so well after ten years' disuse, he reflects that no doubt many people in England will believe that what he is doing is folly, but that he has waited ten years for the chance of committing just such follies; and one to Dumouriez in which he concludes that the position in Catalonia is bad but not desperate, that Cadiz is strongly defended ("but whoever sticks exclusively to the defensive is bound in the end to be defeated") and that what is wanted is for Dumouriez to appear on the scene and modernize the Spanish army which still looks like those of Berwick and Vendôme.

But once again his exaltation was short lived. Downing Street regarded the proceedings as much worse than folly. On July 28th Admiral Keat anchored in Cadiz in the *Implacable* which he had driven furiously from Portsmouth, and told the Duc d'Orléans that Lord Liverpool[1] ordered him to go back to Great Britain immediately. On Louis-Philippe's refusal, Henry Wellesley, British ambassador at Cadiz and Wellington's brother, applied the necessary pressure to the Council of Regency which on August 25th politely asked him to leave Cadiz. An appeal to the Cortés merely resulted in the discouraging statement that "the Cortés considers your Highness' departure necessary for the safety of the country you have come to defend". By the end of October the adventure was over and Louis-Philippe on his way back to Palermo. It was no consolation, though perhaps something of a relief, for him to set down his views on the Foreign Office in a letter to d'Antraigues that summer. Much as he loves England he finds the activities of English diplomats consistently disastrous. Foreign affairs are not taken seriously and as for British Foreign Office officials in general their only concern is to dominate and they hardly ever understand the language or the character of the nationals to whom they are accredited. He was to return to the theme more than once in later life.

[1] Secretary of State for War with Palmerston as his subordinate.

V

Although at the time six months pregnant, Marie-Amélie had actively encouraged the Spanish adventure. Before Louis-Philippe returned to Sicily a new Duc de Chartres, Ferdinand-Louis-Charles, was born on September 3rd, 1810. In view of the infant's tragic destiny it is ironical to read of his mother writing just before his birth "everybody calculates that your son will be the heir presumptive to the throne of France".[1] But for the moment all was happiness in the family and soon Louis-Philippe was able to report enthusiastically: "Little Charles is coming on splendidly. He has the big Orléanic head (*la grosse tête orléanique*)." Two daughters followed – Louise, the future Queen of the Belgians in 1812 and Marie, the future Duchess of Württemberg in 1813 – before a second son would be born in France. In these years Louis-Philippe developed the strong vein of domesticity which was henceforth so predominant a trait in his character. He devoted much energy and detailed care to restoring the dilapidated mansion which the family inhabited outside Palermo, sending a stream of letters back to England for the purchase (preferably at knock-down prices) of household effects of one sort and another. It was as well that he found evident satisfaction in these domestic preoccupations since internal Sicilian politics were not only unedifying but dangerous, and wider horizons now seemed permanently closed to him. He and another underemployed prince, the Duke of Kent, concocted plans to topple Murat's Kingdom of Naples ("castles in Spain which make my mouth water", as Kent rather oddly described them[2]), and even as late as 1814 Dumouriez was urging some such plan in London on the grounds that "it would be an act of injustice, if the other

[1] There were as yet no children of the third generation in the elder branch.
[2] Brit. Mus. Add. MSS. 37290/131.

Bourbon princes are allowed to appear in the other armies, nay, it would be most impolitic, to exclude from them the prince who is the most capable". But nothing came of all this and in fact the art of mere survival in Sicily was at this time exacting enough, with the British plenipotentiary Lord William Bentinck and Queen Marie-Caroline on the worst possible terms and the crowd shouting for a Constitution under the King's windows. Louis-Philippe's equivocal position on the island impelled him to play the double game which was becoming dangerously second nature to him. For family reasons he had to maintain a semblance of loyalty to the régime but he was a personal friend of Bentinck's and sympathized with the islanders' demands for some sort of constitutional protection from the capricious fantasies of the Queen. He had no illusions as to the probable outcome. He wrote to his friend the Vicomte de Rohan Chabot, an officer in the English army, at the beginning of 1812:

> Our position here is precarious. We are surrounded by the sort of moral crises one forgets in the happy island where Twickenham is (Twickenham, whose memory I still love though my position there was not exactly brilliant). We can't tell what's going to happen. Therefore I haven't yet built up a permanent staff. Kirchner is still in Malta with my things; I simply don't know from one day to another what's going to happen to me. So one isn't exactly in a position to suggest to anyone that they should leave their gout, their friends and the country they're used to to come and embark on a *sea of troubles*.[1]

The anticipated crisis was not long delayed. Bentinck fathered a constitution on the island in 1812: Marie-Caroline propelled her husband into an attempted coup d'état; and although Louis-Philippe did his best to act as a peace-maker and persuaded Ferdinand to leave Palermo for his country retreat, Bentinck had had enough and Marie-Caroline was soon on her way, via Constantinople, to Vienna where she died of apoplexy in 1814.

[1] The last phrase was characteristically in English. Louis-Philippe always enjoyed airing his Shakespeare.

Nor did the Constitution survive 1814, although it would be heard of again – notably in 1848.

Either because news reached Sicily slowly of the final convulsions of the Napoleonic Empire in the winter and early spring of 1814 or because he failed to appreciate rapidly the significance of what was happening, Louis-Philippe remained inactive in Sicily, while Artois moved nervously from Basle to Nancy, and his eldest son, Angoulême, trailed along behind Wellington's army, until the royalist revolt in Bordeaux of March 12th at least suggested that there was at any rate some semblance of enthusiasm in France for a Bourbon restoration. Two days later Napoleon was proclaiming: "I am still the man I was at Wagram and Austerlitz" and Alexander of Russia told Vitrolles, Louis XVIII's emissary, that as far as he could see the alternatives lay between giving the crown to Bernadotte, Eugène or the Duc d'Orléans or establishing "a wisely organized republic". But within a fortnight Castlereagh, Hardenberg and Metternich drank together for the first time to the success of the Bourbons. On the 30th Napoleon heard of Marmont's defection and on the morning of the 31st the rulers of Russia and Prussia rode into Paris. On April 5th Alexander was still suggesting to the members of Talleyrand's provisional government[1] that they should accept the King of Rome, but the next day the Senate adopted unanimously a constitutional draft by which "the people of France call freely to the throne of France, Louis-Stanislas-Xavier of France, brother of the last King and after him the other members of the house of Bourbon in the old order". Artois, back in the Tuileries, and looking wonderfully handsome in the inappropriate uniform of the National Guard, was made Lieutenant-General pending Louis XVIII's acceptance of the constitution. On the 23rd of April an armistice convention gave Europe its first day of formal peace since the rupture of the Peace of Amiens.

That day an English frigate, the *Aboukir*, landed at Palermo with news of these events. Bentinck immediately put it at Louis-

[1] Which included Beurnonville, whom Louis-Philippe had met in such peculiar circumstances in 1793.

Philippe's disposal and by May 1st he left for France accompanied by White, his valet de chambre, a week after Louis XVIII had left Dover on the *Royal Sovereign* escorted by eight ships of the line.

By the time Louis-Philippe was able to present himself to his cousin on May 18th, the royal declaration of May 2nd from St. Ouen, with its preface "Louis, by the grace of God, King of France and Navarre", had shown clearly that the Restoration was to be a restoration of divine right with no unnecessary concessions to the principle of popular sovereignty. Nor was it perhaps a happy inspiration for an inscription to be placed on the statue of Henri IV on the Pont-Neuf which read "Ludovico reduce, Henricus redivivus"; nor yet encouraging for the Old Guard lining the route of the King's triumphal re-entry to the capital to observe the Duc d'Angoulême riding beside the royal carriage in an English general's uniform. But for all the returned exiles it was a joyous moment and one in which old rivalries and suspicions, at least amongst themselves, could easily be overlooked. Louis-Philippe's reception was gracious and the King told him affably, "my cousin, you were a lieutenant-general twenty-five years ago;[1] I restore you to your rank with twenty-five years' service". And with it he received the appointment and emoluments of Colonel-General of Hussars. The next day by royal ordinance he resumed his possession of the Palais-Royal and the Parc de Monceau. After twenty-one years' exile he was home again.

The scene which confronted him at the Palais-Royal, where he describes himself as falling on his knees and kissing the first step of the marble staircase, was horrible. The palace had been used since 1806 as a store-house for unwanted furniture for which large orders had been placed to provide employment for out-of-work Paris manufacturers. In addition the shops and trading booths of Egalité's day had spread themselves all over the precincts. He began rapidly transforming it to its former grandeur as a home for his wife and children, still in Sicily. He appointed as his

[1] A slight exaggeration, but time had not passed quickly for either of them.

A.D.C.'s two officers of the Imperial army, Atthalin and de Sainte-Aldégonde, and renewed some old acquaintanceships, notably with Lafayette and Macdonald. Paris was almost as strange to him as London had been in 1800, but a common factor was always the Comte d'Artois – extremely vivacious and genial these days amidst his vapid entourage which was rashly encouraged to believe that while his clever elder brother did the thinking for the new régime (or perhaps, properly speaking, the old one) he and his friends would do the acting. When he pointed out his surprise at seeing Louis-Philippe sporting a white cockade, he laid himself open to the rejoinder that it was equally unexpected to see the Comte d'Artois in National Guard uniform.

After a short trip to England for business purposes and to plead the cause of his father-in-law with the allied sovereigns in London, Louis-Philippe brought from Sicily his wife, once again pregnant, his sister and his three children and by September 22nd they were all installed in the Palais-Royal and Marie-Amélie was soon afterwards received at the Tuileries with great kindness, even by the Duchesse d'Angoulême. A second son, the Duc de Nemours, was born in October. In addition to all these family preoccupations, Louis-Philippe had to address himself to the enormously complicated task of sorting out the Orléans estate. His father had died bankrupt with innumerable creditors. His mother who had now returned to France, after parting from the family circle in Palermo with some rancour four years earlier, had her own needs and those of M. Rouzet de Folmont to press. Although it seemed probable that a great part of the family patrimony would be recoverable, it would be a slow process discharging the debts with which it was encumbered. The King himself took a benevolent interest in all this and Marie-Amélie, who after all was a niece of Marie-Antoinette, was primarily instrumental in creating a better atmosphere between the Tuileries and the Palais-Royal than can ever have seemed likely. While during the winter the Palais-Royal salon included rather more savants and disgruntled heroes of the Empire than can have been considered suitable by Artois' immediate circle at the Pavillon de Marsan, it was still altogether respectable and Châteaubriand was among the guests as well as Constant and Guizot. Reconciliation was the mood of the moment. Louis-Philippe, for instance, called on a well-known literary lady who had really done very well for herself under the Empire, but who was now writing: "I, who as my works prove have always loved them, saw the return of the Bourbon family with an inexpressible joy." Having broken a good many years' ice, Louis-Philippe brought along his wife to be introduced to the interesting sexagenarian Madame de Genlis. Marie-Amélie carried off the honours of the encounter by saying that there were two products of Madame de Genlis which she loved passionately – her pupils and her books.

But while in court circles the restored Monarchy seemed to be taking root, more than one of its enemies was actively plotting its overthrow. One of the least committed adherents of the régime was Fouché, Duke of Otranto, who, observing that he had been unaccountably overlooked for ministerial appointment, was the centre of intrigues which in the winter of 1814–15 involved him in correspondence with figures as diverse as Davout, Lafayette, Metternich and the officer commanding the 16th division at Lille, Drouet d'Erlon.

VI

It was not difficult to see that many people in France wished the overthrow of the Bourbons. How to replace them was more difficult and a discreet approach to the Duc d'Orléans by Talleyrand before he left for the Congress of Vienna evoked no response. The troops at Lille began an insurrection on March 7th, only to be disarmed without difficulty by Marshal Mortier. But already before that, on March 1st, 1815, Napoleon had landed at Cannes with a thousand men while Wellington, Metternich, Talleyrand and Hardenberg were discussing the settlement of Europe at Vienna.

On March 5th at eleven o'clock in the evening, Louis XVIII's unpopular favourite, the Comte de Blacas d'Aulps, arrived at the Palais-Royal and insisted on taking the Duc d'Orléans straight to the King without even giving him time to change into uniform, Louis-Philippe learning for the first time en route for the Tuileries of Napoleon's landing. "This is immensely dangerous," he said immediately, to which Blacas replied: "The King doesn't see it like that and you will find him very calm." From the armchair to which he was confined by an access of gout, Louis XVIII explained his preliminary dispositions – the garrisons of Grenoble and Valence to block the path of the invader, de Berri to go to Besançon, Angoulême to Nîmes, Artois to Lyon with Orléans to assist him. Louis-Philippe suggested that he would be better employed raising a mobile reserve between Lyon and Paris, inwardly resenting the prospect of being employed as Artois' A.D.C. But the King was adamant. "I don't say you've got to go this evening, but get your boots greased and come and see me tomorrow morning."

On the 8th, Louis-Philippe was joined by another veteran of Jemappes, Macdonald, Duke of Taranto, who was also on his way to Lyon to supplement the somewhat uncertain military potential of the Comte d'Artois, similar roles having been allotted to Ney and Gouvion de Saint Cyr in respect of the other princes. The next day he reported immediately to Artois' headquarters in the Archbishop's Palace to be met with the news of Napoleon's triumphal entry into Grenoble. Both Macdonald and Louis-Philippe suggested withdrawing the troops from Lyon, but the Comte d'Artois was always a master of supremely dignified but total indecision in moments of crisis. Eventually, in the small hours of March 10th, they heard that Napoleon's advance-guard was rapidly approaching the suburbs and felt it highly desirable to report the fact to their superior commander. This was less easy to achieve than might reasonably have been expected as Artois' command post turned out to be the archiepiscopal bedroom, where he was fast asleep in a curtained four-poster, the key being in the hands of the captain of the guard, who was nowhere to be found. Neither Louis-Philippe nor Macdonald had any intention, if they could avoid it, of falling into the hands of Napoleon. Consequently, when they eventually effected an entry, Macdonald decided to ignore conventions of etiquette and prefaced an extremely frank statement of the situation with the words "Mais, Monsieur, levez-vous donc." They were all soon on their way to Paris, none quicker than Louis-Philippe, who, with a prudence born of similar experiences, had his horses ready. That evening Napoleon entered the city to cries of "Down with the nobles! Down with the priests! The Bourbons to the scaffold!"

On his return to Paris, Louis-Philippe relayed these rather humiliating proceedings to Louis XVIII who, no doubt already sceptical of Marshal Ney's capacity to deliver Napoleon in an iron cage, nevertheless showed commendably calm and courage amid the turmoil of the capital. He then rapidly effected the escape of his wife and children to England, and was shortly afterwards visited by the Prefect of Police who informed him that it was considered desirable that he should leave Paris. But with the news of Ney's desertion to his old master, it became all too clear that it was in any case highly desirable for everybody in any way associated with the régime to leave Paris as quickly as possible. Macdonald's counsels eventually prevailed at the Tuileries and a general retreat to the north, directed on the fortress of Lille, was decided upon. In these circumstances Louis-Philippe found himself offered by the newly appointed War Minister, Clarke,[1] the command of the Army of the North, with Marshal Mortier as his second in command. The terrain would be far from unfamiliar to him. On the 19th he was inspecting the fortifications of Lille. Towards midnight that evening, Louis XVIII in carpet-slippers crossed the Tuileries between lines of weeping courtiers to the waiting berline which was to carry him to yet another exile.

On the 22nd the King arrived in Lille as Louis-Philippe and Mortier were discussing the insoluble problem of how to defend a strong-point, whose garrison showed no inclination to fight. After a four-hour conference in the King's presence attended by three Napoleonic marshals, Berthier, Macdonald, and Mortier, it was decided on Louis-Philippe's advice that a stand should be made at Dunkirk, which was still on French territory, was comparatively easy to defend and from where it would be possible to maintain contact with England. But by the next morning Louis had gone back on this decision and taken the road to exile at Ghent. The Marshals were thanked for their services before his departure, but when Louis-Philippe asked what he was expected to do, he received the discouraging answer: "Ma foi, Monsieur, you can do just what you like." Left in effect in command of the royal army without any orders, he took a decision, understandable in itself in a veteran soldier to whom leaving his troops without orders was unthinkable, but which nevertheless opened a chasm between himself and the older branch of the family which was never to be bridged. He wrote out an order which he gave to Mortier to transmit to the troops which read: "I must inform you that the unhappy circumstances in which we find ourselves having led the King to leave France this afternoon, I release you from the orders which I have transmitted to you in his name. I leave it to

[1] Once a *habitué* of Madame de Genlis' salon.

your judgement and to your patriotism to do what you think most suitable in the interests of France." He then set out, not for Ghent, but for Twickenham. It was a parting of the ways, which Louis XVIII never forgave, followed as it was by a correspondence which made it abundantly clear how much their respective views differed on the causes and probable outcome of the catastrophe of the first Restoration.

The choice for Louis-Philippe at this crisis lay between committing himself irrevocably to the life of a virtually powerless social luminary in a palace society which distrusted him and which he in his turn despised or keeping his freedom of action by withdrawing into a retirement from which events might summon him. But freedom for what action? Certain aspects of the situation in the spring of 1815 were clear enough. For the returned émigrés the King had been more important than the constitutional Charter, for the majority of the nation the Charter was more important than the King; there was a vigorous and articulate Liberal Opposition in Paris to any form of autocratic and repressive government (as Napoleon was already finding to his cost) and finally the allies were uncertain and divided amongst themselves as to how order was to be restored in France and peace in Europe. All else was obscure in a world in which Napoleon's Minister of Police was in the habit of leaving his master's presence to engage immediately in brisk correspondence with Metternich and Talleyrand at Vienna and with the Duc d'Orléans at Twickenham. Louis-Philippe knew perfectly well that his name was being freely canvassed in the highest circles. Wellington had a good opinion of his character and abilities and had once written to Dumouriez: "I have often lamented the lot of the Duke of Orleans. He is a prince of the most estimable character, great talents and deserved reputation." Talleyrand wrote from Vienna in April 1815 to Louis XVIII, reporting a conversation between the Tsar and Lord Clancarty in which Alexander said: "I see no one so fitted to conciliate all parties as the Duc d'Orléans; he is a Frenchman, a Bourbon, and he has sons. He also, when young, served the constitutional cause. He has worn the tricolour cockade, which

I often maintained, when in Paris, should never have been discarded. In him all parties would be united." Talleyrand, it is true, added reassuringly: "The Emperor Alexander hardly understands the principle of legitimacy." But it was known in Vienna that the Duc d'Orléans had been heard to say: "If they had listened to me not so many stupidities would have been committed", and he had sent the Congress two carefully phrased memoranda on the subject. The Tsar felt that the Congress should give serious consideration to his claims.

But once Waterloo was won,[1] the principle of legitimacy began to carry the day. Fouché, who had been urging on Wellington "the personal qualities of the Duc d'Orléans, the remembrance of Jemappes, the possibility of making a treaty which would conciliate all interests, and the name of Bourbon which might serve outside, but not be pronounced within", had by now concluded that "nothing can be done with a Bourbon who has neither a mistress nor a confessor", and placed himself at the head of an Executive Commission of five, of whom only two, Carnot and Quinette, favoured the Orléanist solution. Soon Wellington had made his decision, Louis XVIII and Talleyrand were back in Paris and the second Restoration had begun.

On July 26th Louis-Philippe wrote to Chabot, "Like a mortar-bomb I'm going to be hurled from Twickenham – the peace of Twick – to fall on the agitated ground of Paris. I've had a number of letters from Paris, all urging me to come as soon as possible. It isn't that the King has condescended to advise me or send a message. No; I'm still *sent to Coventry*." He was only in Paris a short time (receiving a chilly welcome at the Tuileries) and wrote again at the end of August: "Here I am again at old Twick, my dear Viscount, without knowing exactly when I will leave it. Everything has been ruined for a long time to come in that unhappy country and I don't know what one's going to see happen there." What was happening in fact in that unhappy country was a ruinous military occupation, savage legitimist reprisals in the

[1] Dumouriez always liked to point out the exact spot on a London pavement where he danced with joy when Louis-Philippe told him the news.

South, and the election of the notoriously reactionary *Chambre Introuvable* in August. "Mercy is not fashionable this season," observed Madame de Rémusat.

The Duc d'Orléans, with the other princes, was nominated by the King a member of the Chamber of Peers and became immediately involved in an issue of political principle, over which he was completely unwilling to compromise his deepest convictions. In their debate on the reply to the address the Peers were pressing for the utmost rigour against their enemies.[1] Louis-Philippe, a little pale and nervous, walked on to the tribune and urged strongly the unsuitability of the Chamber, which under the Charter was empowered to judge political offences, anticipating its judicial functions. Only eight of the peers voted with him, but they included the President of the Council, Richelieu, and the Minister of Justice. Coming from a prince of the blood in the prevalent atmosphere of vicious reaction, this was extremely *mal vu* and it meant that Louis-Philippe had to return to exile in England for a period of nearly two years. The ordinance empowering the princes of the blood to sit in the Peers was withdrawn. In October and January in two letters written to Chabot in the usual odd mixture of French and English Louis-Philippe summed up the situation in France as well as his own outlook and prospects. "Here I am back in *old England* and delighted to be so, because *prospects* the other side of the water are not exactly bright . . . Unhappy France! What evils befall her through the fury of certain individuals and the blindness and bad faith of all. The fact is that in these matters the court party is irresistible although its influence is restricted entirely to the court and it has no influence in the country." And again:

My office has sent me four enormous memoranda on the liquidation of my inheritance which isn't going better than anything else, but which involves me in writing letters like a clerk. This year I have twenty-two cuts of wood unsold through lack of buyers . . . But enough on the business of the wood-merchant; the politician is no

[1] E.g. the Duc de Fitzjames: "The whole electorate demands the punishment of the guilty; the nation is disgusted at the impunity they enjoy."

better; everywhere one sees nothing but misery. What a mess they're in there! I bless heaven, *morning, noon and night* that I'm in my peaceful house in *old Twick*, on the *Banks of the Thames*. I would be delighted, as would my family, to go back to Paris if we had the prospect of being quiet there, but today that would only mean one would be the centre of attention of friends and enemies alike and that's a situation that doesn't particularly attract me.

These are hardly the letters of the restless and ambitious intriguer which legitimist historians consistently depict. When he did return to Paris in the summer of 1817 Villèle observed: "What is singular is that he is not in the least disposed to make himself factious." Louis XVIII with his usual shrewdness summed up the true position as follows: "The Duc d'Orléans remains absolutely still but nevertheless I notice that he is moving forward. This activity without movement alarms me. What does one do to stop a man who does not move? It's a problem I shall have to solve. I certainly wouldn't care to leave the solution to my successor."

VII

The wood-merchant and the paterfamilias predominated in these years at Twickenham, which, despite the early letters to Chabot, were very happy years. For £270 a year Louis-Philippe had leased the riverside house of Mr George Pococke. It consisted of an oriel centre and a long wing carried to an extremely decorative octagonal tower, which still exists. Politics obtruded from time to time – the retention of Atthalin as A.D.C. despite his rallying to Napoleon during the Hundred Days was commented on; Ney's wife persuaded him to write a letter to the Prince Regent urging her husband's acquittal;[1] and Louis-Philippe's name was associated with the Didier conspiracy. Decazes had the family spied on and it was thought a coup had been achieved when a printing press was reported to be operating in Orléans House, although it turned out to be only a toy one, bought to amuse the children. But in general the picture is one of cheerful domesticity and steady business correspondence with the hard-headed agent Dupin, who was busily building up the family patrimony to its former magnificence and driving some very hard bargains in the process.

The not always indulgent Duchesse de Boigne described Louis-Philippe at this period as follows:

> The Duc d'Orléans led a retired life in the society of his family. He was perhaps never at any time so brilliant in his conversation as he was in these days. He had passed the age when his knowledge, as extensive as it was varied, appeared a little tarnished by pedantry. The impartiality of his mind enabled him to grasp all situations and

[1] The Princesse de la Moskowa had emphasized to Louis-Philippe the absurdity of Europe being called in to condemn her husband to death when Bonaparte, "author of all our miseries and the only man really guilty", was allowed to live. The correspondence is in the Royal Archives at Windsor.

to discuss them with generous moderation. The happiness of his home life soothed the occasional vexations caused by his political position and altogether I have never seen him to such advantage or in such a state of contentment as in the little drawing-room at Twickenham.

There were old friends to meet again – the Prince Regent and the Duke of Kent among them – and new ones including Leopold of Saxe-Coburg, who may have noticed in the family circle the blonde and vivacious Louise. Marie Amélie and Adélaïde visited Oxford, Blenheim, Stowe, Hatfield and – not for the last time – Claremont. Between 1816 and 1824, six more children were born – a daughter who died of consumption aged three; Clémentine, who married Augustus of Saxe-Coburg-Gotha and lived to be ninety; François, Duc de Joinville, who lived to be eighty-two; a son, the Duc de Penthièvre, who was mentally deficient and died in 1828; Henri, Duc d'Aumale, who lived to be seventy-five; and Antoine, Duc de Montpensier, who lived to be seventy-six. With a vigorous family of five sons and three daughters to educate and establish, it was worth totting up carefully the proceeds accruing from the activities of the woodcutters and as it happened Louis-Philippe found work of that sort congenial.

By 1817 the whole family was back in the Palais-Royal and it was possible to supervise minutely the legal and commercial activities of Dupin and de Broval. Mountains of legal documents were perused and annotated; capital and income were manipulated with skill and perseverance; and to him who had already abundantly, more was being continually added. In 1821 Marie-Adélaïde died of cancer of the breast and left her enormous fortune to her children, two-thirds to Louis-Philippe and one-third to Adélaïde; his aunt the Duchesse de Bourbon died the next year; and in 1825 Louis-Philippe acquired seventeen million francs, as a result of Villèle's much criticized measure of compensation for the émigrés. As if all this were not enough, the last of the Condés, the depraved old Duc de Bourbon made a will leaving Chantilly and his other possessions to the young Duc d'Aumale at the instance of his imperious mistress, who had started life as Sophie Dawes, a fisherman's daughter from the Isle of Wight, and who found it socially helpful to use the Palais-Royal as a stepping-stone to the Tuileries. The enormous wealth of the Orléans family invited both envy and criticism, not all of it unjust. Louis-Philippe had known poverty and in-security and now wished himself and his family to live in princely magnificence with their futures assured.[1] He had nothing else to do, but at the same time the mental concentration and re-sourceful ingenuity which he devoted to the process of making money to some extent hardened his character and developed a dangerous aspect of it – his growing conviction that there was nobody who could outwit him in the management of men and affairs. In all other respects his attitude and activities under Louis XVIII and Charles X were impeccable. Although Artois and Berri treated him affably, the old King was deeply distrustful of him and seemed to rejoice in inflicting social humiliations on him. One folding-door at the Tuileries would be opened for Louis-Philippe, two for his wife; at Notre-Dame their prayer-stools would be removed so that they had to kneel further back on the carpet; at the baptism ceremony of the Duc de Bordeaux the Chancellor was about to hand the Duc d'Orléans the pen with which to sign the *acte de naissance* when the King sent that digni-tary away and insisted in a loud voice that he be replaced by a junior member of the ceremonial staff. These trivial but exasperat-ing humiliations bitterly hurt Louis-Philippe's pride, and must have reminded him of his father's stories of the attitude of Versailles in the old days. All the time venomous rumours were being circulated about him in the Faubourg Saint-Germain. When the Duc de Bordeaux, *l'enfant du miracle*, was born after the assassination of his father, the Duc de Berri, an article casting aspersions on his legitimacy appeared in the *Morning Chronicle* and its authorship was inevitably attributed (as it has been by subsequent generations of legitimist historians) to Louis-Philippe.

[1] He wrote to Vatout in 1823: "When one remembers the time of Saint Gothard, one puts up with the inconveniences of the Palais-Royal."

He would in due course have plenty of opportunity to evaluate the morals of the Duchesse de Berri, but there is no evidence whatever to associate him with an action of this sort which is totally out of character.

But a return to Paris meant for Louis-Philippe the attention of friends as well as the suspicions and malevolence of enemies. Voluble and gregarious in middle age, his width of interests attracted to the Palais-Royal, where the entertainment provided in the way of dinners and concerts was anything but meagre, a clientèle which recalled the brilliant constellation of the seventeen-eighties. There were his old comrades in arms, Mortier, Valence, Macdonald and Beurnonville; Foy, Gérard, Sébastiani, lesser lights of the Napoleonic epic, but of greater political significance; amongst the Peers, the ageing Talleyrand, the austere Duc de Broglie, the courtly and dignified Comte Molé; among prominent deputies, critical of the régime, the two bankers, the vain and vulgar Laffitte and the formidable Casimir-Périer; members of the *corps diplomatique*, Pozzo di Borgo, Rostopchine and Apponyi; and, amongst prominent intellectuals, the poet Casimir Delavigne, the historian Guizot and the journalist Paul-Louis Courier. The latter wrote of Louis-Philippe in 1822: "I should like him to be *maire* of the *commune*. He would keep things quiet, not only through the wisdom which God has given him, but through a virtue no less considerable and too little appreciated – economy. A bourgeois quality if you like . . ."

Bourgeois is a word which has had a bad press in this century and is a great deal overdue for a historical revaluation. The history of social amelioration in Western civilization owes something to aristocrats like the Earl of Shaftesbury and even more to cloth-cap visionaries like Keir Hardie, but it owes more still to the enlightened elements in the middle classes. In the eighteen-twenties in France it became steadily clearer that Talleyrand, in backing the principle of Legitimacy, had backed the wrong horse. The reactionary doctrines of de Maistre and de Bonald, the rhetorical and gloomy fanaticism of Châteaubriand, the much-vaunted alliance of Throne and Altar, and the activities of legitimist firebrands like the Chevaliers de la Foi were not only anachronistic, but seemed in the eyes of the younger members of the bourgeoisie, nurtured on romantic liberalism, both wicked and – what is even more dangerous in France – ultimately ridiculous. The once frivolous and dissipated Comte d'Artois had somehow been metamorphosed into Charles X, the descendant of Clovis, stretched out on the Coronation cushions at Rheims and pricked seven times with a gold needle. Parliamentary government on the basis of an electorate of 90,000 under the adroit management of Villèle seemed to hold out little prospect for those who, like Guizot, were proud to proclaim "I am one of those whom the *élan* of 1789 has raised and who will not consent to descend."

Time was to show that the bourgeois solution under the July Monarchy was in fact unable to contain the revolutionary *élan*. But for the moment the Duc d'Orléans seemed a prince notably unlike his increasingly unpopular relatives. "Je me moque absolument de l'étiquette," he observed, and he outraged the Court by sending his sons to school at the Collège Henri IV, considering that "college life seems to me the best apprenticeship in humanity which princes can serve".[1] Visitors to the Palais-Royal and the favourite family residence at Neuilly saw an intimate and united family circle. Tom Moore was invited to dinner to talk over old times and found Louis-Philippe's English a little rusty, so that he was greeted affably with the words, "I wish you a very good night, Mr Moore." "Though the thing was at first rather royal and formidable, I soon found myself perfectly at ease among as unaffected and domestic a circle as ever I witnessed in any station." After dinner "four or five fine children were admitted with whom the Duke played most delightedly, making polichinelle caps for them etc." At holiday times the whole family rumbled off in a charabanc with twelve seats in it to Aunt Adélaïde's château of

[1] In 1823 he wrote to Vatout about a prize-giving, "I had altogether forgotten about the possibility that my son might get a prize, because in that case I should like whatever journal reports it, to stress the difference of age between him and his competitors . . . they are all sixteen and he is only thirteen." The letter is in the Musée Condé.

Randan in Auvergne or to the Château d'Eu. If domesticity was a bourgeois virtue, then here was a model family in the eyes of the bourgeoisie – friendly, modest and accessible. Dumouriez, in receipt of a pension[1] which enabled him to keep a horse and carriage in his old age, wrote familiarly, "Take plenty of exercise, especially on foot, go in for even a little manual or tiring work, in order to avoid corpulence, to which you are prone. Love your old friend and write to him as often as your affairs will allow you to." The Duke of Kent, in the year before his death, wrote from Kensington Palace, describing the arrival of his daughter, the Princess Victoria, rather unflatteringly, "La petite is rather a pocket Hercules than a pocket Venus." [2] Louis-Philippe's own surviving correspondence for this period is for the most part business-like and prosaic, though it occasionally comes to life as in a letter to Vatout, his librarian, in 1824 where there is more than an echo of the pedagogue of Reichenau. "*Version à faire.* 'Haste me to know it, that I with wings as swift as meditation or the thoughts of love may sweep to my revenge.' That's what Hamlet said on the terrace to his father's ghost,[3] and which I quoted to you yesterday without you understanding it." More characteristic perhaps is a letter ending, "it's past midnight. Voltaire used to say that that is the hour of love, but I say it's the hour for sleep, and I'm going off to bed." All in all it was a peaceful, uneventful, happy existence.

[1] As was Madame de Genlis. She died at the very end of the year 1830, just in time to acclaim her old pupil as King of the French.
[2] Royal Archives Windsor C.F.P., Vol. II, M 3/4.
[3] He too had a father.

VIII

In August 1829 Charles X handed over the government of France to Prince Jules de Polignac with as Minister of the Interior the hated La Bourdonnaye and as Minister of War de Bourmont, a veteran of the Vendée and the chief witness for the prosecution at the trial of Ney. It was effectively a coup d'état and immediately seized on as such. Lafayette was loudly acclaimed in Lyon and the *Journal des Débats* wrote, "What France has gained in forty years of labour and misery is being taken from her, what she repulses with all the vigour at her command . . . is being imposed on her by force." But the Duc d'Orléans was quietly engaged at Randan checking the catalogue of the Palais-Royal library, and as late as October 11th he wrote from there: "Although I lead a very peaceful life here which suits me very well, it's a very active life too. I ride every day and carry out the duties of an engineer in tracing out the routes in this charming forest which will soon be cut up criss-cross by them like the Bois de Boulogne. Those already made have produced this year an increase of about 25 per cent in the profits of wood-cutting and that isn't bad." His existence was to be neither bourgeois nor peaceful much longer and he would soon be concerned with graver worries than the price of wood.

In December, two young journalists, the illegitimate Provençal Adolphe Thiers and Armand Carrel, who had written in 1827 a life of James II of England, went to a small château in Touraine to sound Talleyrand, who was in his seventy-eighth year, about the possibility of raising funds for another opposition newspaper. They succeeded, and the first number of *Le National* appeared in January 1830, the money emanating from Jacques Laffitte, the immensely wealthy banker who was Louis-Philippe's financial adviser. All that needed doing, suggested the editors, was to imitate what had happened in England in 1688. "England was so unrevolutionary at that time that she chose the family most closely related to the fallen prince." On March 2nd, 1830, both Chambers were listening to the speech from the throne. As Charles X read the menacing phrases "if guilty intrigues raise for my government obstacles which I do not wish to foresee, I should be able to overcome them in my determination to maintain public order", he threw his head back and his hat fell off. It was picked up and held for the rest of the speech by the Duc d'Orléans.

Events moved fast in the spring. On March 19th the Chambers were prorogued till September 1st, but not until 221 Liberal Deputies had voted a hostile address to the Crown for its choice of an unrepresentative government. In May the Government resorted to the unoriginal expedient of a bellicose foreign policy. The fleet sailed for Algiers (which in due course capitulated in four days to Bourmont's army) and the Chambers were dissolved pending new elections in the summer. Two of Louis-Philippe's A.D.C.'s, Atthalin and Rumigny, wished to stand for election but were forbidden to do so by their master, who said he did not wish to appear to have agents in the new Chamber. The energies of the Palais-Royal were devoted instead to celebrating the state visit of the King of Naples, Marie-Amélie's brother. A magnificent ball was held on May 31st. In the interior of the Palace, brilliantly illuminated, there was an immense concourse of guests, drawn alike from court and opposition circles, Charles X himself appearing about eleven o'clock. Outside, the gardens were thrown open to the citizens of Paris who soon produced rival illuminations of their own, burning piles of chairs and having eventually to be dispersed by troops. It was a magic evening, but with an atmosphere of the faintly menacing about it. "A Neapolitan night; as at Naples we are dancing on a volcano", observed Louis-Philippe's friend, de Salvandy, as they listened to the shouts from the gardens of "*à bas Polignac! à bas les aristocrates*". When all was over by six in the morning, and even the indefatigable Duchesse de Berri was tired of dancing, the only material damage turned out to be a slight charring of the base of Apollo's statue, but those who remembered 1789 were beginning to feel uneasy.

The first election results at the end of June for the electoral colleges indicated a great Liberal triumph despite strong governmental pressure on the prefects. Before the final results came in, giving the Liberals 274 seats to the Government's 143, Charles and Polignac had decided that the new Chamber was not to meet. In a conversation with Louis-Philippe the King explained that he had no intention of violating the Charter but merely of utilizing Article XIV which entitled him to issue "regulations and ordinances necessary for the execution of the laws and the safety of the State", arguing that this was the appropriate legal countermeasure to the defiance of the royal power by the 221 opposition deputies. "This article is incompatible with the Charter of which it would be the negation," warned Louis-Philippe in vain. The news on July 9th of the fall of Algiers and the fatuous optimism of Polignac made Charles X certain that he could succeed in avoiding the fate of Louis XVI by a show of firmness.

On July 25th at eleven o'clock at night, four ordinances, drawn up in great secrecy by the King and his Ministers, were taken to the offices of the *Moniteur*, whose editor Sauvo commented after reading them: "God save the King and France! Gentlemen, I am fifty-seven, I have lived through the worst days of the Revolution, and I resign in profound terror."

On Monday morning, July 26th, Louis-Philippe, staying at Neuilly with his family, read in the *Moniteur* the text of the ordinances which suspended freedom of the press, dissolved the newly elected Chamber, narrowed the franchise,[1] convened the electors for September, and appointed notorious reactionaries to the Conseil d'Etat. On reading them, Louis-Philippe went very pale and was heard muttering, "They're mad, they'll get themselves driven out . . . as far as I'm concerned I've been exiled twice and I don't want any more. I shall stay in France." Marie-Amélie was

[1] As M. Bertier de Sauvigny points out, a rather more astute politician would have *enlarged* the franchise so as to outnumber the bourgeoisie with peasant proprietors of more conservative sympathies.

in tears, but no one was left much in doubt about where the sympathies of Madame Adélaïde lay. That evening news reached Neuilly of the protest of forty-four journalists led by Thiers, Carrel and Mignet of *Le National*, de Rémusat of *Le Globe* and Cauchois-Lemaire of *Le Constitutionnel*, the last of whom had already in 1826 published an open letter to Monseigneur le Duc d'Orléans which read: "Come, Prince, a little courage, change your ducal habiliments for the civic crown. There is a place to take up in our monarchy, the place which Lafayette occupied during the Republic, that of first citizen of France." The protest declared that obedience had ceased to be a duty and that it was for the nation to judge how far resistance should go. But apart from certain angry demonstrations by compositors and students in the Place du Carrousel, little happened that night. It was as if the capital was stunned. Marshal Marmont, Duc de Raguse, already selected to maintain order in the city despite the unpopularity he had incurred by betraying Napoleon, had as yet received no orders from his royal master.

In the brilliant sunshine of the 27th, the citizens of Paris, fed largely on rumours the day before, now became aware of what was really afoot as they read the newspapers and were harangued by excited orators in the gardens of the Palais-Royal. By afternoon the attempts of the police to break up the printing presses provoked clashes, and after some shooting in the Rue Saint-Honoré, Marmont, at last told what his duties were, deployed his troops with an issue of sixty cartridges a man. By six o'clock, the first barricade went up in the Rue de l'Echelle. The traditional Parisian activity of looting gunsmiths' shops was by now well under way, and later in the evening the first tricolour flags appeared on the streets. But with the onset of darkness all seemed quiet, though there had already sprung into existence twelve insurrectionary committees, which worked feverishly through the night organizing food, arms and ammunition.

At dawn on Wednesday the 28th, another day of blazing sunshine, what had seemed the day before to be a potentially ugly printers' lockout had become another French Revolution. A crowd composed of workmen, former members of the National Guard (dissolved by Charles X in 1827), old soldiers and students began pulling down the white flags on the *mairies* and dragging them through the gutters, cutting down trees, pulling up paving stones and shouting according to personal predilection, "*Vive la République!*" or "*Vive l'Empereur!*" Early that morning the mob seized the Arsénal, the Hôtel de Ville and Notre-Dame, and Alexandre Dumas observed a well-dressed gentleman distributing powder at the sacred portal of the *Institut de France* in the Rue Mazarine. Before the end of the morning elements of the 53rd and 5th regiments had joined the insurgents. The Duc de Raguse had already written to Charles X at Saint-Cloud: "This is no longer a riot, it's a Revolution. It is urgently necessary for Your Majesty to take steps to pacify it. I am taking the necessary measures. The troops will be ready at midday, but I await with impatience the orders of your Majesty." He received none and so sent out four columns in the afternoon to seize the principal areas in the hands of the insurgents and to sweep the approaches to them. The students of the Ecole Polytechnique hurled themselves into the struggle and everywhere a rain of missiles descended on the troops of the line, painfully struggling to clear the barricades composed of upturned omnibuses, carriages, carts, furniture, wine-barrels and paving stones. Meanwhile the leaders of the Opposition met at the house of the Radical deputy, Audry de Puyraveau. The elderly Lafayette and the banker Laffitte had just arrived there after hurrying in from the country. They decided to send to Marmont a deputation of five, which included Casimir-Périer and Laffitte. Marmont was already resigned to the ultimate hopelessness of his task, but having abandoned Napoleon, he felt himself in no position to lay down his command once again without fighting and Polignac, who was in an adjacent room, simply refused to see the deputation. By five o'clock the troops had seized their objectives, including the Hôtel de Ville, but in their rear the barricades had gone up again, they had no rations and they were running out of cartridges. As the bewildered deputies met again and Laffitte began for the first time to talk of an approach to the Duc d'Orléans at Neuilly, Marmont withdrew his forces to concentrate them around the Louvre and the Tuileries. 2,500 of them, mostly deserters, were missing. The firing had been audible all day at St. Cloud where Charles X had felt it unnecessary to put off his usual game of whist.

On the 29th six thousand barricades were up, and when the insurgents profited by a badly organized relief to force the soldiers out of the Louvre, Marmont was compelled to fall back, first to the Champs-Elysées and then to the Etoile and the Bois. Talleyrand, watching the proceedings from an admirable vantage point at the window of his house in the Rue Saint-Florentin, drew out his watch and observed: "At five minutes past twelve the elder branch of the Bourbons has ceased to reign." By the afternoon the fighting had stopped, the troops having lost about a thousand killed and wounded, the insurgents 1,800 killed and 4,500 wounded. About midday the opposition deputies, assembled at Laffitte's house, found themselves confronted with the spectre of an imminent triumph of mob-rule. Unless they took control of the situation Paris would be in the hands of whatever republican leaders the streets threw up, such as the obscure General Dubourg, who had dressed himself up in epaulettes borrowed from the wardrobe of the Opéra-Comique, and was busy issuing proclamations from the Hôtel de Ville, an assumption of power scarcely justified by his experience of the 1812 campaign, sandwiched between an early career as a Chouan and his unsuccessful attendance on Louis XVIII at Ghent. Lafayette was accordingly put in charge of the National Guard and proceeded to take over the insurgent headquarters in the Hôtel de Ville, being followed there by a municipal commission of five – Laffitte, handicapped by a sprained ankle which he afterwards attributed to jumping over a barricade, Casimir-Périer, General Mouton, Schonen and Audry de Puyraveau. For Lafayette it must have seemed like 1791 all over again.

At much the same time three peers, Sémonville, Vitrolles and d'Argout[1] were urging Charles X to revoke the ordinances and

[1] Who was rumoured to have had a tricolour burnt in 1815 by the public executioner.

7. The Council of Ministers at the Tuileries, August 15th, 1842; *by Jacquand*. (The figure on the extreme left is Guizot. Marshal Soult is presenting to the King the text of the Regency Law. Behind Soult with the portfolio is Duchâtel.)

appoint a conciliatory ministry under the Duc de Mortemart which should include Casimir-Périer and Gérard, who had commanded a corps at Waterloo. Charles agreed after dismissing Marmont and replacing him by the Duc d'Angoulême, who immediately ordered the remnants of the army to fall back on Saint-Cloud. At 6 o'clock the three peers returned to Paris with the news of the royal concessions only to be told by Lafayette in the Hôtel de Ville, "It is too late."

What meanwhile had been happening at Neuilly? On the 27th Louis-Philippe showed the elderly Mrs Forbes, a neighbour at Twickenham, round the château and some of the children went into the city to bathe in the swimming-school.[1] The atmosphere in the château was sombre on that beautiful starlit night, the distant sound of rifle-shots dying out about midnight. On the 28th, the decisive day, all was uncertainty, except that a great struggle was going on in Paris. A shell landed in the park and deserters drifted into the grounds from time to time. Adélaïde and the children were excitedly discussing the prospects of the insurgents, but Louis-Philippe unemotionally calculated that whichever side was victorious there was a serious risk that he might be captured and taken as a hostage. Accordingly at dawn on the 29th he left on horseback by a devious route for Le Raincy, one of his mansions just outside the city. Shortly after he left, one of the Palais-Royal circle, Ary Scheffer, the painter, arrived at Neuilly with the news that the royalists were winning. An hour later news of the true situation arrived and Adélaïde busied herself and the princesses in sewing tricolour cockades. The 30th was to bring a startling change in the family fortunes.

On the night of the 29th Charles X went to bed without signing the concessions he had agreed to during the day and so Polignac's successor, the Duc de Mortemart, remained necessarily inactive at Saint-Cloud. At 2.30 in the morning de Vitrolles and d'Argout on their return from Paris went to the King's bedroom and woke him up, as Macdonald and Louis-Philippe had done

---

[1] Louis-Philippe recalled that Montpensier had tried to do just this on another fateful day, August 10th, 1792, but had been unable to gain admittance.

fifteen years previously, and by seven Mortemart at last left Saint-Cloud. When he got to Paris he saw the walls plastered with placards, the results of the nocturnal activity of two of the editors of *Le National*, Thiers and Mignet. They read:

> Charles X can never return to Paris. He has caused the blood of the people to be shed.
>
> A republic would expose us to terrible divisions; it would embroil us with Europe.
>
> The Duc d'Orléans is a prince devoted to the cause of the Revolution.
>
> The Duc d'Orléans has never fought against us.
>
> The Duc d'Orléans was at Jemappes.
>
> The Duc d'Orléans bore the tricolour flag under fire; the Duc d'Orléans alone can bear it again; we will have no other flag.
>
> The Duc d'Orléans has declared himself; he accepts the Charter as we have always wished and understood it.
>
> It will be from the people of France that he will hold his crown.

Three of these propositions were untrue or at best half-truths. If by "devoted to the cause of the Revolution" was meant opposed to the theory of divine right and in favour of a constitutional monarchy, in which the King would be a great deal more than a mere figurehead, then in that very limited sense Louis-Philippe could be said to be a devotee of the Revolution. It was true that he had not borne arms against the French but he had tried to at least twice. He had certainly not declared himself, but was doing his best to keep right out of the centre of events in the obscurity of Le Raincy. Finally it would not be from the people of France that he would hold his crown but from the politically conscious middle classes, in revolt against an anachronistic and priest-ridden régime, and fearful of republican anarchy. But in spite of, or perhaps because of, these highly dubious assertions, Thiers' placards with their skilful reiteration of a name which meant in 1830 very little to the average Parisian effectively opened the road to an Orléans monarchy. That is if the Duc d'Orléans could be persuaded to seize the opportunity of which he had not yet even been apprised.

IX

Thiers was never the bravest of men during a Revolution. When the July Revolution broke out, the first of the long series with which he would be intimately associated, he took refuge at Bessancourt, only returning to Paris on the 29th. In the early morning of the 30th he succeeded in persuading the Liberal deputies at Laffitte's house – now known derisively as *le Conseil de l'Hésitation* – that he was the ideal man to send to Neuilly to exercise the necessary powers of persuasion on Louis-Philippe.[1] He chose as his companion Ary Scheffer and as his steed a pony called Cob, belonging to the son of Marshal Ney, since the animal was of a stature to accommodate his very short legs and his decidedly limited equestrian skill. Scheffer found no difficulty in jumping the barricades, but Thiers frequently had to be lifted over them, pony and all. These rather incongruous messengers of fate duly arrived at Neuilly only to find that Louis-Philippe was absent – a desperate development at a moment when it seemed that it could only be a matter of hours if France was to be saved from not only the Republic, but the Terror. Thiers in his strong southern accent painted a lurid picture to Marie-Amélie of power being seized by mad demagogues while Lafayette and the moderates at the Hôtel de Ville were hourly watching the situation slip from their grasp. All this seemed to make little impression on Marie-Amélie who replied: "My husband can't accept. They will call him a usurper. He is the most honest of men . . ." But Adélaïde, who from her girlhood had suffered little but neglect and scorn in legitimist circles, felt very differently and Thiers, sensing that here

[1] On the 29th in Laffitte's house Sébastiani was arguing in favour of accepting Mortemart and the revocation of the Ordinances in one room, while in another Thiers and Mignet were comparing Louis-Philippe with William III. Professor Toynbee would approve the triumph of historical mimesis.

was somebody who properly appreciated the true gravity of the moment, turned on her all his persuasive powers of advocacy. "We must have a new dynasty which owes its crown to us. . . . Everyone will be aware that you haven't looked for the crown because it's certainly too perilous a possession today for anybody to seek . . . all authority is gone. . . . Anything can happen. Only hurry!" Madame Adélaïde rose and replied: "If you believe that the adherence of our family can be useful to the revolution, we will give it you willingly. A woman is nothing in a family, she can be compromised. I am ready to go to Paris." "Madame," replied Thiers gratefully, "you are today accepting the crown for your family." Thereupon an A.D.C., de Montesquiou, was sent off to Le Raincy with a message while Vatout in the next room explained the situation to the children to be greeted with cries of "Our poor papa! Mon Dieu, how terrible! He is lost! And we are all lost with him!" By one o'clock in the afternoon Thiers was back in Paris to learn that his colleagues had been persuaded by the cautious Liberal grandee, the Duc de Broglie and by Talleyrand to offer Louis-Philippe for the moment not the crown but the Lieutenant-Generalcy of France. Meanwhile the increasingly restive heroes of the Revolution, now dominated by the formidable Godefroy Cavaignac, were urging on Lafayette the desirability of proclaiming the Republic the next day.

The hour of decision had struck for Louis-Philippe. At fifty-six it was not an easy decision. On the one hand, here was the apparent culmination of the ancient ambitions of his family; and to refuse would in all probability mean exile, of which he had already experienced close on a quarter of a century, as well as disinheritance, not only for himself but for his heir, now grown into a magnificent young man, who would soon be of age and was at this moment with his regiment, the First Hussars; and, perhaps the strongest consideration of all, how could he resist the messages pouring in from Paris, including one from Talleyrand, all of which indicated that he alone stood between France and a renewal of the horrors of '93, which had left such an indelible mark on him during those miserable months at Reichenau? On the other hand, he had sworn oaths of allegiance to Charles X, who had always treated him well according to his lights. And in any case would a crown of this sort, picked up in the gutter, be worth wearing, worth exchanging even for the peace of Twick? In the end he made up his mind that he would have to go – but having set out, he turned back once on his tracks, before finally steeling himself to the necessary pitch of decision. He reached Neuilly towards nine o'clock that evening and took leave of his wife and family by torchlight in the summer-house called Les Poteaux Ronds. He then set out for Paris in civilian costume with a tricolour badge in his hat to pick his way on foot past the Etoile and over the barricades to the Palais-Royal, which he entered dusty and exhausted at eleven o'clock through the entrance of 216, Rue Saint-Honoré.

Much had happened that day, both in Paris and Saint-Cloud. Mortemart, arriving on foot in Paris in the early morning, encountered an opposition deputy in the Rue des Mathurins who persuaded him to go neither to Laffitte's nor to the Hôtel de Ville, but to try his luck with the Peers in the Luxembourg. One of the handful of peers assembled there agreed to take the documents revoking the Ordinances to the Hôtel de Ville, only to be met with hostile contumely. During the day the *National* group began to make common cause in support of the Orléans solution with the more articulate deputies – Laffitte, Casimir-Périer, Guizot, Constant and Odilon Barrot – together with a handful of peers of which the most prominent were de Broglie and the young Montalivet. An influential figure in these reunions was the ballad-monger Béranger with his romantic moustachios who was in the habit of apostrophizing Louis-Philippe as either *le sage Ulysse* or the Louis XIV of the bourgeoisie. Lafayette was slowly coming round to the idea of a popular monarchy, surrounded by republican institutions, as the contiguity of the more ardent republicans – *les combattants de la veille* – led him to reflect on the liabilities attached to being once again the hero of two worlds. At Saint-Cloud confusion and disaster reigned. Angoulême lost his temper with Marmont. He accused him of having perpetrated a second great betrayal and tried to seize his sword. Marmont pushed the half-disengaged blade back into its scabbard and cut Angoulême's fingers, whereupon the latter shouted, "Arrest him!" and sank down weeping on the sofa. As news of more and more desertions came in, the royal family left first for Trianon and then Rambouillet, the Duchesse de Berri clasping in her arms the nine-year-old Duc de Bordeaux, *héritier du sang d'un martyr*, who, they still hoped, might be proclaimed Henri V.

Almost as soon as Louis-Philippe entered the Palais-Royal he sent an A.D.C., Oudard, to summon the Duc de Mortemart and then lay down on a mattress on the floor of one of the smallest rooms to snatch what sleep he could, leaving two candles alight on the table. At 3 a.m. on the 31st Oudard knocked, Louis-Philippe awoke and Mortemart was shown in. No episode in his career is more mysterious than this clandestine interview in which he is alleged to have told Mortemart that if he saw Charles X he must tell him that he, Louis-Philippe, would never accept the crown.[1] One recalls the turning-back at Le Raincy. At three in the morning after a row of sleepless nights morale is low. And there were by now two fatal weaknesses in Louis-Philippe, which age would consistently accentuate – hesitancy in decision and a desire to be liked and admired by anyone he happened to be talking with at the moment, which is the shortest way to be thought a hypocrite. His actions on August 2nd in any case lend credit to the story – as long as he was only Lieutenant-General the die was not irretrievably cast.[2]

Next morning in the Palais-Royal, however, things seemed very different. It would have been noisy under any circumstances as the palace was full of decorators, profiting by the proposed sojourn of the family at Eu.[3] But the staircases were thronged with students, National Guardsmen and workmen, mostly un-

[1] According to one account he gave Mortemart a letter to Charles which the former was never able to deliver.

[2] See page 148.

[3] That day Mme de Boigne went to see Marie-Amélie at Neuilly and heard her sobbing aloud: "What a catastrophe! And to think we might have been at Eu!" A week later she was still talking about a crown of thorns.

aware that the duke was in his palace, and the hubbub and stink were indescribable. Louis-Philippe sent a messenger along the street to ask Talleyrand whether he ought to accept the Lieutenant-Generalcy and received the answer *"qu'il accepte"*. At eight a deputation of twelve deputies, among whom Sébastiani was prominent, harangued him about the growing anarchy. Louis-Philippe after a short hesitation accepted the Lieutenant-Generalcy and a document was drawn up which concluded with the words: "Returning to the city of Paris I wore with pride the glorious colours which you have assumed again and which I myself had carried long ago. The Chambers are about to meet; they will discuss means of assuring the rule of law and the maintenance of the rights of the nation. The Charter will henceforth be a reality – Louis-Philippe d'Orléans." Sébastiani took this back to the Palais-Bourbon, where the Chamber took cognizance of it, and then proceeded en masse to wait on the Lieutenant-General in the Palais-Royal where, if one is to believe the inimitable, if generally mendacious, memoirs of the Gascon Laffitte, tears and mutual embraces were the order of the day.[1] The Chamber was doing its best to take over the revolution. As M. Roger Priouret observes, to the King of France by the grace of God succeeds the King of the French by the grace of the deputies. But there was still the Hôtel de Ville and the Marquis de Lafayette, who seemed consistently to ignore messages from the Palais-Royal inviting him to come there for consultation. The mountain it seemed would have to go to Mahomet. Consequently about two o'clock a procession set out for the Hôtel de Ville, the somewhat undignified nature of which has been cruelly immortalized by Châteaubriand. It was led by one of the heroes of what were now known as the Three Glorious Days of July, brandishing a tricolour; there then followed Louis-Philippe in general's uniform on a white horse; then two hot and dusty deputies; then Benjamin Constant, the creator of *Adolphe*, carried in a sedan-chair by two Savoyard

---

[1] Of Louis-Philippe's partiality for embracing all and sundry Laffitte characteristically observed: "It's good for morale, it's also a good method of government and is easy on the pockets of the taxpayer".

porters who did not seem to appreciate the true dignity of their burden; the whole being enlivened by a half-drunk drummer and a pack of deputies bellowing "Vive le Duc d'Orléans". Near Saint-Germain l'Auxerrois a figure in shirt-sleeves and brandishing a carbine, who might have served as a model for Géricault, violently harangued the procession on the subject of Marshal Ney from the top of a barricade. Even in the Hôtel de Ville there were hostile shouts and the histrionic Dubourg pushed himself forward to demand menacingly a republican oath from the Lieutenant-General. The destiny of France was at that moment in the hands of Lafayette, of whom Talleyrand wrote in his memoirs: "in a novel the author gives some intelligence and a distinguished character to the principal personage; fate takes less trouble; mediocrities play a part in great events simply because they happen to be there." Despite the mediocrity about which neither Jefferson nor Talleyrand nor Napoleon were ever in doubt, Lafayette possessed one priceless gift for occasions of this sort – *panache*.[1] When he and Louis-Philippe and an outsize tricolour appeared on the balcony, the combined emotional weight of so much symbolism was decisive. The Duc d'Orléans returned in glory to the Palais-Royal amidst an immense ovation.

[1] "That wonderful man Lafayette is the anchor of our liberty," wrote Stendhal a fortnight later. "I was enraptured by those July days . . . I shall never forget the lovely sunshine and the first sight of the tricolour."

Book Three

Uneasy lies the head that wears a crown.

HENRY IV PART II (III. i)

I

On August 9th the curtain was rung down on the Revolution of 1830 when the Duc d'Orléans appeared before the Chambers and accepted the crown as Louis-Philippe I, King of the French.[1] But in the events of the intervening week it is possible to discern a great deal in the attitude and aspirations of the new King and his heterogeneous clique of supporters which goes far to explain the troubled history of the July Monarchy. Talleyrand, although having no illusions about the elder branch, had observed at the time of the Restoration that one can do anything in France with a principle. What was altogether deficient in the entirely new situation of August 1830 was any demonstrable principle at all. It was all very well for the doctrinaires to grope about for something they liked to call "quasi-legitimacy" and for a deputation from Vedoul asking for a flag for their battalion of the National Guard to describe the new dynasty as "more than legitimate because it is necessary for the welfare of the country"[2] – if sovereignty is not legitimate it must be based either on conquest or widespread consent, neither of which conditions precisely obtained. No one was more worried about this than the new king, as can be easily illustrated from his dealings during this difficult week both with Charles X and the republican leaders.

Charles X at Rambouillet during the night of August 1st/2nd – a night during which Paris was shaken by a heavy thunderstorm – issued an ordinance appointing Louis-Philippe Lieutenant-General, to which the latter replied that he already held that post from the representatives of the nation. During the morning of the 2nd, although his military resources were by no means negligible vis-à-vis the unregulated cohorts of the Revolution, Charles abdicated the crown for himself and for Angoulême

---

[1] The title borne by Louis XVI in the autumn of 1789.
[2] Archives Nationales F 1c 1. 32.

and instructed Louis-Philippe to proclaim Henry V. Before the act of abdication reached Louis-Philippe later that night, he sent four commissioners to Rambouillet to urge Charles X to remove himself further from the capital, but they received very short shrift from Charles, who had an understandable distaste for discussing his affairs with M. Odilon Barrot. Some time during the night Louis-Philippe sent for an attaché at the British Embassy, Colonel Caradoc. Either that night or the following morning he gave Caradoc a short note to sew into the collar of his coat which read: "Believe, Sire, what Colonel Caradoc tells you from me." The message Caradoc was to convey to Charles X (and which in fact he was only able to deliver in Normandy on the night of the 7th) was to the effect that if the Duc de Bordeaux' rights were to be proclaimed he must be smuggled into the city as soon as possible. Once again Louis-Philippe was to be woken up in the small hours, this time at 4 a.m. by Barrot and his colleagues urging him to overcome Charles' hostile attitude by staging a popular demonstration against Rambouillet. "How do you expect me to take forcible measures against the royal family?" asked Louis-Philippe in despair. However, in the early morning Lafayette was ordered to call out the National Guard and by mid-day in response to rumours that Charles X was planning to march on the capital and crown Henry V by force, a tumultuous armed procession of about 15,000, little better organized than the march to Versailles of October 5th, 1789, set out for Rambouillet in a fantastic assortment of impressed vehicles. By 8 o'clock they were within a few miles of their destination and General Maison, going on ahead of the rabble, persuaded Charles X and his court to decamp rapidly in the direction of Maintenon, whence via Dreux and Saint-Lô and with the active connivance of the government he reached Cherbourg on August 15th to start the next day his last exile which after years in Holyrood ended in Prussia in 1836.[1]

---

[1] Madame de Boigne relates that on the way Charles and his entourage stopped to eat at the private house of one of their loyal adherents. *Les officiers de la bouche* informed their hostess that a square table must be provided. Since one could not be found they sawed up a beautiful round mahogany table.

During the late evening of the 3rd the crown diamonds were handed in to the Palais-Royal, whose master that afternoon had announced in the Palais-Bourbon before 240 deputies and 60 peers the abdication of Charles X without any reference to the Duc de Bordeaux. With that omission Louis-Philippe stepped finally outside the narrow circle of legitimacy. Colonel Caradoc's mission suggests that he may have done so with a lingering regret.[1] Sovereignty must now lie with the people – no doubt as represented by deputies elected on a limited franchise. Or was there another solution of a sort less painfully reminiscent of '93? If so he would have to tread very carefully indeed.

Already he had had a somewhat discouraging encounter with the representatives of the sovereign people. Thiers, anxious to rally as much of public opinion as possible to the new régime which he regarded as his particular brain-child, brought along to the Palais-Royal three fierce and dedicated Republican *combattants de la veille* – Cavaignac,[2] the son of a regicide of the Convention, Bastide and Thomas. Without giving Louis-Philippe time to exercise on them his celebrated charm as a conversationalist, they launched into a demand that the tricolour should be carried across the Rhine in a crusade for liberty, that the second Chamber should be suppressed and that there should be universal suffrage. Louis-Philippe was then sharply reminded that he had been a Jacobin and when he began to talk of the principles he hoped to adopt – peace, prosperity, reconciliation – he was met with the scornful rejoinder, "Oh, well, we needn't worry; with a programme like that you'll only last four years!"[3] As his uncompromising visitors were about to leave in disgust, Louis-Philippe said genially: "*Allons*, you'll come back to me in the end. You'll see, you'll see . . . ." "Never!" shouted Cavaignac. *La politique du juste-milieu* was going to be hard work.

[1] Sébastiani and Molé, who were frequently in and out of the Palais-Royal at this time, favoured the idea of Louis-Philippe being Regent for the Duc de Bordeaux.

[2] Of whom his mother observed accurately: "Godefroy, c'est un Brutus."

[3] Châteaubriand was nearer the mark when he said: "This will last fifteen years, then the deluge."

The deputies, too, were busy that week. There was to be no Constituent Assembly, but rather a revision of the Charter which this Rump-Parliament, most of whose members had originally wished to do little more than frighten Charles X, was determined to effect with the least possible concession to the susceptibilities of M. Cavaignac. The modifications to the Charter approved on August 7th amounted in themselves to comparatively little, but, as with the provisions of the prototype Bill of Rights of 1689, they were susceptible of development. Much was in fact specifically left over for further legislation – the electoral qualification, the constitution of the National Guard, the press laws, the nature of the peerage and liberty of education; much also would evolve, more or less tacitly, and à l'anglaise, as time went on. Divine Right, extraordinary tribunals, press censorship, the suspending and dispensing powers and mid-term elections were all swept away at the outset. The Chambers were henceforth to share with the King the right of initiating legislation. Subsequent legislation within just over a year filled in the gaps. A series of laws on the press enabled editors to publish their opinions freely, provided they could afford to pay caution-money and stamp-duty, but if they infringed the laws of libel they were liable for trial by juries drawn from the upper-middle classes and selected by the prefects.[1] The electoral law of March 1831 increased the number of electors from 94,000 in 1830 to 166,000, a figure which rose by 1848 to 241,000 as increased prosperity enabled more people to pay the necessary qualification in direct taxes.[2] This restriction of the *pays légal* to the upper section of the middle-classes arbitrarily divided the bourgeoisie on whom the régime depended and the fiscal qualifications in fact favoured the landowner rather than the industrial and commercial classes.[3] The municipal law of March 1831 extended the same principles to the communes in a manner which Louis Blanc described as "basing the executive power on

[1] See the very full and interesting treatment of this complex subject by Irene Collins in *The Government and the Newspaper Press in France, 1814–1881*.

[2] 200 francs with certain exceptions.

[3] See Peter Campbell, *French Electoral Systems and Elections 1789–1957*, pp. 61–3.

nearly 34,000 little bourgeois oligarchies".[1] Lafayette was for opening the ranks of the National Guard to all and sundry, but another law of March 1831 restricted its membership to those paying direct taxes and able to pay for their own uniform. The resultant corps of grocer-janissaries became the pride and prop of the régime and was to fight passionately in the streets on its be-half in 1832 and 1834. Finally the law of December 1831 abolished the hereditary peerage, reserving the nomination of life peers within certain defined categories to the King; the *haute bourgeoisie* was not backward in pressing its claim to replace Ultra bishops and barons in an assembly whose duties were dignified rather than onerous. Seventy-six prefects and seventy-five generals were the most important casualties in an extensive purge of supporters of the old régime. The press of applicants for places was on a heroic scale. A musical comedy soon depicted a chorus of place-hunters in the ante-room of a ministry intoning in chorus:

> *Qu'on nous place*
> *Et que justice se fasse!*
> *Qu'on nous place*
> *Tous en masse!*
> *Que les placés*
> *Soient chassés!*

and Louis-Philippe had to write to Guizot: "I am angry at having to write and tell you that two of our new *sous-préfects* arrived yesterday at the Palais-Royal completely drunk and were mocked by the National Guard. My A.D.C.s will tell you their names which I have forgotten but which you will keep quiet out of consideration for their patrons. A choice of that sort doesn't reflect credit on us and we will replace them." The Palais-Royal throughout the reign resembled a high-grade labour exchange in public offices and Guizot, a close student of English methods, was to show himself a master of all the arts and crafts employed by Newcastle and Robinson – or for that matter *la république des*

---

[1] The king or the prefect appointed the Maire and adjoints according to the importance of the commune.

copains. But the deputy, as well as the *fonctionnaire*, had his way to make and was determined never again to be treated as he had been by Charles X. On November 6th, 1830, Mauguin, one of the more strident of the left-wing leaders, demanding information from the government on a question not on the order of the day, secured a debate a week later and so *le droit d'interpellation* – one of the strongest weapons in the armoury of the opposition deputy – was established. In September 1831 an order of the day was voted expressing confidence in the government's foreign policy. But it might equally have been one of no confidence and on April 1st, 1834, the Duc de Broglie resigned in the face of a hostile vote by the Chamber. Although none of Louis-Philippe's Chambers lasted their full five years he never governed with a ministry which could not, by one means or another, command a majority. At first glance it might seem that a constitutional monarchy, in the sense that we now understand the term, had been achieved. But appearances were deceptive. M. Roger Priouret, writing in 1959, analyses Louis-Philippe's interpretation of his own particular function in the constitution as follows: "He had a conception of his role which approximates curiously enough to that which General de Gaulle brought back with him to the liberated France of 1944 and which he succeeded in inserting into the Constitution of 1958 . . . above parties, there is the whole which transcends them, which has an autonomous existence, which has its own demands. All this is personified in the Chief of State who, for Louis-Philippe as for de Gaulle, must be an arbiter and never lose control of diplomacy, the Colonies or the Army." Experience had taught Louis-Philippe above all else how to wait and not to show his hand too soon, but inwardly he was not impressed by Thiers' theory of a King who reigns but does not govern, since he felt that if he must reign he could govern France much better than M. Thiers could.

8. Thiers; *by L. Bonnat*

9. Molé; *a lithograph from the picture by Ingres*

10. Casimir-Périer; *by Mme Desnos*

11. Louis-Blanc; *a photograph published in 1876*

12. Lamartine; *by Cattier*

II

The nation over which Louis-Philippe was called to reign and which he intended to govern was already in the grip of two inter-related revolutions, which as a man of the eighteenth century he was never able to understand – one in the sphere of economics and one in that of thought. The conjunction of social romanticism with industrial expansion under conditions of unregulated capitalist enterprise combined to produce new tensions in society which were beyond an imagination nurtured on the Physiocrats and Adam Smith. Yet Louis-Philippe owed his throne and many of the difficulties of his first two years' occupancy of it in some measure to the slump that persisted from 1828 to 1832, while that of 1846 contributed appreciably to the final collapse of the régime; and grotesque and chimerical as were many of the ideas of the social romantics, yet throughout the reign he and his supporters would always be on the defensive in the war of ideas. It was perfectly natural to underestimate the explosive potential of these two movements when one's days and nights were passed in ceaseless application to foreign affairs and home politics, since the outward signs of a radical transformation of society were not yet easy to discern. In a nation of 32 millions 22 still lived by agriculture; the Paris population of 750,000 still included 50,000 domestic servants; the first passenger railway was only built in 1837 and by 1840 only 270 miles had been laid down; labour was so cheap under the Restoration that few French industrialists had bothered to acquire the new machines; letters from Paris to Bordeaux in this slow-moving society took 45 hours to arrive; workers' combinations were illegal and Jean-Baptiste Say was preaching the virtues of absolute freedom of contract between employers and workmen. And what was the significance after all of these bizarre new theories that urged the total reorganization of society and undermined the revealed truths of Adam Smith and Malthus? Louis-Philippe had an early lesson about their probable practical consequences during August 1830 when the Palais-Royal was still pullulating with the heroes of the barricades[1] and he was forced to emerge several times a day to beat time to the refrain of La Marseillaise and La Parisienne.[2] Late one night two young men, emissaries of the secret society *Les Amis du Peuple*, demanded to see him, drawing the A.D.C.'s attention to their filthy and bloodstained shirts with the boast: "We were covered with blood in the fighting and we aren't changing our shirts till it's all over." When Louis-Philippe came in, they told him: "Society is dissolved, nothing which has been ought to exist any more and we have come to warn you that the people want everything to be made new." Louis-Philippe replied to them benevolently: "How do you know the opinion of the people and by what right are you their spokesmen? Society has, it is true, been shaken, but it exists; and the dreams of your imagination are not going to alter it in a flash." It seemed to him as time went on that the practical outcome of the new social theories appeared to be the endemic street-rioting which persisted till 1834 and the eight attempts to assassinate him. The theories in themselves, which permeated the working classes in attenuated and mangled form, were for the most part hardly calculated to appeal to a man who had known and talked with Mirabeau and Washington and William Pitt. There was sustained argument (and for that matter the very greatest prophetic genius) in the writings of Saint-Simon, who had after all been patronized by Laffitte, with his emphasis on the value of industrial co-operation, managerial efficiency and a technocratic élite. But it hardly seemed that his

[1] They seemed to multiply astonishingly in numbers as memories of the actual fighting became more indistinct. There were also a surprising number of surviving *vainqueurs de la Bastille* in needy circumstances to be dealt with.

[2] A verse of which ran:

> *Pour briser leurs masses profondes*
> *Qui conduit nos drapeaux sanglants?*
> *C'est la liberté des Deux Mondes*
> *C'est Lafayette en cheveux blonds.*

followers, Enfantin and Bazard, need be taken seriously with their peculiar church at Ménilmontant, presided over by Enfantin in red fez, white trousers and blue coat with a sash inscribed *le père*, preaching free divorce and what he called "religious promiscuity" and "the rehabilitation of the flesh".[1] The movement in any case was broken up in 1832 and Enfantin and his friends went off to Egypt in pursuit of *la femme Messie*, eventually achieving something nearer the founder's heart by inspiring de Lesseps with the idea of the Suez Canal. Nor were Fourier's ideas of the regeneration of mankind by association in phalansteries any more likely to be translated into reality, although he, too, like Saint-Simon could be prophetic, e.g. in his insistence that the Sahara could be put to good economic use. He also solved, in theory, the perennially difficult problem of who is to do the dirty jobs in the perfect society by allotting them to small boys who anyway like dirt. Perhaps by way of consolation his co-operative millennium envisaged oceans of lemonade across which ships would be steered by anti-whales. The ideas of Etienne Cabet, Pierre Leroux, Constantin Pecquer, Victor Considérant, Louis Blanc, Auguste Comte might be suitable for export to the United States where there was room to experiment with cranky social systems, but for the moment there was enough to do in France reconstituting society and closing the era of revolutions without bothering about romantic concepts like communism, social workshops, universal suffrage and "l'equitable égalité du point de départ". If Leroux was right in saying "république et socialisme, c'est un", then the thing to avoid was the republic.[2] "Vous êtes de braves jeunes gens," Louis-Philippe told his bloodstained visitors, "but seduced by some theory or other on which you've been nourishing yourselves for a long time." As to the new movement in literature, Louis-Philippe disliked *Hernani*, although its author made a popular and decorative Peer, and if M. Petrus Borel decided to

[1] When Enfantin after bombarding Louis-Philippe with memoranda eventually secured an interview he was offered a job as a sous-préfet.

[2] For a detailed examination of this subject, see D. Owen Evans, *Social Romanticism in France 1830–48.*

call the King of the French "a gigantic lobster with no blood in its veins, but whose shell is the colour of spilt blood", he and his fellow Bouzingos could safely be allowed to let off steam until they became middle-aged and accepted quiet jobs in the civil service.

In thinking in common with the aristocratic Whigs across the Channel that a steady volume of middle-class support and a little judicious and gradual reform would enable his government to contain the rising tide of working-class agitation, Louis-Philippe made an ultimately disastrous miscalculation. It is true that the policy, which was to be initiated in 1831 by Casimir-Périer and carried on by his successors of tackling the symptoms without touching the underlying causes of social distress in Paris and Lyon achieved a considerable measure of success. Perhaps if Guizot had shown a vestige of flexibility in 1846 he might even have emulated Peel's triumph. But the conditions of working-class life in Paris and certain other industrial centres were such that the visionary social programmes of even the most Utopian reformers could hardly fail to command a hearing. In 1830 the wages of the Lyon silk-workers were a third of what they had been in 1810. Some 64,000 inhabitants of Paris had no stable employment, being dependent on charity or crime.[1] The average wage for a man in 1842 was 1 franc 78 centimes, for a woman 1 franc, which meant that many earned a great deal less. Children of four were employed for long hours in the mills. In 1834, 32,000 cotton-workers in Lille were living on charity. It is not to be assumed, however, that all were ardent revolutionaries, eager to play their part in the class struggle. Except when a bad harvest drove them beyond their normal destitution to the point of starvation they were as a rule apathetically resigned to their misery. The indefatigable agitator Flora Tristan lamented just before she died in 1844, "the workers are for the most part indifferent to social ideas . . . What can one do if these miserable people are so base and cowardly that they won't even demand what's due to them?" Organized resistance to law and order seemed to be broken in both Paris

[1] The demography of nineteenth-century France is best studied in C. Morazé, *La France Bourgeoise.*

and Lyon by 1835. But it would be on this submerged reef of proletarian misery, irreducible according to prevailing political science on both sides of the Channel, that the régime was finally shipwrecked. In the secret societies, which flourished at the beginning of the reign, revived for a moment in 1839 and finally triumphed so unexpectedly in February 1848, there was always a revolutionary cadre which was eventually able to fuse successfully the three elements essential to the republican cause – the mystique of 1793, the misery of the industrial workers and the revolutionary theories of the social romantics. The two most celebrated secret societies were *Les Amis du Peuple* and *Les Droits de l'Homme*. The latter took over the leadership in 1833 after the suppression of *Les Amis du Peuple* by the government, but by May 1835 it too had been destroyed and in large part discredited. But although the government, as will be seen, could dissolve the societies under one legal pretext or another, the leaders remained active in the propagation of revolutionary doctrine. The appearance of Cavaignac in a law-court was always a source of acute embarrassment to the régime.[1] Raspail, an eminent chemist, was beloved by the people of Paris and although in no sense an advocate of the class war, he advocated universal suffrage, pacifism and graduated taxation in *Le Réformateur*, whose editorials tended to make observations like "the people of France despise the peerage like the mud on their shoes". Other irreconcilables were Filippo Buonarotti, who was a survivor of Babeuf's conspiracy of 1796; the romantic and wealthy Creole, Armand Barbès, whom Proudhon called "le Bayard de la démocratie";[2] Ulysse Trélat, another doctor; Armand Marrast, editor first of *La Tribune* and then of *Le National*, who became notably more moderate as the reign advanced, but remained a most formidable opponent; and the greatest of all nineteenth-century revolutionaries, Auguste Blanqui, who had already been wounded three times on the streets as a young student in 1827.[3]

[1] He even succeeded in making John Stuart Mill tremble on one occasion.

[2] Gambetta's balloon in 1871 was called "Armand Barbès".

[3] De Tocqueville's souvenirs contain the following celebrated description of Blanqui on May 15th, 1848: "He had wan, emaciated cheeks, white lips, a sickly, wicked and repulsive expression, a dirty pallor, the appearance of a

The opposition to the régime from the legitimist Right was as dedicated and vitriolic as that from the Republican Left, for whereas usurpers are often a success in England they arouse passionate hostility in France. Châteaubriand, after a last dramatic speech in the Peers, had abandoned public life, as did many other Legitimists in what was called *"l'émigration à l'intérieur"*, but the cause of the exiled monarchy had a powerful and eloquent spokesman in the person of the forty-year-old barrister Pierre-Antoine Berryer, whose magnificent oratorical gifts and obvious sincerity made him a consistently impressive advocate of a cause, which though hopelessly lost, was a source of great embarrassment to Louis-Philippe. Berryer's strength lay in the moderation with which he stated the Legitimist case. Prepared to admit Polignac's mistakes, he lost no opportunity to stress the instability and inconsistency of a régime founded on broken oaths and alien alike to the genius of the ancient monarchy and the triumphant Revolution and Empire. For the moment the partisans of Henri V lay low, but their mischief-making potentiality proved almost as great as that of the Republicans, with whom they were not above making common cause.

There were two other dangerous sources of ideological hostility to the July Monarchy, dangerous either in their own right or in alliance with the Republican or Legitimist opposition – the Church and Bonapartism. Outwardly Bonapartism seemed to have few formal adherents,[1] but as a half-formulated creed it could evoke passions even stronger than those associated with '93. It linked hands with Republicanism in its unappeasable yearning for an aggressive foreign policy, the *guerre libératrice*, promising revenge for the humiliation of 1815. This idea was an emotional obsession with the most fiery newspaper editor of the day, Armand Carrel, editor of *Le National*, until his death in a duel in 1836. Carrel, a passionate Liberal under the Restoration, ini-

mouldy corpse; he wore no visible linen; an old black frock-coat tightly covered his lean, withered limbs; he seemed to have passed his life in a sewer and to have just left it."

[1] Montalivet described it in 1830 as a religion with a few priests and no congregation.

tially supported the monarchy of Louis-Philippe, but by 1832 was castigating it as inglorious and corrupt. His disdain for the anarchic made him a dubious ally of the extreme Left, but his advocacy of orderly government at home and a crusade for liberty in Europe evoked a ready response among veterans of the Empire and young romantics alike. A sane and pacific foreign policy was to become appallingly difficult to carry out in a society all too ready to applaud editorials which proclaimed: "France is not happy when she is insufficiently glorious" and dismissed the entente with England in the phrase "England's honour is based on the dishonour of France".[1]

The revolution of July was directed as much against the altar as it was against the throne and it was followed by anti-clerical measures including the reduction of episcopal salaries, the abolition of regimental chaplains, the banning of processions and the removal of crucifixes from the court-rooms. Louis-Philippe agreed readily with the Duc de Broglie, his first minister of Education and Religious Cults, about the need to dissociate the monarchy from militant anti-clericalism. "One should never put one's finger into Church affairs," he observed, "because one never gets it out; it stays there." But when early in the reign he used the word "providence" in an address to the Chamber he was accused by Le Constitutionnel of a tendency to mysticism. "The old religion is completely dead and is already in a state of putrefaction," wrote Heine, "the majority of Frenchmen don't wish to hear the corpse spoken of and hold a handkerchief in front of their nose when anyone talks of the Church." The Archbishop of Paris, Monseigneur de Quélen, had once pronounced from the pulpit of Notre-Dame that "not only was Jesus Christ the Son of God, but he was also of very good family on his mother's side and there are excellent reasons for seeing in him the heir to the throne of Judaea." Now he was in hiding, from which he did not emerge

---

[1] A little before Carrel's death, Louis-Napoleon sent Persigny to see him. During their conversation Carrel remarked: "The name he bears is the greatest in modern times; it is the only one capable of arousing a strong response among the French people."

until 1831.[1] The bourgeois, anti-clerical supporters of the monarchy might well have concluded that a policy of rigour against the Jesuits, a cool and legalistic observance of the Concordat and eventually perhaps some fulfilment of the promise in the Charter about educational freedom would suffice to appease for good and all the persistent religious quarrel which had divided France since the Revolution.[2] That nothing of the sort happened was certainly not the fault of Louis-Philippe, who went to Mass quietly every Sunday and by his moderation and tolerance earned the enthusiastic approbation of Gregory XVI. That the religious question was to remain difficult and at times dangerous throughout the reign was due to a number of complex and interrelated issues – the rapidity with which the Catholic religion revived in France after the disasters of 1830 and 1831; liberal sympathy for the suffering of Catholics in Belgium, Poland and Ireland; the fundamental nature of the debate on religious education; and the individual genius of Lamennais, Montalembert and Lacordaire. The revival was largely an upper and middle class affair, appealing especially to the younger generation, many of whom found sceptical Voltaireanism and the fashionable eclectic philosophy of Cousin equally unsatisfying and became progressively more sympathetic to the claims of a Church no longer associated with the prevailing political régime. They were to find their spokesman in Henri Lacordaire, whose own path to religious conversion as a young man had been traced through the thickets of the romantic agony common to his generation. In an increasingly sympathetic atmosphere the almost hypnotic compulsion of Lacordaire's Lent sermons of 1835 filled Notre-Dame to overflowing. By 1837 a strong religious revival appeared to be under way, although it had scarcely touched the apathetic peasantry of eastern and central France and made virtually no impact on the swelling industrial population. That it had not spent its momentum even

[1] *Le National* on August 1st, 1830, reported: "Mgr. de Quélen has been arrested by the soldiers of the nation. He was carrying off with him a million in gold and many diamonds."

[2] Although three prelates fled the country after the Revolution there were only 300 objectors to the new régime among 29,000 priests.

by the end of the July Monarchy is apparent from the popularity of the priesthood in the early days of the Second Republic. Lacordaire admonished his congregation never to forget that the first tree of liberty was planted in the earthly Paradise. In the Spring of 1848 the republican trees of liberty were in the event blessed by the curés, for, paradoxically, the revival of Catholicism among the well-to-do proved to be in no sense a source of support to the established order of the July Monarchy. This was primarily due to the fact that of the three outstanding religious figures of the period, Lacordaire and Montalembert were advanced Liberals and Lamennais an extreme Republican. It was shortly after the July Revolution that the first number of *L'Avenir* appeared in October 1830 with the motto "Dieu et la Liberté". The editor was Félicité de Lamennais with, as his assistants, Lacordaire and the twenty-year-old Comte de Montalembert. Already under the Restoration Lamennais had aroused the unfavourable attention of the Gallican orthodox with his advocacy of an extreme Ultramontanism. In those days he was a convinced monarchist. But by 1830 his obsession with the abstract idea of liberty and his burning zeal to eliminate every intermediary power between Pope and people had led him to become an equally extreme republican. *L'Avenir* preached daily a radical programme of reform in Church matters. Church and State must be completely separated. The University, the state organization responsible for all education in France, had failed in its strenuous attempt under the Restoration to secure Catholic control of education; therefore education must be free with no restrictions on the teaching activity of the religious orders. But if education was to be free, so in the sacred name of liberty should be the right of expression. Freedom of association must be granted to all religious orders and therefore in the name of liberty to the workers also. If there was to be proper liberty then there must be universal suffrage. And if Frenchmen were to enjoy liberty, so must the oppressed Catholics in Poland, Belgium and Ireland. Lamennais proclaimed "liberty does not offer itself, it has to be seized"; and, furthermore, seized from the régime he described as "a miserable compromise between material power and justice", even if the nation had to undergo "purification in the fire of a fearful war". By the autumn of 1831 *L'Avenir* ceased publication while its editors set out for Rome as "pilgrims of Liberty". Gregory XVI whom Lamennais would soon feel free to call "a cowardly and imbecile old man" condemned their movement in the encyclical *Mirari Vos* and by 1834 Lamennais had celebrated his last mass and published *Les Paroles d'un Croyant*, which Professor Laski once called "a lyrical version of the Communist Manifesto". His voice became indistinguishable from that of the most extreme social revolutionaries.[1] But Montalembert who submitted to the papal censure with Lacordaire, kept alive in the Peers the problem of religious education, essentially the struggle for the souls of the coming generations. It was all very well for Louis-Philippe to dismiss the whole question as "a quarrel of beaks and beadles", but his government was perpetually harassed by the twin problems of what to do with the Jesuits and how to establish an educational order that would satisfy a church incongruously talking about "the true and generous spirit of the French Revolution". As Lacordaire put it, the victory of religious liberty would be won "under the banners of civil liberty". The victory was not won until 1850 and by that time the leaders of the Catholic party had seen the passing of the July Monarchy without regret.

[1] E.g. "While the upper classes, softened by pleasure and luxury, are drunk with their fandango, everywhere in the distance a dull rumbling announces the Pyrrhic victory of the peoples."

III

In the face of hostility of such depth and variety, Louis-Philippe might reasonably have expected a high degree of unity and loyalty among his own supporters. In fact they were divided amongst themselves by a deep cleavage of opinion about ends and means. On the one hand there were those who were soon to be called *le parti du mouvement*, who saw in the July Revolution a starting-point in the advance towards some rather ill-defined regeneration of the social order, to achieve which it was more important to maintain the revolutionary impetus than to be at all precise about the ends to be achieved. Their adversaries in the so-called *parti de résistance* would for the most part have been satisfied with a change of heart on the part of Charles X or a regency for the Duc de Bordeaux and held strongly that the revised Charter represented the ultimate that need be conceded to the principle of popular sovereignty. By December Guizot expressed their position perfectly when he pronounced that "the spirit of revolution, the spirit of insurrection is a spirit radically contrary to liberty". Personal rivalries and unsatisfied egoisms accentuated the disharmony between and within the two groups. Louis-Philippe, like William III in circumstances not altogether dissimilar, hoped initially to govern through a coalition ministry with a preponderance of conservatives. But at the same time he did his best to come to terms with the more amenable revolutionary elements to which he owed his throne. It was a hesitant and devious policy, characteristic henceforth of his attitude to politics, which Guizot described to Nassau Senior years later when he said: "He preferred cunning to force and always tried to turn obstacles rather than attack them frontally." But truth to tell he could hardly do otherwise in the immediate aftermath of the Revolution. Government of some sort there had to be and it could hardly be left to Lafayette; equally there was no means of avoiding the attentions of the populace, since not only was he unhedged by any sort of divinity but there were no locks on the gates of his palace. In creating, partly consciously and partly by sheer force of circumstances, the myth of a popular monarch, perpetually prepared to wring the hands of his subjects and happy to substitute an umbrella for a sceptre, Louis-Philippe raised for himself more problems than he solved. The height of absurdity was reached when the ineffable Lafayette took it on himself to lead into the Palais-Royal a deputation of former political prisoners, announcing: "Here are the political prisoners; they are presented to you by one of their accomplices." Among them was Fieschi.[1]

It is impossible not to admire the stamina and invariable good humour with which Louis-Philippe supported the treadmill of his daily existence. A deputation from Nemours about to leave Paris on September 13th found Lafayette too busy to see them but reported that "the King received us with a kindness above all expression and promised to take into particular consideration the various demands with which the town of Nemours may decide to present him". On February 14th, 1831, to take another example, he received in audience successively the maires of the 7th arrondissement, National Guard deputations from Saintes, Montluçon, Aubenas, Honfleur (introduced by Guizot), more Parisian maires, then once again the National Guards of Cette, Villevaude, Condé (to whom a special flag had to be presented), Eu and Livry. Undoubtedly, though at a heavy cost, his unforced affability and more or less continuous accessibility earned him the sustained loyalty of a great many honest middle-class grocers.[2] But in Paris everything quickly turns to ridicule. The bourgeois monarchy soon became a huge joke, a joke which in the skilful hands of its enemies was easily turned to satire and thence to cruel and libellous caricature. Irksome as it all became,

---

[1] See pp. 230–233.

[2] After the December riots of 1830 the National Guard of Saint-Brieuc wrote: "Say only the word, Sire, and we fly to share with our brave comrades of Paris the honour of serving as a rampart for your throne." (Archives Nationales.)

Louis-Philippe was to some extent responsible for the progressive deterioration of his own prestige, as a result of his fatal urge for easy popularity. Greville recorded as early as August 14th: "The new King, too, conducts himself in a way that gives me a bad opinion of him; he is too complaisant to the rage for equality, and stoops more than he need do; in fact he overdoes it."

While the Palais-Royal was seething with this odd mixture of loyal and grubby citizens, place-hunters and sightseers,[1] acutely difficult problems confronted the harassed and divided ministry which was appointed on August 11th. Of the *parti de résistance*, Molé, a very rich and cultivated individual who had inherited the lustre of a name famous in the annals of the Parlement of Paris, was Foreign Minister. His record as a Liberal peer in opposition to Villèle was considerably discounted by the fact that he had held office under both the Empire and the Restoration. He could be labelled a Politique rather than a Doctrinaire, an appellation which did however apply to two other members of the Cabinet, Guizot (Minister of the Interior) and the Duc de Broglie (Education and Religious Cults). Both had been stern critics of the previous régime and both had had their moments of popularity. They had consistently confined their opposition within the limits of the Constitution, which they had wished to see progressively liberalized in the English manner. Royer-Collard, the archpriest of the small group of high-minded political theorists to which both men belonged, was once asked whether he had called Guizot "an austere intriguer" and replied, "I did not say austere", though in fact he might well have done. A Protestant and the son of a Nîmes bourgeois, who had been guillotined in 1794, Guizot as a young man translated Gibbon and Shakespeare and in 1812 secured the chair of modern history at the Sorbonne.[2] During the first Restoration he was secretary-general of the Interior and visited Louis XVIII at Ghent. From 1815 to 1820 he was secretary to the Minister of Justice. But it was his work as a historian

---

[1] One of Louis-Philippe's friends apologized acidly for entering the royal presence without first muddying his boots.

[2] He was originally trained to be a carpenter.

and political philosopher which first earned him the sort of reputation which despite all his subsequent failures led Acton and Morley to agree one day together that Guizot was the greatest all-round statesman of the nineteenth century. A man of superb intellectual endowments, he was essentially disinterested for himself while capable of complete ruthlessness in the interests of his own class, which was in his opinion the repository of all political wisdom. Like Ferry and Clemenceau he despised popularity and defined his political creed as "faith in providence, the sanctity of duty, submission to paternal authority and the imperishable principles of morality and reason without which the social order is in peril". With this went a belief in royalty which he expressed thus in his *Histoire de la civilisation européenne*: "Royalty is something quite different from the will of one man, though that is the form under which it appears. It is the personification of the sovereignty of law, of a will which is essentially reasonable, enlightened, just and impartial, which rises above all individual wills and is for that reason entitled to govern them." Time was to show how precisely Guizot's view chimed in with Louis-Philippe's own conception of the monarchial power, though for the moment differences of temperament kept them apart. The Duc de Broglie resembled Guizot in his personal austerity and high-mindedness but a vein of aristocratic disdain for political manœuvre and a justifiable lack of confidence in his ability to handle politicians limited the effectiveness of one of the most distinguished Liberals of the age. Baron Louis, who was in large part responsible for the prosperity France had enjoyed under the Restoration, was put in charge of finance at a moment when the *Journal des Débats* was proclaiming: "the imminence of a great commercial catastrophe" and *Le National* was deploring "the lack of confidence which is killing business". Other conservatives were Sébastiani in charge of the Navy and Louis-Philippe's pertinacious, but uninspiring legal adviser, Dupin, and Casimir-Périer as ministers without portfolio. No ministry thus constituted could have survived in the early months of the Revolution and it was necessary to dilute it with certain elements more calculated to appeal to the masses in the streets clamouring for the overthrow of the existing order in Europe. The Napoleonic general, Gérard, who was soon to become one of the pillars of the régime, had the War office, and the stiff and uncompromising Dupont de l'Eure[1] the Ministry of Justice. Laffitte and Bignon were ministers without portfolio and Laffitte was much incensed when he was defeated for the Presidency of the Chamber by Casimir-Périer. No Prime Minister could hope to weld together such a coalition and none was appointed. It was far from certain that the cabinet even commanded effective power for there was always Lafayette in his headquarters at the Hôtel de Ville basking in his new-found popularity,[2] Lafayette of whom Charles X had said "he and I are the only men in France who haven't changed". And as Prefect of the Seine, responsible for order in the city, was M. Odilon Barrot, like Lafayette sublimely confident in his own generosity and wisdom and intoxicated with the sound of his own advocacy, interpreting his task as that of a benevolent tutelary deity to the good people of Paris, who must be allowed to riot happily as long as there was anything left to riot about. These were the resources with which Louis-Philippe had to confront an angry and suspicious Europe, an empty treasury, a disordered capital, a disaffected civil service, and an entirely uncertain political future. No wonder Marie-Amélie still pined for the peace of Neuilly.

The ministry survived only to the beginning of November, but before it expired Louis-Philippe had ensured the triumph of the pacific foreign policy which, while still only Lieutenant-General, he proclaimed to the world in his address at the opening of the Chambers on August 3rd in the words: "France will show Europe that concerned only with her own internal prosperity she cherishes peace as much as liberty and only wishes the happiness and repose

[1] This rather formidable mandarin of the Liberal Left had been a member of the Five Hundred in 1798. He was known as the Aristides of the Assembly.
[2] Among the complimentary addresses from National Guard companies from all over France which poured in on the Hôtel de Ville was one from Rodez, bespattered with rather vinous signatures, ending, "*Vive la Liberté! Vive notre Wasington* [sic]! *Vive Lafayette!*" (Archives Nationales F [1c] 1. 32).

of her neighbours." In the century of Palmerston, Bismarck and Napoleon III the blessings that the Gospel promises to the peace-makers were not notably forthcoming in this world. Louis-Philippe's love of peace was none the less sincere and creditable for being mixed with a thoroughly realistic appraisal of the prob-able consequences for France of European war. That on more than one occasion (and notably in 1830) it earned him the oppro-brium of the majority of his subjects never deflected him from an objective which seemed to him his first duty, even if it involved considerable national and personal humiliation.[1] He has been censured, and with some justice, for falsifying the conception of constitutional monarchy by his continual personal intervention in affairs of state. But, while not always as expert in the handling of foreign affairs as he liked to think himself, his extraordinarily wide knowledge of European nations and languages rendered him better equipped than anybody in France, except Talleyrand, to keep the peace and to ensue it, and he knew all too well how little he could rely on the skill and discretion of the politicians with their susceptibility to dangerous currents of popular opinion. "We must not only cherish peace," he told one of the endless deputa-tions to the Palais-Royal, "we must also avoid everything which could provoke war." This took courage at a moment when the "patriotic" Left was emulating Brissot in the intemperance of its language.[2]

Both his principles and practice were soon put to the test. On July 27th Metternich and the Russian foreign minister Nesselrode were engaged at Carlsbad in what looked like being abortive diplomatic conversations. By July 30th they rapidly discovered an identity of interests which had eluded them for a long time in the need to take some sort of action to neutralize the dangerously contagious consequences of the new French Revolution. The

[1] Metternich once told him that the entente between Great Britain and France was like that between the horse and the rider and warned him not to be the horse.

[2] E.g. Edgar Quinet: "All the Rhineland is only awaiting a signal to reunite itself with France." He was clearly suffering from one of the persistent illusions of the Left – the assumed existence of "l'Europe Peuple".

Prussia of Frederick William III readily concurred and the Holy Alliance suddenly appeared to have taken on a new lease of life. Nicholas I told his ambassador in Paris, Pozzo di Borgo, to withdraw all Russian nationals from France and to tell Louis-Philippe that he would never be recognized in Saint-Petersburg. Metternich, who considered the monarchy of Louis XVIII dangerously republican, gave its successor a probable duration of three months, but although he planned for the necessary intervention at the end of that period, neither he nor Frederick William III were as anxious as Nicholas to play the part of an international fire-brigade. Intent on calming as quickly as possible both apprehensions and rancours, Louis-Philippe despatched a series of reliable generals to London, Vienna, Saint-Petersburg and Berlin armed with reassuring messages which he himself composed late at night after the community-singers had left the Palais-Royal. Atthalin took to Russia a letter reading: "I groan for the unhappiness that has afflicted the elder branch of my family. My only ambition would have been to prevent it and to remain in the position in which Providence had placed me; but circumstances dictated otherwise and I had to obey. The least hesitation on my part would have plunged the country into disorder of which one could not foresee the end." There was very little, if anything, insincere in this letter but it made no impression on Nicholas and its indiscreet publication in Paris aroused a storm of protest. However the ice soon broke in London. The Duke, still Prime Minister after a troubled summer, had not been an admirer of Polignac, whom he knew well and was very angry about Algiers. But, while it was true that ever since 1808 the Foreign Office files had suggested that the Duc d'Orléans was a dangerous person, the one thing to avoid with Reform agitation looking so ugly was any sort of threat to the peace of Europe and a very real threat had now broken out in Belgium.

The union of Holland and Belgium was no more popular in Belgium than it was in France, where it had been popularly described by the republican General Lamarque as a bridgehead which kept the road to Paris open to the coalition powers. The unpopularity of the Hague government succeeded in uniting Belgian Liberals and Belgian Ultras in a resistance which aroused the strongest emotional sympathy in France on grounds of religion, language and political sympathy. The news of the July Revolution seemed initially to have little effect on the citizens of Brussels, who were busily occupied with an industrial exhibition. But as the month of August went on tension mounted. On August 25th a performance took place of La Muette de Portici,[1] an opera by Scribe and Auber, and by the time the audience began to sing in unison about "l'amour sacré de la patrie", another revolution had effectively broken out. A moderate Committee of Public Safety soon gave way to an extremist Provisional Government. By September 27th the Dutch hold on Belgian territory was limited to Antwerp and on October 4th the Provisional Government declared Belgium an independent State and their delegate in London informed Wellington that if the powers intervened to restore the *status quo* of 1814, the Belgian reaction would be union with France. In these circumstances William IV's government decided to recognize the upstart French monarchy by the end of August and on September 20th Louis-Philippe's inspired choice as ambassador to London, the Prince de Talleyrand, set out for the country from which he had been expelled thirty-six years before. On August 11th Aberdeen, Wellington's foreign secretary, had written: "The tricolour flag and the setting aside of the Duc de Bordeaux may sanctify the title of the Duke of Orleans in the eyes of many; but I cannot think that even the charms of republicanism and usurpation will enable him to last long." But the diplomatic charms of Talleyrand were another matter and by October 2nd the ambassador was able to write to the Princesse Adélaïde the following reassuring despatch: "I think that the Duke is now quite convinced that the movement of the French in July was not due to any one person but that it was entirely caused by the state of general dissatisfaction; that there was no single intrigue; that M. le Duc d'Orléans was forced to become Lieutenant-General of the Kingdom and subsequently to accept

[1] The subject is Masaniello's rebellion.

· 178 ·

the crown; that in so doing he has fulfilled a duty; and that in fulfilling this duty he has rendered an essential service to the whole of Europe. The King has many admirers here and many who love him." Before leaving Paris Talleyrand had arranged to correspond regularly with the King's sister, a device which enabled Louis-Philippe to conduct in concert with him a personal diplomacy, which by-passed the ministry of Foreign Affairs and fully justified itself in the difficult first six months of the reign.

Austria and Prussia pessimistically and Russia with the worst possible grace, followed the British lead in accepting the situation in France but the Belgian crisis threw everything once more into the melting-pot. Nicholas threatened armed intervention with sixty thousand men and the Prussians moved an army corps into the Rhine provinces. Louis-Philippe had an extremely difficult hand to play and played it with coolness and resource. If he took no action and the Powers set about crushing the Belgian revolution he could not hope to restrain the Left. On the other hand the French could at most put into the field an army of 250,000, many of whom could hardly be expected to regard the new monarchy with the necessary crusading zeal. However the government proclaimed its adherence to the principle of non-intervention by the Powers in Belgium and in face of Prussian threats Molé at the end of September warned the Prussian ambassador that intervention would mean war with France. Despite the protests of Metternich, who likened the principle of non-intervention to burglars protesting against the police, or incendiaries against the fire-brigade, a combination of bluff and the diplomatic persistence of Talleyrand achieved the desired result for France. By agreeing to renounce any plan to annex Belgium, rectify the frontier or establish a French prince in Brussels, Talleyrand secured the British consent to the whole problem being settled by the conference of ambassadors which was already in being in London to discuss the Greek question. At the first session Talleyrand remarked placidly: "I am not the diplomatic mouthpiece of France. I'm only a man of some experience who has come to sit with old friends to talk of general affairs." Soon Palmerston, who had replaced Aberdeen at the Foreign Office after the fall of the Tories, was protesting uncharacteristically that "we are fully sensible of the value of the friendship of so liberal and intelligent a power as France". This did not stop him keeping Talleyrand waiting for an hour or two outside the office and when the latter edged gingerly towards the subject of a little frontier rectification, Palmerston's reaction prefigured the shape of things to come in a memorandum which began: "The moment we give France a cabbage-garden or a vineyard we lose all vantage ground of principle." However, the independence and neutrality of Belgium secured, there only remained the problem of giving her a monarchy and coercing the recalcitrant Dutch. Louis-Philippe's renunciation of the crown offered by the Belgians to the Duc de Nemours in February 1831 left the way open for Leopold of Saxe-Coburg in the summer of the following year. There was to be more trouble with the Dutch and the uneasy concert of Europe was to be disturbed in Poland and Italy before the first year of the July Monarchy had elapsed, but an excellent beginning had been made.

IV

"One daren't go into a shop to buy anything when the streets are full of agitators. But whenever one of these agitators is arrested one finds in his pocket a petition requesting that he should be made a prefect." Thus Dupin described the explosive mixture of social disintegration and unsatisfied material aspirations which characterized Paris in the last months of 1830. While the ill-assorted members of the Ministry of August 11th exercised their powers of rhetoric on the King and on each other in a cabinet room, whose windows gave them an uncomfortably good view of the July heroes in the gardens below, *Les Amis du Peuple* in the rue Montmartre were holding tumultuous sessions at which Blanqui and Cavaignac contrasted the bourgeois pusillanimity of the new régime with the great days of '93. Every Tuesday in the rue d'Artois, Lafayette was at home to a grimy, if patriotic, rabble, which he liked to describe as "that noble population of the barricades whose sublime conduct has placed them in the front rank of French society". But not everyone could be in the front rank of even Lafayette's army. As bankruptcy succeeded to bankruptcy and more and more unemployed and dangerous vagrants wandered the streets, the more responsible members of society began to look for a lead to the King, the Ministry and the Chambers, only to find that none was forthcoming.

Louis-Philippe was, as has been seen, much preoccupied with foreign affairs and in addition he was kept ceaselessly at work reviewing battalions of the National Guard,[1] receiving deputations and drinking toasts with all and sundry. He had his

---

[1] Which he did very well, once he became accustomed to a tendency among the more eager patriots to break the ranks in order to wring the monarch's hand. Alfred de Vigny, whose battalion he reviewed, even compared him in dignity to Louis XIV.

moments of exaltation, as when he urged Guizot to remind all Frenchmen that now "individual liberty exists for everyone on the widest possible scale – for travellers of all sorts to go where they wish, for all opinions, for all parties". For a short time he entertained the illusion that under what Heine called his "vast sentimental umbrella" Frenchmen might be free, prosperous and glorious. This mood led to indiscretions, such as an uncalculated but disastrous over-adulation of Laffitte and Lafayette, which he was soon to regret. Thoroughly enjoying the congenial role of being all things to all men, he talked a great deal and he talked too loudly. Marie-Amélie would whisper in English: "Take care. We are not alone," to which he would reply: "So much the better; I would like all France to hear me." But he was speedily to discover that the concept of a united France ready to listen to the benevolent counsels of a wise, experienced and liberal monarch bore no relation to reality. On the Right and on the Left were irreconcilable enemies. By March of 1831 he diagnosed the prevalent disease of French society with his usual shrewdness as follows: "The misfortune of our country is that we never stop thinking; no one is prepared to see things as they really are; we feed on the chimerical and this mental unbalance communicates itself to the entire body of society; and that is how it will die." [1] The King's political inactivity in the early months of the reign was not entirely attributable to false optimism. By one false move he could either finally alienate the vociferous forces of the Left or alternatively precipitate the revolution beyond a point of no return. The same fear paralysed the Chambers, in which the preponderating moderates were uneasily aware how little they represented the dominant public opinion of the capital. As for the Ministry, even Guizot at the Interior felt impelled to placate the spirit of popular insurrection in referring to the streets of Paris as "the most noble of battlefields". In his administrative appointments he had the unpleasant choice of either being branded as a

---

[1] Guizot described the mood of the day as "reflecting excessive confidence in human intelligence"; Alfred de Musset, with even greater precision, ingeminated "La politique, hélas! voilà notre misère".

counter-revolutionary, or promoting to office people whom he knew to be perfectly unfit for it. Any move on the part of the conservative elements in the cabinet to exploit its majority was countered by pompous reminders from Laffitte of his decisive role as king-maker, or by surly threats of resignation from the austere and disagreeable Dupont de L'Eure, who passed on cabinet secrets to the leaders of the clubs and flatly contradicted Louis-Philippe to his face. Disorders in the streets elicited obsequious proclamations from Barrot and if regular troops appeared in public they had to be preceded by detachments of the National Guard, who, adopting a policy of keeping order as and when they chose, did at last break up an open session of Les Amis du Peuple on September 25th, only to drive it underground as a secret society.

The first internal crisis of the reign centred round the fate of Polignac and three other ministers of Charles X, who were incarcerated in the fortress of Vincennes. Their trial was duly voted on September 27th in a debate in which Guizot had the courage to aver that "France has made a revolution, but she hasn't agreed to put herself in a condition of permanent revolution". The crucial question was whether Polignac and his confederates after trial for treason by the Peers would incur the death-penalty. The entire Left was united in demanding death as the appropriate expiation of the crimes of the fallen régime.[1] Few men realized better than Louis-Philippe the lamentable consequences of political executions. Apart from his own personal memories of the Terror, the execution of Ney was a discouraging precedent and there was also European public opinion to consider. So, faithful to his policy of turning obstacles rather than confronting them head-on, he persuaded the Chambers to vote him an address, requesting him to abolish the death-penalty for political offences, which they duly did on October 8th. In giving his consent Louis-Philippe declared: "Witness in my youth of the frightful abuse of the death-penalty for political offences, I have constantly

[1] In which oddly enough they had the support of The Times and the Edinburgh Review.

and most genuinely desired its abolition." The obstacle apparently turned, the Chamber of deputies adjourned on October 10th to enable complementary elections to fill its empty benches.

The consequent outcry in the clubs and in the press left no doubt about the sanguinary intentions of the agitators. On the 17th an angry crowd surrounded the Palais-Royal, demanding death for the imprisoned ministers. On the evening of the 18th the demonstrators broke into the gardens and quadrangles of the palace. When the guard had with great difficulty ejected them, the shout went up "*A Vincennes!*" and a torchlit rabble set forth in that direction. When they arrived they found themselves confronted by an imperturbable and wooden-legged Napoleonic veteran, General Daumesnil, who threatened to blow up the powder-magazine and thus accompany his visitors back to Paris via the Porte Saint-Antoine. At two o'clock that morning, Adélaïde was woken by the sound of the drunken mob, back again in Paris, surging into the palace, shouting, "Death to the ministers, or the head of King Louis-Philippe!" A providential reinforcement of the National Guard saved what might have become a very ugly situation, but not before some of the demonstrators had started to move up the great staircase.[1] The panic-stricken ministry immediately issued a note which appeared in the *Moniteur* to the effect that an immediate abolition of the death-penalty was not possible and Barrot, the Prefect of the Seine, issued a proclamation to the effect that in his view it had been "an inopportune step".

Government in France seemed to have capitulated completely to mob intimidation. Since it was impossible in the inflamed state of public opinion to get rid of Barrot or Dupont, de Broglie suggested to Louis-Philippe, whose mind was already turning in that direction, that the best plan was to allow the politicians of the Left to reap their own whirlwind. De Broglie, Guizot, Casimir Périer, Dupin, Molé and Louis resigned and a new ministry was formed on November 2nd with Jacques Laffitte as President

[1] Thereafter for the first time since the Revolution the gates of the Palais-Royal were locked at nightfall.

of the Council and finance minister, and Dupont as Minister of Justice. But the composition of the new cabinet reveals clearly that for Louis-Philippe and the Doctrinaires this was not a surrender to the Left but a tactical withdrawal. Louis-Philippe insinuated into the key-post of the Interior the twenty-nine year old colonel of the 4th Legion of the National Guard, the Comte de Montalivet, acceptable as the son of a Napoleonic minister and on account of his unimpeachably Liberal antecedents, but very much a personal adherent of the King. By November 17th after a cabinet reshuffle, Foreign Affairs were entrusted to Sébastiani, an execrable speaker and limited in his political range, but a devoted confidant of the Kings, fully prepared to do what Talleyrand told him to do from Hanover Square and perfectly happy to by-pass Laffitte. Nor was Soult, the Marshal Duke of Dalmatia, at the War Office likely in the evening of his years to countenance any rash romanticism in foreign policy. Had Laffitte had any equipment for high political office other than his own boundless vanity and ephemeral popularity he would not have accepted as colleagues men with whose outlook he had nothing in common. It was an unpromising beginning for a ministry whose obituary would be pronounced four months later by the exasperated Carrel in the contemptuous phrase: "Monsieur Laffitte has tried not a system, but the absence of all system, that is government by default." Louis-Philippe and the moderates, aware that things had to get worse before they could get better, were prepared to allow him sufficient rope with which to hang himself.

While finance and administration ran steadily downhill, Laffitte's ministry was almost exclusively occupied with the insistent public clamour for the execution of Charles X's ministers and for a war of revenge against the victors of 1815. The revolt of the Poles, which began at the end of August 1830 and was to last far into 1831, provoked a species of romantic obsession which united otherwise diverse elements in a demand for what would have amounted to national suicide. The bellicosity of Carrel's editorials was almost matched in extravagance by Montalembert's passionate pleading in *L'Avenir* for relief for the sufferings of the Catholic Poles; Lafayette irresponsibly countenanced the aggressive instincts of his admirers; Petrus Borel sported a cloak which he described as being of the colour of Polish blood; and Casimir Delavigne reinforced his success with 'La Parisienne' by composing 'La Varsovienne', in which the heroic Poles demanded of their old allies:

> Pour de vieux frères en armes
> N'aurez-vous que des larmes?

As well as Poland there was Belgium and, early in the new year, popular risings in Italy. It soon became all too clear that the generous bellicosity of the emotional Left would provoke war with Russia over Poland, with Austria over Italy, and with Prussia, Holland and England over Belgium and the left bank of the Rhine. It was no doubt intoxicating for Frenchmen to hear of the president of the revolutionary government in Bologna comparing in importance the three days of July with the six days of the creation, but fortunately Louis-Philippe and Talleyrand kept a firm grip on the situation, concealing despatches from Laffitte and using the impassive Sébastiani as a convenient chopping-block in the Chamber. England, France's only ally, true to her invariable policy of not helping the Poles against the Russians, was not even prepared, under her new Whig government, to make a diplomatic démarche. So, not for the last time, it was necessary, however much unpopularity it incurred, to sacrifice the unhappy Poles to prevent a general European conflagration. Louis-Philippe was at least able to reflect in exile that his successors in 1848 were able to do no more for the Poles and the Italians than he had done in even less auspicious circumstances.

His other main object, as has been seen, was to save the lives of Charles X's ministers. Street processions, carrying murderous placards, indicated all too clearly how difficult a task this would prove. When the trial opened in the Luxembourg on December 15th, the surrounding gardens were filled with demonstrators, fraternizing with members of the National Guard, the majority of which (and notably the artillery) was known to favour the exaction of the death penalty. Lafayette in his heart wished to avoid bloodshed but lacked the moral courage to say so publicly. The conduct and bearing of Polignac and his fellow-ministers during the trial was extremely impressive, and they were brilliantly defended.[1] But by December 20th the demonstrations outside the Luxembourg became so ugly that Pasquier, the President of the Peers, suspended the sitting before the final vote was taken, so that the government could deliberate on the probable consequences the next day of any verdict being pronounced other than death. Montalivet summoned a conference, at which on Pasquier's suggestion it was agreed that the National Guard should be withdrawn from the Luxembourg and replaced by line troops. Lafayette, who was present at the conference, at first agreed. Then, unable to resist the members of his entourage, he subsequently went back on his decision and allowed unruly elements of the National Guard to enter the gardens, while Soult rendered himself carefully inaccessible in the War Office. After a night of general terror and apprehension throughout the city, the situation on the 21st seemed desperate, only to be saved by a brave and brilliantly executed *coup de main* on the part of Montalivet. Before the Peers had finished deliberating, he extracted the accused ministers from the custody of their gaoler, bundled them into a carriage and with an escort of chasseurs, riding himself on the horse of one of the N.C.O.'s, he escorted them at top speed to the safety of Vincennes. As the news spread through the gardens of the Luxembourg the crowd, baulked of its prey, roared its disapproval, but was soon placated by an insistent rumour that the death penalty would after all be exacted. By the time the announcement was made at ten o'clock that the sentence was in fact life imprisonment,[2] the mob-impetus was spent and Louis-Philippe, much relieved at another desperate corner being turned, warmly embraced the intrepid Montalivet.

New and menacing crowds carrying black flags assembled in

[1] Polignac was defended by his predecessor in office, Martignac, who was a dying man.
[2] Polignac was also condemned to civil death.

the streets on the 22nd, but by now even the students of the Ecole Polytechnique were proclaiming the virtues of public order and on the 23rd the King, reviewing National Guard detachments in the streets, received an encouraging ovation.[1] Over the next few days Montalivet's police reports indicated a general slackening of tension, and the King was able to seize a sudden opportunity which presented itself to get rid of Lafayette whom a cartoon had recently depicted as saying to a bare-headed Louis-Philippe with hat in hand, "Sire, you may put on your hat." The Chamber decreed the abolition of the emergency post of Commander-in-Chief of the National Guard, while decreeing that Lafayette might continue to hold the honorary title. The great man took umbrage, resigned and, resisting the adulatory caresses of Laffitte, refused to withdraw his resignation unless the Ministry resigned, the Chamber of Peers was abolished, and the franchise widened nearly to the point of universal suffrage. Louis-Philippe, strengthened by the firmness of Marie-Amélie,[2] called his bluff and replaced him as Commander of the National Guard of the capital by Marshal Lobau, who had saved the French Army after Essling. The disbandment of the mutinous National Guard artillery and the resignation of M. Dupont de l'Eure followed and 1830 ended with Guizot and the other partisans of order going over to the attack in the Chamber. Of Lafayette's career under the July Monarchy Wellington observed with some justice: "I have always considered Lafayette as a striking instance of how seldom men in politics profit by experience. After all that he had said and done in 1789, and seeing the results, he was beginning to play exactly the same part after 1830; and if Louis-Philippe had not

[1] Greville recorded in his entry for December 26th: "The King of the French has put an end to the disturbances of Paris about the sentence on the ex-ministers by a gallant coup d'état. At night when the streets were most crowded and agitated he sallied from the Palais-Royal on horseback with his son the Duc de Nemours and his personal cortège, and paraded through Paris for two hours. This did the business; he was received with shouts of applause and at once reduced everything to tranquillity. He deserves his throne for this and will probably keep it."

[2] Montalivet observed of her at this stage: "One can see she is the grand-daughter of Maria-Theresa."

been a very different man from Louis XVI, and had not had the firmness first to check and then to dismiss him, he would a second time have overturned the government . . . it was the same unswerving adherence to principle, and the same insufficient control of circumstance, that shaped the whole of his political course."

Laffitte was soon to follow Lafayette into political obscurity. The patience of the King and the Doctrinaires with a Prime Minister who smiled and smiled and did precisely nothing was finally exhausted as a result of a particularly savage outburst of anti-clericalism, which took place in February 1831.[1] It was provoked initially by the Legitimists, who very misguidedly chose to celebrate ostentatiously the anniversary of the assassination eleven years previously of the Duc de Berri, Charles X's younger son, by celebrating a mass in the Church of Saint-Germain-l'Auxerrois, conducted by the priest who had attended Marie-Antoinette on the scaffold. Within a comparatively short space of time the church was reduced to a heap of débris, whereupon the unappeased mob made for the thirteenth-century Archbishop's palace in the shadow of Notre-Dame, which had already been damaged in the July fighting. Before nightfall great bonfires of furniture and ornaments lit up the dark river-side and the frenzied rioters openly announced their intention of returning the next day. They did so with a vengeance, hurling the finest ecclesiastical library in France into the Seine and gutting the building until nothing was left of it but broken walls and rubble. The Archbishop's country house at Conflans was looted and seminaries and episcopal palaces at Lille, Nîmes, Dijon and Angoulême suffered similarly. Drunken rioters, dressed up in ecclesiastical garments, openly parodied the Mass. More than one observer noticed that an appreciable number of young bourgeois were to be found among the rioters. Neither Barrot, nor the Prefect of Police, nor Thiers, who visited the Archbishop's palace and prevented the National Guard

---

[1] The riots began on February 14th. As an example of how old myths die hard, a distinguished recent contribution to the English historiography of the period tells us in its opening paragraph how Louis-Philippe at dawn that morning "dozed peacefully in the Tuileries" [sic].

intervening, took any effective action to check the proceedings until Notre-Dame itself was threatened. Montalivet's political immaturity was revealed in a feeble attempt at exculpation in the Chamber; Barrot pontificated about the legitimate indignation of the affronted heroes of July; and Laffitte's only contribution was to impel Louis-Philippe to remove the fleurs-de-lys from the royal arms.

V

It was time to call a halt. At the end of eight months of the new reign commerce everywhere in France was stagnant, unemployment growing, a deficit mounting monthly, civil servants idle or mutinous and the European powers again contemplating intervention to check the excesses of a revolution, which was fast appearing to justify Wellington's gloomy opinion "that a democracy once set going must sooner or later work itself out in anarchy". On March 2nd the mob was shouting for "bread or work" outside the Palais-Royal, and on the 10th a false rumour of the capture of Warsaw led to a volley of stones breaking the windows of the Russian embassy. The *parti du mouvement*, under a leader, who suffered from the fatal disadvantage of not knowing in which direction to lead, was played out. Everyone knew that if Laffitte's ministry were to be replaced by a combination dominated by the conservative *parti de la résistance*, any such ministry would inevitably be led by the one man strong enough through force of character to be acceptable as the regenerator of French society, in default of the military hero usually called on by the nation in a crisis of this sort. This was a fifty-four year old banker from Dauphiné, a veteran of the parliamentary struggles of the previous reign and now president of the Chamber, Casimir-Périer.

Louis-Philippe hesitated momentarily. He was well aware of the services he had himself rendered to France and Europe in keeping the peace. His personal conduct of foreign affairs had led the English ambassador, Granville, to describe him as "the ablest man in France" and Metternich had recently told an English visitor that in his opinion "Louis-Philippe is the ablest statesman the French have had for a great while". He undoubtedly wished to extend his personal control to home as well as foreign affairs and he knew perfectly well that Casimir-Périer would monopolize all power in any government of which he was the head.

But equally Casimir-Périer was the only man remotely capable of giving France peace and internal security as matters then stood. On March 11th, 1831, he began his herculean task, which he knew perfectly well from his doctor's advice was bound to kill him, and proceeded in the short space of just over a year to transform the internal and external situation of France almost beyond recognition. There is a superficial resemblance between Casimir-Périer and Chatham – the same indomitable wrestling of the spirit with the flesh, the same haughtiness and impatience with compromise and colleagues who counselled compromise and something of the same strength and quickness of decision in foreign affairs. Casimir-Périer was not particularly well-educated, he had nothing of the oratorical fluency which Guizot already possessed and Thiers was at this stage rapidly acquiring, and he was impatient of the tendency of French assemblies to elevate anything they discussed to the status of a political principle. But he had a vibrant personal force and sincerity, and differed from both his supporters and his opponents in both proclaiming and achieving clear and realizable objectives. He was certain in his own mind, and rightly, that the riotous republicans in the streets of the capital and their provincial supporters were at this stage quite unrepresentative of the nation at large and must no longer be allowed to paralyse government either at the centre or in the provinces. A firm supporter of the principle of constitutional monarchy, he was initially suspicious of Louis-Philippe as being too easily influenced by revolutionary pressures and too fatalistic about the weakness of the régime. At the same time he and the King were agreed on strictly relating the legality of their actions to the letter and spirit of the Charter. It was, and is, possible to view his foreign policy differently from the opposite sides of the Channel, but it succeeded by a mixture of adroitness, common sense and some good fortune in both preserving the peace and enhancing the status of France, an achievement which was subsequently to elude both Thiers and Guizot. All this he promised in his first great speech to the Chamber on March 18th when he proclaimed his policy to be: "at home, order, without the sacri-

fice of liberty; abroad, peace, without the sacrifice of honour".
And within limits, he came very near to performing what he
promised, a feat rare enough in nineteenth-century politics to
entitle him to high rank as a statesman.

From the outset, Périer was determined to dominate the King,
the cabinet, the civil administration and the Chamber. The
cabinet would deliberate without the King being present before
submitting agreed measures for Louis-Philippe's signature; the
Duc d'Orléans, the dashing heir to the throne, who was given to
romantic flirtations with the idealistic Left, was to be excluded
from all cabinet meetings; cabinet approval would henceforth
be necessary for any insertions in the *Moniteur*. As to the ministry
itself, Périer insisted on Baron Louis as the only man capable of
restoring financial confidence in face of the fifty-one million franc
deficit accumulated by M. Laffitte, now popularly known as M.
Faillitte, owing to the failure of his own banking business following hard on that of his administration. Montalivet sensibly
offered to give up the vital post of Minister of the Interior to
Périer himself, so that the all-important problem of policing the
country properly should be in the ablest hands.[1] Soult agreed to
stay at the War Office, when it was tersely pointed out to him by
Périer that it would be a perfectly simple matter to replace him
by the slightly less illustrious Marshal Jourdain; Talleyrand stayed
in London and Sébastiani at the Foreign Office. Périer's views on
cabinet solidarity were sharply exemplified when on one occasion d'Argout, the Minister of Works, making some critical references to cabinet policy in the Chamber, was sharply interrupted
by a cry of "Ici, d'Argout" from the terrible President of the
Council and had to slink back to his seat from the tribune with
his tail between his legs.

All this was not very much to the liking of the Palais-Royal.
Adélaïde was frankly disgusted. Although solicitous about the
great man's health and continually urging him to have fewer
sleepless nights, Louis-Philippe only really recovered his aplomb

---

[1] Melbourne was carrying out the same functions as Home Secretary in
Great Britain with rather greater ruthlessness.

when he escaped to make a comparatively triumphant tour of the North and East in June and July of 1831.[1] There was a significant episode at Metz when both the mayor and the commander of the National Guard attempted to harangue him on national politics. Louis-Philippe interrupted them curtly to the effect that he was not prepared to listen to them on subjects that were beyond their competence. He was, in fact, won over in this summer by the force of events and the personal triumph of Périer to the *politique de la résistance*, the moderate conservatism which was to characterize the remainder of his reign. The choice lay simply between support of Casimir Périer or capitulation to the revolution and European war. For the moment this would involve many humiliations, but gradually the two men came closer together, each realizing the other's merits. It was probably an exaggeration on Louis-Philippe's part, born of wounded vanity, which led him in a characteristic indiscretion to say shortly after Périer's death: "Périer gave me some trouble but in the end I was able to ride him." But there was to be more truth in his later development of this equestrian metaphor – "A ministry is a staging-post. I sometimes have good horses and the voyage is easy. But then I arrive at a post where I have to take mettlesome and restive horses; then one has to get on with the journey and after all it's only one relay."

In control of the cabinet and the King, Périer set about the civil service and the Chamber of Deputies with equal decisiveness. Provincial administrators were left in no doubt that there was now a central government and that it intended to be obeyed. A ruthless purge was initiated of all servants of the crown, who, under the aegis of Lafayette, had joined the so-called National Association, an organization rather imprecisely dedicated to developing "the consequences of the Revolution." Among those dismissed were General Lamarque, a hero of the last stages of the Napoleonic epic,[2] whose nuisance-value as a rhetorical advocate of a war of

---

[1] Included in his itinerary was a visit to the hill of Valmy.

[2] The Emperor, who had used him to crush a revolt in the Vendée during the Hundred Days, had sung his praises at Saint-Helena. He had had four horses shot from under him at Wagram.

revenge on Europe was almost unparalleled and one of Louis-Philippe's A.D.C.'s. Barrot had already been got rid of and the new Prefect of Police, Gisquet, one of Périer's former bank-employees, knew his business thoroughly even to the point of securing volunteer assistance from a number of Parisian workers. In securing a firm grip on the prefects, Périer was able to exploit increasingly the conservative instincts of the French countryside, where by and large Legitimism and a semi-articulate, sentimental Bonapartism represented more of a threat to the July Monarchy than republicanism.

The volatile and undisciplined nature of the Chamber made the maintenance of a firm parliamentary majority a very difficult undertaking. Périer's personal ascendancy again and again rallied just sufficient supporters to save the government from extinction. His plan to make the elections in July a vote of confidence in himself was negatived by the ingenious tactics of Carrel and the Left who succeeded in having the election fought primarily on the issue of whether the peerage should be hereditary or not. Confronted by a Chamber with many new members of uncertain political allegiance, Périer staked his future on the election of the President of the Chamber, which he insisted on treating as an issue of confidence. When his candidate only secured a majority of one vote over Laffitte, Périer resigned and Louis-Philippe had already approached Molé, when the international crisis precipitated by the Dutch invasion of Belgium saved the situation. On his great days Périer was able to carry conviction as he vigorously defended his own actions and castigated the irresponsibility of his enemies, but by no means everybody was prepared to agree with him that "there is more glory for those who finish revolutions than for those who begin them". The Chief spokesman of the Left, the barrister Mauguin, voiced an alternative view on September 19th when he proclaimed: "The people can do no wrong without the government being to blame." [1] Consequently, although the cause of a hereditary second Chamber was defended

---

[1] It was Louis-Philippe's opinion that "very few barristers understand the nature of government". But perhaps he had Barrot in mind.

in the Chamber by the combined oratorical skill of Guizot, Thiers and Berryer, Périer admitted defeat on this issue, Louis-Philippe being in the event allowed to nominate life-peers among certain selected categories. It seemed to Greville at the end of August 1831 "pretty evident that France is rapidly advancing to a republic. Her institutions have long been republican, and though very compatible with a despotic Empire, incompatible with a constitutional and limited monarchy".

VI

The republican impetus was maintained throughout Périer's ministry by three factors – continuous war-fever, a sustained campaign of vilification of Louis-Philippe and the ministers in the Press and more or less serious insurrectionary activity in Paris and Lyon, all three aided and abetted by the irreconcilables of the secret societies, notably *Les Amis du Peuple*. While it is difficult not to admire the skill and courage with which Périer dealt with the symptoms of social unrest in France, his inability to penetrate to its root causes prevented him establishing the monarchy on an ultimately stable basis. This was, of course, primarily due to the disturbed history of France over the preceding forty years, but partly due also to the fact that neither he nor his successors, nor *a fortiori* Louis-Philippe himself, were able to transcend the Liberal orthodoxies of their day. Perhaps one million out of thirty-five million inhabitants of France constituted what the bourgeoisie were inclined to describe as "the dangerous class", whether employed in factories or living on their wits in urban slums.[1] It was generally felt that any attempt to alter their conditions of employment or to interfere with the free exercise of the iron economic laws of supply and demand could only result in making their lot worse. As the Poor Law Commissioners across the Channel put it in 1834: "Every penny bestowed that tends to render the condition of the pauper more eligible than that of the independent labourer is a bounty on indolence and vice."[2] An orator at the Academy of Moral Sciences pointed out that "nothing is really

[1] Their numbers were swollen by appreciable numbers of foreign immigrants, especially in Paris.

[2] Cf. the opposition of *The Economist* to the Public Health Act of 1848: "Suffering and evil are nature's admonitions; they cannot be got rid of; and the impatient attempts of benevolence to banish them from the world by legislation . . . have always been productive of more evil than good."

less astonishing and less unjust than the different rates of profit realized respectively by the capitalist and the worker". Voltaire, after all, had pointed out that property was an inalienable right, and not even the men of '93 had been prepared to gainsay him. There was no force in nineteenth-century France comparable to Evangelicalism in its ability to soften the rigours of the class war in the industrial areas, despite the well meaning efforts of the charitable organizations. If government action had no place in the regulation of the economic condition of the urban proletariat, it was considered self-evident that the latter could enjoy at best civic, but not political rights. They were not sufficiently responsible, it was felt. As an article in *Le Temps* of 1836 indicated: "the poor man lacks the art of applying his store of wealth to his real needs, being without the ability to envisage the concept of the future . . . and from that cause, more than any other, his unhappiness is due." The future of Liberal institutions could be safely left to the great middle class, whose justifiable claims to political advancement Casimir Périer and Guizot had championed under Charles X, the class whose solid merits Louis-Philippe had learned to appreciate in America and in England, and which saw in the July Monarchy the predestined guardian of its material and moral interests. It should be remembered that Guizot held a more favourable view of middle-class morality than did either Balzac or Flaubert, or for that matter Molière. Time was to prove, however, that it was an egregious error on the part of the July Monarchy to conclude that the political base of the régime was rendered sufficiently wide by a very limited extension of the franchise, on the comfortable assumption that for every voter another five or six might feel themselves more or less adequately represented by the local deputy.[1] It would admittedly have been a considerable feat of imagination to foresee in 1831 the tendency of French electorates to return under conditions of universal suffrage (whether plebiscitary or not) politicians of sheep-like dispositions. But even in 1831 a rather bolder leap in the dark would have disarmed a good deal of the opposition.

[1] The electoral law of April 1831 extended the franchise to some 190,000.

"What society needs is legalized order and power." For all Périer's dictum on March 18th, street-rioting continued unabated in Paris. On April 10th he passed a riot act, enabling any crowd to be forcibly dispersed after three warnings, which was to remain in force throughout the reign. That same month nineteen young men, leaders of the National Guard artillery, were brought to trial for treasonable activities during the trial of Charles X's ministers. The proceedings which lasted for ten days made it abundantly clear that the forces of order would have to pay a high price for the constitutional provision of the right of trial by jury for political offences. They were all acquitted and tumultuous cheering greeted the passionate speeches of the bald little defence counsel, Michel de Bourges,[1] and the theatrical affirmation of his republican sentiments by Godefroy Cavaignac. Less impressive was the fate of another noisy demonstration on May 5th, this time with a Bonapartist flavour, which was dispersed by Marshal Lobau with half a dozen firehoses. Louis-Philippe endeavoured to pacify the heroes of July by offering them as an anniversary emblem a commemorative medal. When the republican leaders discovered that the medal was inscribed "given by the King", they ordered their followers not to accept it and it had to be withdrawn. Louis-Philippe was hurt by this, but he was soon to suffer much worse indignity, as, for instance, when during the anniversary illuminations of July 28th a Parisian citizen underlined what seemed to him the true status of a King of the barricades by displaying in his window a portrait of Louis-Philippe alongside one of himself with the legend:

> Il n'est point de distance entre Philippe et moi;
> Il est roi-citoyen, je suis citoyen-roi.

Only gradually was Périer able to control the rioters who, as late as September, were still looting jewellers' shops, pulling up railings and smashing lamp-posts. But no sooner was the situation in the capital comparatively quiet than an insurrection of extremely

[1] With whom Georges Sand proceeded to fall in love. She was soon writing to him: "J'ai envie de mordre, mais où est la chair qui attire mes dents?"

formidable proportions broke out in Lyon, the second city of the Kingdom.

The fortunes of the silk-industry in Lyon with its 10,000 small masters and 40,000 *canuts*, dependent on the prosperity of the big manufacturers, had run into strong competition with Switzerland and Spitalfields. A workman paid 4 to 6 francs a day under the Empire was now in receipt of some 2 francs for a 15-hour day. In defiance of the law against employees' associations formulated in 1791,[1] the workmen grouped together and proposed to negotiate a wages scale with the manufacturers. The prefect of the Rhône, Bouvier-Dumolard, convened a meeting of manufacturers and workers' delegates, which succeeded in drawing up with his approval a minimum wage-scale. Fearing perhaps that he had overstepped the mark, he reported this remarkable achievement to Périer, who replied on November 8th that no such scale was or could ever be binding and that it was his duty as prefect, while preserving liberty, to prevent disorder in the city. About a hundred manufacturers had already decided that a wage-scale with no legal backing was not an innovation with which they were inclined to concur. By November 21st the enraged *canuts* assembled on the hill of Croix-Rousse and marched into the city where they immediately collided with a half-hearted detachment of the National Guard. Within forty-eight hours, after sharp fighting, the city was in the hands of the silk-workers assisted by a large part of the National Guard, which had gone over to their side in opposition to the regulars of the garrison. Black flags were hoisted with the menacing legend: "Vivre en travaillant ou mourir en combattant." [2] Périer reacted sharply. On December 2nd (a personal anniversary of some importance to him) Soult, with the Duc d'Orléans in support, entered the city with a force

---

[1] *La Loi le Chapelier*, which proclaimed somewhat naïvely that in industry there were no intermediary or group interests, merely "the particular interest of each individual" and the general interest.

[2] There was a certain imprecision about the *political* objects of the rioters. Talleyrand told Greville that shouts were heard for Henry V, Napoleon II, the Republic and Bristol (the latter a reference to contemporary Reform riots in England).

comprising nearly a tenth of the whole French Army and restored order without encountering any resistance. Périer's explanation to the Chamber of these untoward events was in perfect accord with the fashionable analytical technique of the *haute école* of classical economics – it was all a matter of population increase, the simplification of the means of production and increased competition. However, he suggested that the Chamber might be stimulated to study the root causes of industrial unrest. But even the opposition deputies felt that there were more politically urgent matters to discuss and the Chamber voted an address to Louis-Philippe which ran: "We hasten to express to your Majesty the unanimous wish of the deputies of France that the government should oppose with all legal force these deplorable excesses ... Personal safety has been violently attacked; the principle of property has been threatened; the freedom of industry has been menaced with destruction. Such outbreaks must be severely repressed." The unanimity is interesting and Périer had more general support than he had earlier enjoyed in breaking up a republican plot to burn down one of the towers of Notre-Dame in January 1832 and a Legitimist conspiracy to assassinate the whole royal family during a ball at the Tuileries in February. The prison of Sainte-Pélagie now housed with a fine lack of political discrimination fanatical adherents of the divine right of Kings with equally rabid advocates of the sacred duty of regicide. Louis-Philippe continued to extol, with decreasing optimism, the merits of political moderation.

When Périer assumed control of foreign affairs the Russians and the Poles were in deadly conflict near Warsaw, the Austrians were in occupation of Modena and marching on Bologna, and the Belgians and the Dutch were quite unreconciled. Within a fortnight the chancelleries were clear that France would not engage in aggressive war for ideological reasons as long as Périer was able to withstand the frantic clamour of the Left.[1] Many even of his supporters were given to second thoughts on the matter and as

---

[1] Including references by General Lamarque to the unhappy memories of Crécy, Poitiers and Agincourt.

late as June Talleyrand was writing to Sébastiani about "my favourite idea of dividing up Belgium, in which case France would
undoubtedly find the part which suited her best". That Périer was
able to ride the storm was due to his realistic determination not to
break with London, his ability to make peace sound almost as
dramatic as war in his speeches in the Chamber and a series of
fortunate incidents which enabled him to secure resounding
prestige successes with comparatively little risk. Thus when Dom
Miguel, the precarious occupant of the Portuguese throne, refused to compensate French nationals for outrages committed
against them, he sent a squadron into the Tagus which captured
the fleet of England's oldest ally in July. That same month as a
result of Pope Gregory XVI reaching a temporary *modus vivendi*
with his subjects, Louis-Philippe was able to incorporate into his
speech at the opening of the first session of the new Chamber the
not very tactful observation: "Just as I asked, the troops of the
Emperor of Austria have evacuated the papal states." A more
spectacular coup was achieved in February 1832 when Gregory
XVI once more felt impelled to ask the Austrians to return to his
support. The very morning he heard of the occupation of Bologna, Périer ordered a line regiment and a battery of guns to
embark at Toulon for a secret destination. They disembarked at
night in the harbour of Ancona and to the surprise of the local
inhabitants and the general perturbation of the European powers
the tricolour was flying alongside the papal flag on the citadel of
Ancona by the following morning. The Vatican comment was
that nothing like it had been seen since the days of the Saracens.
Certainly the military despatch, with which the expedition was
effected, outran the diplomatic representations Périer had intended, but haranguing the assembled ambassadors in his dressing-
gown with a red handkerchief round his head he managed to
persuade them that French intentions were limited to sharing
with the Austrians the sacred duty of protecting the Holy Father.
And the French remained in Ancona for seven years.

As Louis-Philippe had always realized, nothing could be done
for the Poles, despite Lafayette's vehement pleas to the contrary.

When Sébastiani announced on September 16th the final capitulation of Warsaw,[1] the news was greeted by large crowds assembling under the adjacent windows of Lafayette and the Russian embassy. Every time Lafayette appeared on the balcony a fusillade of stones crashed through his neighbours' windows. Street processions demanding instant war and the heads of Louis-Philippe and the ministers continued for three days before Périer dispersed them with cavalry. Similarly, the Belgian problem continued to be both harassing and hazardous. Having eventually accepted Leopold of Saxe-Coburg as their King in default of Louis-Philippe's second son, Nemours, the Belgians acquiesced in the frontier arrangements which the London conference proposed, though with some reluctance. King William of Holland was even less satisfied and, suddenly denouncing the armistice, threw his troops into Belgium on August 2nd, just as Périer had announced his resignation. The Belgians rapidly and completely overcome, appealed for aid to London and Paris. Périer withdrew his resignation and sent 50,000 men under Marshal Gérard into Belgium by forced marches, which resulted in the Prince of Orange withdrawing his army ten days later from all Belgium except Antwerp. Talleyrand inadvisedly began to talk of the advantages of partition, which prompted Palmerston to observe that "one thing is certain, the French must get out of Belgium, or we have a general war, and war in a given number of days . . ." It was a tempting situation for the French, more especially as the Dutch made it clear that they preferred partition to King Leopold. But after some face-saving concessions were extracted from the Belgians in terms of the dismantling of frontier forces, the French troops were withdrawn by the end of September. It was not the end of the story, but another awkward corner had been turned.

[1] What he actually said was not "l'ordre règne à Varsovie" (the legend surmounting a caricature by Grandville, depicting a Cossack smoking a pipe while trampling on a heap of corpses), but "au moment où l'on écrit, la tranquillité règne à Varsovie" (J. T. De Mesmay, *Horace Sébastiani*).

VII

As a background to all these alarms and excursions, a sustained and vitriolic campaign in the columns of the free press was continually undermining the prestige and popularity of the monarchy. The opposition journalists fostered the limited circulation of their newspapers by a remarkable disregard for truth, justice or elementary decency in their attacks on Louis-Philippe. Juries, sometimes intimidated by the threat of reprisals against them in the press or on the streets, were loth to convict for press offences and of 520 prosecutions in the first four years of the reign 322 resulted in acquittals.[1] Caricaturists of malignant genius like Philipon, with his famous discovery that Louis-Philippe's increasingly venerable countenance was becoming more and more pear-like in shape, Daumier, Charlet and others displayed ceaseless ingenuity in representing the King in undignified or illiberal postures. One day he would be depicted as the assassin of the liberty of the press, with cutlass in hand pulling France along by the hair; or holding his hat under the backside of a cow representing Poland, which Russia was milking, while Austria and Prussia held her by the horns; or again, he might be Judas, or a parrot, continually croaking about Valmy and Jemappes. The Queen's natural goodness and dignity spared her from similar treatment, but Adélaïde whose complexion grew richer with the years, was always assumed to have a partiality for the bottle and to be involved in an adulterous relationship with General Atthalin.[2] A good deal of the money behind this campaign came from legitimist sources and juries proved much less inclined to convict journalists accused of the so-called "*offense au roi*" than those who directly threatened

[1] See Irene Collins: *The Government and the Newspaper Press in France 1814–81*, especially chapters VII and VIII.
[2] She was consequently often referred to in the press as "la princesse Athalie".

middle-class interests by inciting to violence in the streets. A good many citizens of Paris regarded their new monarch primarily as "a useful lightning-conductor to protect the shops". Louis-Philippe, although greatly upset by all this, tried hard not to lose his equanimity and on one occasion, observing a small gamin industriously chalking the outlines of a pear on the wall, he helped the child to finish his drawing and gave him a piece of silver, pointing out to the young artist that he would find the pear depicted on the coin. But he had no illusions about the ultimately fatal effect of the campaign of disrespect. Years after, in exile, he pointed out with justice: "During my reign I was the victim of that weapon which Voltaire called the printed lie, a cowardly and treacherous weapon which strikes often without our knowing where the blow comes from, a weapon which inflicts wounds that never heal, because they are poisoned."

Nothing pained him so much as the continual allegations made against him in the press of personal avarice. A munificent, if singularly tasteless, patron of the arts and, despite the natural simplicity of his manners, a generous host, Louis-Philippe was never able to persuade the majority of his subjects that his very real concern for the future prospects of his own family was anything but a culpable manifestation of miserliness and greed. Certainly he had displayed an assiduity in building up his family fortunes under the Restoration, which had already aroused a good deal of unfavourable comment. This was greatly intensified by two episodes early in his reign. On August 7th, 1830, two days before his coronation oath, Louis-Philippe made over his fortune to his children, reserving for himself the income, a device which ran counter to an edict of 1607, whereby the property of a hereditary monarch had to devolve on the crown. On August 27th the wicked old Duc de Bourbon, the last of the Condés, whose senile devotion to Sophie Dawes had long been a scandal in court circles, died in circumstances so mysterious that they continue to be a stock subject of rather scabrous speculation among those interested. His enormous fortune, together with the Château of Chantilly, was inherited by the eight-year-old Duc d'Aumale,

Louis-Philippe's fifth son. Legitimist circles were not slow to point out how carefully the Orléans family had cultivated the unspeakable Sophie Dawes. Louis-Philippe, in his capacity as *père de famille* was certainly a model French bourgeois, but whether many of his subjects were entitled to point the finger of scorn at him in this respect is at least open to doubt.

These events explain in part the disgraceful scenes, which took place in the Chamber when the debate on the provision of a Civil List began in January 1832. Charles X had enjoyed a Civil List of 40 millions. Périer now proposed 18 millions. That the debate would be a stormy one was evident from the wide circulation of some venomous little pamphlets composed by de Cormenin.[1] Montalivet, irked by the pettiness of some of the opposition arguments, committed himself to the observation that: "if luxury is banished from the palaces of the King, it will soon be abolished in the home of his subjects". At the word "subject" an incredible *tapage* developed – deputies banged on their desks and shouted: "We are not subjects! It is we who have made the King! Withdraw!" Barrot demanded a solemn written protestation which soon received a hundred and sixty-five signatures. Eventually a Civil List of 12 millions was voted, after a series of lamentable debates.[2]

Périer's ministry drew to a close in an atmosphere of gloom and apprehension which temporarily concealed the real nature of his achievements. There was continued uproar in the courts which the republicans used with great bravado as an arena in which to ventilate their opinions. In March 1832 the city of Paris with its 774,000 inhabitants was struck by a devastating epidemic of cholera which it is estimated eventually carried off some 20,000 victims. Day after day carts and carriages were piled high with corpses. Needless to say, the government was accused of deliberately poisoning the wine-supply and several revolting murders

[1] A somewhat ambiguous type of politician. A viscount, he had held office under both the Empire and the Restoration, and lived to be one of the framers of the constitution of 1848 and a councillor of state under Napoleon III.

[2] Including allegations of corruption, with chapter and verse specified, against Benjamin Constant, Armand Marrast and even the redoubtable Mauguin.

were perpetrated openly in the streets. The royal family never left the city for a moment, and when Périer and the Duc d'Orléans visited the cholera wards they were denounced by the opposition for wanting to have a closer look at the misery of the people. Périer himself was struck down and after six weeks' agony died on May 16th.

There was no one either willing or qualified to take over the onerous duties of Prime Minister amongst Périer's ministerial colleagues and Louis-Philippe seized rather too eagerly at the chance of emerging from the comparative obscurity, to which he had been relegated for more than a year. Still immensely energetic and perfectly happy if he managed four hours' sleep in the twenty-four, he relished the idea of immersing himself in the day-to-day detail of administration, for which he had a misguided enthusiasm. Furthermore, he was temperamentally unsuited to the exercise of power behind the scenes, his vanity demanding public recognition of his services to the country, recognition of which he felt he had been unfairly deprived. In deciding that he would not replace as Prime Minister the man whom he had called Casimir Premier among his intimates, he chose a particularly difficult moment to expose the royal person in the forefront of the political firing-line. At the beginning of June the régime was suddenly subjected to violent assaults from its enemies both on the Right and on the Left. On May 28th thirty-four opposition deputies celebrated the death of Périer by drawing up a formal indictment of the alleged iniquities of his policy at home and abroad, which was perfectly calculated to encourage the leaders of the secret societies, who were actively planning a revolutionary insurrection in Paris as soon as a good occasion presented itself. On the same day, the Duchesse de Berri, the mother of the Duc de Bordeaux and Marie-Amélie's niece, landed near Marseilles and announced her plan for raising the Midi in her capacity as Regent for Henri V. The rising, such as it was, petered out in two days, but, quite undaunted and ignoring the advice of her supporters in Paris, she declared her intention of proceeding to the Vendée, where she felt confident she could ignite the traditional civil war. Meanwhile in Paris General Lamarque died of cholera on June 2nd, murmuring as he expired: "I die regretting not having avenged France for the infamous treaties of 1815." The funeral of one who had been the incarnate symbol of both Bonapartist and Republican glory seemed to the secret societies a decidedly promising occasion for effecting another revolution.[1] By June 4th red flags and red bonnets were prominent in Ménilmontant, portraits of Robespierre were being widely circulated and precise operation orders were distributed to some two thousand of the faithful Neo-Jacobins.

June 5th, the day of the funeral, was grey and overcast, with a drizzle of rain, but from eight in the morning huge crowds assembled and at half-past eleven the cortège set out, the hearse being accompanied by, among others, the venerable Lafayette (leaning on the arm of one of his working-class friends), Laffitte and Mauguin. By the time the cortège reached the Place Vendôme, round which the leaders insisted it should wind itself three times, there were shouts of "Long live the Republic! Down with Louis-Philippe! Down with the sleepy pear! He'll die on the scaffold like his father!" Enthusiasts proceeded to break the windows of the Foreigners' Club, after failing to persuade Edouard, Duc de Fitzjames, to take his hat off to the illustrious remains. By a preconcerted plan the procession drew to a halt on the Pont d'Austerlitz, where a young man on horseback, dressed in black, made a fiery speech, which was the signal for the conspirators to seize the coffin and attempt to drag it to the Panthéon. The police, warned of this, cut the procession in two, but amid mounting disorder the hearse was covered with Polish and Italian flags and a shout went up that the Republic must be proclaimed and Lafayette taken to the Hôtel de Ville and thence to the Tuileries. That veteran, finding not for the first time in his career that circumstances were out of his control, was bundled into a fiacre, looking more dead than alive.[2] At this juncture the dragoons arrived and

---

[1] In earlier years the funeral processions of General Foy (1825) and Manuel (1827) had given rise to notable street disorders.

[2] He had the alarming experience of hearing one of the conspirators suggest

13. The July Revolution

a general street battle began. Barricades went up in many parts of the city, including one nine feet high in the Faubourg Saint-Antoine. Soult rather gingerly moved in troops and some guns and from every quarter the National Guard hurried on to the scene. For nearly two years now these worthy citizens had never been certain that they would get a night's sleep without suddenly being summoned to seize their muskets and buckle on their belts. With half Paris in the hands of the insurgents by the afternoon, the National Guard were becoming both angry and frightened. Louis-Philippe was at Saint-Cloud that day when in the early evening an A.D.C. arrived on horseback. Turning to his wife, he said: "Amélie, there's trouble in Paris. I'm going." "I'm coming too," said the Queen. Within an hour he was in the Tuileries, interviewing the prefect of police, whom he thoughtfully urged to snatch a few hours' rest. He then rode out into the Cour du Carrousel, reviewed detachments of infantry and National Guard and exhorted them with confidence and serenity to do their duty. By midnight the imperturbable Lobau had swept the outlying quarters of the city, but the insurgents were still in possession of a great deal of the centre. The fighting started again at four o'clock on the morning of the 6th. As the day wore on, the attitude of many of the National Guard changed appreciably. The news of the King's presence and the sight of him riding genially through the streets and stopping to shake hands with officers and privates alike provoked in them feelings of personal loyalty, which were to persist unbroken for the next fifteen years. By midday the boulevards cleared and although stubborn fighting was still going on in the cloister of Saint-Merry, the issue was no longer in doubt. It was a moment of heady personal triumph for Louis-Philippe, who was vociferously cheered as he rode along the quays, and from his own account he began to feel like Henri IV. When three of the opposition leaders, Laffitte, Barrot and Arago, the distinguished astronomer, called on him at the Tuileries, he cut short their metaphysical arguments about the superior merits of

that they should throw him into the Seine in order to compromise the government.

moral force and harangued them at characteristic length with a rather excessive use of the first person singular and a not altogether appropriate quotation from Racine beginning: "Heureux qui, satisfait de son humble fortune . . ." [1] The interview was punctuated by the noise of heavy explosions of gunfire from the direction of Saint-Merry where the fighting ended by nightfall with a total of some eight hundred victims, almost equally divided between the two sides.

Meanwhile the Duchesse de Berri had arrived in the West, disguised as a rather highly-coloured peasant called Petit-Pierre, with a chestnut wig and what Madame de Boigne called "the tiniest feet imaginable". Unfortunately the Vendéens were not the force they had been in '94 and had become rather static peasant-proprietors, unwilling to sell their lives for a romantic escapade, however much it might appeal to imaginations in the Faubourg Saint-Germain nurtured on Sir Walter Scott. After one or two minor skirmishes, the duchess went into hiding in Nantes, so successfully that she defied all the attempts of Louis-Philippe's police to track her down throughout the summer.

Both wings of the opposition soon recovered from these disasters. The Legitimist *Gazette de France* proclaimed, by way of boxing the political compass, on August 10th: "Those who adhere to legitimacy by sentiment or principle and those who believe in the sovereignty of the people, although differing about ends, must agree about the complete nullity of all that has been done." The government received a rude shock when the Appeal Court denied the competence of the courts-martial, which had been set up under proclamation of a state of siege, to try the June offenders and this despite some very lenient sentences.[2] Even the death of the King of Rome at Schönbrunn on July 22nd merely had the result, as Metternich pointed out, of transmitting the fortunes of the Bonaparte dynasty to distinctly shadier characters under much

---

[1] This was certainly an occasion when he might have remembered Talleyrand's dictum: "il n' y a rien de si éloquent que le silence."

[2] The accused suffered a good deal worse when, as a consequence, they were subjected to trial by jury.

less reliable supervision. It was true that the new session of the Chamber was not to open until November, but the day would assuredly arrive when the government would need a spokesman of some ability to defend its actions against M. Mauguin and M. Barrot and M. Berryer and, as Louis-Philippe remarked sadly, the constitution debarred him from making his own speeches at the tribune. To make matters worse, the affairs of Belgium were still troublesome. In defiance of the Concert of Europe, King William of Holland refused to leave Antwerp and this had become increasingly important for Louis-Philippe, since the new King of Belgium had married his beloved daughter Louise in August.

VIII

In all these circumstances, Louis-Philippe found it necessary to abandon his experiment in direct personal government. He first approached the wily Dupin, long associated with the fortunes of the House of Orléans, but found him unwilling to accept what was decidedly a thankless responsibility. Eventually, on October 11th, a new ministry was formed under the Duc de Broglie, whose sense of duty overcame his temperamental dislike for the parliamentary arena. De Broglie had stipulated, as a condition of taking office, the inclusion in the ministry of Guizot, whose academic interests made him a wise choice as Minister of Education and Religion. Baron Louis, now a tired man, was replaced as Finance Minister by Humann. Soult, whose political views were of an almost perfect nullity, was nominally President of the Council, but de Broglie as Foreign Minister was effectively the leader of the government. A new star on the horizon was Adolphe Thiers. Since the July days he had served a comparatively arduous political apprenticeship as financial under-secretary in the first two administrations of the reign and, despite a far from auspicious maiden speech in November 1830, his debating powers were beginning to attain something of the ultimate brilliance which would enable him to hold the rapt attention of the Chamber for three hours at a stretch. Gradually more and more people found themselves prepared to overlook both his vanity and his undeniable vulgarity.[1] For the moment he seemed a decidedly useful supporter of the *politique de la résistance* and he earned his reward by being appointed Minister of the Interior. So began at thirty-

---

[1] Not, however, the magnificent M. Hugo, in whom Thiers inspired "an indefinable feeling of aversion and disgust". Madame de Genlis' old friend the Terrorist Barère, back again from exile, dismissed him, almost as contemptuously, as "just another Girondin".

five the ministerial career of the supreme virtuoso of the Left-Centre, a past-master of the art of applied ambiguity in parliamentary politics.

Thiers was immediately ordered to find the Duchesse de Berri, *la duchesse introuvable*, without any further delay. He was soon the fortunate recipient of an anonymous letter inviting him to a rendez-vous by night in a secluded part of the Champs-Elysées. Arriving with two pistols in his pocket, he found himself confronted by a curly-headed German Jew called Deutz, who after some face-saving protestations offered to give the lady up for cash. This was a language Thiers understood and he closed for five thousand francs. After the soldiers had broken down the door of the house in Nantes, indicated by Deutz, they ransacked it from cellar to attic without finding any trace of the Duchess. The following morning as one of the gendarmes lit some newspapers in the fire-place to warm himself, the Duchess and three other women emerged from some sixteen hours confinement in the chimney. Thiers was very pleased with himself, but when Louis-Philippe heard the news he burst into tears, realizing that he was now involved in a horrible family dilemma. He was not the man to contemplate with equanimity the trial for high treason of his wife's niece. While this disagreeable problem was temporarily shelved, the Duchess was confined to the Castle of Blaye under the martial care of General Bugeaud. Blaye rapidly became a centre of legitimist pilgrimage, but what looked like becoming an impossible problem was dramatically solved by the discovery that the lady was pregnant. She announced that she had secretly married a Sicilian nobleman, Count Lucchesi-Pali, who with a certain apparent reluctance, soon appeared on the scene, only to be nicknamed "Saint Joseph" by the more ribald Paris bourgeois. Bugeaud had the not particularly rewarding task of escorting the Duchess back to a quieter life at Palermo.[1]

The new parliamentary session opened on November 19th. As

[1] On his return, he recorded that the indefatigable lady was much less seasick than the rest of the passengers on the voyage and showed a marked propensity to flirt with one of the midshipmen.

Louis-Philippe was riding across the Pont-Neuf to the Palais-Bourbon a pistol shot was fired at him. He instinctively ducked over his saddle and saluted to show that he was unhurt and riding on to the Chamber delivered the speech from the throne.[1] It ended characteristically as follows: "A few efforts more, and the last traces of the anxieties inseparable from a great revolution will disappear. The feeling of stability will return to all minds . . . and then will be realized the most cherished of my wishes, that of seeing my country raise itself to the height of prosperity to which it has a right to aspire, and of my being able to say, that my efforts have not been useless in the fulfilment of its destinies." There was loud applause and Dupin, the ministerial candidate for the chair of president, defeated Laffitte by 234 to 136. Calmer waters seemed at last to have been reached.

Certainly 1833 was to prove a much happier year both for Louis-Philippe and the nation at large. Paris was still full of angry young men[2] and the republican newspaper *Charivari* had a remarkable piece of good fortune when the police arrested a common pickpocket, who turned out to be authentically called Louis-Philippe, for the theft of an umbrella in the Rue de Rivoli. But a general return of prosperity and the combined talents in office of de Broglie, Guizot and Thiers did much to consolidate the régime in the eyes of the ordinary, peaceful citizen after the difficulties and dangers of 1832. Although Louis-Philippe continued, as usual, to keep his eye closely on foreign policy, his effective political intervention was necessarily limited by the outstanding ability of his ministers. He remarked, somewhat ruefully, to his intimates, that if the three ministers were in agreement the King's views counted for little, vis-à-vis what he called "Casimir Périer

[1] A young man called Bergeron who was arrested on suspicion was acquitted through lack of evidence. The republicans ingeniously suggested that the whole thing was a put-up job on the part of the police.
[2] Their grotesque activities are described in detail in Miss Enid Starkie's "Petrus Borel, the Lycanthrope", who certainly spoke for the avant-garde of the Romantic Movement when he said: "If I talk of republicanism it is because that word represents for me the greatest amount of liberty which civilization and society can provide. I need an enormous amount of liberty."

in Three Persons". The legislative record of the ministry was impressive. Guizot's great law on primary education was a notably progressive measure by the standards of the age. In February the great Doctrinaire permitted himself the following observation (as events turned out considerably in advance of the facts): "the riots are dead, the clubs are dead, revolutionary propaganda is dead; the revolutionary spirit, a spirit of blind faction, which seemed for a moment to have gripped the entire nation, is dead". What was necessary now was to build up "the moral order" in the minds of the coming generation. In his circulars to the teachers he advocated "faith in providence, the sanctity of duty, submission to paternal authority, imperishable principles of morality without which the social order is in peril". This was a far cry from the recent experience of a school inspector, who, when interviewing a headmaster about the progress of religious and moral instruction in a provincial school, was met with the rejoinder: "I don't teach stupid things like that". A local government act gave elected councils to the departments and *arrondissements*; there was a law on expropriation and compensation in connection with public utility schemes; and Thiers secured the necessary credits for the completion of the Etoile, the Madeleine and the Place de la Concorde. In foreign affairs de Broglie showed himself at the outset of the ministry to be both decisive and effective. As the result of an Anglo-French agreement in October 1832, Marshal Gérard was directed on Antwerp the following month at the head of an army of 70,000 men, with Orléans and Nemours in the vanguard, and the siege of the city began on November 19th, the day the new parliamentary session opened. On December 28th the Dutch capitulated and, its task completed, the French army was immediately withdrawn. The activities of Mehemet Ali, the Sultan of Egypt, who liked to call himself *"un enfant de France"*, when it seemed profitable to do so, resurrected the Eastern Question in a dangerous form at the end of 1832. His desire to wrest from his Turkish master, the Sultan Mahmoud, the provinces of Palestine, Syria and Arabia, had resulted in a crushing defeat for the Turks in December and a threat to the whole stability of the

Ottoman Empire. By the time de Broglie's emissary, Admiral Roussin, arrived at Constantinople in February a protective Russian squadron was anchored off the Golden Horn. Roussin persuaded the Turks to send home the Russians, as Palmerston put it, "with a flea in their ear", but only on the basis of a highly suppositious proposal that French prestige would be sufficient to bring Mehemet Ali to heel. This proved to be an illusion and although Talleyrand and Palmerston co-operated energetically on the problem, the Turks, who had to make massive concessions to Mehemet Ali,[1] were thrown back into the arms of the Russians. By the time the Russians had withdrawn from Constantinople they had in their pocket a mutual defence treaty with the Sultan which seemed likely to give them a considerable measure of control over his foreign policy.[2] This was no more a success for French diplomacy than it was for English but despite the tensions between the two allies, born of traditional suspicion and conflicting interests,[3] the entente held. It would be very different next time the Eastern Question became difficult. For the moment things were going tolerably well, despite the temperamental lack of sympathy between Louis-Philippe and his imperious and aloof foreign minister. Talleyrand recorded that summer that "the fact is we have appreciably the most enlightened King in Europe and the Duc de Broglie is gaining every day in peoples' estimation".

But already, before the end of 1833, there were further premonitory symptoms of revolutionary disorder. Louis-Philippe's speech from the throne in December contained the warning "an unceasing vigilance is still necessary; insensate passions and culpable manœuvres are at work to undermine the foundations of the social order". What the ministers had in mind was not only

[1] He was left in control of all the country from the Nile to the Euphrates and the Taurus range, and his son Ibrahim was given Adana.

[2] Unkiar-Skelessi.

[3] Thus William IV made a speech that year in which he said: "Talking of France I must say that whether at peace or war . . . I shall always consider her as our natural enemy". Greville commented: "What can you expect from a man with a head like a pineapple?"

continued violence in the press, especially *La Tribune* and *Le National*, but the activities during 1833 of the *Société des Droits de l'Homme*.[1] Although nominally a secret society, it operated largely in the open, somewhat to the disgust of its Italian, German and Polish supporters, accustomed to working under very much more repressive régimes. Two deputies, Audry de Puyreveau and Voyer d'Argenson, openly boasted of their membership of a society whose proclaimed activities were evidently too seditious to be compatible with their oaths of loyalty. Cavaignac, Raspail and Trélat were the leaders of an organization which claimed some 4,000 members and was subdivided into sections with names clearly evocative of its professed aims – Marat, Robespierre, Babeuf, Louvel, la Guerre aux Châteaux, etc., etc. An order of the day was issued, as the anniversary of Lamarque's funeral approached in June, to the effect that "the cypress of liberty must be watered with blood, not tears" and attempts were made to infiltrate the ranks of the National Guard. But little or nothing came of some rather half-hearted demonstrations on that occasion, nor yet of a campaign of strike-fomenting in the autumn. Carrel, although he continued to attack the government with every weapon in his armoury, admitted privately that the American type of Republicanism he professed was incompatible with this sort of thing and even Lafayette declared in November that "associate of Washington, Franklin and Jefferson, I'm not tempted nearly sixty years later to change my parish for that of Robespierre, Saint-Just and Marat". Thiers, who would in 1871 earn immortal fame by his remark that "the republic is the régime which divides us least", fulminated from the tribune: "France has a horror of republics; when she hears the word spoken, she recoils in fright. She knows that this form of government turns to blood or imbecility." But within three months of Louis-Philippe's speech, the régime's need for "unceasing vigilance" was to be horribly exemplified.

In January, General Bugeaud felt that a personal attack on him

---

[1] It had succeeded *Les Amis du Peuple* in the leadership of republican conspiracy at the end of 1832.

in the Chamber by Dulong, a bastard of Dupont de l'Eure, demanded restitution with pistols in the Bois de Bologne. In a duel which resulted in the death of his adversary, he had employed as one of his seconds General Rumigny, an A.D.C. of the King. A lithograph depicted a clearing in winter and behind Bugeaud with his pistol the profile of Louis-Philippe directing his aim. In February the government was confronted with the problem of dealing with some fifteen hundred public criers whose already seditious tendencies were cleverly exploited by the *Société des Droits de l'Homme*, which furnished them with material like the Catechism of the Rights of Man, with such passages as: "What punishment ought to be accorded to him who usurps sovereignty? Those who usurp sovereignty should be killed by free men." According to *La Tribune*, six million broadsheets were distributed in three months, mostly dated "the forty-second year of the French Republic". On February 20th the government was impelled to proceed on the first step of a campaign to repress freedom of expression, when carried to these lengths, and all public criers had henceforth to be authorized by the police and subjected to the jurisdiction of the municipal magistrates. This was followed on February 24th[1] by a law designed to restrict the activities of secret societies, which Louis-Philippe justified by reference to contemporary English practice. The authorities were permitted to proceed against unauthorized societies, even if they were divided into sections of less than twenty members, by means of correctional tribunals. Crimes against the state by such societies were now to be tried before the Chamber of Peers. The *Société des Droits de l'Homme* had thus succeeded in goading the government into action clearly infringing the spirit of the Charter, which required "political offences" to be tried by jury. The distinction between "political offences" and "crimes against the state" was at best a convenient legal term. The measure passed by 246 votes to 154, but that the ministry was driven back on the defensive is illustrated by Guizot's attack on the opposition: "it is we who have conceived the highest hopes of the progressive

---

[1] An ill-omened date for the July Monarchy.

development of our liberties and our institutions. It is you who have compromised them."

Carrel demanded in *Le National* that the suspension of liberty should be met by the suspension of law and order, and, although Cavaignac hesitated, the more desperate elements in the *Société des Droits de l'Homme* openly announced that they would not obey the law and were preparing for the decisive struggle. They were very active in the provinces and boasted, quite inaccurately, that "all France is with us, all the big cities only wait our signal". Unfortunately for the government, trouble had recently broken out at Lyon. Since 1831 the city had been relatively calm, but an embryonic workers' council had abandoned recently its original quasi-mystical character and become revolutionary with obvious affinities to the *Société des Droits de l'Homme*. In February 1834 the manufacturers in response to a temporary depression in trade made a small reduction in the prices paid to certain grades of silk and velvet weavers. A general meeting of silk-workers was summoned and a proposed strike throughout the trade was put to the vote and carried by 1,297 votes to 1,044. During ten days, while funds lasted, 50,000 workers were idle in the streets and the secret societies found an excellent opportunity to disseminate their doctrines, although political agitators on several occasions were expelled from the workers' lodges. The trial of a few rioters, who had broken the law by actual violence or by convoking unauthorized assemblies,[1] was the signal for the leaders to arm the sections and on April 9th a savage five-day battle began in the streets of the city between the insurgents and the soldiers who had been ordered by Thiers to "let them fire first, but once you've been shot at react vigorously". An already horrible shambles was rendered more lurid by a fall of snow on the 12th and the drifting of a burning barge down the canal, which ignited the piers of the bridges. The last bastion of the insurgents – their Saint-Merry – was the Church of the Cordeliers, which they had converted into a powder

[1] Processions in the streets were singing the songs of '93 – *La Carmagnole* and the *Ça ira*.

magazine and dressing station. It was not yielded up until artillery fire had blown in the façade of the Church. There were over a thousand casualties and it was remarkable that among the dead and prisoners, and those of the wounded who submitted to be taken to hospital, only one out of ten was a silk-worker and indeed only one out of six a Lyonnais at all. During the fighting a green Carlist flag was observed among the red ones.

The desperate courage of the Lyon insurrectionaries had been sustained in the last throes of the struggle by false news from the Paris leaders to the effect that Louis-Philippe had been killed, the Republic proclaimed and Lucien Bonaparte[1] elected First Consul. The central committee of the *Société des Droits de l'Homme* had decreed a sympathetic detonation in Paris and on April 13th, while *La Tribune* published the false news that "the victory of the people is being confirmed daily" the Robespierre, Marat and Louvel sections erected thirty barricades in the city and proclaimed a general uprising. There was notably little response among the Parisians, and the troops and National Guard attacked the barricades vigorously in the evening and renewed the battle before dawn the next morning. After some fierce fighting the last of the barricades were overturned, but some of the insurgents continued to fire on their enemies from the windows of houses. This particular aspect of street fighting has a peculiar savagery all its own and when a company of infantry saw their most popular officer shot dead by a marksman concealed in number 12, Rue Transnonain, while he lay wounded on the ground, they went berserk and slaughtered some twenty men, women and children, many of whom were probably innocent victims. This incident was to have two important consequences in that it inspired Daumier's powerful lithograph "*La Massacre de la Rue Transnonain*", the most telling visual indictment of the régime ever employed by the opposition, and earned for the already unpopular Bugeaud the title of the Butcher of the Rue Transnonain, although in fact he was not commanding in that sector. Bugeaud himself was not backward in condemning those who instigated

[1] At this time living quietly in retirement in Italy.

sanguinary street fighting of this sort. "They prate of Liberty? What Liberty? That of five hundred journalists, generals of the insurrection, who play a strange role, pushing miserable men forward and letting them be killed." [1] Even Lamartine, whose sensitivity to the injustices of a laissez-faire social order was already highly developed, was so revolted by the irresponsibility of the revolutionary leaders, that he wrote at this time: "If Dante had known them, he would have added a new circle to Hell . . . As for me . . . I would fight with any weapons and under any flag against them."

[1] The casualties on April 13th and 14th, 1834, in Paris were not high – probably under a hundred all told.

IX

The government felt impelled to destroy the *Société des Droits de l'Homme* root and branch. Many of the ringleaders were arrested and the society's archives were seized in the house of a certain Signor Facconi. Further riots had been touched off in Saint-Etienne, Grenoble, Marseilles and Clermont-Ferrand. In all these places working-class combinations had been involved and it was to prove of devastating consequence for the social history of France that the cause of working-class solidarity was thus early compromised by its association with revolutionary conspiracy and bloodshed.[1] For the moment the forces of order seemed to have triumphed. Once again, as in 1832, the populace had cheered Louis-Philippe as he rode out of his palace at the moment of danger (though, on this occasion, after an angry altercation with his family he yielded to the suggestion that he should merely ride round the Tuileries) and the National Guard had reaffirmed their loyalty to the régime in a moment of danger. Even the death of Lafayette in May passed off almost without comment.

It was a distinctly unfortunate moment, therefore, for the King to commit two serious errors of political judgement in allowing what had proved his most successful ministry to disintegrate and at the same time to lend his vigorous support to the idea of a mass trial before the Chamber of Peers of all those accused of complicity in the April risings. He very much disliked being at the

[1] Cf. the proclaimed object of the London Working Mens' Association of 1836 "to seek by every legal means to place all classes of society in possession of their equal political and social rights". And even as late as 1839, when "physical force" Chartism was gaining some limited successes, Louis Blanc commented: "For the vast majority of the nation the meetings were rather a show than a serious demonstration, the audience gathered to hear the speakers as an agreeable pastime, and traffic could move freely across the public places where they were held."

receiving end of a lecture and de Broglie and Guizot, as befitted Doctrinaires, had a great deal to say about the wisdom of their own policies. While de Broglie was a consistent advocate of the entente with Great Britain, Louis-Philippe was beginning to feel that if he could get his own hands on the conduct of foreign affairs he might well be able to thaw out the rather chilly relations that existed between Paris and the courts of Vienna, Berlin and Saint-Petersburg and thereby, without upsetting relations with London, recover for France a little more diplomatic freedom of manœuvre. A good many of the deputies were inclined to find de Broglie's aristocratic superiority rather unamiable and this was particularly true of an element in the Chamber, imprecise in both composition and aims, which was now labelled the third party. Grouping themselves loosely round Dupin, they excelled in being unpredictable and unconstructive and were the despair of Guizot, who pined for the comparative rigidity of English political parties.[1] When on March 28th de Broglie in perfect confidence submitted his eminently reasonable solution of a long-standing dispute with the United States over compensation for vessels seized between 1806 and 1812, the third party seized its opportunity and the Chamber divided against the government by a majority of eight votes. De Broglie immediately resigned, commenting to Talleyrand that "there are things and men in this world which cannot be treated lightly". This inaugurated almost a year of ministerial crises and an even longer period of general ministerial instability and political in-fighting, which recalls the situation in the early years of the reign of George III in England. No sooner was the great triumvirate dissolved than Thiers and Guizot banded together to get rid of Soult, who was an increasingly embarrassing, if nominal, President of the Council. His replacement, Marshal Gérard, was not a success and the elections in the summer produced a good deal of very suitable human material for the third party to offset the fact that no overt republicans at all were elected. Gérard's resignation in October coincided with some rather disagreeably ribald disclosures about the

[1] Admittedly, not altogether a characteristic of English politics in the thirties.

propriety of M. Thiers' conduct, when enjoying a party with his friends,[1] and since Louis-Philippe was still not prepared to favour the idea of the Duc de Broglie being persuaded once again to answer the stern call of duty, and Molé was unable to form a cabinet, it seemed that the hour of the third party had struck. But Dupin was not to be cajoled into office. On November 10th a ministry composed of political nonentities (with the exception of Bresson, the able ambassador at Berlin, who was given the Foreign Office without being consulted) was formed under Maret, Duc de Bassano, once Napoleon's most submissive and docile civil servant. The unfortunate Bassano was extremely hard-up at the time and his appointment as Prime Minister was greeted with an enthusiasm on the part of his creditors equalled only by the derision of the public, which succeeded in killing the ministry in three days. Most of the original ministry of October 11th, 1832 (but of course without de Broglie) had to come back, this time under the friendliest of all Napoleon's marshals, Mortier, Louis-Philippe's old companion-in-arms in the army of Dumouriez. Mortier was unfortunately practically incapable of speaking in public and even less capable of patching up a growing rift between Guizot and Thiers. The latter was beginning to see himself as a predestined Foreign Minister and was certain at any rate that he could improve on the performance of the existing holder of that office, Admiral de Rigny, whom Louis-Philippe noted as being seriously deficient in a knowledge of geography. Thiers was not yet ready to break with Guizot but among his supporters he was inclined to make remarks like: "M. Guizot is a great speaker, but – don't be surprised by this – in politics M. Guizot is stupid."[2] The Mortier experiment broke down in February 1835 and Louis-Philippe in a last desperate effort to avoid the return of de Broglie unavailingly approached in turn Molé, Dupin, Soult, Sébastiani, Gérard and once again, Soult. Finally in March he submitted, with surprising good humour, to what

[1] The so-called "orgie de Grandvaux".
[2] Royer-Collard, Guizot's political mentor, was rather of the same opinion: "His gestures are better than his words, his words than his thoughts."

14. Queen Victoria's visit to the Château d'Eu, 1843: a luncheon à l'Anglaise

he called "the yoke of the doctrinaires". De Broglie, before agreeing to be both Prime Minister and Foreign Minister, laid it down that the King should not attend cabinet meetings when it was thought inadvisable. Thiers and Guizot continued in office and ironically the first measure brought successfully before the Chamber by the restored triumvirate was that regulating the indemnity payable to the United States.

Nothing could have illustrated more clearly than this year of political chaos the prevalent uncertainty in France about the proper functioning of constitutional monarchy. There was imprecision about the appropriate constitutional functions both of the King and of the Prime Minister, there was no tradition of cabinet solidarity and no certainty of a stable parliamentary majority except under the stress of imminent revolution. The extent to which Louis-Philippe disliked the idea of a genuinely effective Prime Minister is illustrated by his remark to Guizot and Thiers after the resignation of Mortier – "Why do you need a Prime Minister? Aren't you in agreement with each other? And am I not in agreement with you?" – as also by the transparent device of continually filling that constitutionally vital office with elderly and inarticulate soldiers. As M. Paul Bastid has observed, Louis-Philippe would have made a good Prime Minister himself, but that very fact was incompatible with his existing position as Chief of the State.[1]

Admittedly, Louis-Philippe's more or less personal conduct of foreign affairs during the year (March 1834-March 1835) when de Broglie was out of office was, as usual, shrewd and reasonably successful. This was partly due to the fact that diplomatic interest was centred on the Iberian peninsula, an area in which earlier experience had reinforced Louis-Philippe's natural prudence. Both in Spain and Portugal the problem was to sustain juvenile queens and their liberal supporters against predatory uncles with absolutist predilections. In Spain Ferdinand VII left his crown in September 1833 to his three-year-old daughter Isabella under the regency of Queen Maria Cristina. Don Carlos, his brother,

[1] See *Les Institutions Politiques de la Monarchie Parlementaire Française*, p. 181.

contested the legality of a female succession and had himself proclaimed in the Biscay provinces. Louis-Philippe, a good deal less liberal than he had once been on issues of this sort, would have closed for Don Carlos and thus avoided the awkward problem of an eventual Spanish marriage, an opinion which events were to justify all too painfully. However, there could be no doubt about the attitude in London of the political heirs of George Canning, and France duly declared her sympathy for Queen Isabella and grouped a not very vigilant army of observation on the Pyrenees. The English preoccupation with the necessity of assisting Queen Maria of Portugal to drive out her uncle Dom Miguel, with whom Dom Carlos was closely associated, led England to form a Triple Alliance with the two legitimate queens. Talleyrand achieved his last diplomatic coup in London before his resignation in the summer of 1834 in securing the Whig cabinet's agreement to this being converted into a Quadruple Alliance and soon Dom Miguel was finally eliminated. The next year, Louis-Philippe allowed the French Legion to fight in Spain against Don Carlos, resisting strongly however Marshal Gérard's plea for an unequivocal war of liberation. Louis-Philippe was convinced, and rightly, that the Spanish monarchy could save itself. "I know the Spaniards," he said. "They are indomitable and will not be governed by foreigners . . . if we take on this burden, they will make us carry it on our own shoulders alone and then make it impossible for us to do so." Soult, who knew even more about Spain, supported him and in the end Don Carlos fled the country in 1839. But Lord Palmerston was becoming more and more difficult and it was not altogether surprising that Louis-Philippe began in 1834 to enjoy exchanging confidential views with Metternich, whose diplomatic manners were a great deal more agreeable.

However, ministerial instability during this year halted the legislative programme, which had made such promising beginnings in 1833, and left the régime peculiarly ill-placed to compete with the appalling situation which developed as a result of the decision to convert the trial of the April conspirators into a sort of Grand Assize of the nation. Eventually it was decided to try a hundred and twenty-one of the fifteen hundred arrested in Paris, Lyon and the other centres of revolt. But even this involved the organization of over eight hundred witnesses and an almost inconceivable mass of paper. The opposition rightly concluded that so cumbersome a procedure gave them a marvellous opportunity to convert a political trial into a mass demonstration. The Republicans convened an imposing array of left-wing intellectuals, who under the guise of defence counsels would have a unique opportunity of displaying their oratorical prowess – Carrel, Barbès, Blanqui, Auguste Comte, Buonarotti, Ledru-Rollin, Pierre Leroux, Michel de Bourges, Jules Favre,[1] Raspail and the Abbé Lamennais. If it was to be a trial, it would be a trial of political strength. However, the July Monarchy possessed in the Duc de Pasquier, the President of the Chamber of Peers, one of the coolest and least impressionable political figures of the epoch. A prefect of police under Napoleon in 1810 and Minister of Justice under Louis XVIII, he had exactly the qualities of sceptical, patient humour calculated to keep what was to become a virtually intolerable situation under control. By applying article 295 of the Civil Code he pronounced that only professional advocates could be admitted as defence counsels. Even so when the trial, which was to last for nine months, duly opened on May 5th, 1835, the cacophony was unprecedented. Two hundred guards were required for the one hundred and twenty-one accused. No progress at all was possible, as each accused defended himself by a violent harangue, entirely unrelated to the judge's questions. Soon it became necessary to clap into the Sainte-Pélagie prison anyone impeding the proceedings in court. For the first few days, while the soldiers with fixed bayonets surrounded the Luxembourg Gardens, holding at bay a mass of amused spectators and hirsute students, it seemed that the whole process would end in a damaging fiasco for the government; and Louis-Philippe, who felt there was no going back on this particular decision once taken, found himself strenuously resisting counsels of despair. But suddenly the situation altered. On May 11th there appeared in both

[1] Prominent in the Lyon rising.

La Tribune and *Le Réformateur* of Raspail a letter, addressed to the public and the accused, with ninety-one signatures. It concluded with the startling phrase "the infamy of the judges makes the glory of the accussed".[1] Two of the signatories appeared to be deputies, Audry de Puyraveau and Cormenin. On the 13th the Peers voted that these two should be summoned to the bar of the house to explain what seemed to be a prima facie breach of privilege. Cormenin thereupon denied that he had any knowledge of the letter. The next day Trélat and Michel de Bourges wrote to Pasquier to the effect that they were responsible for the letter, adding "we took it on ourselves to have printed after our names the names of colleagues who we were sure would not disavow us . . ." They had reckoned without M. de Cormenin. Trélat, who defended himself distinctly injudiciously, was sentenced to three years emprisonment and a fine of 10,000 francs, Michel de Bourges to a similar fine and a month's emprisonment and *La Tribune* was finally put out of business. This disclosure significantly altered the reaction of the public, which in any case was beginning to tire of the rhetorical tournament in the Luxembourg. The contumacious prisoners in Sainte-Pélagie found confinement rather tedious after the heady excitements of impeding the course of justice in the Chamber of Peers and their notorious mutual antipathies began to intensify.[2] Barbès organized the escape, via an underground tunnel, of Cavaignac and other leaders in July, which somewhat disillusioned the rank and file. Pasquier had already hit on the ingenious device of trying and sentencing the non-Parisian elements among the accused, who were a good deal less vocal than their metropolitan associates. By the time the court adjourned in August public interest had been largely dissipated. The case was finally wound up in January 1836. There were no death-sentences, only a few deportations, and at the beginning of 1837 every one was released under a political

[1] Among other references to the Peers was a description of them as "l'appareil de la force et de la terreur".

[2] Cavaignac loathed the gentle Dr Raspail, who in turn disliked the aristocratic habits of Marrast, who enjoyed consuming champagne and truffles during his captivity.

amnesty. Those whom Raspail chose to call "legislative butchers" had not behaved with undue severity.

Long before the trial had ended, the inhabitants of Paris had had occasion to observe at close quarters that the Republicans had at least one alternative method of achieving their ends after the failure of the insurrections of 1832 and 1834. For some time Louis-Philippe had been sadly reading police reports of assassination plots directed against himself and the royal family. In July 1835 *Charivari* followed up the news-report that "yesterday, the King returned to Paris with his superb family without being in any way assassinated" with an illustration depicting the King, as usual in the guise of a pear, but this time with his limbs formed of chained, mutilated and massacred human beings, under the heading "Victims of despotism". There were widespread rumours that the King would not survive the great military review which would be held on July 28th to celebrate the anniversary of the revolution.

X

On the evening of July 27th the police were informed by one Suireau, a copper merchant, of the existence of an infernal machine in the vicinity of the Théâtre de l'Ambigu which was planned to destroy the King and the members of the royal family. This information had reached Suireau from his son, who was a drinking companion of an ironmonger called Boireau. The police duly ordered the arrest of Boireau at one o'clock on the morning of the 28th, but through culpable negligence the arrest was not carried out until eight the following evening. The houses in the vicinity of the Théâtre de l'Ambigu in the Boulevard Saint-Martin were duly searched without anything untoward transpiring. A little more thoroughness might have served to remind the police that there was another Théâtre de l'Ambigu in the Boulevard du Temple and had they searched the neighbouring houses in that area they would certainly have unmasked one of the most diabolical assassination plots of the nineteenth century.

Louis-Philippe had already met Joseph Fieschi in 1830 when Lafayette had introduced him to the Palais-Royal among a group of political prisoners "presented to you by one of their accomplices". A closer investigation of M. Fieschi's antecedents than was easily feasible at that time would have revealed that this animated, if unprepossessing, Corsican had served a ten-year prison sentence for theft and forgery. Incurably corrupt and vicious, he was not even a success in a short career as a police spy between 1832 and 1834 and towards the end of that year he begged a roof over his head from an elderly saddler called Pierre Morey. Morey was a very different, if equally dangerous, character. Now nearly sixty, he had served six years in the artillery, had fought on the streets in 1830 and had been an enthusiastic member of the *Droits de l'Homme*.[1]

---

[1] At different times he had professed himself to be a Bonapartist or even a Carlist.

While Fieschi was an unbalanced and depraved megalomaniac, utterly without sincere political convictions except his hatred of society as such, Morey was a taciturn and dyspeptic fanatic with an obsessive devotion to the creed and image of Robespierre and a corrosive hatred of Louis-Philippe. The infernal machine – originally to be ninety rifles mounted on a frame and touched off simultaneously – was Fieschi's brain-child. But it was the venerable, white-haired Morey who improved on Fieschi's idea that the machine would be an admirable weapon for the barricades by rapidly appreciating its possibilities as an instrument of assassination. Needing money, the conspirators had recourse to another member of the *Droits de l'Homme*, a wealthy grocer and wine-merchant called Théodore Pépin. He had also been a police-spy, but before 1830, and was now full of bombastic Republican valour, although at heart he was a great coward. In January 1835 Pépin was sufficiently impressed by a small-scale model shown him by Fieschi (the original ninety barrels now reduced to twenty-five) to advance five hundred francs towards the construction of the machine. He also paid for the hire of the third floor apartment of an inconspicuous house, number 50 Boulevard du Temple (near the Théâtre de l'Ambigu), with a good escape route over adjacent roofs, where Fieschi installed himself with his one-eyed mistress. The machine was constructed by April,[1] but there remained the awkward question of paying for the rifles. Pépin, who enjoyed boasting about his distinguished associations in the higher ranks of the Republican movement, made several unsuccessful attempts to enlist the financial support of Godefroy Cavaignac, whom he visited in Sainte-Pélagie,[2] and finally himself paid for the rifles which were brought from a dealer. On July 26th Fieschi, needing some iron clamps, went to see an ironmonger friend, Victor Boireau, whose addiction to the bottle made him a markedly unsuitable accomplice. Boireau thought the

[1] Louis-Philippe took time off at the beginning of that month to pick violets at Neuilly.

[2] M. Lucas-Dubreton is of the opinion that Cavaignac was almost certainly apprised of the details of the plan; see *Louis-Philippe et La Machine Infernale*, p. 259.

whole project most exciting, talked to a good many café associates, and took over from Pépin the task of riding slowly past number 50 Boulevard du Temple at six o'clock on the evening of the 27th to help Fieschi correct his elevation. Pépin at the same time characteristically took the opportunity of dropping in at the local police-station and asking if the police would protect him the following day since, if anything should happen to the King, he might suffer for his well-known political views. During the night Morey and Fieschi mounted the machine; Morey, who liked to leave nothing to chance, carefully adjusted it so that once Fieschi set it in motion he would inevitably be blown up himself. As the first soldiers lined the streets of the anniversary procession on the morning of July 28th, Fieschi was ready at his post behind the drawn curtains of number 50.

Louis-Philippe rode out of the Tuileries at nine in the morning at the head of a magnificent military and civil procession. On his right was Joinville, on his left Orléans and Nemours. Behind rode Marshal Mortier, Rambuteau, Prefect of the Seine, de Broglie, Marshal Maison, de Rigny, Thiers, suffering from his usual equestrian difficulties, and behind them a big cavalcade of general and staff officers of the army and the National Guard. They were all grave and apprehensive. Thiers had been early at the Tuileries urging the princes to abandon the procession, only to be told, as he expected, that the King would not hear of the idea. Lobau, commanding the National Guard, had secured the King's assent to an order that any petitioners approaching the King en route would be looked after by the A.D.C.'s. "But," said Louis-Philippe, "you can be certain that if there is any danger it will be from a window and not from the street." It was agreed that the Queen should await the return of the procession from the Chancellery in the Place Vendôme.

The volume of applause from the bystanders grew as the column rode slowly along. By midday it passed safely along the Boulevard Saint-Martin, many of the riders raising apprehensive eyes to upper storey windows near the Théâtre de l'Ambigu. Suddenly in the Boulevard du Temple a thick cloud of smoke appeared from the window of a house and the King just had time to cry out to Joinville "This is for me!" when they heard a shattering noise resembling the concentrated fire of a whole platoon of infantry. Louis-Philippe's horse was wounded and reared up and a bullet grazed the King's forehead; Mortier, shot in the left ear, fell dead across Rambuteau's saddle. The latter cried out: "Ride on, Sire, and get in front of the firing." Surrounded by his sons, the King rode forward and standing up on his stirrups waved his plumed hat in the air and cried out: "Here I am!" An immense cry went up of *Vive le roi!* The scene immediately behind him was one of confusion, smoke, blood and dust. After a short consultation with de Broglie who had just removed a spent bullet from his cravat, Louis-Philippe gave the order for the procession to advance and the cortège moved off slowly towards the Bastille, amid almost frenzied acclamations from the National Guard, leaving behind them fourteen dead, including a fourteen-year-old girl and an old man, and twenty-two wounded.[1] They eventually returned along the prescribed route past the scene of the crime and returned to the Place Vendôme where Marie-Amélie was almost out of her wits, refusing to be consoled by the news that her family had survived.[2] After a short rest, Louis-Philippe emerged with a blue and yellow bruise on his forehead and reviewed troops for two more hours in torrid sunshine. He burst into tears that evening at the Tuileries when the Chambers came to offer him their congratulations on his escape.

The funeral of the victims on August 5th became, not unnaturally, something of a counter-revolutionary demonstration. Louis-Philippe took the aspergillum himself from the hands of

[1] Eventually eighteen people died. A Virgilian ode composed by a French hand – "L'auteur a presque tout emprunté à Virgil" – describes the scene as follows:

> Matres atque viri, defunctaque corpora vita
> Magnanimum heroum, pueri, innuptae que puellae
> Sternuuntur . . .
>   (Archives Nationales BB 17A90)

[2] She is recorded as exclaiming: "What horrible people! What a frightful nation! We are surrounded by assassins!"

the priest and, leaning over Mortier's coffin, said with tears in his voice: "Goodbye, my old friend," and on seeing the coffin of the little girl he broke down completely. After seven hours of funeral celebrations he reviewed detachments of the National Guard and received an ovation of unprecedented warmth. The Luxembourg trials and Fieschi had combined with the still vivid memories of 1834 to rally the great majority of Parisians fervently behind the monarchy. It was a moment of triumph – but also ultimately of disaster. Louis-Philippe was by now profoundly sceptical of the merits of a constitutional monarchy, exposed to the merciless onslaught of a press continually inciting to murder and forced to shelter behind politicians whose capacities he regarded as inferior to his own. If by temperament or antecedents he could have contemplated overt dictatorship, this would have been a moment as propitious as 1851 was for Napoleon III at which to have made a clean sweep of his political opponents.[1] Instead, he was heard to remark: "If things are ever going to work, I must be the director of everything and the master of nothing." It was this decision which was ultimately to destroy the Orléans dynasty. As Thiers said long afterwards to Nassau Senior, when commenting on Louis-Philippe's foreign policy: "The King's great fault was his timidity. He was personally a hero but politically a coward." The French nation understands, and periodically responds to dictatorship, whether of the Right or Left. But a veiled dictatorship, whose title-deeds and merits are continually under public discussion, is not a durable form of government in France or anywhere else, and it was precisely this unhappy compromise which Louis-Philippe now decided to adopt. That he managed to preserve a not unimpressive façade of parliamentary government and was so far from conforming to the conventional image of a dictator that he was incapable of signing a death-sentence without acute pangs of conscience merely earned him a reputation for duplicity. Thiers understood his character and the dilemma with which he was confronted. Describing him to Senior on one

[1] As early as March 1834 Orléans considered that the army was so discontented with the Chamber that an 18th Brumaire could easily have been mounted.

occasion as *fin et rusé* he later modified it as follows: "So he was, but those words, without explanation, convey the idea of falsehood, and *false* he was not. He had a strong will and fixed plans, and though the means which he used to effect those plans were often indirect, often indeed morally wrong, they were not *treacherous*. The great error of his life was that he never would submit to be a constitutional King. To work a constitutional government the different powers should be in equilibrium. The King and the Chambers should resemble the passengers in a wherry, they should be constantly endeavouring to trim the boat. If either party destroys its balance it oversets. Now he would never submit to sit still; he was always getting up to seize the rudder." There is substantial justice in this, although if it were a question of whose hand was to be on the rudder there was more than one occasion when Europe could be grateful that it was the King's and not M. Thiers'.

Whatever the future might bring, both the King and his ministers were at one in deciding to muzzle an opposition press which was capable of commenting, as one newspaper did, on the very day after the crime of Fieschi: "This time the Republic missed arriving by half a second; so powerful a cause which failed so narrowly to succeed doesn't seem to us so desperately badly placed." [1] On August 4th de Broglie introduced the three bills which, known as the September Laws, were to last for the duration of the reign. The Prime Minister explained their purpose by introducing them in the words: "All parties are free within the framework of the constitutional monarchy. Once they go beyond those bounds they are not entitled to liberty." Since censorship was impossible under the Charter, a new Press Law tightened up the laws of libel. It would now be a criminal offence to refer to the King, even indirectly, in a political article or to indicate a wish to overthrow the constitutional monarchy or to restore a former dynasty; inciting members of the public to attack the King or overthrow the régime and any attempt to provoke hatred or

[1] It was generally surmised that the time it took Fieschi to draw the curtains was just sufficient to save the King's life.

contempt of the King could now be classified as treason and so tried before the Peers; fines and caution money were increased; and caricatures required official authorization. A verdict of guilty could now be pronounced by a simple majority of the jury (whose names were not to be published) instead of, as previously, a majority of two-thirds; if the accused parties refused to come into court the trial could proceed in their absence, a procès-verbal being read to them after each sitting; and a similar procedure could be adopted in respect of accused persons misbehaving in court. All these measures were passed by big majorities, despite considerable rhetorical displays by Lamartine and Royer-Collard and a long and tedious discourse from the astronomer Arago, which endeavoured to demonstrate that the superiority of a jury convicting by eight to four over one convicting by seven to five was a matter of precise arithmetical calculation. On a short view, the results were impressive, especially the proscription of caricatures. Raspail's *Réformateur*[1] ceased publication in November and *Charivari* soon followed it.[2] Carrel was killed in a duel in 1836 by Emile de Girardin, a pioneer in the production of cheap newspapers tricked out with serial stories, and it was some time before *Le National* recovered its former impetus under Armand Marrast. The September Laws were not on the whole vigorously enforced and the first treason trial for a press offence occurred only in 1841 after an assassination attempt on the Duc d'Aumale. By 1837 *La Mode*, a scurrilous Legitimist production, was openly referring to a mysterious villain dressed as a woman who had guided the mob to Marie-Antoinette's bedroom on October 5th, 1789, and *La France*, the self-styled journal of the "monarchical and religious interests of Europe", began its leader of October 24th, 1837 with the comment that "the deputy is essentially corrupt; he is born in corruption and lives for corruption; he is a moral pest . . ." [3] Mrs

[1] Fieschi testified at his trial: "When I used to see Pépin in the mornings I used to read *Le Réformateur*; and when there was something against the government he showed it to me saying: 'Look at this frightful outrage! Isn't there anybody who will rid us of a scoundrel like that?'"
[2] *La Tribune* had collapsed in May after its 111th lawsuit.
[3] Archives Nationales BB 17A 98.

Irene Collins concludes that "on the whole the result of the Government's efforts was to anger the press without silencing it. In 1847 the newspapers were 'pouring forth daily fire on all public measures' to the surprise of the American Minister to Paris, who could not see what their anger was about when prosperity and contentment were obvious everywhere around him".[1] If comment was not altogether free, neither were facts particularly sacred. As Lord Chief Justice Camden observed in his great judgement in the case of Entick v. Carrington in 1765: "All civilized governments have punished calumny with severity; and with reason; for these compositions debauch the manners of the people; they excite a spirit of disobedience, and enervate the authority of government; they provoke and excite the passions of the people against their rulers, and the rulers oftentimes against the people."

[1] *The Government and the Newspaper Press in France, 1814–1881*

XI

Before Fieschi, Morey and Pépin were executed on February 19th, 1836,[1] de Broglie's ministry of all the talents had fallen. Louis-Philippe did not appreciate a foreign minister who did his best to conceal ambassadors' confidential despatches and even made difficulties about letting him see any diplomatic documents at all. With the winding up of the Luxembourg trial and the passage of the September Laws, he was not alone in feeling that the internal danger was temporarily allayed and felt less than ever inclined to submit to the yoke of the Doctrinaires. Furthermore, old Talleyrand was consistently stressing the limitations of a foreign policy which consisted almost entirely in a rigid adherence to the entente with Great Britain, coupled with occasional unavailing attempts to detach Austria from Prussia and Russia. The alternative was to try a rapprochement with the three Continental Powers, more especially if the dynasty could be fortified by an Austrian marriage. The Doctrinaires, despite their individual ability, were not strong in the Chamber and, when times were quiet, were the object of much sniping from the third party. In January 1836, the Finance Minister, Humann, without previously consulting de Broglie or the Cabinet, declared his personal support for a proposed debt conversion. De Broglie, when asked his opinion, snapped out tersely: "I am asked if it is the government's intention to propose this conversion during the session. I reply: no. Is that quite clear?" This time the Chamber felt it had had enough of the austere superiority of the Duc de Broglie, and the ministry, defeated by 194 votes to 192, was forced to resign on

[1] Boireau was sentenced to twenty years imprisonment. Pépin conducted himself lamentably throughout the investigation and trial, but Fieschi, horribly wounded as he was, revelled in the drama of the occasion and Morey converted himself into a Republican martyr by his taciturn stoicism.

February 5th.[1] Dupin, as usual, not being prepared to accept responsibility, the King concluded it was time to give M. Thiers an opportunity to display in high office the gifts which he was never backward in publicizing. Thiers, after all, seemed a good deal more malleable than de Broglie or Guizot. Louis-Philippe always found him amusing, even if he had to put up with some rather tiresome meridional habits in a Prime Minister who sucked olives in cabinet meetings and spat out the stones in the royal presence. Thiers, for his part, eagerly espoused Louis-Philippe's proposed new orientation of foreign policy and indeed told his friends: "I've gone all Holy Alliance." Overestimating his own ability vis-à-vis the King's, he believed that by securing an Austrian marriage for Orléans he might so ingratiate himself over and against his rivals that he would soon bring about a situation in which Louis-Philippe reigned and M. Thiers governed. It was certainly encouraging when Talleyrand, who had acidly observed that the true vocation of the Duc de Broglie was not to be foreign minister, greeted his successor with the phrase: "Monsieur, Europe awaits you." Perhaps the historian of the Revolution might succeed in reviving by his own efforts some of the glories he had chronicled.[2]

Internally, Thiers' ministry of just over six months amounted to very little. Some railway bills were passed; gaming houses were closed at midnight; largely inconclusive debates took place on tariff reductions. The Prime Minister oscillated tactically between the Right and the Left, taking care to spare the susceptibilities of Guizot, without unduly upsetting Odilon Barrot. His colleagues, with the exception of Montalivet, were nonentities, and although Guizot in opposition was guarded, the solidarity of the old *parti de la resistance* was breaking up in a manner which suggested that the only beneficiary in the foreseeable future would be the King himself. It was in foreign affairs that Thiers hoped to pull off some

[1] Guizot, who could turn an epigram, called de Broglie "at one and the same time the proudest and the most modest man I knew".

[2] Even as a historian Thiers incurred enemies. Soult once complained: "I thought I won the battle of Toulouse according to my own plan; Thiers insists on demonstrating that I won according to his."

outstanding coup to consolidate his personal supremacy. Without protest, he allowed the three Northern powers to coerce revolutionary elements in Cracow; he resisted a suggestion from Palmerston for joint intervention in Spain; he joined with Austria in compelling the Swiss diet to expel refugee republicans. In Vienna and Berlin the July monarchy was fast becoming an object of unqualified admiration and even Czar Nicholas began to unfreeze a little. The moment seemed ripe to break the matrimonial blockade and secure for the brilliant Duc d'Orléans, who had already proved his manhood under the tricolour in Algeria, the hand of the Austrian archduchess, Theresa, daughter of Napoleon's great adversary, the Archduke Charles.

Orléans and Nemours after a triumphal visit to Berlin reached Vienna in March, where Orléans won all hearts, including that of the archduchess, but encountered stubborn opposition from Metternich, who kept referring unhelpfully to Marie-Antoinette and Marie-Louise and was unimpressed by either the cajoling or vague menaces of M. Thiers. Denied the Archduchess Theresa, Orléans, still hopeful, went to Milan, whose viceroy, the Archduke Renier, also had another marriageable archduchess as a daughter. While there he heard the appalling news that on June 25th, just as the King, the Queen and Princess Adélaïde had entered the royal coach,[1] a young man had fired a bullet at point-blank range from a weapon disguised as a walking-stick. The carriage was filled with smoke and the bullet narrowly missed the King. Alibaud, a commercial traveller, who had perpetrated the crime, was immediately arrested, and in the fortnight before his execution could speak only in stock republican sophistries.[2] Louis-Philippe, as usual on these occasions, behaved with admirable calm, but he was observed to look sad, old and tired, and put up no resistance when the annual July review was cancelled. Inevit-

[1] Now a large yellow berline with armoured panels.
[2] He told the priest who visited him in prison that: "Jesus Christ was a democrat like me and if it had been necessary he would have become a regicide." *Le National* was fined for trying to elevate him to the status of a hero.

ably, it was the end of the Austrian marriage project, the Archduke Charles telling the French ambassador: "My daughter doesn't feel strong enough to compete with the dangers to which the French royal family remains unhappily exposed."

Thiers at this juncture lost his head and in an attempt to exact some sort of revenge did his best to stir up the hornets' nest in Spain. The Regent Cristina and the child Queen Isabella were confronted not only by the adherents of Don Carlos, who enjoyed the support of Austria, Russia and Prussia, but also by vigorous liberal revolutionaries. Thiers proposed armed intervention on behalf of the Queen by a corps of French volunteers under the command of General Bugeaud. But Louis-Philippe was not to be drawn into adventures of this sort. "I know Spain better than anybody," he said, "since I found myself there in comparable circumstances and I know what a foreigner exposes himself to if he mixes himself up in their quarrels . . . Any intervention on our part would compromise European peace and my crown." Thiers tried to insist, Metternich began to talk of 1808, and Louis-Philippe told the ambassadors privately: "My minister is talking nonsense." On August 25th Thiers' ministry was dissolved.

Louis-Philippe's new President of the Council was the fifty-five-year-old Comte Molé, who was to be the central figure in the parliamentary arena until 1839. As a child of twelve he had seen his father go to the guillotine and had grown up to be a man whose political scale of values placed administrative expediency before abstract principle. He had been a favourite correspondent of Napoleon, had voted for Ney's execution and had held ministerial rank under three régimes. Although Guizot, Thiers and Berryer appreciably surpassed him as orators, he was an easy man to underestimate, as events were to show. Disraeli described him as: "A grand seigneur, of the highest breeding; courtly, finished, dignified if necessary, but easy and simple; excellent talents, very general information, a complete political culture, and not a mean orator when under pressure." Essentially a Conservative, he was no admirer of the Doctrinaires, nor they of him, but he appreciated that if his ministry was to survive he needed the support of

Guizot in the Chamber and his cabinet therefore included the latter in his old post of Minister of Education with two other Doctrinaires, Duchâtel and de Gasparin, in charge of Finance and the Interior. But it was not to prove a success. Guizot's greatest disservice to the July Monarchy lay in his refusal to co-operate loyally with Molé at this decisive juncture. The conventional basis of parliamentary debate for the next two and a half years was for all parties to taunt Molé with having no policy. But in fact his policy was both simple and sensible – social conciliation combined with developing prosperity at home, and a pacific foreign policy conducted largely by Louis-Philippe himself (although the King's active participation in government would be discreetly veiled). Guizot, as time was to show, was perfectly capable of appreciating that a country is happiest when it has no history – if anything, too much so – but his ambition and his awareness of his own outstanding parliamentary skill made him incapable of serving in a subordinate role or of withdrawing into splendid isolation like de Broglie. At the very moment when the July Monarchy had a chance to stabilize itself after six stormy years, the lure of opposition was altogether too strong for its ablest parliamentarians. The function of the opposition, by a sort of political retardation, came to resemble that with which we are familiar in eighteenth-century England in that it was always considered obligatory to cry up the constitution in danger. Nothing suited the particular talents of Guizot and Thiers better than to play Burke and Fox, and to elevate a discussion on some inoffensive paragraph of the address to the throne into an impassioned debate full of abstract nouns. And if Molé resembled Shelburne rather than North, that only added to the excitement. The essential difference, however, lay in the fact that whereas the parliamentary paladins of George III were as a rule debating real issues and could safely call the constitution in question without endangering it, in France the issues debated were only a transparent veil for naked political ambition – and everybody knew it – and the constitution was far too fragile to be continually exposed to public analysis.

Molé began by assuring the European powers that all danger of intervention in Spain had disappeared with Thiers and then released a number of Republican prisoners and emptied the fortress of Ham of Charles X's ministers. He concluded, reasonably enough, that this was a sufficiently comprehensive gesture towards the enemies of the dynasty. But on October 31st a semaphore despatch arrived from Strasbourg which read: "This morning about six o'clock, Louis-Napoleon, son of the Duchesse de Saint-Leu, who had in his confidence Colonel of Artillery Vaudrey, has been abroad in the streets of Strasbourg with a party of . . ." The rest of the message had been lost because of autumn mist on the line, but its purport was quite clear. Fortunately it hardly seemed necessary to take the obscure, twenty-eight-year-old Bonapartist pretender very seriously, since it transpired that his attempt to raise Strasbourg had fizzled out ignominiously by eight o'clock that morning, when the 46th Regiment of Infantry showed themselves disinclined to turn out of their barracks in support of an Artillery coup d'état. Louis-Philippe, remembering the trouble they had had with the Duchesse de Berri, decided that the best thing to do with this strange young man was to put him aboard the *Andromeda* at Lorient bound for New York.[1] He told the Sardinian ambassador that his unexpected visitor was very pleased not to have suffered the fate of the Duc d'Enghien. Unfortunately for themselves, however, the government decided to arraign his motley gang of supporters before the Assize Court at Strasbourg.

After this somewhat inauspicious beginning, Molé had to confront his first session of the Chamber on December 27th, 1836, with Thiers, revived by a holiday in Italy, busy building up a Left Centre opposition, based on the members of the old third party and such parliamentary flotsam as he could muster, to combat what he chose to call the "anti-national system" of the new ministry. As Louis-Philippe with three of his sons was crossing the Quai des

[1] When Louis-Napoleon arrived at Lorient the sub-prefect asked him if he would have any resources in the United States. On receiving a negative answer the sub-prefect handed him a wallet with 15,000 francs in it, thoughtfully provided by Louis-Philippe.

Tuileries for the opening of the session, a pistol shot was fired into his carriage, grazing his chest and scattering broken glass over Orléans. Louis-Philippe and the duke, his clothes spattered with blood, were loudly cheered in the Chamber and the old King read the speech from the throne with his usual firmness and composure. The criminal turned out to be a young debauchee called Meunier, who might be described as a victim of literacy in that his only defence was that: "What I have read has taught me that the Orléans have always made France unhappy." The Peers sentenced him to death which Louis-Philippe promptly commuted to exile, taking care to see that he had some money to live on in America.[1] Shortly afterwards, the police discovered a nearly complete infernal machine in the home of one Champion, who strangled himself in his cell.

[1] It is pleasant to record that Meunier, unlike Louis-Napoleon, was grateful for his benefaction.

Book Four

Il y a des gens destinés à être sots qui ne font pas seulement des
sottises par leur choix mais que la fortune même contraint d'en
faire.

LA ROCHEFOUCAULD (Maximes)

I

Despite continuing evidence of submerged revolutionary plotting, 1837, the year of Queen Victoria's accession, proved to be
perhaps the happiest and most flourishing of Louis-Philippe's
reign.[1] Great general prosperity, as well as allaying bourgeois
rancours, minimized the unregulated unemployment which was
the most dangerous social factor of the age. On May 8th, with the
active concurrence of the King, Molé pronounced an amnesty for
the political prisoners of 1835 and 1836 and Blanqui emerged for
one of his rare periods of exposure to the fresh air. On May 15th
Louis-Philippe went for a quiet walk in the Jardin des Plantes,
accompanied by two ministers, an A.D.C. and the Prefect of
Police, and found himself cheered at close quarters by some of his
fellow-citizens who looked so indescribably villainous that his
companions were terrified. Ten days later the Duc d'Orléans'
affianced bride, the Princess Hélène of Mecklenburg-Schwerin,
arrived at Fontainebleau. Intelligent, graceful and dignified, she
was an instantaneous success and only Legitimists were prepared
to cavil at her German Protestant origins. During the marriage
celebrations Louis-Philippe decided not to sleep in Napoleon's
bed, because he found it too soft. After three marriage cere-
monies – civil, Catholic and Protestant – there was a state entry
into Paris on June 4th, a day of superb sunshine. The King and the
princess rode on horseback down the Champs Elysées with the
Queen, the duchess and the princesses in an open carriage behind,
and all Paris seemed to cheer. The *Journal des Débats* proclaimed
it as "the first day of a new era . . . The July dynasty, peaceful and
glorious, appears to be surrounded by the respect of Europe and
the grateful love of France." With a good instinct for stage-

[1] At Victoria's coronation in June 1838 old Marshal Soult was an unexpected
success.

management, the government arranged on June 10th the official
opening by Louis-Philippe of the restored Versailles on which he
had been working since 1833 and on which he spent 23 millions
from his civil list without any charge being laid on the national
budget. The restoration, "to all the glories of France", can hardly
be said to have transcended the limitations of the aesthetic canons
of the period, but Louis-Philippe must at least be given some
credit for his observation that "after me people will do better
those parts which I have only been able to do imperfectly". He
insisted also that pictorial justice in the galleries should be done
not only to the splendours and triumphs of the ancien régime, the
Revolution and the Empire, but also to those of the Restoration.
There was a banquet for 1,500 guests,[1] a performance of *Le
Misanthrope* with Mlle Mars as Celimène, at which the King's
striking facial resemblance to Louis XIV was much commented
on,[2] and a splendid torchlight promenade. Among those invited
were Balzac, Hugo and Dumas, the two latter attending in
National Guard uniform. The previous year had seen the opening
of the Arc de Triomphe and the erection of the prodigious obelisk
of Luxor, a present from Mehemet Ali, on the site where Philippe
Egalité's head had been severed by the guillotine.[3] It was widely
felt that the monarchical principle was successfully reasserting
itself in France. Finally, the year was crowned with the news from
Algeria that after a deadly battle General Lamoricière, with the
Duc de Nemours in the van, had planted the tricolour on the
heights of Constantine.

But the political scene had become more sombre than ever.
Greville had visited France early in the year and concluded:
"There appears to be something rotten in the state of this country
. . . I see only a confusion and caprice of passions, prejudices and

[1] At which Madame de Boigne cattishly observed that Louis-Philippe sat
under a large picture with an inscription in gold letters: "Le roi gouverne par
lui-même".
[2] See Greville: "The King is too civil; he has a fine head and closely resembles
the pictures of Louis XIV" (January 25th, 1837).
[3] Among other architectural enterprises put in hand by Louis-Philippe was
the restoration of the palaces of Fontainebleau and Saint-Cloud.

opinions which are only reduced to anything like order by the strong sober sense of the King, who is far the ablest man among them." By the spring Molé's original ministerial team had disintegrated. Guizot's friends and the newspapers he controlled were continually putting it about that Molé was not personally up to the job and would assuredly not last long. Maladroitly, the government introduced five bills simultaneously at the end of January – one to provide for the unpaid dowry of the Queen of the Belgians, one granting Rambouillet to the Duc de Nemours and three concerned with the law on political offences, of which the most important[1] arose out of the acquittal by the Strasbourg jury of Louis-Napoleon's accomplices.[2] Among those acquitted were members of the army, and the new law required that soldiers accused of political offences of this sort should be judicially separated from their civilian associates and tried by court-martial. After a parliamentary fracas, much envenomed by de Cormenin producing another of his vicious little pamphlets purporting to demonstrate Louis-Philippe's parsimony, the government was defeated on the courts-martial issue by 211 to 209. During March and April all sorts of political combinations were mooted, including one, which Louis-Philippe strongly supported, for a revival of the ministry of October 11th, 1832, under de Broglie, an indication that the King was, if necessary, perfectly prepared to submit himself to both Thiers and Guizot combined and even surrender his grip on foreign policy. However, Thiers felt himself too committed to his new friends of the Left and nothing came of the project. Consequently Molé shed Guizot and his two Doctrinaire colleagues and with Montalivet at the Interior,[3] braced himself to lead a party of mediocre Conservatives against the opposition forces of Guizot, Thiers, Berryer and Barrot. He had to drop the proposed Nemours settlement, but

---

[1] The two others were concerned with deportation and misprision of treason.

[2] The defence, conducted mostly by lawyers with Radical affiliations, was reasonably enough based on the fact that the principal conspirator had already been let off.

[3] Who, as a former Intendant of the Civil List, was able to rebut, without rejoinder, de Cormenin's charges about Louis-Philippe's personal expenses.

showing unexpected firmness and adroitness, he slowly began to gain ground and with the five per cents resilient and the news from Algeria improving he overcame in September Louis-Philippe's doubts about the advantages of a dissolution and election. What Molé wanted was a majority of Conservatives prepared to support him as against Guizot and Thiers, but the distinction was too subtle a one for the electors to grasp and the Chamber returned was of almost identical political complexion with that of 1834. It was noted that Barrot's dynastic Left, in constituencies where it had no candidate, was not above making common cause with Republicans and Legitimists. Confronted therefore with the probability of continued personal and parliamentary conflict, Louis-Philippe in his speech from the throne on December 18th, 1837, urged political unity in the words: "Let us learn, gentlemen, how to conserve by our unity and wisdom what we have conquered by our courage and patriotism", but the parliamentary annals of 1838, if conspicuous for a prodigious output of words, were to be characterized by neither unity, wisdom nor patriotism. Thiers led his skirmishers of the Left-Centre in the struggle for what he decided to call "the reality of representative government" and told Guizot that he considered Molé's ministry "the most disgraceful which ever existed". But Guizot was still inclined to draw up his skirts when being wooed from this particular quarter and this enabled Molé to hang on precariously, growing slowly in personal prestige and tactical skill, and maintaining by skilful management a parlous majority, which included a great many of the 191 civil servants in the Chamber, whose allegiance to the ministry actually in power was not invariably disinterested. While Molé daily confronted his enemies at the tribune, Louis-Philippe made a quiet and sensible job of foreign policy and, his appetite whetted, also supervised Montalivet at the Interior.[1] Fortune temporarily favoured them. The country

[1] Dupin records in his memoirs once asking Louis-Philippe: "Isn't it essentially an advantage to the Crown to cover itself with the English axiom – the King can do no wrong?" To which Louis-Philippe replied animatedly: "Ah! that's because he does nothing. In France a King like that would be treated as a sticking-pig."

seemed daily to be getting richer, foreign trade was excellent, roads were being built and although the police seized at the end of September the printing presses of a mysterious secret society called *Les Saisons*, disorders in the streets seemed a thing of the past. In October an inexpensive attack was made on the Mexicans, who had been ill-treating French residents, a naval squadron, including the corvette *La Créole* commanded by the twenty-year old Prince de Joinville, storming the fort of San Juan d'Ulloa, a name hitherto more familiar in English than in French naval history.

None of this suited the political aspirations of either Thiers and Guizot. It was a narrow-minded, if virtuous young lawyer with a passion for the minutiae of constitutional law, Duvergier de Hauranne, who was to forge an opposition coalition, more infamous than that of Fox and North, because more widely based on ultimately irreconcilable political attitudes. What was wanted he felt was a rallying cry capable of bringing together not only Thiers and Guizot – the Left-Centre and the Right-Centre – but also the dynastic Left under Barrot and he found the ideal formula in his demand that France should "substitute parliamentary government for personal government". Deputies under the July Monarchy were just as enthusiastic for government exclusively by deputies as were their successors under the Third and Fourth Republics. Even Berryer's fifteen Legitimists and Garnier-Pagès' nineteen Republicans were prepared at this trumpet-call to enlist whole-heartedly under the same colours, shoulder to shoulder with the Doctrinaires. If the country was too prosperous and contented to be interested in politics,[1] it was evidently high time to make politics more interesting. So the austere M. Guizot arrived unannounced one evening at the residence of M. Odilon Barrot and said: "You're surprised to see me; I have come to unite with you to attack this personal government which is dishonouring and destroying our country; it is time to finish with court favourites." The infamous coalition was forged.

The battle – perhaps the most extraordinary in French parliamentary history – opened on January 7th, 1839 and lasted twelve

[1] As was indicated by reports from the prefects all over the country.

days, Thiers speaking thirteen times, Guizot twelve and Molé seventeen. The occasion chosen was the debate on the reply to the address from the throne. This was always drafted by a commission chosen from the nine standing committees of the Chamber and the defection of Dupin, the President of the Chamber, enabled the leaders of the opposition to combine to produce a draft reply which was almost an overt attack on the King's use of his prerogative. Molé decided to defend himself by contesting the draft, paragraph by paragraph. Determined not to yield and drawing on unexpected reserves of energy and stamina, he held his narrow majority almost intact. Many hitherto rather invertebrate ministerial supporters were frankly disgusted by the unscrupulousness of the coalition, and cheered the Prime Minister tumultuously as he returned again and again to the tribune. Guizot led the opening attack amid continual interruption and built up his peroration to a climax by quoting a phrase from Tacitus – *omnia serviliter pro dominatione* – as illustrative of his thesis that the cabinet was nothing but a set of courtiers. During a short adjournment, Royer-Collard betook himself to the library, checked the reference and enabled Molé to begin his reply by quietly pointing out that in the passage quoted Tacitus was referring not to courtiers but to ambitious politicians. The coalition's onslaught on the government's foreign policy was largely sheer political dishonesty, as Guizot virtually admits in his memoirs.[1] When Metternich withdrew his troops from Bologna the French had evacuated Ancona, as had been clearly stipulated at the time of the occupation under Casimir-Périer; there had been difficulties with the Swiss when Louis-Napoleon returned there from America; and a resurrection of the Belgian problem had ended in a final settlement of the frontier, with France acting in conjunction with the four great European powers.[2] Yet, although the government secured a small

[1] Vol. IV, p. 292.
[2] The King of Holland had at last agreed to the settlement of 1833 but in return asked that the Belgians should restore parts of Luxembourg and Limburg which they had been holding in surety. The Belgians proved aggressive and difficult but Louis-Philippe handled King Leopold, his son-in-law, with considerable skill and secured for the Belgians a financial *quid pro quo*.

majority on each individual paragraph of the address relating to these problems, they were defeated by nine votes on what was known as the ensemble of foreign policy, something of a demonstration that in French representative chambers the parts added up do not always equal the whole.[1] But it was the only success the coalition achieved. In a mounting crescendo of excitement (on one occasion when Molé inadvisedly admitted that he was nearing the end of his strength one of his opponents shouted: "die, dog!")[2] the government secured majorities of 7, 4, 29, 13, 7, 9 and finally, on the whole amended draft, 13. It was by any standards a remarkable feat of endurance on the part of Molé, whose only effective supporter was the poet Lamartine. On the fifth day Louis-Philippe wrote to him: "I am only too happy when I can convey to you how much I appreciate the courage, talent and devotion you are displaying in this inconceivably bitter struggle. I hope more than ever that it will end happily." But that was clearly impossible and the Chamber was dissolved on February 2nd after only just over a year's existence and new elections were ordered for March 2nd. The Chamber was due to meet on March 26th.

The coalition set up three election committees under Thiers, Guizot and Barrot, which worked in close consultation with each other and Garnier-Pagès and Berryer agreed that their followers should support coalition candidates in constituencies where Republicans and Legitimists were not standing. Molé and Montalivet worked the administrative machine as hard as they could, but the coalition, not to be outdone, published "A Notice to Civil Servants" warning them that since the ministry would be defeated "it would therefore be wise of them to appreciate on which side they would be advised to act." It would be difficult to imagine anything more damaging to the stability of the country and its new institutions than an electoral campaign fought on the issues of an allegedly weak foreign policy and the abuse of the royal

[1] Thiers, apparently forgetting his ministry of 1836, even accused Molé of weakening the English alliance.

[2] The French – crève, chien – is rather more expressive.

prerogative, since the stock arguments advanced inevitably recalled the social turmoil of 1831.[1] Such a campaign was a godsend to Legitimists and Republicans and time would amply demonstrate to both Thiers and Guizot the inadvisability of professed supporters of the dynasty associating with its irreconcilable enemies. Metternich, now more than ever sceptical of the monarchy's survival value, wrote on February 9th: "France today is back in 1830 . . . and all because MM. Thiers and Guizot wish to be ministers at all costs and – note this – one in spite of and at the expense of the other! Long live modern representative government!"

The coalition's electoral tactics succeeded. As the results came in, it transpired that Molé's supporters had dropped in number from 221 to about 190, and the opposition of all colours and sizes membered about 240. On March 8th Molé resigned. Louis-Philippe had suffered a severe emotional shock at the beginning of this political crisis when his liveliest and most talented daughter, Marie, Duchess of Württemberg, had died of tuberculosis on January 2nd. Having followed the struggle daily in a mood of gloom and anxiety, not always unmixed with an ironic scepticism, he now braced himself to accept a ministry drawn from the coalition, only to discover immediately that, as Metternich foresaw, neither Thiers nor Guizot were prepared to serve under each other. Soult was instructed to try and build up a Left-Centre ministry under Thiers. When the latter presented the list to Louis-Philippe, the King objected to two names – those of Passy and Dufaure. Thiers said: "The King is mistaken; he doesn't know these gentlemen; let him summon them; he'll find they're worth more than I am." Louis-Philippe looked quizzically at him for a moment and replied: "Oh, you think so. I dare say it's quite possible." Thiers was then asked to formulate a programme. Inevitably his programme included a measure of intervention in Spain. Louis-Philippe did not dissent, but asked for a day to consider this. When finally the members of the proposed cabinet were

[1] In fact it was rather worse even than that in that Molé was frequently likened to Polignac.

assembled in the presence of the King, and just as Soult was about to sign the document announcing the formation of the new ministry, Thiers interrupted the proceedings and emphasized his determination to act vigorously in Spain. Three of his colleagues immediately objected and so the cabinet could not be formed.

It was by now March 24th and the new Chamber was due to assemble on March 26th with no Prime Minister and no cabinet. The Third and Fourth Republics have accustomed us to this sort of situation, but in 1839 it was sufficiently novel to shake the commercial credit of the country disastrously. The streets filled with workers paid off by their employers and heavy withdrawals were made from the banks. The opening of the session was adjourned until April 4th and Louis-Philippe sent for de Broglie, who tried unavailingly to mediate between Thiers and Guizot. A so-called provisional ministry of minor political figures was scratched together for the opening of the session, the *Moniteur* announcing that it was taking office "on the express condition of ceasing as soon as a definite ministry was formed". The Chamber proceeded to vote a humble address to the King asking him to use his prerogative and nominate a permanent ministry, but before this could be achieved the sound of shooting was heard once again in the streets of Paris on Sunday, May 12th.

II

The so-called *Société des Saisons*, numbering perhaps six hundred members, had been working underground for some three years under the leadership of Blanqui, Barbès and a compositor called Martin Bernard. Blanqui, who like most fanatics had a tendency to over-estimate the general popularity of his ideas, concluded that the unprecedented ministerial confusion and the deepening commercial crisis presented him with the ideal opportunity to raise the streets. At two o'clock in the afternoon the conspirators assembled in the Rue Saint-Martin and in the traditional fashion broke open an armourer's shop, whence Barbès led them to the Palais de Justice where they murdered some soldiers, whom they took by surprise. A more ambitious onslaught on the Prefecture of Police was strongly resisted and there was nothing left for it but to withdraw behind barricades, as there seemed to be little or no popular response to a fiery proclamation read out by Barbès. Detachments of soldiers and National Guards had comparatively little difficulty in taking the barricades and locking up the leaders.

This episode brought the politicians to their senses and ended a ministerial interregnum which had now lasted more than two months. "Marshal," Louis-Philippe said to Soult, "the waters are troubled. We must fish for ministers." The fish landed were all rather little ones – three from the Left-Centre, two from the Right-Centre, and one of Molé's supporters.[1] Soult was himself to be Prime Minister and Foreign Minister, which was a clear enough indication that there was no immediate intention on the part of Louis-Philippe to renounce the control of public affairs.

Unfortunately for France, the world could not stand still while

[1] Respectively Passy, Dufaure, Teste; Duchâtel, Villemain; Cunin-Gridaine.

her legislators allowed themselves the luxury of dancing elaborate political quadrilles. Soult's ministry found itself confronted immediately with a resurgence of the Eastern Question in a peculiarly dangerous and complicated form. On April 21st, 1839, the Sultan Mahmoud was rash enough under the impact of *delirium tremens* and with the encouragement of Lord Ponsonby, the British ambassador, to send a Turkish army across the Euphrates with the object of wreaking a final revenge on Mehemet Ali, who since 1833 had been in control of Syria and Adana.[1] This was followed in rapid succession by a catastrophic defeat of the Turks on the plain of Nezib, the death of Mahmoud and the appearance of the entire Turkish fleet at Alexandria, where it surrendered itself to Mehemet Ali. Although a French representative succeeded with some difficulty in persuading Ibrahim not to cross the Taurus and complete the destruction of the Turkish Empire, the French admiral, Lalande, had been decidedly instrumental in facilitating the surrender of the Turkish fleet. Louis-Philippe, in common with almost the entire nation, saw in these events a striking confirmation of their conviction that their client Mehemet Ali was invincibly powerful and must without question be encouraged to stake out his claim to add the hereditary pashalik of all Syria to his Egyptian possessions. Lord Palmerston, on the other hand, strongly abetted by Ponsonby, disliked both Mehemet Ali and the prospect of extended French influence in North Africa and the Eastern Mediterranean. For the moment, however, both powers were above all anxious to ensure that Russia did not take it on herself in the spirit of 1833 to come to the rescue of the Turks without reference to the other European powers. As it transpired, the Russians having made no objection, all five powers agreed to send a note to the seventeen-year-old Sultan on July 27th undertaking to settle the question, just as the Turks were engaged in negotiating direct with Mehemet Ali, who was naturally at that moment in a particularly strong position. In the long run, this was to prove a serious, if understandable, mistake on the part of Louis-Philippe and Soult. They were trying at one and the same

[1] See p. 216.

time to secure Mehemet Ali in his conquests and to prevent any danger of Russian predominance at Constantinople, but what they failed to appreciate was that Palmerston had no intention, once he was clear that Russia was prepared to act in concert with the other powers, of assisting in the aggrandizement of Mehemet Ali. French satisfaction at the British Foreign Secretary's description of Marshal Soult as a jewel soon gave way to an uneasy awareness that things were not going at all well. Had the Turco-Egyptian negotiations proceeded undisturbed, Mehemet Ali could not conceivably have been fobbed off with anything less than the possession of all Syria (even perhaps on the hereditary basis he was demanding), while now the impossible Lord Palmerston was asserting that he should be allowed the hereditary possession of Egypt only and be compelled to restore the Turkish fleet. The Czar, appreciating perfectly well that here was a unique opportunity to prise apart the Anglo-French entente, lent the support of Russia to Palmerston's proposals, and the slightest hint of Louis-Philippe and Soult weakening in support of Mehemet Ali was enough to cause violent chauvinistic clamour in the French press. The perspicacious French ambassador at Vienna, Saint-Aulaire, saw disaster to be imminent and demanded: "Must we quarrel with all our allies over Mehemet Ali? That man is France's evil genius." But Louis-Philippe not only shared in the general over-estimation of the "new Alexander", who had given Egypt 38,000 water-wheels, but pointed out that if the conditions imposed on the Pasha were too severe he might march on Constantinople, which in turn might lead Russia to precipitate a general war. Palmerston was not without his difficulties in that there was a strong Francophil element in the cabinet,[1] but after Nicholas' special envoy, Baron Brunnow, had been to London in September, Soult was offered as a maximum concession for Mehemet Ali Egypt and the hereditary pashalik of Acre, except the fortress itself, provided France would join in coercing the Pasha, if he made difficulties. As things turned out, the French should have accepted this offer and they would never again have so good an oppor-

[1] Notably Holland, Clarendon and Russell.

tunity of extricating themselves with comparative dignity from a position which was to become less and less tenable. When they in fact turned the offer down, convinced wrongly that an Anglo-Russian alliance was too unnatural to endure, Palmerston immediately withdrew the offer of Acre and henceforth planned his campaign with the primary object of isolating and mortifying France. By the end of 1839 Soult was writing to Sébastiani "they want to smash the Anglo-French alliance, to which Europe owes ten years of peace" and, although Louis-Philippe was becoming distinctly worried, the new parliamentary session was about to open and public opinion was adamant against any concessions.

As might have been foreseen, the politicians chose this perilous moment to bring down the ministry. Almost everybody seemed to be for a tough line over Syria, except Lamartine who was for a tough line on the Rhine, and as a result of a heavy vote of confidence the government was committed more deeply than ever to the support of Mehemet Ali, Soult telling the British government on January 26th that he thought "the proposal to impose Lord Palmerston's conditions on Mehemet Ali dangerous and impracticable". But by this time Thiers and Guizot had tired of the historical studies, which had engaged their enforced leisure during the summer,[1] and, whereas Guizot found himself appointed ambassador to the Court of Saint James's, Thiers was quite unable to resist engineering the overthrow of the government by six votes in February. The issue selected was a drearily familiar one – the proposal to vote a marriage settlement on the Duc de Nemours. Once again, de Cormenin, unabashed by his exposure three years earlier, produced a pamphlet – "Questions scandaleuses d'un Jacobin au sujet d'une dotation" – and once again there was an anti-monarchical hullabaloo in the press. Neither de Broglie nor Molé was prepared to step into the breach and Louis-Philippe had no option but to subject the country to another experience of Thiers. It was hardly calculated as an appointment to suit the exigencies of a particularly delicate international crisis. As Lord Melbourne observed: "He is a strange quicksilver man,

[1] Thiers began his history of the Consulate and Guizot his life of Washington.

this Thiers, he puts me in mind of Brougham." Lord Melbourne, it will be recalled, had no high opinion of Lord Brougham.

"I am signing tomorrow my own humiliation," said Louis-Philippe and when he was told that Thiers was having difficulty in finding a finance minister he said: "That won't be difficult; let M. Thiers present me if he wishes with one of the doorkeepers at the ministry; I am quite resigned to that." However, he over-came his not unjustifiable resentment and the new Minister of the Interior, the Doctrinaire de Rémusat, wrote to Guizot on March 13th: "The King treats us perfectly well and lends us real support." It was very much a patchwork cabinet – two ministries were held by Doctrinaires, three by obscure figures of the Left-Centre, and there was even an under-secretary from Barrot's dynastic Left. Nor was there any likelihood of a stable majority, unless Thiers himself, who was in charge of foreign affairs as well as being Prime Minister, could create one on the basis of a per-sonal triumph, which in the circumstances was not going to be easy. It was, of course, always possible for the Prime Minister to give encouraging and intimate interviews to left-wing journalists while he was shaving and to proclaim: "I am a child of this revolution. I am the humblest of the children of the revolu-tion . . .", but Guizot made it clear he would only stay in London if there were no dissolution and no move towards electoral reform, and Thiers had thus to placate his right-wing supporters by making it clear that electoral reform was an issue "for the future". But to many this particular future was beginning to appear unduly delayed. On May 14th the great astronomer François Arago made a long and impressive speech, in which he declared that in his opinion universal suffrage was desirable not only in itself but because it was the necessary prelude to socialism. The scientist turned political radical is a commonplace of our times, but Arago's learned reputation lent added force to his pro-phetic words: "In Turgot's day the principle of *laisser-faire* and *laisser-passer* represented real progress. This principle is now out-worn and indeed vicious in the presence of the powerful machines, which have been created by man's intelligence. If you do not modify this principle we will see in our country great evils and great misery." The principles of the eighteenth-century Enlightenment in which Louis-Philippe had grown up were under heavy fire now and he, the last of the Enlightened Despots, the crowned Jacobin, was fast becoming an anachronism. Electoral and social reform were becoming two linked causes and their supporters that spring were busy organizing banquets at which to popularize their theories, a device which the Conservative bourgeoisie would one day learn to be not quite so harmless as it appeared.[1] The newspaper war was intensified when Thiers, as a concession to his supporters on the Left, allowed Armand Marrast to return to France and take over the editorship of *Le National* which had languished since the death of Carrel. Marrast had learned caution during the years of exile in England, which had followed his escape from Sainte-Pélagie in 1835, and, avoiding the excesses which had led to the demise of *La Tribune*, he set himself to educate his readers in the virtues of republicanism. He did it well enough to find himself eight years later President of the Constituent Assembly of a new French Republic.

Just as in 1836, Thiers displayed prodigious virtuosity in endeavouring to persuade mutually irreconcilable factions that he was their man.[2] But in due course it became necessary to do something – and preferably something theatrically effective. So, reviving an old project which had been pigeon-holed since 1834,[3] he announced on May 12th that with the concurrence of the English government the Prince de Joinville would embark for Saint-Helena in his frigate and return with the ashes of the great Napoleon, which would be ceremoniously interred in the Invalides. The trick worked splendidly to begin with, though a speech by Lamartine in which he pointed out that it was perhaps not particularly wise to blow on the sparks of ashes which were

[1] The Minister of the Interior, de Rémusat, used his discretionary powers to ban a large banquet due to be held on July 14th.
[2] Heinrich Heine commented: "This man knows everything; it's a pity he hasn't studied German philosophy; he could have explained even that."
[3] In 1830 the Chamber had rejected the idea and Victor Hugo lamented: "Dors, nous t'irons chercher! Ce jour viendra peut-être!"

not yet extinct had a dampening effect on a proposed public subscription. But France was feeling warlike over Mehemet Ali and Louis-Philippe was indulgent about a project which seemed likely to appease the national desire for glory without any attendant risk of actual war. Nobody gave much thought to Prince Louis-Napoleon Bonaparte who reissued in London his pamphlet of 1839, *Des Idées Napoléoniennes*, with a new foreword pointing out that "it is not only the ashes but the ideas of the Emperor which must be brought back". On July 7th Joinville set sail in *La Belle Poule*, complaining that while his elder brothers were allowed to win glory in Algeria he had to act as an undertaker. Before he returned, Louis-Napoleon had left England to invade France.

III

Lord Palmerston had assented to the return of the ashes with his usual imperturbable good humour, but he had other and more important matters in hand, which he proposed to conceal from Guizot, who was acting in London rather unwillingly as Thiers' agent. The very day the Chamber adjourned, July 15th, it was learnt that Great Britain, Russia, Austria and Prussia had signed a treaty pledging themselves jointly to settle the Eastern Question without reference to France. Furthermore, the terms of the treaty required Mehemet Ali within a stipulated period of ten days to accept a settlement whereby he remained hereditary ruler of Egypt, but was granted only southern Syria with the pashalik of Acre for life. If he did not accept this within ten days, the offer of Acre would be withdrawn; and if he did not submit within a period of another ten days after that, the Sultan would be at liberty to withdraw even the hereditary government of Egypt. The news was a shattering blow to French national self-esteem and it comes as something of a surprise that two such astute politicians as Louis-Philippe and Thiers were as surprised as any-one else, despite several warning signals transmitted from Guizot in London. A glance behind the diplomatic scene during Thiers' ministry will serve, however, to indicate the causes of so serious a miscalculation. A fortnight before Thiers took office, Brunnow wrote to Saint-Petersburg: "The best course for our plans is not to conclude, but to let negotiations drag on; the greater the delay, the more painful will be the relations between France and England." Those relations were in fact bound to become strained, because of a fundamental difference of outlook on the whole situation. Louis-Philippe and Thiers believed that a close alliance between the Whig party and the Czar was too unnatural to endure, and that Mehemet Ali would be strong enough to secure what he wanted directly from Constantinople. Palmerston, on the other hand, believed that he could continue to manage the Russians, that Syria was essential to a strong Turkey, that Mehemet Ali was an impostor[1] and that in the last resort France would not be prepared to take on all Europe in arms for his sake. Thiers, sublimely confident of the outcome and happily aware that public opinion was behind him, twice rejected suggestions based on a partition of Mehemet Ali's conquests. By June energetic French representations in Constantinople resulted in the overthrow of the Russophil Grand Vizier. This prompted Palmerston to react quickly and effectively. Overcoming the hesitations of Lord Melbourne by suggesting that the Ottoman Empire was about to be divided into two halves, one a satellite of Russia and the other a satellite of France, he profited by a revolt of the Syrians against Ibrahim, which had been carefully brewed up by English agents, to send Admiral Stopford to the scene of the proceedings.[2] It was something of an achievement for a Foreign Secretary, who had once said: "No man in this House attaches greater value than I do myself to the intimate alliance of Great Britain and France."

Paris rang with cries of *"perfide Albion"* and *"à bas les Anglais!"* and for two months the populace was in the grip of a war-fever from which only the Legitimists were exempt. Louis-Philippe was initially very angry. "For ten years I have been the dyke against the revolution," he shouted so loud that Marie-Amélie had to shut his study door, "and this at the expense of my popularity and my peace of mind, even at the risk of my life. They owe to me the peace of Europe, the security of their thrones and this is how they thank me! Are they absolutely determined to make me wear the *bonnet rouge*?" "You are devoid of gratitude," he told the ambassadors. "But this time don't think I'm going to be separated from my ministry and my country. You want war and you shall have it and if necessary I will unmuzzle the tiger.

[1] He called him "that aged afrancesado freebooter".
[2] Clarendon and Holland dissented from the rest of the Cabinet and Palmerston had to threaten resignation.

He knows me and I know how to play with him. You'll see if he will respect you as he does me." Orléans was even more aggressive, pointing out that he would prefer to die on the banks of the Rhine than in a gutter of the Rue Saint-Denis, an observation which was lent some colour by the prevalent unity of patriotic and revolutionary emotion. Many thought, perhaps with justice, that the French Mediterranean fleet could win at least one battle with their ancient enemies. As for Thiers, he remained convinced that Mehemet Ali could not be coerced and would in all probability march on Constantinople. In that event, if the allies came to the rescue of the Turks, the French must throw an army across the Alps into Austrian Italy. But by the end of July, as Thiers was calling up the classes of 1836 to 1839, the old King recovered his usual caution. He told Saint-Aulaire in a private audience: "For your personal guidance you must be aware that I will not allow myself to be carried too far by my little minister. Basically he wants war and I don't; and if he leaves me no alternative I will break him rather than break with all Europe." But for the moment it was as well to use the opportunity for building up French defences, to await developments in Syria and by maintaining a warlike posture not to allow Thiers to pose as a martyr sacrificed on the altar of the notorious royal pacifism. As Bulwer wrote to Palmerston from Paris: "The position of the King and the Minister is most curious. Playing the game together as partners, each is jealous of the cards and skill of the other and afraid that he will find some means of pocketing the whole of the stake which should be divided between them." Palmerston knew his man and wrote to Granville, the British ambassador in Paris, in August: "He is far too prudent to meddle in such a hornets' nest."

Before the climax was reached there was a diversion from an unexpected quarter. On August 6th Louis-Napoleon landed at Wimereux in the *Edinburgh Castle* with fifty followers, nine horses and two carriages, some chests of muskets, batches of proclamations and a tame eagle bought in Gravesend. The proceedings lasted only an hour longer than they had at Strasbourg, before the regulars and the National Guard rounded up the whole expedition on the beach. Recidivism of this sort could not now be overlooked. While Louis-Napoleon was transferred from the fortress of Ham to the cell in the Conciergerie, formerly occupied by Fieschi, arrangements were made for his trial before the Peers and Louis-Philippe paid a state visit to Boulogne to thank the army and the National Guard.[1] On October 6th the pretender was sentenced to perpetual emprisonment in a French fortress, but not before Berryer in defending him had used all his eloquence to vilify the July Monarchy and Louis-Napoleon had gone some way to belie his own gloomy and uninspiring appearance by a spirited defence of his antecedents and aspirations. It was scarcely an opportune prelude to the return of the ashes, although for the moment it aroused comparatively little public interest.

Meanwhile, Thiers was observed lying on his stomach sticking blue and green pins into maps of Italy, just as Napoleon had done. The army was considerably increased, the fortification of Paris set in hand and M. de Tocqueville was showing himself to be unexpectedly bellicose. There were more reform banquets, a series of strikes which, despite their illegality the authorities refrained from suppressing, and a good deal of public discussion of the theories of M. Louis Blanc, a dwarf-like figure described as having "the quick and fiery glance of a Spaniard and a sonorous voice", who the year before had produced a little book called *L'organization du travail* which as well as preaching the virtues of collectivism had a chapter entitled "Free Competition necessarily ends in a life and death struggle between France and England". Guizot reflected gloomily that it only needed an English sailor to bump into a French one for "the most terrible war the world has seen to break out".

It was the prophecy of Palmerston and not that of Thiers which was fulfilled. As Commodore Napier was patrolling the Syrian

---

[1] As far back as December 1830, the Boulonnais had sent a loyal address to Louis-Philippe, proclaiming that he would always find them "above all in the hour of danger at the head of your most faithful subjects" (Archive Nationales F 1c I. 32).

coast and inviting the inhabitants to revolt against Ibrahim, the Turks presented Mehemet Ali with the ultimatum of the Quadruple Alliance, only to be told that what had been acquired by the sword would only be relinquished at the sword's point. The Pasha had second thoughts, it is true, and under French pressure[1] tried to bargain his way out of his dilemma, only to find the Turkish attitude stiffened by the intervention of Ponsonby. Palmerston at this juncture suggested to Bulwer, the chargé d'affaires in Paris, that it would be as well to let Thiers know, amiably and inoffensively, that in the event of war France would lose her fleet, her colonies and her commerce and Mehemet Ali would "just be chucked into the Nile". He had endless difficulties with Melbourne, with the cabinet, with Leopold of the Belgians, even with the Queen,[2] but he knew he had won when on September 11th Napier bombarded Beirut and Ibrahim's allegedly invincible army remained supine on the heights above the town. By November 2nd the fortress of Acre had fallen and although *Le National* was urging a march on the Rhine and all Germany was singing "Sie sollen nicht ihn haben, den freien deutschen Rheim", Louis-Philippe had finally realized that Mehemet Ali was a broken reed and that Thiers must go. The decision was taken to recall the Chambers for October 28th. Thiers realized that the old *parti de la résistance* was about to reassert itself with a unity it had never known since 1831 to repel the combined spectre of war and revolution and expostulated to the King: "But the Chambers, that means peace!" Louis-Philippe did not contradict him.

As the King drove along the Quai des Tuileries on October 15th his carriage was suddenly enveloped in a cloud of smoke. A man at the foot of a lamp-post had just discharged an overloaded firearm which had burst and wounded him in the hand. When the culprit, Darmès, a destitute and evil-living floor-polisher, was

---

[1] From Walewski, Napoleon I's grandson and Napoleon III's foreign minister.
[2] Who, being enceinte, was far from anxious for a war at this particular juncture.

asked his profession, he replied: "Exterminator of tyrants" and when asked if he repented he said: "I only repent for not having succeeded." In 1870 there was to be no one prepared to discountenance the cries of "*à Berlin!*" But now, thirty years earlier, Louis-Philippe struck out a belligerent passage in the draft copy produced by de Rémusat of the speech from the throne, accepted Thiers' resignation, summoned Guizot back from London and, writing to Dupin that he appreciated that the newspapers would be very angry, concluded: "Never mind. My conscience is clear that I am being true to my royal oath in devoting myself to preserving France from a war which in my opinion would be without either cause or object and consequently without justification in the eyes of God or man. I will no more yield to the factious clamour to which people try to subject us than I will to the bullets of assassins." Lord Palmerston had won and would make sure everyone knew it, in case "the French nation would believe that we gave way to their menaces, and not to the entreaties of Louis-Philippe".

IV

It was not until the elections of 1842 that it began to dawn on both Louis-Philippe and the nation at large that the discomfiture of Thiers and Guizot's assumption of effective power in the new cabinet, nominally headed by Soult, had introduced an entirely new factor of stability and permanence into the troubled history of the parliamentary monarchy. Louis-Philippe was under no illusions about the sombre outlook both in Paris and abroad, but he soon came to realize that in Guizot he had acquired the greatest parliamentary manager of the age and not merely a transient politician, conceivably capable of liquidating a diplomatic bankruptcy. At the age of sixty-six, after surviving twenty-one years of exile and six attempted assassinations, the old King had become set in his ways, both public and private. His political outlook was by now confined to three almost obsessive principles – the establishment of his dynasty, the maintenance of European peace and the suppression of the revolution. That such a programme had its limitations was obvious not only to frustrated Utopians, those of whom Guizot wrote "they yearn for events, immense, sudden and strange; they busy themselves with making and unmaking governments, nations, religions, society, Europe, the world". Louis-Philippe's own heir, the Duc d'Orléans, confided to the painter Scheffer in 1840: "the present epoch is prosperous and peaceful, but it is too dull not to become soon stagnant and consequently corrupt; innumerable vulgar and mean little interests seethe under an apparently united surface which can perhaps only be disturbed by the most violent upheavals." Hugo's criticism of Louis-Philippe as being "excellent at making the smallness of day-to-day realities an obstacle to the immensity of ideas" was equally applicable to Guizot. Both of them were aware that nothing could ultimately check the momentum of the democratic movement. Both saw it as their duty to contain and harness the tide. "Property, family and all the bases of society are attacked everywhere," wrote Guizot – "they must everywhere be vigorously defended." There was indeed much to defend, enough to elicit a grudging tribute from Stendhal in 1838: "I do not know how to find prudent terms to describe the growing prosperity which France has been enjoying under Louis-Philippe; I fear to appear as a hireling. I see at every step builders at work; very many houses are being built in towns, in boroughs, in villages . . . in the fields you see on all sides hedging and ditching being carried out and walls being erected." For the seventy-five per cent of the population which lived and worked in the villages and fields, more and more of them owning their own land, there seemed no pressing need to overturn society.[1] To the workers of Paris and Lyons, as we have seen, things looked very different, but it was not difficult for employers of industry to argue that new machines and new processes were bound in the end to alleviate the lot of the workers, even if there would inevitably be a transitional period of distress in doomed industries like that of the handloom weaver. Above all there must be no departure from the great liberal orthodoxy through any attempt, except in dire emergencies, to interfere in existing relations between capital and labour. For the *haute bourgeoisie*, whom Balzac and Flaubert caricatured as Philipon caricatured Louis-Philippe, thrift and enterprise commended themselves as alike personal and public virtues. If one became rich, all would be added – power, social prestige and even the right to vote like-minded men into the Chamber of Deputies. Here, in the railway age, was the true significance of the *carrière ouverte aux talents*. Guizot spoke for his natural supporters when he wrote: "Some by their intelligence and good conduct create for themselves capital and enter the road of ease and progress. Others, without proper vision, lacking moderation or lazy, remain in their light and precarious condition based exclusively on wage-earning."

Louis-Philippe was, of course, not ill-adapted by nature and

[1] See J. L. Talmon, *Political Messianism – The Romantic Phase*, pp. 344–6.

usage to preside over the destinies of a ruling class of successful businessmen, though they continued to grumble at him whenever anything went wrong. An American visitor to the Tuileries in 1840, General Lewis Cass, described him as follows: "The King is now about sixty-six years of age. His constitution, however, is vigorous and there are no marks of declining years about him. His frame is large, but there is much ease in his movements and his whole carriage is marked by that happy address, which good taste and the polished society where he has moved have enabled him to acquire. He is very ready in conversation and displays great tact and judgement in his observations." There is almost complete unanimity amongst those who knew him well, whether admirers or critics, that this famous readiness in conversation was anything but tedious.[1] Indeed, it could be decidedly pointed. When told of the death of Talleyrand, Louis-Philippe asked: "Are you quite sure he's dead? Because with Talleyrand one must never judge by appearances and I ask myself what interest he can have in dying at this particular moment." Like all extreme extroverts he was fascinated by the vices and foibles of other human beings and enjoyed reading secret police reports. One day in 1840 Thiers was unaccountably missing from an important session of the cabinet. The King laughingly indicated that a visit to a certain specified number in the Rue Vaugirard might prove profitable. The house indicated was a very large building and the emissary was in some doubt as to which floor was likely to be occupied by M. Thiers' hostess. A stentorian shout of "Adolphe! Adolphe!" duly produced the startled apparition at a third floor window of the Prime Minister in spectacles and very considerable undress. Half an hour later at the Tuileries Thiers was greeted by

[1] De Tocqueville is something of an exception, although even he admits that though the royal conversation was "prolix and diffused . . . it gave all satisfaction which one may find in intellectual pleasures where delicacy and elevation are absent". It may perhaps be surmised that both of them were experts in monologue – it is certain that on one occasion Louis-Philippe preferred to talk himself about America than to listen to de Tocqueville on that inexhaustible topic, though no doubt he thereby missed a discourse of great delicacy and elevation.

the King with the words, "You are late, Prime Minister." "I must apologize, Your Majesty, but I was preparing myself." "I am sorry to have upset your preparations," replied the King laughingly, whereupon the cabinet addressed itself in some confusion to the immediate agenda. Invariably affable, unpretentious and entirely devoid of the dignified but vacuous impersonality which is so often characteristic of high breeding unless allied to high intelligence, he yet managed to convey an impression of genuine majesty. Hugo described him as combining something of Charlemagne and something of a country solicitor.[1] There was in all probability a good deal that was studied in all this, in that it conformed so exactly to the exigencies of his peculiar position, but it was firmly enough grounded in the man's nature, in his genuine kindliness, in his unremitting devotion to his duty and in the stability, simplicity and happiness of his remarkable family life.

The basic routine for the royal family and their visitors at the Tuileries as it remained for many years is described in a letter from Leopold of the Belgians to the future Queen Victoria in November 1835:

> I shall begin with the breakfast which is ten o'clock, then, all unite as they would do for a dinner which in reality it is. After the breakfast the company adjourns to the inner salon where the ladies sit round a large table and work and talk. The King generally does not assist at the breakfast . . . At six precisely we return to the Pavillon de Flore for dinner which takes place in the Galerie de Diane, a fine long room furnished and painted by command of Catherine de Medici. Dinner lasts about an hour and a half as it is almost always numerous. After that there are constant arrivals in the salon of all sorts of people . . . by regular entrée or by appointment. When we do not go to the play we remain till after ten at the salon which is a constant circle and as such rather fatiguing for my poor mother-in-law.[2]

Within the framework of the life of a palace, which was more an open house than a court, Louis-Philippe's immensely long

---

[1] See the interesting historical excursus *Quelques Pages d'Histoire* in Part IV of *Les Misérables*.   [2] Royal Archives Y/6/27.

15. As Duc de Chartres

16. A cartoon by Daumier.   The caption reads:
Tiens peuple, tiens bon peuple, en veux-tu, en voilà

working-day had of necessity to follow a precise pattern. He rose at seven, winter and summer, lit his own fire, shaved himself, and then Richard, his coiffeur, organized the celebrated wig. He then received the A.D.C. on duty for the day, the Controller of the Tuileries and Montalivet, Intendant of the Civil List. There followed a reading of *The Times* and other English papers, a predilection which, he once explained to one of his aides, arose from the fact that some of the French newspapers did nothing but blame his government and the others did nothing but praise it, and "therefore I have nothing to learn from them and would waste my time reading their more or less recreative lucubrations." He then breakfasted rapidly, invariably off boiled rice, an *échaudé*[1] and a glass of water. After chatting with the family he would usually go out, sometimes alone, but very often with his architect, Fontaine, who had served in the same capacity the Convention, the Directory, the Empire, Louis XVIII and Charles X. They would wander round the Louvre or the Palais-Royal or cross the river to the Ecole des Beaux-Arts. As a patron of the arts, his taste was totally vitiated by a passion for photographic verisimilitude, but his enthusiasm was boundless and large sums were allocated from the Civil List to museums, architects and painters, especially for the restoration and embellishment of Versailles, Saint-Cloud, Fontainebleau, Neuilly and the Palais-Royal.[2] Around midday he normally presided over a cabinet meeting and then talked it all over with Adélaïde, if not required to receive provincial delegations in the throne-room. If time permitted, he would then go for an outing, either by carriage to Saint-Cloud or on foot to Neuilly. At six he would return for dinner, which was restricted to the family only on Wednesdays and Fridays. He laid it down that no one should get up when he arrived and often

---

[1] The nearest Anglo-Saxon gastronomical equivalent is a waffle.

[2] He possessed 30,000 historical portrait engravings in several hundred volumes. Vatout, who was responsible for cataloguing them, had to mind his p's and q's, just as if he were a pupil at Reichenau. "Everyone has his own ideas of spelling. I believe one should write horison and not horizon. S between two vowels is pronounced like z, but here the s seems more in accord with etymology and is I believe justified by usage."

came in during the second course. He was usually brought four or five different soups, which he mixed up into a special potion of his own; then some roast meat, a few vegetables and finally a plate of macaroni and a glass of Spanish wine. But for those who liked it, there was plenty of good food and wine. Then followed the famous reception, at which with great ease and familiarity Louis-Philippe talked with his guests, who might range from members of the diplomatic corps, marshals and ministers to provincial mayors. By ten o'clock they all departed, the ladies of the family retired to their rooms and the young princes played billiards. The King would then go alone into his study and settle himself down till two or three in the morning to work on state papers and personal and public correspondence. In addition to his other preoccupations, he paid meticulous attention to anything connected with his prerogative of mercy. The number of his relations who had died on the scaffold had imprinted on him a deep hatred of the guillotine and like a true son of the Enlightenment he had read his Beccaria and annotated it in detail. One of his most deadly critics, Louis Blanc, felt impelled to testify to his humanity in these matters as follows: "He was more human than any prince of his time, because of his respect on principle for the inviolability of human life, by natural benevolence and by philosophy. Reared in the eighteenth-century school, admirer of Voltaire and a rationalist, he loved tolerance *un peu en esprit fort*, *un peu en bel esprit*. If his ministers had let him have his way, he would have eliminated the scaffold as Voltaire destroyed torture." Late one evening Montalivet, entering his study, found him bent over a notebook, of which several pages were already covered in his huge, spidery handwriting and asked him if he was composing his memoirs. "*Mon Dieu, non*," replied Louis-Philippe, "you see me occupied with something a great deal sadder. In this notebook I enter the names of criminals condemned to the death-penalty, those whom my prerogative of mercy has not been able to protect against my conscience or the decision of my ministers." Montalivet noticed an entry which read: "Alibaud, to my great regret." At last in the small hours he would make his way to his bedroom, where a lamp burned all night and two loaded pistols lay, ready for eventualities, beside a bed with a horse-hair mattress and a wooden plank.[1]

The treadmill of the monarchical existence was not endurable in the nineteenth any more than it is in the twentieth century, without a secure and happy domestic background, and here Louis-Philippe was immensely fortunate. Marie-Amélie consoled herself for a nerve-wracking existence in the care and contemplation of her children and on her knees in the church of Saint-Roch. As the years went on, her daughters disappeared one by one. Louise, Queen of the Belgians since 1832, highly intelligent, kindly and universally popular in her adopted country, remained a faithful correspondent of her father, to whom like the rest of his children she would refer as "*le père*", or even "*l'excellent père*";[2] Marie, a great beauty and a talented sculptress by the standards of the age, after a marriage lasting only two years to the large if unintelligent Duke Alexander of Württemberg, died of consumption at the age of twenty-six; the virtuous Clémentine, who married Prince Augustus of Saxe-Coburg-Gotha in 1843, was to become the mother of Ferdinand, King of Bulgaria.

A celebrated work of Louis-Philippe's favourite painter, Horace Vernet, depicts the King riding proudly on a white horse out of the Palace of Versailles with a cavalcade of his five handsome and gorgeously bedizened sons. Orléans, mounted on a rather restive chestnut, and Joinville are on his right, Nemours

[1] He wrote apologizing to Queen Victoria in May 1846 for a delay in replying to a letter: "Every day and I can honestly say every night I've been finding myself obliged to leave my sad desk without having been able to do what I've been nevertheless in a great hurry to do."

[2] e.g. in a letter written from Buckingham Palace to her mother in August 1843, when she was acting as intermediary between the two courts in connection with Queen Victoria's visit to Eu, she writes: "Victoria would rather see him as the *Père de famille* than as the King. You will appreciate the distinction. *L'excellent père* ought therefore to be natural, paternal, patriarchal and simple as he always is . . . But I would recommend prudence as and when *l'excellent père* shows signs of being carried away in conversation by the '*furia française*' [*sic*]. All the outbursts of vivacity to which *l'excellent père* is prone, despite the very contradictions they abound in which are a proof of his perfect sincerity are interpreted as falseness and calculation."

and Aumale on his left and the more boyish Montpensier a pace to the rear. They all inherited the intrepidity which had characterized their father's youth. Orléans saw active service at Antwerp in 1831 (where as the first bullet flew over his head he took off his hat and observed "one must be polite with new acquaintances"), and in Algeria between 1835 and 1840; Nemours was also at the siege of Antwerp and in the thick of the fighting in Algeria between 1836 and 1841; Aumale made his début in the field in Algeria at the age of eighteen in 1840; Joinville, the sailor of the family, as well as fighting as a soldier in Algeria, was on active service at sea off Mexico in 1838 and off Morocco in 1844;[1] Montpensier was wounded in Algeria in 1844 at the age of twenty. The uncertain fortunes of the French army in Algeria were at all times a major preoccupation of the July Monarchy. But from 1835 to very nearly the end of his reign Louis-Philippe's heartfelt pleasure in the genuine military exploits of his sons was mixed with periods of great anxiety for their personal safety. Except for a quiet period in 1838 and 1839, the possibility of a major disaster was never far distant from the autumn of 1830, when General Clausel celebrated his short-lived conquest of Medea with the order of the day: "Soldiers, the fires of your bivouacs, which from the peaks of the Atlas seem to mingle with the lights of the stars, announce the victory you have just won . . ." to the December day in 1847 when the elusive Abd-el-Kadr, in token of final surrender, ceremoniously handed over his favourite mare to the Duc d'Aumale. There is a sombrely prophetic note about some of the comments of the day on the Algerian problem. Marshal Bugeaud foresaw grimly: "it will cost us something to keep that barren soil"; and de Tocqueville considered, "there is no half-way house between evacuation and full dominion".

Orléans arrived in Algeria just after Trézel's horrible defeat in the defile of La Macta in 1835 and in Clausel's expedition of revenge to Mascara was heavily bruised in the thigh by a bullet. Nemours a week after his arrival in the theatre in October 1839, joined the

[1] In 1870, under an incognito, he served with d'Aurelle des Paladines on the Loire.

march to Constantine, where the French army was only saved from total annihilation by Changarnier's epic rear-guard action. He was a shy, haughty young man, who studiously shunned publicity and never shared the comparative popularity of his brothers, but was his father's favourite son. There is little doubt that he was a soldier of considerable merit. When General Damrémont set out in the autumn of 1837 for Constantine, Nemours commanded a brigade, Orléans having generously yielded place to him although he desperately wanted to take part. After riding alongside Damrémont and his chief of staff when both were killed by enemy bullets, he followed hard on the heels of Lamoricière and his Zouaves as they successfully assaulted the mountain fortress. In 1843 it would be Aumale's turn to distinguish himself in a decidedly rash but brilliant cavalry action, in which he raided and overthrew Abd-el-Kadr's *smala*, or mobile desert headquarters, and earned himself a lieutenant-generalcy. This dashing exploit particularly pleased Louis-Philippe and he wrote to Aumale: "I can tell you honestly that the nation and the army are electrified. I enclose three newspaper cuttings, whose articles seem to me the most striking; because on this occasion I have set aside my rule of not reading them." Aumale insisted on giving the royal family an Arab feast at Neuilly a few weeks after his return with roast sheep and conserves, but it was not much to his father's taste and elicited the observation: "Aumale, I prefer my own dinner. I am for civilization." The hero returned to Algeria and the anxious parent was soon urging him not to risk his reputation and end up like Charles XII at Poltawa, pointing out the dangers of assaulting strong mountain defensive positions, as witness the fate of the Austrians at Morgarten.

Algeria was a tragedy, for though the fighting there trained a good breed of officers like Changarnier, Lamoricière and above all Bugeaud, the lessons acquired were not applicable to even more deadly French battlefields in Europe in the years to come and the vacillations and contradictions of governmental policy contributed greatly to the instability of the régime. Louis-Philippe, steadfastly pacific in Europe, was inclined to regard Algeria as an opportunity to acquire on the cheap the military glory which so many of his critics vociferously demanded, though it should be remembered in partial extenuation that he could not conceivably have relinquished the sole military conquest of his predecessor, By the end of his reign over 100,000 European colons were established there,[1] very considerable trading profits having accrued to the mother country. Guizot, in one of his luminous moments of historical insight, told the English economist Nassau Senior in 1860: "Avarice, or rather cupidity, created the germ of your distant empire, vanity created ours; and the ignorance and perverseness of semi-barbarous neighbours may oblige us, as they obliged you, to extend it. Africa has given us good soldiers and India has given you good generals. There the advantages to the dominant countries end . . . In Algeria we have put an end to the civil wars of the tribes; we have made the country safe; we distribute impartial justice; its produce has enormously increased . . . Never was a conquered country more benefited by its conquest; yet it requires the constant presence of a French army . . ."

[1] Of which, however, less than half were Frenchmen.

V

The advent of the Soult-Guizot ministry of October 29th, 1840, was greeted by a rise in government securities and a notable diminution of bellicose utterances on both sides of the Channel. The Concert of Europe was slowly re-established, while the public interest was largely centred on the murder trial of Madame de Genlis' grand-daughter, Madame Lafarge, and the pompous but extremely chilly ceremony at the Invalides on December 15th when the great Napoleon's ashes were finally laid to rest. Palmerston continued to make as many difficulties as possible, but the Whig cabinet was on its last legs and France was duly included as a signatory to the Straits Convention of July 1841, whereby the Powers affirmed their "unanimous determination to conform to the ancient rule of the Ottoman Empire, by which the Straits must always be closed to foreign warships, so long as the Porte is at peace". Mehemet Ali was left with the hereditary possession of Egypt and nothing else. Palmerston added insult to a good many injuries by going out of his way to address his electors at Tiverton on the iniquity of French tactics in Algeria as compared with those of the British army in Afghanistan. The success of the Tories and the appearance of Aberdeen at the Foreign Office were not unnaturally therefore greeted with evident relief at the Tuileries. For the next five years Anglo-French relations were to be improved out of all recognition.

If the peace of Europe was for the moment assured, the prospects of constitutional monarchy in France remained fragile. The legitimist press sank to a lower level than ever in publishing three letters alleged to have been written by the King, in which he appeared to advocate the evacuation of Algeria, the extinction of Poland and the employment of the new fortifications of Paris for the suppression of Parisian insurgents. The letters had been purchased from a veteran prostitute called Eselina de Jongh, rejoicing in the pseudonym of Ida de Sainte-Elme, who in her palmy days had been associated with Ney and Moreau, but was now out of a job in London. Despite the blatant nature of the imposture, a jury acquitted the editor of *La France*, after Berryer had pleaded that he had acted in all good faith in accepting the letters for publication. In the summer of 1841 troubles beset the government thick and fast. An attempt to impose a stricter tax régime by checking evasion of the wine-duties and re-assessing the property-tax resulted in provincial rioting, notably at Toulouse. The death in June at an early age of Garnier-Pagès, the intelligent and respected leader of the extreme Left, led to the election of Ledru-Rollin. A young lawyer with an imposing bust and a stentorian voice, he saw himself consistently as a re-incarnation of Danton until his final discomfiture in June of 1849, when he had to flee the country because of the mistimed activities of rioters, whom he had incited for years, remarking characteristically: "I am their leader, I must follow them." He composed an election address, which attacked with the greatest violence nearly all the social and political institutions of the country, and was condemned to four months in prison. Before the outcry about this had subsided, the secret societies attempted another assassination. On September 13th the Duc d'Aumale rode into Paris at the head of his regiment, the 17th Light. Orléans and Nemours met the cortège to pay honour to the regimental colour, torn and blackened after seven years' continuous service in Algeria. As the cavalcade reached the Rue Saint-Antoine, Quénisset, a half-witted member of a society calling itself *Les Egalitaires*, fired a pistol almost point-blank at the three princes, killing the lieutenant-colonel's horse. The crowd, which had been applauding the cavalcade, were with difficulty prevented from lynching the culprit, who under interrogation confessed himself a communist and much influenced by the communist paper, *Le Journal du Peuple*. The obsession of his fellow-conspirators with the political philosophy current in 1793 was revealed by the fact that among the cries that were to be raised in the street if the attempt succeeded was: "Down with the accomplices of Dumouriez!" Since Quénisset declared that he had been "lost" by his persistent perusal of *Le Journal du Peuple*, it was perhaps not altogether unreasonable that its elegant and bejewelled editor, M. Dupoty, should be condemned for complicity by the Peers and sentenced to five years, but the government was on dangerous ground in utilizing the relevant article of the September Laws which classified serious press offences as treasonable. The outcry was such that these perfectly legal powers were not used again. When condemned to death, Quénisset was reprieved by Louis-Philippe.

Although Guizot was able to utilize all this evidence of continued social instability to build up his position amongst conservative elements in the Chamber, his majority remained precarious and he had to yield to a combination of factiousness and Anglophobia by refusing against his better judgement the ratification of an Anglo-French convention on the Right of Search to prevent slave-running. Peel observed, perhaps a little sententiously considering the comparative political background of the two countries: "Guizot makes lots of concessions to his friends, I only make them to my enemies." But that he was making a point of some substance was revealed in the crucially important debates of February 1842 on parliamentary and electoral reform, during which Louis-Philippe and Guizot adopted a fatally rigid position, from which, as long as they were associated, they felt themselves unable to withdraw. It was in a very real sense the point of no return for the monarchy and it is peculiarly instructive to analyse how it came about.

The reform proposals of the opposition were on the face of it eminently modest. It was proposed that the great majority of servants of the crown should not be eligible for election as deputies and that no deputy could accept an office of profit under the crown for the duration of his mandate and one year after;[1] and that the franchise should be slightly extended to include anyone eligible to sit on a jury. Support for these proposals

[1] In 1842 there were 149 salaried servants of the state among 459 deputies, but only 80 held posts dependent on the government in power.

came not only from the extreme and dynastic Left but from Thiers and the Left-Centre, despite the fact that Thiers, as we have seen, had repudiated reform as late as 1840.[1] Thiers' volte-face undoubtedly played its part in influencing Guizot and Louis-Philippe to see the proposals as nothing but a parliamentary manœuvre, calculated to catch votes at the forthcoming elections. But both of them were utterly averse to any reform calculated to call in question the legal and constitutional basis of the régime. Guizot accused the opposition of seeking "to alter the stability of power and the laws and sowing uncertainty everywhere." It was for him the first step on a road which would inevitably lead to universal suffrage and he proclaimed: "For my part I am a decided enemy of universal suffrage. I regard it as the ruin of democracy and liberty." This was, of course, a sound Whig principle, differing not even in force of expression from Macaulay's dictum that universal suffrage is "utterly incompatible with the existence of civilization". In his Memoirs Guizot makes much play of the fact that the electorate, 99,000 in 1830, had risen to 224,000 as a result of increased prosperity making for a higher number of eligibles. Furthermore, it was always his contention that the 200 franc elector represented perfectly the interests of the 100 franc elector, indeed of every intelligent man, anxious to stabilize and develop the achievements of 1830. "All the great conquests have been made, all the great interests are satisfied; our present dominant interest is to assure for ourselves the firm enjoyment of what we have conquered." Universal suffrage might in certain exceptional and temporary circumstances be suitable for bringing about great and fundamental social changes, but for the existing task of consolidating French society it was a thoroughly bad political instrument. Dufaure, on behalf of the dissident Conservatives, besought the ministry not to set its face against even the modest measures of reform suggested and Lamartine, hitherto a decided if unpredictable Conservative, rejoiced the opposition benches with a celebrated peroration, which ran: "It seems that the genius of politicians consists only in one thing, to

[1] See page 260 above.

rest secure in a situation afforded them by chance or a revolution and to stay there motionless, inert, implacable.... Yes, implacable against any improvement. And if that is, in effect, the entire genius of a statesman charged with the conduct of government, then there is no need for a statesman, since a boundary-stone would be perfectly sufficient." But Guizot had his majority and Louis-Philippe, approaching his seventieth year, was becoming more and more ready to equate the survival of his dynasty with the parliamentary prospects of a Prime Minister, who seemed armed against every contingency with an inexhaustible array of magisterial and peremptory political theory and a superb technique in debate. As Guizot proceeded to busy himself with the congenial task of bringing order and energy into the backward and financially chaotic French railways,[1] Thiers returned gloomily to his history books.

The elections in July of 1842 were on the whole quietly conducted, the opposition finding no more stirring electoral issue than the Right of Search. The first results from Paris indicated that ten seats out of twelve had been won by Left candidates of one complexion or another. But the provinces, as usual, restored the balance, just as they were to do in later elections under universal suffrage. In the event Soult and Guizot appeared to have a rather uncertain majority of seventy, whereupon Guizot wrote revealingly to a friend: "I don't despair of victory, but I'm tired of the fight. But don't worry, I'll act as if I weren't tired."

Before the election returns were in, Louis-Philippe suffered the cruellest personal calamity of his long life since the disgrace and execution of his father, as a result of the accidental death of his eldest son. On the morning of July 13th Orléans set out in a fast and very low phaeton drawn by two horses from the Tuileries to say good-bye to his father at Neuilly, before leaving to inspect

[1] By 1840 only 433 kilometres had been laid. By 1848 1,592 kilometres were usable and 2,144 more were being constructed. The financial solution adopted was a mixture of state ownership and private enterprise. In the middle of the debate on the bill, on May 8th, 1842, a very serious accident, costing 150 lives, took place on the Paris-Versailles line, which temporarily robbed the government of any credit for a far-seeing measure.

regiments at Saint-Omer. Near the Porte-Maillot the horse that the postillion was riding took fright and galloped. "Are your horses out of control?" shouted the Duke. "No, Monseigneur, but I am still driving them," came the reply. "But you can't hold them back?" asked the Duke, standing up in the carriage. On receiving the reply, "No, Monseigneur", Orléans jumped out of the carriage with his legs together and fell violently on the pavement, fracturing his skull. He was carried unconscious into a grocer's house just opposite Lord Seymour's stables.

Louis-Philippe, Marie-Amélie, Adélaïde and Clémentine were the first to arrive, shortly followed by other members of the royal family, but the Duchesse d'Orléans was far away at Plombières. On her knees by the couch of her dying son, Marie-Amélie wept frantically. The state dignitaries, who filed, one after the other, into the tiny room, observed Louis-Philippe standing motionless with his eyes fixed continually on the couch during the long slow hours of agony which elapsed before the end came mercifully at half-past four. The King and Queen embraced their dead son for the last time and four non-commissioned officers carried the corpse back to Neuilly on a stretcher, the royal family following on foot. A week later Louise of the Belgians, who had hurried to Neuilly on receiving the news, wrote to Queen Victoria:

My parents show great fortitude and resignation, but their hearts are for ever broke. They are only sustained by their feeling of duty. My poor mother bears up for my father, and my father bears up to fulfil his duties of father and of King. Their health is, thank God! good, and my father retains all his strength of mind and quickness of judgement; but they are both grown old in looks, and their hairs are turned quite white. The first days, my poor father could do nothing but sob, and it was really heartbreaking to see him. He begins now to have more command upon his grief, and the presence of your uncle,[1] whom he dearly loves, seems to do him good. The poor children are well and merry and seem unconscious of their dreadful loss . . .[2] The remainder of the family is, as you may easily

[1] Leopold.
[2] The Comte de Paris, born in 1838, and the Duc de Chartres, born in 1840.

imagine, in the *deepest affliction*. Nemours especially is quite broken
down with grief. Chartres was *more* than a *brother* to him, as he was
more than a second father to us all. He was the *head* and the *heart*
and the *soul* of the whole family. We all looked up to him, and we
found him on all occasions. A *better* or even *such* a brother was never
seen; our loss is as great as irreparable; but God's will be done! He
had surely His motives in sending on my unfortunate parents the
horrid affliction in their old days, and in removing from us the being
who seemed the *most necessary* to the hope and happiness of us all . . .
We expect on Saturday poor Joinville. My father will thus have his
four remaining sons round him for the opening of the Session, which
takes place on the 26th,[1] and at which he must preside in person.
It is a hard duty for him.

There was widespread mourning and grief in France and even
Lord Palmerston said that the death of Orléans was "a calamity
for France and for Europe". Something of the young prince's
aspirations for the future of the country and the dynasty can be
surmised from that section of his will, drawn up in 1840, in
which he laid down the principles which should govern the upbringing of his heir, the young Comte de Paris:

> To prepare the Comte de Paris for the destiny which awaits him
> is a great and difficult task; because no one can know at present
> what the prospects of this child are when it will be necessary to
> reconstruct on a new basis a society which rests today only on the
> mutilated and ill-assorted remnants of its previous forms of govern-
> ment. But whether the Comte de Paris turns out to be one of those
> instruments which are broken before they have begun to be of
> service or whether he becomes one of the artisans of that social
> regeneration which can at the moment only be glimpsed across the
> barrier of great obstacles and perhaps torrents of blood; whether he
> becomes King or whether he remains an unknown and obscure
> defender of a cause to which we all adhere, he must above and
> before all else be a man of his generation and of his country; he is
> to be a Catholic and a passionate and single-minded servant of
> France and of the Revolution.

[1] i.e. less than a fortnight after the accident.

This is clearly not the language of Guizot.[1] As Joinville pointed out sadly, for ten years all France had seen Orléans as the "*chef de demain*", the leader in the great days to come. Now the old King was seventy and Cuvillier-Fleury noticed that his eyes had lost their vivacity and that his cheeks had gone thin and hollow. His heir was a boy of four. "Providence is becoming furiously republican," said Béranger to Châteaubriand.

[1] Of whom Orléans had not been an admirer.

VI

The Charter of 1830 made no provision for a regency and a short-lived national unity, born of disaster, gave way rapidly to furious political wrangling about the respective claims of Nemours and the widowed Duchesse d'Orléans, which broadened into a more fundamental argument as to whether the regency was of right or elective. The King at the opening of the Session had difficulty in holding back his tears, but although he had learnt, as never before, to appreciate the courage and dignity of his daughter-in-law in those first weeks of her bereavement, he and Guizot were determined to secure the regency for Nemours. Thiers' support of a government, which he concluded over-optimistically to be in its death-throes, swayed the balance decisively, despite the opposition of Odilon Barrot. The consequent estrangement of Left-Centre and dynastic Left enabled Guizot to anticipate with greater confidence the next parliamentary session in January 1843, more especially as 1842 ended on a note of evident and widespread prosperity. During the prorogation between August and January, the government was hard at work, building up support among the more hesitant Conservatives by a process euphemistically known as "individual conquests". Guizot liked to hold himself aloof from personal participation in traffic of this sort, which is inseparable from parliamentary life conducted on a narrow franchise, leaving it in the competent hands of his *chef de cabinet*, Génie, and the Minister of the Interior, the Comte Duchâtel, a corpulent and cynical individual, who knew every man's price. It was said that one of Duchâtel's permanent officials unguardedly let out the remark: "We needed to gain about twenty votes and we gained them; but they cost us a lot." There was nothing particularly new about this – Molé, too, had regarded the prefects as electoral agents – but it consorted ill with Guizot's irritating and ostentatious high-mindedness.

The successive votes of confidence secured with unexpected smoothness at the opening of the new session by what the *Annual Register* of 1843 significantly called "the admirable government of which M. Guizot is the virtual head" were offset to some extent by a notable defection from the Conservative ranks in the person of Lamartine. Lamartine's estimate of himself as a politician appreciably exceeds that of posterity.[1] But he had a considerable talent for phrase-making, was not only a great poet, but looked the part, and could even convince himself, despite the chaos of his private finances, that he was an economic expert on railways and beet-sugar. According to Sainte-Beuve he replied to the allegation that he was distrusted by most of the eminent politicians of the day with the rejoinder: "What does it matter? I have on my side the women and the young people; I can do without the rest." [2] Neither Guizot nor the Chamber in general were much affected. Louis-Philippe was frankly impatient ("Don't speak to me of poets who get mixed up in politics") and one of Barrot's papers commented disrespectfully: "M. de Lamartine has come over with his baggage of poetic oratory into the ranks of the Left; he would like to be its chief, but the place is already occupied." However his reputation outside the Chamber, especially in intellectual circles, was considerable and France, which he had declared in 1839 to be "a nation which is bored", became increasingly addicted to his rather imprecise social romanticism.

Certainly the government's legislative record in 1843 was not inspiring, being concerned almost exclusively with beet-sugar, solicitors' deeds and traffic police. Guizot's attempt to achieve something constructive in foreign affairs by bringing about a Customs Union with Belgium foundered on the opposition of French heavy industrialists and the British Foreign Office. It was left to Louis-Philippe himself to play the central part in a notable

---

[1] His letters include the following phrases – "J'ai eu un grandissime succès" (June 1836); "you have no idea of the effect of my last speech at the tribune" (March 1837); "there has never been so marvellous a success at the tribune since the great debates of the Restoration" (April 1838); "I have just had a success of a sort I have never seen equalled since 1830" (1839).

[2] After all, Lady Hester Stanhope had picked him as a possible Messiah.

J'abdique cette couronne
que la voix nationale m'avait
appellée à porter, en faveur
de mon petit fils le Comte de
Paris. Puisse t'il réussir
dans la grande tâche qui lui
échoit aujourd'hui.

Louis Philippe

24 Fevr 1848

17. The Letter of Abdication

improvement in Anglo-French relations, amounting to what he himself continually referred to in speeches and letters as *une entente cordiale*. Early in the year relations were decidedly strained, despite the general goodwill of Peel and Aberdeen. As so often before, mutual suspicion existed between the two countries over Spanish affairs. The moderates, supporting Queen Cristina's regency, had been overthrown by a Liberal revolution in 1840 and the Liberal leader, General Espartero, having assumed the regency, Cristina fled to France. This state of affairs was only to endure for three years, but the crucially important long-term question was the eventual marriage of the child queen, Isabella. Court circles in Spain were at this stage known to favour the dashing Duc d'Aumale, but Louis-Philippe let it be known clearly that although he was determined Isabella should marry some Bourbon descendant, Spanish or Italian, of Philip V, he would not countenance her marriage into the French royal family, which would be all too likely to involve a new war of the Spanish Succession. Unfortunately, in 1841, the candidature was mooted of Prince Leopold of Saxe-Coburg, whose elder brother had been King of Portugal since 1836.[1] Whoever originally advanced this suggestion, a prince of that name was obviously a highly acceptable candidate at Windsor. In all the circumstances, it was not surprising that French opinion was highly sensitive to any suggestion of this sort. Louis-Philippe enjoyed contemplating his own moderation in successively refusing the Belgian crown for Nemours and the Spanish marriage for Aumale. Now to be confronted with a close relative of the English royal family at the court of Madrid was clearly intolerable and matters were not improved by cool remarks from Aberdeen and Metternich that since the Spaniards had every right to choose a husband for their own Queen, France was not in a position formally to exclude any candidate. A counter-revolution in July 1843 involving the disappearance of the "progressive" Espartero in a British ship suggested, however, to a Tory government that the prospects of

[1] His younger brother married Louis-Philippe's daughter Clémentine in 1843 and his sister was Duchesse de Nemours.

the Coburg candidate had "lost their best support",[1] and Aberdeen suggested to Guizot joint action to maintain some sort of equilibrium in Spain.

It was against this somewhat strained background that an announcement was made towards the end of August that Queen Victoria proposed to cruise off the southern coast of England and would like to take the opportunity of visiting the French royal family in residence at Eu in Normandy. The proposal was largely due to the Queen's own initiative, though the closeness of her relationships with two of Louis-Philippe's daughters, Louise of the Belgians and Clémentine, played its part.[2] Louis-Philippe was in ecstasies at the prospect of a ruling sovereign of Britain at last emulating Henry VIII at the Field of the Cloth of Gold and hurriedly ordered sixty new beds to be despatched from Neuilly. At a quarter past five on the afternoon of September 2nd the firing of guns announced the arrival at Tréport of the steam-yacht *Victoria and Albert*, under the command of Lord Adolphus Fitzclarence, son of William IV and Mrs Jordan. Louis-Philippe set out with his entourage in a whaleboat propelled by 24 oarsmen in scarlet belts, leapt aboard the yacht with an agility which reminded an observer of an elderly pirate and warmly embraced the blushing young queen. The Château d'Eu, the favourite residence of the old Duc de Bourbon-Penthièvre, and formerly a possession of the Guises, made an attractive setting for a five-day meeting, which turned out to be a triumphant success. The Queen's letters and diary make it perfectly clear that she enjoyed herself thoroughly from the day she landed in purple satin and an ostrich feather to what she called "the sad moment" of her departure. It was all so very friendly and not at all exotic – "The countryside reminds me of Brighton, but the houses and people are different"; "the King's gaiety and vivacity charm and amuse

[1] The wording of a despatch from Cowley, the British ambassador, to Guizot.

[2] Leopold, for example, wrote to Queen Victoria: "Personal contact will remove some impressions on the subject of the King which are really untrue. Particularly the attempt of representing him as the most astute of men, calculating constantly everything to deceive people."

me"; "I do like these dear people and feel so gay and so happy in their company". The first evening there was dinner for forty with Louis-Philippe dressed as a general; on the 4th there was a picnic in the forest with a splendid cold collation and forty carafes of wine; on the 5th Louis-Philippe took the Queen for a tour of the gardens and, offering her a peach, solved her embarrassment about eating it by drawing a large pen-knife out of his pocket, observing: "When one has been like me a poor devil living on forty sous a day one always carries a knife in one's pocket". That evening Louise of the Belgians set off a general fit of royal giggles during a horn solo, forming part of a concert arranged by Auber. On the 6th there was a fork-luncheon in the forest; and as they sailed away on the 7th, Albert and Victoria enjoyed the indiscreet company of Joinville, who accompanied them back across the Channel.

It had all been a far cry from Twickenham days. But a fatal imprecision in the political discussions between Guizot and Aberdeen, which accompanied the royal festivities, was eventually to undo all the good work. Aberdeen after a long interview with Louis-Philippe expressed himself as "content with the views and political intentions developed by the King, especially on the subject of Spain" and "struck with the abundance of his ideas and memories, of the rightness and freedom of his judgement, with the natural vivacity and gaiety of his language". But although everything seemed perfectly harmonious, the Coburg candidate was not explicitly ruled out, out of deference to the principle of allowing the Spaniards an unfettered freedom of choice, and although Guizot told Aberdeen that "the appearance of the Prince of Coburg would entail the resurrection of the Duc d'Aumale", no engagement was entered into of sufficient strength to bind Lord Palmerston in days to come. But this particular difficulty lay ahead and for the moment public opinion in France seemed generally disposed to view the entente favourably.

The Duc de Bordeaux, grandson of Charles X, now twenty-three, chose this moment to visit London and the hope was entertained in legitimist circles that he would be received by Queen Victoria.

At a hint from the Tuileries, Aberdeen wrote: "The Queen doesn't want to see the prince and as for me I would take the responsibility of advising her not to." The concern of Guizot and Louis-Philippe arose from the fact that large numbers of Legitimists, including Châteaubriand, had gone over to London on what they called a pilgrimage to present their duty to the Duc de Bordeaux in Belgrave Square. They were noisy and ostentatious and Greville recorded that at their arrival: "the town has ever since swarmed with monstrous beards of every cut and colour." On November 29th the Duc de Fitzjames delivered an address to "his King" amid shouts of "*Vive Henri V!*"

The government's wisest course would have been to ignore this pantomime. But Louis-Philippe took it violently amiss that amongst the "pilgrims of Belgrave Square" were two peers and five deputies, who had of course taken oaths of loyalty to him. Consequently, somewhat overconfident after their triumph at Eu, the King and Guizot not only made so effusive a reference to the entente in the speech from the throne that Thiers was able to stigmatize it as unfitting to the dignity of the nation, but proceeded to madden the Legitimists by attacking them on the Belgrave Square episode. A furious debate developed over a sentence in the draft of the address – "the public conscience utterly condemns guilty demonstrations." The Legitimists pretended that "utterly condemns"[1] was excessively strong language and the Left were perfectly happy to use even as thin a stick as this with which to beat Guizot. It was a classic demonstration of the unity in pure, unconstructive factiousness of extreme Right and extreme Left, the phenomenon which emerged in the 1846 elections and was known to the government as Carlo-republicanism. Guizot's visit to Louis XVIII in exile at Ghent during the Hundred Days was seized on as the central issue in an incredible demonstration. "If we can't conquer Guizot we must tire him out" observed one deputy. For an hour and a half he defended himself at the tribune, for a long time being unable to proceed further than the single sentence, "Yes, I went to Ghent", which was

[1] The French word, thus inadequately translated, is *flétrir*.

greeted with howls and cat-calls. Once he obtained a hearing, he summed up the irresponsibility of the opposition in the words: "You have never been able to establish either power or liberty. You have in fact always destroyed both power and liberty", and, utterly exhausted, he finally left the tribune with a last withering glance of disdain at his enemies and the characteristic phrase: "And as for insults, calumnies and demonstrations of bad temper, you may repeat them and heap them up to your hearts' content, but they will never rise to the level of my contempt."[1] Guizot was master of the parliamentary battlefield and for Louis-Philippe that was enough. But a victory in the Palais-Bourbon was not necessarily a victory in the country and it was highly significant that, when the five Belgrave Square deputies, having resigned their seats, submitted themselves for re-election, all five were successful as a result of the combined voting strength of Legitimists and Republicans.

[1] Disraeli's friend, George Smythe, described Guizot as "transcendentally bumptious".

VII

On March 18th, 1844, Louis-Philippe wrote to Guizot: "My dear Minister, fifty-one years ago today I was at the battle of Neerwinden. At this precise moment, it was going well; an hour later, it was completely lost. That was worse than this. Thank God, we have only to sustain battles for peace and that's in every way a better trade, although often it's no gentler." It has been said that most men in their lifetime go through three discernible stages – an angry youth, a complacent and confident middle period, and a defeated old age. Louis-Philippe had by now traversed the first two stages and although not yet defeated, he was an old man, and old age was accentuating certain aspects of his character – the curious, self-defeating combination of prudence and uncontrolled loquacity and his notorious tendency to try and outflank or postpone a problem which required confronting directly. He was by now won over, heart and soul, by Guizot's personal ascendancy, in which he saw the possibility of realizing his one remaining ambition – to end his days securely and at peace. "My dear Minister, you will die like me in harness" was the expression of his dearest wish, but a sadly inaccurate prophesy. He gave way increasingly to moods of depression and defeatism, but consoled himself with the contemplation of Guizot's steadfast domination of the political scene. "A liberal government faced with absolutist traditions is very difficult; it needs liberal conservatives and there are not enough of them. You are the last of the Romans."

Until the year 1846 when dangerous storm-signals began to appear, there seemed on the whole some justification for what Guizot described as "my habit of optimism and hope". Since the opposition made no attempt to preserve even a semblance of what we would now call a bi-partisan policy in foreign affairs, both the Chamber and public opinion were disproportionately concerned with the ups and downs of Anglo-French relations. The year 1844 witnessed an almost continuous state of crisis between the two countries, because of two simultaneous disputes, which broke out in Tahiti and Morocco.

The Tahiti affair involved a dashing French admiral, Dupetit-Thouars, Pomare, the Queen of that island paradise, and a truculent Birmingham missionary called George Pritchard. The chain of events was so grotesque that it is surprising, in view of the advantageous setting, that the story has not suggested itself as a scenario for musical comedy. Dupetit-Thouars had annexed the Marquesas Islands for the July Monarchy in 1838 and in September 1842 persuaded Queen Pomare that she would do well to place Tahiti under the protection of the tricolour. In so doing he reckoned without the redoubtable Pritchard who, although absent on leave at the crucial moment, normally acted as British consul and, if one is not to discount the anti-Protestant bias of the Admiral, as the Queen's lover, chaplain, *accoucheur* and Home Secretary. Pritchard's evangelical zeal soon succeeded in indoctrinating the natives against Romish practices and the Admiral, entirely on his own initiative, proceeded to land sailors and annex the island in November 1843. The news reached France in February 1844 and Guizot, strongly supported by Louis-Philippe, rapidly disclaimed the annexation. All would have been well had not the natives proceeded to attack and disarm a French sentinel in March, whereupon the French authorities on the island bundled Pritchard most unceremoniously into gaol and then sent him home to England via Valparaiso.

The news of what Sir Robert Peel called "a gross outrage coupled with gross indignity" reached both governments in July at a moment of maximum tension over Morocco, across the frontiers of which Bugeaud had driven France's redoubtable enemy in Algeria, Abd-el-Kadr. The Moroccans had not only given Abd-el-Kadr a safe refuge but had set up on the frontier the apparatus of what looked uncomfortably like a Holy War and were continually mounting raids into French territory. On June 12th Guizot issued an ultimatum to the Moroccans and

Joinville was put in command of a fleet of twenty-eight warships and ordered to cruise off the Moroccan coast. To most English opinion all this looked very much like the prelude to a full-scale French occupation of Morocco, which is in uncomfortable proximity to Gibraltar. And now there was Pritchard as well. On August 6th Joinville, who early in the year had produced a rather indiscreet pamphlet on the comparative strengths of the British and French navies, destroyed the fortifications of Tangier and on August 14th Bugeaud won the battle of Isly against a Moroccan force six times larger, capturing eighteen flags, eleven guns, the tent, parasol and personal correspondence of the Emperor of Morocco's son and some heavy chains destined for enslaved French prisoners. A nine-days' war was triumphantly concluded when Joinville landed the next day at Mogador.

In England, the Francophil Lady Holland considered as a result of all this that "everyone is resigned to war and prepared to support it, even if it means a ten per cent income-tax"; the Duke of Wellington observed that "the disposition of the French was to insult us whenever and wherever they thought they could do so with impunity"; and Queen Victoria, replying to Leopold's congratulations on the birth of her second son, wrote: "The only thing almost to mar our happiness is the heavy and threatening cloud which hangs over our relations with France. . . . The whole nation here are very angry . . . God grant all may come right, and I am still of good cheer; but the French keep us constantly in hot water." However, a good deal of the trouble had originated in inflammatory opposition speeches and newspaper articles on both sides of the Channel and neither Aberdeen nor Guizot was prepared to go to war for issues of this sort. Thus wiser counsels prevailed and after the peace-treaty with the Moroccans had demonstrated that the French had no intention of proceeding further in that quarter and Guizot had promised an indemnity for Pritchard (which was never in fact paid), the clouds blew over and plans could be set in hand for a promised visit of Louis-Philippe to Windsor.[1]

[1] When Leopold wrote to him about the prospect of war, Louis-Philippe

A brisk preparatory correspondence developed between Victoria and Louise about the old King's habits. There was talk of the horse-hair mattress with the plank of wood under it and Louise wrote: "You know he can take a great deal of exercise and everything will interest and delight him, to see as to do; this is not a compliment but a mere fact." Marie-Amélie had her anxieties for the well-being of her septuagenarian husband – "and what makes my mother uneasy is the fear that, being at liberty and without control, he will make too much, as she says, *le jeune homme*, ride, go about, and do everything as if he was still twenty years old. If I must tell you *all the truth*, she is afraid also he will eat too much." However, all went off perfectly and, the visit concluded, the Queen wrote to Leopold: "What an extraordinary man the King is! What a wonderful memory, and how lively, how sagacious! He spoke very openly to us all, and is determined that our affairs should go on well. He wishes Tahiti *au fond de la mer*." The King, accompanied by Guizot was met at Portsmouth by the Duke and Albert on October 8th, spent the following day at Windsor and enormously enjoyed a visit to his old house at Twickenham on the 10th, followed by lunch at Claremont, which he was soon to revisit in very different circumstances. On the 11th he was made a Knight of the Garter and Albert was given the Grand Cordon of the Legion of Honour. On the 12th he was acclaimed with what the Queen described as "a veritable delirium" by the pupils of Eton, whose predilection for champagne on these occasions had aroused the unfavourable comments of Guizot at the time of his London embassy. The 14th was scheduled for the return journey to France from Gosport. The sea turned out to be very rough and although Victoria and Albert lunched on board with the French admiral, Louis-Philippe was conveyed by train to Dover for a shorter crossing the following day. A large building turned out

replied: "I have no patience with the manner in which people so often magnify miserable trifles into *casus belli* . . . If you knew as I do what bellum is, you would take good care not to listen as you do to the sad catalogue of *casus belli* . . ."

to be on fire at New Cross station and the King had to pick his way over hosepipes, characteristically observing to the directors that he hoped they were well insured.

Although the opposition continued to press Guizot hard, continued prosperity at home and peace abroad made it difficult to upset him. On September 8th, 1845, Victoria was again received at the Château d'Eu for a twenty-four hour visit on her return journey from Germany, and Guizot and Aberdeen took the opportunity to discuss the still unsolved affair of the Spanish marriage. Guizot made it clear that France favoured the candidature of either a Neapolitan Bourbon or one of Isabella's cousins, the Duke of Cadiz or the Duke of Seville. But for some time now, the Tuileries had entertained the idea that Louis-Philippe's youngest son, Montpensier, should marry Isabella's sister, the Infanta Luisa. This idea was not popular in London, but the two statesmen appeared to have settled the problem amicably, Aberdeen writing to Peel from Eu on September the 8th:

> With respect to the Infanta, they (Louis-Philippe and Guizot) declared in the most positive and explicit manner, that *until the Queen was married and had children*, they should consider the Infanta precisely as her sister, and that any marriage with a French prince would be entirely out of the question. The King said that he did not wish that his son should have the prospect of being on the throne of Spain; but that if the Queen had children, by whom the succession would be secured, he did not engage to preclude himself from the possibility of profiting by the great inheritance which the Infanta would bring his son. All this, however, was uncertain, and would require time at all events to accomplish; for I distinctly understood, that it was not only a marriage and a child, but *children that were necessary to secure the succession*.

There was now no need for Louis-Philippe to "profit by a great inheritance", despite the habits he had acquired before 1830, and he would have done better to leave well alone and to remember that Spain was not a lucky country for France to meddle in. However Lord Palmerston was still in opposition, there was less talk now of Prince Leopold of Coburg and a marriage of this sort for Montpensier was an attractive consolation prize.[1] Guizot in his conversations with Aberdeen had reminded him that in the French view only Bourbons were eligible, this being the condition on which Louis-Philippe had agreed not to marry the Queen herself into the French royal family, despite the fact that Cristina, the Queen Regent, was continually suggesting it. Louis-Philippe was thus encouraged to hear from Aberdeen: "As to the candidature of Prince Leopold of Saxe-Coburg you needn't worry on that score; I guarantee that it will be neither admitted nor supported by England and that you won't be embarrassed by it."

To make sure there would be no ambiguity arising from these conversations, Guizot sent a memorandum, drafted in February 1846, to Aberdeen in which he specified that "if the marriage of the Queen with Prince Leopold, or with any prince other than a descendant of Philip V became probable or imminent, the French government would consider itself quit of all engagements and would regard itself free to demand the hand of the Queen or of the Infanta for the Duke of Montpensier". Aberdeen thought this was going too far in terms of limiting Spanish freedom of choice, but as long as he was at the Foreign Office there seemed no likelihood whatever of the Coburg candidature being revived in London. Relations between the two courts were now so cordial that Queen Victoria embroidered a fancy waistcoat for Louis-Philippe, who wore it proudly on Easter Sunday.[2]

In Madrid, however, Great Britain had been represented since 1843 by the imperious and ambitious Henry Bulwer, who always considered himself more than a match for the French since the day when passing through Paris on the way to his first post as attaché at Berlin he won £6,000 in a night's gambling. Queen Cristina, who disliked impartially all the suggested candidates, approached him tentatively about Leopold of Coburg and Bulwer grossly transcended his brief by telling her "that a marriage so reasonable and unobjectionable could not be persistently opposed

[1] Aumale had married in 1844 Marie-Caroline of Naples.
[2] Royal Archives Y 48/47.

by the King of the French". Aberdeen reprimanded him severely, but by the end of June the Tories were out of office and the Whig Foreign Secretary was Lord Palmerston. In addition the presence during the year of Prince Leopold in Lisbon, a known centre of English influence, was highly disturbing from Guizot's point of view.

The French ambassador at Madrid, de Bresson, had a marked distaste for Bulwer, which was fully reciprocated, and from a well-established vantage-point in court circles in Madrid, he now began to take up the running, being prepared to exceed his instructions exactly as Bulwer had. Within a fortnight of assuming office, Palmerston sent instructions to Bulwer commenting critically on Conservative rule in Spain and setting out a short list of three candidates, at the top of which appeared the name of Prince Leopold of Coburg;[1] and then coolly showed it to Jarnac, the French ambassador to London, who could scarcely believe his eyes. When Jarnac protested that this was contrary to Aberdeen's constant assurances, Palmerston merely replied that nothing could be done about it as the instructions had already gone out. Meanwhile, de Bresson was not letting the grass grow under his feet and that matters were in any case urgent was revealed by his remarkable despatch of April the 3rd, 1846 – "*la reine est nubile depuis deux heures*". He knew that Queen Cristina was prepared to accept rather unwillingly the Duke of Cadiz as bridegroom for Isabella, provided Luisa was also married to Montpensier, since Bulwer's alternative candidate, the Duke of Seville, was too closely associated with her Liberal opponents. So de Bresson, seizing his chance, told her without reference to Guizot that simultaneous marriages would be acceptable to the Tuileries. It had been strongly rumoured that the Duke of Cadiz was impotent. Had this been the case, a French succession in the Peninsula might have seemed probable, but it seems highly doubtful if this entered into the French calculations in view of the

[1] The other two were the Duke of Cadiz and the Duke of Seville, the former of whom was associated with the Conservative elements in Madrid, the latter with the Progressives.

following uncompromising statement of Louis-Philippe's to Louise: "It seemed to me certain from the information, of a very detailed character, which was collected in Madrid on Don Francisco d'Assiz[1] that he was in a good condition of virility." In any case Louis-Philippe was anxious to adhere to the Eu compact and wrote to Guizot: "a formal disavowal is indispensable . . . give it quickly and clearly on the issue of simultaneity." Unfortunately, just as this happened, Palmerston handed his famous despatch to Jarnac and both Louis-Philippe and Guizot, exasperated by what they considered as a characteristic Palmerstonian coup, boiled over and consented to the double marriage which took place on October 8th.[2] The first *entente cordiale* was irretrievably shattered.

Despite the dubious nature of these transactions, the opposition was able to make very little capital out of a situation which Guizot somewhat misguidedly proclaimed to be a victory for French prestige. But the Spanish marriages are something much more important than an anachronistic dynastic intrigue. To them is largely attributable the establishment of Louis-Philippe's reputation for perfidy, which, hitherto a subject for Legitimist and Republican propaganda, now became an internationally accepted common-place. Historians have largely discounted this – e.g. R. W. Seton-Watson's judgement "The calm verdict of history must undoubtedly be that the charges of gross perfidy and bad faith, levelled against Louis-Philippe at the time and long afterwards, rested in the main upon a misapprehension." But for the moment there was a unanimous chorus of indignation in England. The Queen described "Guizot's conduct as beyond *all* belief shameful and *so* shabbily dishonest"; Greville considered that Britain "had been jockeyed by France in a very shabby underhand way"; and Palmerston described Louis-Philippe to Bulwer as "a pickpocket caught in the act", and told a friend of Guizot's

[1] The Duke of Cadiz.
[2] The Duke of Cadiz proved capable of giving Isabella four children. Montpensier, who lived until 1897, blew out the Duke of Seville's brains in a duel in 1870, after his victim had called him "a puffed-up French pastrycook".

in London that this was the first time a King of France had broken his word. Time and the misfortunes of the dynasty were to mitigate these acerbities, but in two other respects the Spanish marriages were to prove a highly illusory triumph for the French government. To begin with, English foreign policy up to the revolution was conducted by Palmerston with the express object of making things as difficult and humiliating for France as possible, and secondly their preoccupation with foreign affairs during and after 1846 blinded Louis-Philippe and Guizot to the existence of infinitely more dangerous internal problems. To adapt de Salvandy's metaphor of 1830 they signally failed to realize that the diplomatic minuet was being danced on a particularly menacing social volcano.

Initially, Palmerston appeared to have the worst of it. When the three Northern powers took the opportunity afforded by the break-up of the *entente cordiale* to annex Cracow, he rudely rebuffed Guizot's suggestion of a joint protest, but made no headway in his attempt to interest them in the English defeat in Spain and was equally unsuccessful in trying to persuade Isabella to divorce her new husband or abdicate. Although Normanby, the new English ambassador in Paris, was in continual contact with the leaders of the French opposition and frequently showed secret papers to Thiers, the latter seemed incapable of making any inroads on Guizot's majority and Charles Greville, who was sent over to Paris by more moderate Whig elements at the end of 1846 to try and smooth things over, was not far wrong in his judgement that "Thiers thinks of nothing but mischief, of gratifying his personal passions and resentments".[1] But all the same, 1846 was to prove as unhappy a year for the French monarchy in external as in internal affairs. In Italy, Germany and Switzerland there broke out liberal and nationalist movements, which would have

[1] Thiers said to Greville on December 19th: "*Savez-vous ce que c'est que le Roi? Le mot est grossier, mais vous le comprendrez. Eh bien, c'est un J—— F——; de plus il est poltron.*" A few weeks later Greville, received at the Tuileries recorded: "The King looks very well, and is grossly caricatured by *Punch*; he is a very good-looking old gentleman, and seems to have many years of life in him still."

rejoiced the hearts of Laffitte and Lafayette, but were not now to the taste of Louis-Philippe and Guizot, irretrievably committed to a policy of rigid conservatism at home and at odds with Palmerston and Russell. In June the new pope, Pius IX, promised liberal reforms; Tuscany followed his example and Charles Albert of Sardinia was openly sympathetic. In February 1847 Frederick William IV of Prussia granted his subjects a constitution and it became clear in that year that the anti-clerical and liberal cantons in Switzerland were determined to destroy the Sonderbund, the association of Catholic cantons, and to expel the Jesuits. Guizot and Louis-Philippe had no hope, even if their predilections had pointed in that direction, of outbidding Palmerston in support of European liberalism or even of associating with him in its defence. So they took the disastrous decision of trying to secure a prestige success by supporting Metternich in the leadership of European Conservatism. Guizot attempted to achieve a five-power intervention in Switzerland only to be smartly out-manœuvred by Palmerston, who held up the diplomatic proceedings long enough to allow the radical cantons to defeat the Sonderbund in November 1847; and when the Austrians drove the papal troops out of Ferrara in August of that year, he meekly acquiesced in a manner that would have outraged Casimir-Périer. The grant of constitutions early in 1848 by the rulers of Naples and Tuscany emphasized the apparent bankruptcy of a policy which seemed to belie the very *raison d'être* of the July Revolution. Queen Victoria summed the position up well when she wrote to her Uncle Leopold in September 1847: "In my opinion nothing has gone on so well since the *unfortunate* false move of the Spanish marriages and I think you will admit *que cela n'a pas porté bonheur au Roi.*"

VIII

In May 1846 Louis-Philippe wrote to Leopold of the Belgians: "What spoils everything is that as a general rule our politicians have a superabundance of courage and audacity when they are in opposition while when they are in office they are *feigherzig* and always ready to drop everything . . . One must find a Guizot to avoid these evils, a man who knows how to face his adversaries and who also knows how to shake up his friends when they are frightened . . ." But, absorbed in European politics and blinded by an unshakeable conviction in his own wisdom and rectitude, Guizot in the event presided over the demise of the Orléans monarchy with an almost somnambulistic incapacity to read the signs of the times. Observers much further from the centre of affairs saw increasing evidence of an imminent crisis. Lamartine wrote: "This country is dead and nothing can galvanize it but a crisis. As an honest man I fear it; as a philosopher I desire it." Molé said much the same – "our civilization is very ill and nothing would be less surprising than a good cataclysm which would put an end to it all". The most striking evidence of the prevalent disquiet is to be found in a letter of November 1847 from Joinville to Nemours in which he wrote:

> I am writing you a line because I am worried by all the events which I see piling up on every side . . . There are no more ministers, their responsibility is nil, everything comes back in the end to the King. The King has reached an age when he no longer accepts other peoples' observations; he is accustomed to governing, he likes to show that it is he who governs . . . We are confronting the Chambers with a detestable internal situation; and foreign affairs are no better. All this is the work of the King alone, the result of the old age of a King who wishes to govern but who lacks the strength to take a firm resolution. And worst of all I can see no remedy for

all this ... You know my respect and affection for him; but I can't help looking into the future and it rather frightens me.

And yet Guizot as late as May 1847 demonstrated his imperturbability by writing: "For the moment, there is nothing; no grave question; no embarrassing event ... superficial and puerile effervescence."

He was to some extent misled as to the durability of what Louis-Philippe called "our system" by the elections of July 1846. Thiers and Barrot had brought the Left-Centre and the Left formally together in an electoral compact at the end of 1845. They agreed to switch the direction of their attacks from foreign affairs to a demand for electoral and parliamentary reform and wholesale allegations of political corruption. Guizot, as a rule, disdained to engage them himself on this ground, and left the defence of the ministry to Duchâtel, whose election-circular to the prefects urged them to exercise "a frank and loyal influence" on public opinion, while ensuring that "the independence of consciences must be scrupulously respected". The opposition made in fact very little headway in a campaign involving a good deal of obvious misrepresentation and exaggeration and their newspapers had to fall back on stigmatizing ministerial candidates in their columns with the letter P for Pritchardist. Three days before the elections began on July the 29th two long-range pistol shots were fired from behind a statue at Louis-Philippe as he was saluting the crowd from the balcony of the Tuileries by an apparently unpolitical paranoiac called Henri. Apart from this, the elections went off calmly, and although the opposition gained nine out of fourteen thousand votes in Paris and won eleven out of fourteen seats, the rest of France swung over to Guizot in sufficient numbers to give him a majority of a hundred. France was apparently prosperous, peaceful and Conservative – that is if you were inclined to conclude that the electorate faithfully reflected the outlook of the nation at large.

As a political triumph the election was to prove no more durable than the Spanish marriages, which were the main preoccupation of Louis-Philippe and Guizot that summer. The correlation between social unrest and the price of bread is a commonplace of nineteenth-century history and it was to be strikingly exemplified in 1847. The harvest of 1845 had not been good, but that of 1846 was disastrous, and it was followed by almost unprecedented floods in the Loire valley. An economic chain-reaction followed. Large quantities of corn had to be imported, all grain-supplies for the army were secured expensively abroad and the municipalities poured out money to keep bread prices stable. But by this time it was winter, the price of bread continued to rise and there were wholesale withdrawals from the rural savings banks.[1] Gold ran short in the Banque de France, the bank-rate was raised and panic assailed a great many railway speculators. To maintain the level of railway construction, massive state subsidies were required and a heavy deficit incurred on the budget. A government avowedly dedicated to business prosperity did not seem to be making a success of the nation's business.

But the social and political consequences of dear bread were much graver than immediately appeared on the surface. Dissatisfaction on the land was a temporary phenomenon and the régime could have ridden it in due course. But in the industrial centres with no poor law, no cushion against unemployment and with Guizot's legislative record limited to one enactment in 1841 restricting child labour in factories,[2] there was an ideal field for revolutionary agitation. While the secret societies since 1839 had been losing ground, the Utopian theorists had been busy. Three publications of the year 1840 had penetrated in the form of garbled aphorisms deep into the consciousness of proletarian Paris – Cabet's *Voyage en Icarie*, Louis Blanc's *L' Organization du Travail* and Proudhon's *Mémoire sur la Propriété* with its famous definition of property as theft. Proudhon had very little sympathy with the naïf communism of the social romantics – he described Louis Blanc unkindly as "the most ignorant, the vainest, the emptiest,

[1] Wheat was 29 francs a hectolitre in January 1847 and 40 by March.

[2] No children under eight were to be employed; hours were restricted to eight for children between eight and twelve and to twelve for children up to sixteen. Even so, the measure was opposed by the leading philosopher and the leading scientist of the day, Cousin and Gay-Lussac.

the most impudent, the most nauseating of rhetoricians" – but to an empty stomach in a Paris hovel either Proudhon's brand of misanthropic anarchism or the rosy visions of the Utopians were equally attractive in the winter of 1846–7. Marrast's *National* had been outbidden in the ferocity of its opposition to the government by *La Réforme*, founded in 1843 by Flocon, an associate of Marx and Engels, and both papers harped continually on the theme of corruption. In addition 1847 saw a spate of highly coloured histories of the French Revolution – the first volumes of Louis Blanc and Michelet and the eight volumes of Lamartine's *Histoire des Girondins*, a singularly ill-advised attempt to prevent France being bored by the shameless romanticization of her history. These publications were exactly timed to stimulate the psychopathology of Revolution, what Professor Talmon has called "the Revolutionary mysticism, the fatalistic conviction of the inevitability of Revolution, (and) the impersonal deterministic grandeur ascribed to it".

The old King had no patience with this sort of thing. He was obsessed with the idea that any government other than Guizot's would mean war in the then troubled state of Europe, and, as far as he was concerned, he was going to end his days in peace. People noticed a certain tendency in him to senile irritability, although at times he recovered his sunny good nature, as when he remarked after being shot at from behind a wall by a disgruntled gamekeeper called Lecomte in April 1846 in the forest of Fontainebleau "it is only in hunting me that there is no close season". He was in reasonably good spirits when he opened the session of 1847, referring to "the sufferings which this year distress a part of our population" and expressing the hope that "by the firm maintenance of order, by the liberty and security of commercial transactions, by an ample and judicious application of the public resources efficiently aiding the zeal of private charity, we shall mitigate these trials, with which Providence sometimes visits the most prosperous states". The government had a majority on the reply to the speech from the throne of 248 to 84 and if the Chambers were any reflection of the state of opinion at large in the country, there seemed no cause for anxiety. And yet by the time the session ended in August the government was almost universally discredited and the whole basis of the régime seriously undermined.

Conservative governments with large majorities are inclined to have trouble with the rank and file of their supporters. Some of the younger deputies returned for the first time in 1846 tended to resent the heavy hand of Guizot and began to slip out of the clutches of his parliamentary manager Duchâtel, whose efficiency in any case began about this time to be impaired by ill-health and a certain natural indolence. The old issues of electoral and parliamentary reform were debated in March and the adamantine Guizot refused to budge an inch, although nothing more revolutionary was suggested than a lowering of the franchise qualification from two hundred to a hundred francs and the addition of some two hundred thousand specially qualified electors. When a republican deputy affirmed in the debate that the day of universal suffrage would come, Guizot replied testily: "Universal suffrage will never come . . . the question doesn't justify diverting my attention at this moment from what we have on hand." But although the government had a majority of ninety-eight on the issue of electoral reform, when parliamentary reform was debated (for the seventeenth time since 1830) the majority was exactly half. The government was further weakened by the resignation or dismissal of three cabinet ministers, including that of the finance minister, and their replacement by three peers of no particular distinction. Though he little suspected it, this was Guizot's last chance to save the situation by some striking constructive gesture – if not by a Disraelian "leap in the dark" on the franchise issue, then at any rate by a bold legislative programme. Instead of which he laid himself open to the damaging criticism of one of his former supporters who claimed that the diminution of the Conservative majority was due to the total inertia of the government, and proclaimed to the delight of the opposition that "the whole system of government was nothing, nothing, nothing!" In fact, the only legislative operation of the government was of a sort calculated to arouse violent enmity on the Right. This was a belated attempt to appease the indignation of the more ardent Catholics that the promise of full educational liberty contained in the Charter of 1830 remained as yet unfulfilled.[1] Two half-hearted attempts had been made in 1836 and 1844 to reconcile the anti-clerical educational monopoly of the University with the natural desire of many Catholic parents to have their children educated by clerical teachers. Louis-Philippe altogether failed to appreciate the emotional force generated by this question and showed a misguided tendency to tease the Archbishop of Paris, Mgr. Affre, by asking him conundrums about candles. But for Montalembert and his supporters it was now an issue of life and death: "We are the successors of the martyrs and we will not tremble before the successors of Julian the Apostate; we are the sons of the crusaders and we will not yield to the sons of Voltaire." The Minister of Education had gone mad in 1844, suffering from the delusion that he was being hounded to death by Jesuits. Now in the spring of 1847 a new government project was introduced, which once again failed to satisfy anybody and served to weaken the reputation of the ministry in quarters where it might otherwise have commanded valuable support.

Worse was to follow. As has been seen, the opposition had achieved as yet only a limited success in their campaign against political corruption. It was therefore a disastrous moment from Guizot's point of view for a particularly squalid public scandal to be exposed, involving Thiers' Minister for War, a Waterloo veteran called Cubières, and a former Minister of Public Works, Teste, who was now in the peculiarly vulnerable position of being President of the *Cour de Cassation*. Though he tried to brazen it out before the Peers it transpired that Teste had been paid 94,000 francs by Cubières, acting as intermediary for a shady financier called Pellapra, who had thereby acquired the concession of a salt-mine. The trial was sensational and concluded with an attempted suicide on the part of Teste. De Tocqueville's Cassandra-like denunciations of the moral state of the nation

[1] See pp. 168–70.

seemed more than ever justified when this unsavoury affair was followed by one of the most ghastly crimes of the century. The Duc de Choiseul-Praslin murdered his wife, Marshal Sébastiani's daughter, who had borne him eleven children. He escaped the guillotine by taking arsenic and was formally condemned after his death by the Peers. Despite this unorthodox attempt to vindicate the principle of even-handed justice, Sainte Beuve, analysing the causes of the February revolution, recorded his opinion that "the act of M. de Praslin contributed to it as much perhaps as the acts of M. Guizot." As if this were not enough, de Bresson, now ambassador at Naples, cut his own throat, the Prince d'Eckmühl stabbed his mistress, Comte Mortier tried to kill his children and another peer forged the signature of the secretary of the Jockey Club. It was not therefore surprising that at the height of the Teste affair, the Duc de Montpensier's guests returning in carriages from an elaborate party at Vincennes were hooted at by the inhabitants of the Faubourg Saint-Antoine. The long-term record of the July Monarchy for moral probity can easily sustain comparison with either the Third or the Fourth Republic, to say nothing of the Second Empire, but the simultaneous eruption of all these scandals in 1847 was utterly calamitous for the survival of the régime.[1]

The opposition, now understandably convinced that things were running in their favour, had meanwhile decided to employ the parliamentary vacation by organizing a campaign in favour of electoral and parliamentary reform.

The idea of holding political banquets was revived after Richard Cobden, visiting Paris in 1846, had discussed the success of the anti-Corn-Law agitation with Thiers and Barrot. The Left and Left-Centre, still pledged to support of the dynasty, made common cause for the moment with the Republicans, a tactical error

---

[1] De Tocqueville wrote in his Souvenirs: "A few glaring instances of corruption, discovered by accident, led the country to presuppose a number of hidden cases, and convinced it that the whole of the governing class was corrupt; whence it conceived for the latter a silent contempt, which was generally taken for confiding and contented submission."

which they were very soon to repent. Thiers kept himself prudently in the background (although he did attend a politically modest affair in Marseilles, largely devoted to the exaltation of *bouillabaisse* and the vins du pays) but Barrot was naturally unable to resist so admirably an opportunity for displaying his rhetorical powers. The campaign started briskly enough. On July the 9th in Paris during the Teste trial there was a gathering of about a hundred deputies and twelve hundred Parisian electors with much singing of the Marseillaise and a profusion of toasts, notably omitting any reference to the King's health. Shortly afterwards, although it was strictly no part of the campaign, a banquet was offered to Lamartine by his constituents at Mâcon to celebrate the success of the *Histoire des Girondins*. The poet-historian harangued his admirers against a background of crashing thunder and fork-lightning and after agreeably comparing himself to Herodotus being crowned at the Olympic Games he observed that: "If royalty continues to act as it does, after having had revolutions of liberty and counter-revolutions of glory, you will have the revolution of the public conscience and the revolution of contempt." Thereafter, despite frantic efforts by the organizing committee the campaign looked like falling flat. However under the stimulus of the Praslin murder it began to revive in October. All in all there were about seventy banquets and the indefatigable Barrot went to twenty of them, resplendent in his blue coat and gold buttons, sublimely unaware that he was digging the grave of a dynasty, whose passing he would vainly regret less than a year later.[1] Gradually the demagogic republicans wrested the leadership of the campaign from the moderates and even Barrot had to absent himself, if he were not to be fatally compromised by associating with Ledru-Rollin and Louis Blanc. It was a dangerous moment for M. Flocon to sound the cry "to your tents, O Israel" that hungry winter, while the leaders of the underground societies were sedulously distributing Robespierre's

---

[1] Gustave Flaubert watched him in full oratorical flight at Rouen after a feast of cold turkey and sucking pig and was considerably plagued by an over-excited locksmith who kept tapping him on the shoulder at all the good bits.

speeches, Marat's pamphlets and Buonarotti's history of Babeuf's conspiracy.

Guizot continued to be unperturbed. "If like me you had all Europe to worry about, you wouldn't stop to consider the child-ish pranks of the city of Paris." After seven patient years he had at last got rid of Marshal Soult, that ornamental dignitary being retired with the rank of Marshal-General of France, an honour he was perhaps fortunate to share with Turenne, Villars and Marshal Saxe. Louis-Philippe celebrated his seventy-fourth birthday that autumn and found little to console him in the state of either Europe or of his capital, though the appointment of Aumale to be Governor-General of Algeria in succession to Marshal Bugeaud pleased him greatly. He was inclined more than ever to nervous irritability and was quite inaccessible to criticism. When a suc-cession of old friends – Gérard, Sébastiani and Montalivet – hinted at the possibility of a change of ministry or a measure of reform, he would point out that he was behaving perfectly con-stitutionally in that the existing government had only recently been elected by a large majority. As to reform, he saw the matter like this: "I am not hostile to reform in itself, but it would involve me first with Molé and then that would lead to Thiers. Thiers means war! And I'm not going to destroy my policy of peace! And if I'm pushed any further I shall abdicate!" In December he had a sharp attack of influenza and on December the 31st, three days after he had opened the new session, he was cut to the heart by the sudden death of his sister and life-long companion. Louis-Philippe and Adélaïde had come a long way together since their reunion at Portsmouth nearly forty years previously, and he looked a sad and broken figure as he followed her coffin bare-headed at Dreux – as Louise wrote "to him the loss is irretrievable. My aunt lived but for him, one may almost say that her affection alone had kept her alive these last years." [1] Orléans was dead,

---

[1] It was some consolation that this event provoked Queen Victoria to resume the flow of friendly letters, interrupted since the Spanish marriages. When Louis-Philippe received her letter of condolence, "he kissed it tenderly", according to Leopold.

Aumale and Joinville in Africa and even Guizot now broached the possibility of resigning. All the weight, it seemed, would have to be borne on his shoulders. However, he was not going to yield. "All this outcry," he told de Tocqueville, "won't stop me driving my own cart."

His voice was dull and tired when he read his last speech from the throne on December the 28th, but he made a special effort to sound firmer when he came to the decisive paragraph in which he referred to the "agitation fomented by hostile or blind passions". This of course was directed at the organizers of the banquet campaign and could be taken to imply a royal condemnation of the political activities of a hundred opposition deputies. The debates for the first few days were calm – there was much division in the ranks of the opposition, *La Réforme* was dying from lack of subscribers, and nobody quite knew what to do next. The first notable speech was in fact a brilliant two-hour oration in the Peers by Montalembert, attacking the whole concept of Revolution, in which he accused Lamartine of reviving Jacobinism in novels masquerading under the name of history. De Tocqueville in his best prophetic vein forecast the imminence of a revolution (the speedy fulfillment of which prophecy much surprised him by his own admission). Thiers, seeing the moment ripening, endeavoured to set himself up once more as a man of the Left. Another example of corrupt administrative practices came to light, comparatively trivial in itself, but providing an invaluable opportunity to compare Guizot to Tartuffe.[1] But Guizot, although almost deprived of his voice by influenza, held his own and as late as February the 7th de Broglie wrote to his son: "Things here are going slowly but splendidly. The majority is solid."

But as yet neither of the really crucial problems had been dealt with – reform and the question whether the opposition would accept the condemnation of the banquet-campaign implied in the

[1] A minor legal official called Petit had secured the post he wanted by persuading the government to buy out the existing holder, a practice which appeared to be fairly widespread.

King's speech. Barrot, Duvergier Hauranne and other leaders of the dynastic opposition had condemned a suggestion that more banquets should be held in Paris in January. A group of officers of the National Guard of the 12th arrondissement (Panthéon) decided to hold a banquet on January the 19th. A timber-merchant, Captain Roinville, took it upon himself to go to the prefecture to ask for authorization of the banquet. Authorization was refused and it transpired that this was on the orders of Duchâtel, Minister of the Interior. A furious altercation now took place in the Chamber, the opposition claiming that since seventy banquets had already taken place no authorization was necessary. The Minister of Justice observed that the government had every right to prohibit banquets dangerous to public order, but stupidly asserted that since the right of political assembly was not specified in the Charter it therefore didn't exist. Lamartine reminded the government of what another reactionary régime had once suffered by denying the right of assembly in a Tennis Court. The government majority dropped to 43, and then to 33 on a motion by a dissident Conservative that the government should take some initiative on the question of reform, to which Guizot replied in a notably imprecise manner that something might be done at the appropriate time. The debate ended on February the 12th and with it to all intents and purposes the parliamentary history of the July Monarchy.

IX

Despite all auguries and premonitions, the February Revolution in France was one long chapter of accidents and miscalculations. The monarchy survived far more premeditated and violent attacks in 1832 and 1834 and in the long chain of fortuitous events, which was now to bring about its overthrow, the one ultimately determining factor was Louis-Philippe's unwillingness to use regular troops to suppress a riot. This can be interpreted either as a failure of nerve or as the expression of a life-long hatred of bloodshed. Walter Bagehot inclined to the first view when he wrote:

> The failure of Louis-Philippe to use his reserve power as constitutional monarch is the most instructive proof of how great that reserve power is ... The Parisian population ought to have been put down as Guizot wished. If Louis-Philippe had been a fit King to introduce free government, he would have strengthened his ministers when they were instruments of order, even if he afterwards discarded them when order was safe and policy could be discussed. But he was one of the cautious men who are "noted" to fail in old age and, of great ability, he failed and lost his crown for want of petty and momentary energy, which at such a crisis a plain man would have at once put forth.

To Louis Blanc it seemed that the question of avoiding bloodshed was ultimately decisive –

> it is true that in 1848 he let the sceptre slip voluntarily from his hand, because the defection of the National Guard made him believe that even the bourgeoisie was against him ... but if it is true that dominated by this thought he did not feel he had the right to give the signal for throats to be cut and was unwilling to reign by right of assassination, this interpretation of his fall should be considered as the only act of his life which had the mark of greatness and does

eternal honour to his memory. If he did not fall as a King, he knew how to fall as a human being.

The speed and unexpectedness of events was certainly calculated to destroy the judgement of a younger and more flexible ruler than Louis-Philippe. After the conclusion of the debate on the address, a hundred opposition deputies met on February the 13th under Barrot's presidency in the restaurant Durand in the Place de la Madeleine, and decided that the Parisian banquet should after all take place on February 22nd, but that they, and not the committee of the 12th Legion, should take over the organization. Neither the King nor Guizot was particularly disturbed, and it even seemed to Guizot that a mild insurrection might rally support to the throne. Very much against Louis-Philippe's advice it was decided that the government should open negotiations with the opposition through two intermediaries – one of whom was Morny, Napoleon III's half-brother. A formal agreement was drawn up on the afternoon of the 19th, wherein it was agreed that the demonstrators would assemble at the Madeleine and would proceed with unarmed National Guards to the banquet, which would take place in a tent in a quiet part of the Champs Elysées unsuitable for the erection of barricades; that once the guests had assembled a police commissioner would declare that the proceedings were illegal; that Barrot would protest formally in the name of the right of public assembly, but would advise the guests to disperse peaceably; and that then the whole affair would be brought before the courts for a decision. Meanwhile the opposition deputies agreed to play down agitation in their newspapers. It seemed a sensible solution, commending itself both to the government and the parliamentary opposition, which was for the most part rapidly losing stomach for the fight.

Then on the morning of February the 21st, the columns of *Le National*, *La Réforme* and the Fourierist organ *La Démocratie Pacifique* were filled with a detailed operation order drawn up by Armand Marrast for the following day's proceedings. Although Marrast had shown this document to Odilon Barrot just as that supremely incompetent politician was sitting down to dinner,

Barrot had approved it without reading it, merely commenting characteristically – "Add nothing that would compromise the opposition." But the document turned out to give precise marching orders to the National Guard, an assumption of authority which was obviously and flagrantly *ultra vires* for a mere political committee with no constitutional standing. By ten o'clock in the morning, a meeting of ministers assembled under Duchâtel rapidly concluded that both the spirit and the letter of the compact had been broken. Jacqueminot, Duchâtel's father-in-law, an elderly invalid, who had commanded the National Guard since 1842, reminded that body that it could only be mustered on the orders of its superior officers and a proclamation was issued forbidding both the procession and the banquet. A meeting of the opposition deputies was strongly advised to acquiesce by Thiers, who now began to sense that he was not going to find it easy to get anyone to pick his chestnuts out of this particular fire, and it was decided to abandon the whole project by 80 votes to 17. Louis-Philippe was exultant.

The following day it became clear that many of the enthusiasts for the demonstration, especially the students, were furious at being abandoned by their leaders. There was a stormy meeting at the offices of *Le Siècle* where a decision was taken to proceed with an armed demonstration the next day. However, that evening at another meeting in Flocon's office, Louis Blanc strongly counselled the desirability of avoiding a clash with the authorities, as did Ledru-Rollin, who refused categorically to involve himself in any demonstration. The leaders of the secret societies were equally unwilling to risk a trial of strength. Yet this meeting was in the event to prove decisive for the revolution. It was attended by de la Hodde, a spy in the service of Delessert, the Prefect of Police, and his encouraging report of the proceedings resulted in the authorities countermanding shortly after midnight certain agreed precautionary measures including a number of arrests.

At nine in the morning of February 22nd in drizzling rain student demonstrators began to lead a procession from the Panthéon to the Madeleine, composed of elements who either wished to defy the republican leadership or had quite simply not heard that the proceedings had been called off. There were shouts of "Down with Guizot!" and much singing of *La Marseillaise* and the Girondins' chorus. A few demonstrators forced their way into the empty Chamber of Deputies, but were easily ejected in a friendly fashion by a handful of dragoons. The Chamber in a leisurely manner discussed the affairs of the Banque de Bordeaux and put off a censure motion of Barrot's until later in the week. A rather ramshackle barricade went up and a few armourers' shops were looted as darkness fell. It had been a day of mild and rather purposeless disorder, apparently a damp and depressing fiasco. Louis-Philippe observed that the Parisians were not given to winter revolutions.

During the night of February 22nd/23rd there were two indications, however, that all was not quite well. Towards nine o'clock the commander of the Army of Paris, Tiburce Sébastiani,[1] ordered the troops of the line to take up the defensive positions which had been originally agreed on the previous evening, in accordance with a plan of Marshal Gérard's for the defence of the capital drawn up during the Middle East crisis of 1839. Since this plan required the collaboration of certain National Guard contingents, some legions were called out by their officers. Despite reiterated expressions of perfect confidence in the loyalty of the National Guard by the hopelessly infirm Jacqueminot, the response was extremely half-hearted, and a good many of those who turned out were heard to shout: "*Vive la Réforme!*" Furthermore, when Delessert tried to proceed with the arrests countermanded the previous evening, he found that most of the agitators concerned had profited by the delay and were not to be found. However, by midnight the city was absolutely quiet in its pall of wintry gloom and the troops returned to barracks.

At seven in the morning of the 23rd the soldiers marched out of their barracks in the rain and took up their positions. They encountered no resistance, and indeed a good many shouts of "*Vive la ligne!*", until about nine o'clock when in the area of the

[1] Brother of Louis-Philippe's former Foreign Minister.

Temple there was a certain amount of shooting behind a few barricades. Then, with such insurrection as there was well under control and 30,000 regular soldiers deployed, if admittedly rather wet and short of rations, the astonishing decision was taken to call out the National Guard. General Jacqueminot from his sick-bed was still stupidly complacent about their loyalty and, with the unthinking rigidity which tends to afflict the military mind when acting in defence of the civil power, the high command was worried about certain gaps left in Marshal Gérard's defence plan. Louis-Philippe had ceased his annual review of the National Guard, considerably expanded in 1837, since 1840, and it was by now pretty well known that a high proportion of its officers were sympathetic to the dynastic opposition, while a good many of the other ranks were radical or even republican in outlook. What now happened was that the Conservative elements simply failed to turn out, a striking exemplification of the extent to which the régime in general and Louis-Philippe in particular had failed, especially over the last six years, to inspire any spirit of active loyalty. As the Second Legion took post in the Place de la Concorde, the shout of "*Vive la Réforme!*" went up from the ranks; the Seventh split up into isolated detachments and mixing with the insurgents prevented the regular troops firing; the Eight and Ninth hardly mustered at all; the Twelfth, the most actively revolutionary, turned out in great numbers and shouted "*Vive la République!*"; the First and Second were apathetic and only the Tenth obviously loyal.

When this development was reported at the Tuileries, many members of the court, including Montalivet, who were hostile to Guizot, immediately concluded that the peremptory need of the moment was for a change of government, and they persuaded Marie-Amélie to urge this course on the King. Louis-Philippe was overwhelmed by the news, confronted as he was with the possibility of a sanguinary clash between the regular army and the National Guard. "I have seen enough blood," he kept repeating, and under pressure from the Queen and Montalivet he sent Duchâtel to summon Guizot from the Chamber at half-past two.

The latter made it quite clear that he could not carry on without the firm support of the Crown and Louis-Philippe, accepting his resignation with tears in his eyes, announced his intention of summoning Molé – a decision which indicated a collapse not only of his nerves but of his judgement. Guizot returned to the Chamber and announced to the thunderstruck incredulity of the government supporters that he was no longer Prime Minister. It says something for M. Odilon Barrot that he tried to restrain the applause of his supporters. For after all, it was effectively the end of the July Monarchy, of which he had always proclaimed himself a supporter.

Molé was eventually unearthed from the Chamber of Peers and arrived at the Tuileries about four. For the next six hours he vainly pursued a half-hearted attempt to form a cabinet, with Thiers refusing to co-operate, while Marshal Bugeaud sat waiting in the palace hoping that the old King would give him orders to grip a situation with which he felt sure he could compete, given a measure of resolute leadership. Not for the last time, France found itself without a government at a moment of supreme crisis. A good many National Guardsmen felt reassured by the dismissal of Guizot and returned home to their *pot-au-feu* with their shakos on the ends of their muskets. But to the denizens of Saint-Antoine and Saint-Denis, the name of Molé hardly suggested a communist millennium. An unruly crowd attacked barracks and the guard-posts of the unpopular municipal guards. A strong band formed with flags and torches in the Faubourg Saint-Antoine and debouched opposite the Foreign Office in the Boulevard des Capucines. This had been a danger spot for over twenty-four hours and was protected by the 14th Regiment of the Line with in front a protective screen of the National Guard. The latter had unfortunately been recently withdrawn to protect the Chancellery in the Place Vendôme. The mob now pressed heavily on to the soldiers lining the pavement. The colonel commanding forced them back so that his men could fix bayonets. Soon a shot rang out, the origin of which is likely to remain ultimately mysterious, though the most circumstantial account attributes it to an enraged

Corsican sergeant who resented a threat on the part of one of the agitators to burn the colonel's whiskers with a torch. In the subsequent volley some fifty people were killed or wounded and both the mob and the soldiers gave way to complete panic. With a rapidity which certainly suggests a measure of intelligent anticipation, an adjacent yellow cart with a white horse harnessed to it was piled up with sixteen corpses, surmounted with that of a half undressed female, and an angry torchlit procession set off, pausing in front of the offices of *Le National* and *La Réforme* and continuing through Les Halles to the mairie of the 4th arrondissement where the corpses were deposited. The tocsin began to sound from the church steeples and barricades went up everywhere.

This was more than enough to persuade Molé to abandon his uncongenial task. Already, far too many precious hours had been lost. By one in the morning of February 24th Adolphe Thiers was summoned to assume the office of President of the Council with the assistance of Odilon Barrot, and Bugeaud commissioned to come to the rescue of the July Monarchy. The lugubrious procession of sixteen corpses was still rattling over the paving-stones amid cries of "the peoples' blood has been shed and must be avenged."

As he took up his command in the Place du Carrousel the intrepid Bugeaud observed: "It's a bit late, but I've never been beaten and I'm not beginning today." Confronted with a group of utterly demoralized staff officers, he put his watch on the table and said: "It's now two o'clock. By four o'clock we must begin to attack everywhere. I don't want our force split up into little packets. What I want is four columns, sweeping away the mob without waiting to be attacked – the first in the area of the Hôtel de Ville, the second to be directed on the Bastille, the third to follow behind them to prevent the barricades being reformed, and the fourth to sweep the Panthéon area. The reserves will concentrate in the Place du Carrousel." As he was appointing the commanders of these columns, Thiers arrived and Bugeaud, after saying he was charmed to see him, alarmed him considerably by repeating more than once: "After all I shall have the pleasure of killing a good many of these swine." Twenty-three years later M. Thiers was to find himself in a distressingly analogous situation at the time of the third revolution in which he was a principal actor. At this particular juncture he returned about four o'clock in the morning to the Tuileries, where he found the exhausted old King, swathed in flannel, about to go to bed and not unnaturally disinclined to dismiss the fire-eating commander-in-chief, at any rate until daylight. Thiers spent the remaining hours of darkness trying to form a cabinet out of the third-class politicians available.

Meanwhile, Bugeaud's columns set out about 5.30 a.m. and soon encountered a forest of barricades. Sébastiani succeeded in reaching his objective at the Hôtel de Ville, as did the column directed on the Panthéon without undue difficulty. The column commanded by the African veteran Bedeau encountered a rather stronger barricade in the Rue Saint-Denis. Instead of forcing it, Bedeau began to parley with a group of National Guards, who tried to persuade him that if only the populace knew that Thiers and Barrot were now ministers all resistance would cease. Bedeau sent back a pencilled note to Bugeaud urging the issue of a proclamation about the newly constituted ministry. When this arrived at his headquarters, Bugeaud was surrounded by unnerved staff officers and importunate civilians urging the necessity of avoiding a general massacre. He knew in his heart that the new government was not prepared to accept the consequences of a civil war in the capital and being not without personal political ambitions he had already written to Thiers, suggesting himself as Minister of War in the new cabinet. Consequently, in all probability on his own initiative, but thoroughly aware that he was merely registering the wishes of the King and his advisers, he issued a cease fire. The army then proceeded to disintegrate, as first single soldiers and then whole units began to mix with the insurgents and drift off into wine shops. Bedeau with the greatest difficulty led a demoralized remnant back to the Place de la Concorde. Thiers and Barrot had been at the Tuileries since eight o'clock and it was agreed that Barrot and the newly appointed commander of the National Guard, the popular Lamoricière, should go into the streets and harangue the populace, announcing everywhere the formation of the new cabinet. The reception they encountered was the reverse of encouraging, and Barrot, utterly discouraged, went home.

At half-past ten the King with his family, Thiers and some twenty politicians were trying to eat breakfast when a breathless and dishevelled staff officer burst into the room and announced the imminent disintegration of Bedeau's troops and the very real possibility that they were in no condition to defend the Tuileries. While further news was sought, the King asked the assembled politicians what they thought he should do. Thiers suggested they should withdraw to Saint-Cloud, form a force of sixty thousand troops under Bugeaud and recover the city the next day. Marie-Amélie, whose courage and dignity contrasted superbly with the prevalent panic and confusion, declared: "The King and his family must await their fate at the Tuileries and die together if need be." Reports came in of a slightly improved situation in the Place de la Concorde and it was decided that the King should mount his horse and review the troops and National Guards in front of the palace in the Place du Carrousel. About eleven o'clock he rode out in lieutenant-general's uniform, accompanied by Nemours, Montpensier, Bugeaud and Lamoricière on horseback and Thiers on foot. But he was no longer the Louis-Philippe of 1832. Drawn up in front of him were four thousand troops of the line, of whose loyalty there was no reason to doubt, the First and Tenth legions of the National Guard, the most solidly dynastic of all, and certain elements of the Fourth. Mistakenly, Louis-Philippe rode first down the ranks of the National Guard and was greeted by the First and Tenth with shouts of: "*Vive le Roi!*" and "*Vive la Réforme!*" But when he reached the 4th, the men broke their ranks, shouting: "*A bas les ministres! A bas le système!*" And some of them began to surround the cavalcade with menacing gestures. Without a word and to everyone's stupefaction, the King slowly turned his horse's head round and rode back into the palace without even looking at the troops of the line drawn up at the present. Back in his study he collapsed in a chair with his head in his hands, silent and with a glazed, expressionless stare in his eyes.

A few minutes later a band of about six hundred insurgents pressed into the Place du Carrousel and was bloodlessly dispersed by the personal vigour of Bugeaud and Lamoricière. But on the other side of the Tuileries a desperate fight was going on within two hundred metres of the palace, where a detachment of the 14th regiment, vastly outnumbered and short of ammunition, was holding out in a building called the Château d'Eau in the Place du Palais-Royal. The insurgents were preparing to burn down the building with straw collected from the royal stables. The noise of the shooting was, of course, clearly audible in the Tuileries and Thiers kept repeating: "The flood is rising." By now, all considerations of precedence and etiquette had been abandoned and people were coming and going in the palace without reference to the old King, still sunk in his chair. Among them was the radical Jewish lawyer, Crémieux, who strenuously urged the substitution of Marshal Gérard for Bugeaud and Odilon Barrot for Thiers. Bugeaud, now certain that resistance was hopeless, made no difficulty about handing his command over to a man who was as old as Louis-Philippe and an invalid to boot; but Barrot was at this moment engaged in sending off messages to the provinces from the Ministry of the Interior, through the back gardens of which Guizot and Duchâtel had recently escaped on their way to exile. As the noise of the shooting from the Château d'Eau became sharper and sharper, the word "abdication" began to be whispered and then about twelve o'clock the journalist Emile de Girardin burst through the ranks of frightened courtiers and going straight up to the King declared in a peremptory tone that abdication was in fact the only possible solution. Piscatory, a diplomat on leave, said to Louis-Philippe: "Your abdication, Sire, means the Republic within an hour. Don't abdicate." Louis-Philippe from his chair turned towards Sébastiani, Gérard and Soult and asked: "Is any defence possible?" There was no answer. He rose slowly from his chair and said:

"I am a peaceful King. Since all defence is impossible, I do not wish to spill French blood in vain and I abdicate." He moved heavily over to the maple-wood desk – Napoleon's – at which he had for so many years worked alone far into the night, and wrote out with great deliberation: "I abdicate this crown which the will of the nation called me to wear in favour of my grandson the Comte de Paris. May he succeed in the great task which falls to him today." As he was writing, panic-stricken courtiers crowded round his desk urging him to hurry. As the sound of firing quickened Montpensier too asked his father to write more quickly. Louis-Philippe turned round and observed placidly: "I have always written slowly; this isn't the moment to change my habits." The decision taken, his courage was slowly returning and when he was asked by the protesting onlookers to announce in the document the regency of the Duchesse d'Orléans, he shouted at them in a terrible voice: "It's against the law and as, thank God, I have never violated any law, I'm not going to begin at a moment like this."

Old Gérard, in civilian clothes, was bundled on to a white horse and sent out into the thick of the fighting in the Place du Palais-Royal to announce the news of their victory to the people. It was a mission at least as dangerous as any he had undertaken in Spain or Russia in the old days, and, unable to make any impression, he allowed one of the insurgents to grab the act of abdication out of his hand. But even at this late hour, a word of command to the troops in the Place du Carrousel would have resulted in the insurgents being easily pushed back from the vicinity of the palace. Instead, Lamoricière bravely attempted to separate the combatants, was wounded and taken prisoner. With the Château d'Eau already blazing, the fall of the post was imminent and Crémieux rushed back into the palace, shouting breathlessly: "The people are coming . . . they will be here in a few minutes . . . Sire, you must go." Louis-Philippe took off his uniform coat and the royal family began to group round him. Hélène d'Orléans threw herself into his arms, crying: "Don't leave me. I am only a poor, weak woman. What shall I do without your advice and protection?" Louis-Philippe embraced her and replied: "My dearest child, you owe yourself to your children and to France. You must stay."

Twelve carriages had been made ready in the stables, but the fighting in the vicinity had made it only possible for two to be extricated and they had been lost when the groom was shot dead. Fortunately, Nemours had kept his head throughout the crisis and had ordered to the Tuileries two one-horse broughams and a cabriolet, used by members of the royal household. The King, who had just time to burn all his papers, proceeded on foot with the royal family to a point near the obelisk on the Place de la Concorde, where they were soon surrounded by a potentially menacing crowd of spectators, becoming increasingly •dense, when there suddenly appeared an escort of cavalry commanded by General Dumas. Thanks to this, the carriages were able to join the fugitives, who piled into them – in the first Louis-Philippe, Marie-Amélie and three grandchildren; in the second the Duchesse de Nemours and her children; in the cabriolet Montpensier, Dumas and a lady-in-waiting. Escorted by double ranks of cuirassiers this undignified cavalcade clattered off on the road to Saint-Cloud. The revolution had triumphed at the cost of 72 soldiers and 289 insurgents.

The defending troops having moved to the Concorde, the mob poured into the palace, while Marshal Bugeaud rode majestically at walking pace through their ranks. The royal apartments were sacked from top to bottom. Wine barrels were broached so that by nightfall the level of wine on the floors was such that several revellers were found drowned; the throne was ceremoniously burnt; enthusiastic bacchantes dressed up in court robes; the famous yellow carriage was thrown into the Seine and Louis-Philippe's bed was systematically fouled. For nearly a fortnight, the Provisional Government of the Second Republic felt unable to call a halt to these proceedings, which were diversified by the sacking of the Palais-Royal and the burning of the Château de Neuilly and the Château de Suresnes, a Rothschild mansion crammed with art treasures of every description. As Lord

Normanby commented in his diary that evening: "I cannot but hope that tomorrow may bring some signs of a settled future; but nothing can be more gloomy for the prospects of a great country than the complete anarchy which exists at this moment."

X

In the spring of 1793 Louis-Philippe's escape from the authorities of the First Republic had amounted to a quick dash for
freedom; now, fifty-five years later, his escape from the authorities of the Second Republic was protracted, arduous and agonizing. While the Duchesse d'Orléans was making her last brave
stand for the dynasty in the Palais-Bourbon, the King and Queen
were being driven to Dreux, where they arrived at five o'clock,
just as Lamartine was proclaiming the Second Republic at the
Hôtel de Ville. Dreux, the home of the hideous family mausoleum,
is a little hilly town with a chapel begun in 1816 by Egalité's
widow. Louis-Philippe's remains were taken there from England
in 1876. Now Marie-Amélie knelt in prayer before the family
tombs and Louis-Philippe busied himself with plans for the next
stage of the flight, before finally getting to bed at two in the
morning. The rest of the family had already made for Boulogne.
A conference was held at the King's bedside at seven on the
morning of the 25th. With the proclamation of the republic, a
journey to Eu was altogether too hazardous and it was decided
that the King and Queen would make as rapidly as possible for
England, disguised as M. and Mme Lebrun.[1] They set off for
Honfleur, with the sub-prefect on the box of a berline and
General de Rumigny for escort. They stopped only at Evreux,
where one of the agents Louis-Philippe employed to look after
Laffitte's famous forest of Breteuil gave them a good meal and a
thousand francs. At Evreux they were only about fifty miles from
the coast. They decided to proceed in two separate carriages and
travelling all night in filthy weather they reached La Côte de
Grace, just above Honfleur, at daybreak on the 26th, where, as

---

[1] The real name of the Head of the State in comparably disastrous circumstances in 1940.

had been arranged, they were to be hidden in the house of a M. de Perthuis, a relative of General Dumas. De Perthuis' gardener, although he recognized the King, began negotiations to secure a fishing-boat and a friend of the family undertook to persuade the skipper of the English channel-packet *Express* (Newhaven to Le Havre) to sight the fishing-boat as if by chance and take the passengers aboard. The skipper refused.

Louis-Philippe stayed the nights of February the 26th and 27th in de Perthuis' home with nothing to do except to read the papers, while Marie-Amélie lay prostrate with exhaustion on a bed. Eventually there was news of a possible boat at Trouville. When they reached the shore on the 28th in pouring rain over bad roads, the boat was grounded at low tide and the sea mountainous. An immediate start was impossible and the old couple had to take refuge in a house in Trouville, secured by de Rumigny. Rumours soon spread round the little town and at eight o'clock on the morning of March 1st Louis-Philippe was warned that the house was about to be searched. While de Rumigny charged his pistols, the King left by a back-entrance and ran straight into an un-known man, who said: "Sire, a faithful subject is here to conduct you to a place of safety." A few minutes later, Louis-Philippe was respectively greeted by an assembly of the notables of Trouville in the salon of a former mayor. After an agreeable conversation, they escorted him back to de Perthuis' house. Three days had now passed and escape was no nearer.

But at dawn on March 2nd the King received an unexpected visitor, a Mr Jones, Her Britannic Majesty's vice-consul at Le Havre, who informed him not only that the *Express* was at his service but that the Duc de Nemours and the Princess Clémentine were safely back in England. To reach Le Havre unrecognized would be very difficult. The Queen would be, as before, Mme. Lebrun; but the King would be William Smith, an English business man, who was a relative of the British consul, an energetic individual who rejoiced in the rather grander name of Mr Featherstonhaugh. Louis-Philippe cut off his side-whiskers, put on thick goggles and a very Anglo-Saxon greatcoat and talked to Mr

Jones in a volley of admirable English. On the quay at Le Havre he was greeted with much hand-shaking by Mr Featherstonhaugh, his reputed nephew, but began to overact his part, the consul later writing to Palmerston that "my dear Uncle talked so loud and so much that I had the greatest difficulty to make him keep silence". Even after the King and Queen were safely aboard the *Express*, a suspicious port-official came aboard and asked if he could go over the cabins. "Very willingly on my next voyage," replied the captain, "unless you want to make the trip with us." The *Express* steamed out of Le Havre a little after nine o'clock and the port-official, who had had just time to get ashore, asked the consul: "Please tell me who was the person you've put aboard the *Express*?" "My uncle," replied Featherstonhaugh – "Oh, consul, what have you done?" – "What you would have done in my place, monsieur." Just as the fugitives had embarked, a party of gendarmes arrived in the house they had occupied to arrest them. As Mr Featherstonhaugh remarked: "It was a hair-trigger affair altogether."

At seven on the morning of March the 3rd after a terrible crossing, Mr and Mrs William Smith landed at Newhaven. That day from a room with a bow-window in the little seventeenth-century Bridge Hotel, Louis-Philippe wrote to Queen Victoria: "After having given thanks to God, my first duty is to offer to your Majesty the homage of my acknowledgements for the generous assistance you have given us, myself and all my family ... It is only, Madame, as the Comte de Neuilly that I, recalling your former kindness, come to seek under your auspices a refuge and a peaceful retreat and as far from political relations as that which I enjoyed at another time, and of which I have always preserved such a precious memory." The next day Louis-Philippe and Marie-Amélie were in their last home at Claremont, although just as they were about to leave Newhaven they were subjected in The Bridge to addresses in Latin and French delivered by the pupils of the Free Grammar School at Lewes.

Exile at Claremont was in the circumstances a good deal less supportable than exile at nearby Twickenham forty years earlier. But it was mercifully to prove far less protracted. Louis-Philippe's initial reception was mixed. Not everybody by any means had forgotten the Spanish marriages. *The Spectator* wrote: "He comes for shelter with his cajoling tongue in his cheek; he returns to us, even on deposition, 'with pleasure'; he continues to know all sorts of obscure gentlemen by name; he shakes hands all round; and addresses a knot of anonymous sight-seers as 'the British nation'. There is not a puffing advertiser, nor even a playhouse manager, that better understands the art of humbug . . . He has fallen on his true social designation – he is properly one of the Smiths." But it is somewhat in the tradition of *The Spectator* not to err on the side of charity and perhaps a fairer estimate of the fallen King's fortunes was that of Lord John Russell: "After the vicissitudes of a long life, it may be no irremediable calamity if a Prince of great powers of mind and warm domestic affections is permitted by Providence to end his days in peace and tranquility." Queen Victoria's close links with the French royal family enabled her to judge the situation both accurately and charitably. She wrote to old Melbourne on March the 15th:

> The poor King and his Government made many mistakes within the last two years, and were obstinate and totally blind at the last till flight was inevitable. But for *sixteen* years he did a great deal to maintain peace and made France prosperous, which should *not* be forgotten . . . Lord Melbourne's kind heart will grieve to think of the *real want* the poor King and Queen are in, their dinner-table containing barely enough to eat . . . Surely the poor old King is sufficiently punished for his faults?

A month later she wrote to Russell: "Guizot is more to blame; *he* was the responsible adviser: he is *no* Bourbon, and he ought to have behaved differently. Had the poor King died in 1844 after he came here, and before that most unfortunate Spanish marriages question was started, he would deservedly have gone down to posterity as a great monarch. *Now*, what will be his name in history? His fate is a great *moral*!" Disraeli, who had greatly appreciated Louis-Philippe's kindness to him at the Tuileries in 1842, said in the House of Commons: "I have no hesitation in saying that I lament that the late Ruler of France has fallen. Whatever his errors to his people may have been, he was a great prince, a great gentleman (a laugh), a great man ... I cannot forget that for eighteen years he did secure, he did maintain for Europe, the blessings of peace."

Claremont House, near Esher, was built for Clive in 1768 and had been granted in life-interest to Leopold of the Belgians after the death of his first wife, George IV's daughter. It was rather a characterless building, decidedly gloomy in winter, but with a magnificent park. But for a generous gesture on the part of Aberdeen, who surreptitiously gave a thousand pounds to a member of the household, the family's initial financial embarrassment would have been acute. Visitors noticed the extreme simplicity of the ex-King's bedroom and although gradually some sort of establishment was maintained with a few good horses in the stables, and the table-silver from Eu, it was some time before Dupin in Paris was able to recover sufficient funds for the simple needs of the family. One by one, they reassembled, children and grandchildren, including Aumale, who had had to abandon his brilliant career in Algeria, and Joinville. The old people supported a life of enforced leisure with comparative resignation, Marie-Amélie especially finding consolation in the noisy vitality of her grandchildren and in an existence happily devoid of the daily terror of assassination plots. The chronicle of their last years together was uneventful. The first autumn most of the family were poisoned by bad drinking water and three of their entourage died. This necessitated a temporary move to Richmond where they stayed at the Star and Garter, familiar to Louis-Philippe from the old days.[1] A short trip to Saint Leonards followed and they were soon restored to health. Old Cuvillier-Fleury, Aumale's tutor, visited them for the second time in August 1849, and although he thought Marie-Amélie looked

[1] Wandering on foot round adjacent Twickenham he was one day accosted by a man who shook him by the hand effusively. He turned out to be a retired publican. "Surely you remember me, Your Majesty – I kept the Crown?" "That's more than I did," replied Louis-Philippe in a flash.

splendid, he noticed that Louis-Philippe was obviously beginning to fade away, although still eating well and reading *The Times* as vigorously as ever.

His great consolation was to talk about the ups and downs of his extraordinary existence to a sympathetic listener. In December 1849 he much enjoyed dining with Peel at Drayton Manor a few months before they both died, when Peel told him: "Sire, to you we owe the peace of the world; as head of a nation justly sensitive and justly proud of its military glory, you were able to attain the great end of peace, without ever sacrificing any of France's interests." Since Robert Peel was no courtier, this tribute pleased the old man greatly. Wellington spent an afternoon at Claremont and the two veterans agreed that '48 in Paris was a movement that could not have been resisted; another septuagenarian, that indefatigable busy-body, Lord Brougham, sought the ex-King's views on the prospects of General Cavaignac; in November 1848 he told Clarendon how delighted he was with the number of National Guards who called on him, but how irritating it was when they said: "Why did you abandon us?" Croker recalled a long interview with Louis-Philippe, when the old man talked fascinatingly of an evening in the distant past when he dined with Pétion and Robespierre. He recalled that when Pétion teased Robespierre about being so silent and surly and suggested marriage as a solution, the latter opened his mouth for the first and last time with a kind of scream and declared that he would never marry. But more often, as with Molé and de Broglie, the talk would be of the February Revolution and the progress of events in Paris.

As Louis-Napoleon became more firmly established than suited the book of the surviving politicians of the July Monarchy, there was much talk of attempting a fusion between the Legitimist and Orléanist factions in order to secure the throne for the Comte de Chambord as Henri V. Louis-Philippe was quite ready to entertain the idea, though it was well known that the Duchesse d'Orléans was firmly opposed to it. In June 1850 he was trying to recover his fast-fading health at Saint Leonards, when he was visited by an old acquaintance in Adolphe Thiers, who had by this time had more than his fill of Bonapartism. Louis-Philippe embraced him warmly and they had an animated discussion on the prospects of a restoration.[1] But that same month Guizot heard alarming rumours about his old master's health and came hurriedly to pay his respects at Saint Leonards. He wrote: "I found the King better, that is to say less bad than people had told me. He is horribly changed, thin as a sheet of paper, his face has fallen in, but his eye is bright, his complexion clear, his voice firm and his mind as quick and serene as it has ever been. Truly a phenomenon of vitality, kept going by the vigour of his intelligence and the natural solidity of his physique." He added that Louis-Philippe was suffering from an incurable disease of the liver, but was determined to overcome it. In July he seemed to be better and went for long walks on the sea-front, but a visit to London to attend the Comte de Paris' first communion left him drained of energy and he began to deteriorate rapidly at Claremont.

On Saturday, August 24th he sat out on the terrace in bright sunshine and felt well enough to dine with the family, although he ate nothing. But after a feverish night it was clear that a pleurisy was overcoming him and the following morning he asked the doctor to tell him the truth. Seeing the doctor hesitate, he smiled and said: "Je comprends. Vous venez m'apporter mon congé." He still had enough strength to dictate a page of his memoirs, describing the events of 1814, to Dumas and settle a few points in his will. After being alone with the Queen for half an hour, he confessed and received extreme unction. At his bedside through the night knelt Marie-Amélie, the Duchesse d'Orléans and his three sons, Nemours, Aumale, Joinville and their wives. He died at eight o'clock in the morning of August the 26th and was buried in a private Catholic chapel at Weybridge. The next day Charles Greville, looking out on to the sea at Brighton, wrote in his diary: "Yesterday morning L.P. expired at Claremont quite unexpectedly, for though he had been ill for a long time, it was

[1] When he heard of the ex-King's death two months later, Thiers observed: "As for me, I could never help liking him."

supposed he might still live many months. Not long ago his life was the most important in the world, and his death would have produced a profound sensation and general consternation. Now hardly more importance attaches to the event than there would be to the death of one of the Old Bathing-women opposite my window." The world had changed greatly in seventy-seven years since Louis-Philippe had been born. Now the nineteenth century was half spent and Europe was about to enter a new age of violence.

Appendix I: Genealogical Table

LOUIS XIII (1601–1643)

Maria Theresa of Spain m. LOUIS XIV (1638–1715) . . . Mme de Montespan

Maria Anna of Bavaria m. Louis (1661–1711)

Louis, Duc de Bourgogne (1682–1712) m. Marie Adélaïde of Savoy

LOUIS XV (1710–74) m. Maria Leszczynska

Louis m. Maria Josepha of Saxony (1729–65)

LOUIS XVI (1754–1793) m. Marie-Antoinette of Austria

LOUIS XVIII (1755–1824)

CHARLES X (1757–1836) m. Maria-Theresa of Sardinia

Marie-Thérèse m. Louis Duc d'Angoulême (1778–1851) (1775–1844)

Louis b. 1785

Ferdinand, Duc d'Orléans (1810–42) m. Hélène of Mecklenburg-Schwerin

Henri, Duc de Bordeaux and Comte de Chambord (1820–83) o.s.p.

Louis-Philippe, Comte de Paris (1838–94)

Philippe, Duc d'Orléans (1869–1926)

Charles Duc de Berri m. Caroline of Naples (1778–1820)

Marie (1813–39) m. Frederick of Wurtemberg

Louise (1812–50) m. Leopold, King of the Belgians

Prince de Lamballe (1747–68)

Louise-Marie-Adélaïde de Bourbon-Penthièvre (1747–1821)

Duc de Penthièvre m. Maria-Theresa of Este-Modena (1725–93) (1726–56)

Charlotte m. Francis III, Duke of Modena

Comte de Toulouse

Philippe d'Orléans (1640–1701) m. (1) Henrietta Maria of England
(2) Elizabeth Charlotte of the Palatinate

Mlle de Blois (1677–1749) m. Philippe d'Orléans, The Regent (1674–1723)

Louis d'Orléans (le pieux) (1703–52) m. Augusta Maria of Baden

Louis-Philippe d'Orléans (le gros) (1725–85) m. Louise-Henriette de Conti (and morganatically Mme de Montesson, aunt of Mme de Genlis)

Louis-Philippe-Joseph d'Orléans (Egalité) (1747–93)

Louise-Bathilde d'Orléans m. Louis Henri, duc de Bourbon, last of the Condés (1756–1830)

Antoine, Duc de Montpensier (1775–1807)

Adélaïde (1777–1847)

Françoise, died in infancy

Louis-Charles, Comte de Beaujolais (1779–1808)

Louis Antoine, Duc d'Enghien (1772–1804)

LOUIS-PHILIPPE I (1773–1850) m. Marie-Amélie de Bourbon-Sicile (1782–1866)

daughter died in infancy

Clementine (1817–1907) m. Augustus of Saxe-Coburg-Gotha

Ferdinand, King of Bulgaria

François, Duc de Joinville (1818–1900) m. Françoise of Braganza

son, Duc de Penthièvre, died in infancy

Louis, Duc de Nemours (1814–96) m. Victoria of Saxe-Coburg-Gotha

Robert, Duc de Chartres (1840–1910)

Jean, Duc de Guise (1874–1940)

Henri, Comte de Paris (1908–   )

Henri, Duc d'Aumale (1822–97) m. Caroline of Naples

Antoine, Duc de Montpensier (1824–1900) m. Maria Luisa of Spain

Appendix II

The circumstances attending the birth and baptism of Louis-Philippe demand relation in some detail since by a fortunate and brilliant piece of research in connection with them in the Archives Nationales at Paris, M. André Castelot has been able to disprove the famous Chiappini allegations that the future King of the French was a suppositious child, allegations which were to plague him in after-life at a particularly embarrassing moment in his career and which have been regurgitated with varying degrees of malice in almost every book relating to his career. The essentials of this celebrated story are that in the spring of 1773 a mysterious Comte de Joinville was travelling with his wife in Italy; that on April 17th, 1773, in the town of Modigliani the Comtesse gave birth to a daughter; that that daughter was exchanged in accordance with a prearranged plan for the son of the local gaoler Lorenzo Chiappini; that the Comte and Comtesse de Joinville were in reality the Duc and Duchesse de Chartres engaged in a conspiracy to ensure a male heir for the House of Orléans; and that in October 1773 the birth of Louis-Philippe consisted essentially in the passing-off of a five-month old Italian baby as the newly-born heir. To her dying day in 1843 it is probable that Marie-Stella-Petronilla Chiappini, who became first the Countess of Newborough and subsequently Baronne de Sternberg, believed every word of the legend from the moment that she received in 1821 a letter from the dying gaoler of Modigliani which read as follows:

Milady –
I have come to the end of my life without having revealed to anyone a secret which concerns you and me directly.
The secret is as follows:
The day you were born of a person whom I cannot name and who has already passed into another world, a son was born to me also.

I was asked to make an exchange and considering my circumstances at the time I agreed to the profitable proposal which was pressed upon me; and it was then that I adopted you for my daughter in the same way as my son was adopted by the other party.

I see that Heaven has condoned my sins since you are in a better station of life than your true father, although he was almost of the same rank; and so I can end my life in peace.

Keep you this to yourself so as not to make me totally guilty! Yes, in asking you to forgive me I ask you please to keep this a secret so as to stop people talking about an affair that can no longer be remedied.

This letter will only be sent to you after my death.

Lorenzo Chiappini

From then onwards Maria-Stella, who already had some suspicion about her paternity, devoted herself with great assiduity and skill to solving the mystery. Joinville being one of the Orléans family names and one frequently used by Philippe-Egalité, the trail soon led her to the conclusion that the secret was to be found in the comings and goings of the Duc and Duchesse de Chartres in 1773. Gradually a formidable case was built up, the elements of which, seized on by innumerable Legitimist and Republican pamphleteers, were as follows:

1. In 1824 the ecclesiastical tribunal of Faenza after hearing several witnesses gave judgement that Maria Stella was in fact the daughter of the *soi-disant* Comte de Joinville.

2. Dupin, Louis-Philippe's legal adviser, unfortunately drew up a rebuttal of the Chiappini thesis, which was inaccurate in several details and was easily revealed as such.

3. Maria Stella published in 1830 her *Mémoires* in 318 pages entitled "Maria Stella or the criminal exchange of a girl of the highest birth with a boy of the lowest social condition". The July Monarchy allowed this to appear in new editions between 1830 and 1837.

4. In these *Mémoires* Maria Stella built up her case by alleging that Marie-Adélaïde had practically disappeared from view in the winter of 1772-73, her first public appearance being at the Opera

in June 1773 "two months after my birth". Furthermore the ceremony of the private baptism (*ondoiement*) of the new-born prince was carried out in secret at the Palais-Royal on Louis-Philippe's own admission by the palace almoner and in the presence of two valets instead of, as would have been normal, in the parish church of Saint-Eustache, and that the signature on the *acte d'ondoiement* reads "L.P.J. d'Orléans" at a time when that prince was only Duc de Chartres. Finally why did the Duc d'Orléans, the head of the family, not sign the acte? Everything seemed to suggest an atmosphere of dark conspiracy.

M. Castelot by his own admission approached his study of the so-called Enigma of Modigliani with a prejudice in favour of the Maria Stella solution, which was still giving rise to a vigorous anti-Orléanist literature in the nineteen-forties. He has painstakingly succeeded in finally demolishing the legend. In the Archives Nationales[1] he has discovered a document which records that during the final hours of Marie-Adélaïde's accouchement and in her very bedroom at the Palais-Royal (as was the barbarous custom of the day) there were present as well as the Duc de Chartres, the Duc de Bourbon-Penthièvre, the Princesse de Lamballe, the duc de Bourbon, the Prince de Conti and a considerable number of other personages of the household. Shortly after the birth, the Duc d'Orléans, summoned during the night, appeared "and as soon as he had seen his new-born grandson he left and took the road for Fontainebleau . . ." It was at seven o'clock in broad morning daylight that the allegedly dark and conspiratorial *ondoiement* took place not it is true in the parish church but, as was the family tradition, in the palace itself. The "two valets" turn out to be the Comte de Schomberg, chamberlain to the Duc de Chartres and the Comte d'Hunolstein, a gentleman of the bedchamber, and in any case there were present also the Duchesse de Bourbon, the Prince de Conti and the Comte de la Marche. Louis-Philippe-Joseph signed himself "L.P.J. d'Orléans", although he was Duc de Chartres, because this was how he always did sign himself, as can be seen at the foot of the letter addressed

[1] Dossier K 142

to Louis XV in protest against the dismissal of the Parlements. Finally another document reveals the fact that Marie-Adélaïde attended a particularly crowded ceremony six weeks before her alleged accouchement in Italy, her dress, which is described in detail, revealing no indication of an imminent maternity. There can be little doubt that Maria Stella, Baroness de Sternberg, was the daughter of an aristocrat touring Italy under the name of the Comte de Joinville in the spring of 1773. But there is no doubt at all that Louis-Philippe, King of the French, was authentically the son of Philippe-Egalité.

Select Bibliography

A. BIOGRAPHIES

P. de la Gorce, *Louis-Philippe*, 1931.
J. Lucas-Dubreton, *Louis-Philippe*, 1938.
D. Cochin, *Louis-Philippe*, 1918.
C. Gavin, *Louis-Philippe, King of the French*, 1933.
R. Recouly, *Louis-Philippe, Roi des Français*.
M. Aghion, *Les Années d'Aventure de Louis-Philippe*, 1930.
G. N. Wright, *Life and Times of Louis-Philippe, King of the French*, 1842.
P. Gruyer, *La Jeunesse de Louis-Philippe*, 1909.
J. Bertaut, *Le Roi Bourgeois*, 1936.
De Flers, *Le Roi Louis-Philippe, Vie Anecdotique*, 1891.
E. Boutmy, *Histoire Personelle de Louis-Philippe*, 1848.
A. Britsch, *La Jeunesse de Philippe-Égalité*, 1926.
A. de Castelot, *Philippe-Égalité, le Prince Rouge*, 1950.
J. Harmand, *Madame de Genlis*, 1912.
V. Wyndham, *Madame de Genlis*, 1958.
E. Dard, *Le Général Choderlos de Laclos*, 1905.
M. Hay, *Prince in Captivity*, 1960.
A. Trognon, *La Vie de Marie-Amélie*, 1872.
R. Arnaud, *Adélaïde d'Orléans*, 1908.
Duff Cooper, *Talleyrand*, 1937.
C. Nicoullaud, *Casimir Périer*, 1894.
J. Lucas-Dubreton, *Monsieur Thiers*, 1948.
J-T. de Mesmay, *Horace Sébastiani*, 1948.
P. Quentin Bauchart, *Lamartine*, 1903.
J. Lucas-Dubreton, *Lamartine*, 1951.
F. A. Simpson, *Louis-Napoleon and the Recovery of France*, 1923.
W. F. Monypenny and G. E. Buckle, *The Life of Benjamin Disraeli, Earl of Beaconsfield*, 1910–20.

B. MEMOIRS, ETC.

Louis-Philippe d'Orléans, *Mon Journal*, 1849.
Talleyrand, *Mémoires*, 1891–2.

J. Mallet du Pan, *Memoirs and Correspondence* (ed. Sayous), 1851.
Comtesse de Boigne, *Mémoires*, 1922–4.
Prince de Joinville, *Vieux Souvenirs*, 1894.
A. de Chateaubriand, *Mémoires d'Outre-Tombe*, 1849–50.
R. Apponyi, *Journal* (1926).
Sainte-Beuve, *Causeries du Lundi*.
A. A. Cuvillier-Fleury, *Journal*, 1903.
J. Laffitte, *Mémoires* (ed. 1932).
C. de Montalivet, *Fragments et Souvenirs*, 1899.
O. Barrot *Mémoires*, 1875–6.
L. Blanc, *L'Organisation du Travail*, 1840.
L. Blanc, *Histoire de Dix Ans*, 1841–4.
H. Heine, *Lutèce*, 1855.
F. Guizot, *Mémoires pour servir à l'Histoire de mon Temps*, 1858–67.
V. Hugo, *Choses Vues*, 1888–1900.
V. Hugo, *Les Misérables*, 1862.
L. de la Hodde, *Histoire des Sociétés Secrètes et du Parti Républicain de 1830 à 1848*, 1850.
M. du Camp, *Souvenirs de l'Année 1848*, 1876.
L. Blanc, *Histoire de la Révolution de 1848*, 1880.
A. de Tocqueville, *Souvenirs*, 1893.
E. Taschereau, *Revue Rétrospective*, 1848.
Duke of Wellington, *Despatches, Correspondence and Memoranda*.
C. Greville, *Diary and Memoirs*.
The Letters of Queen Victoria.
Lewis Cass, *France, its King, Court and Government*, 1840.
Lord Normanby, *A Year of Revolution*, 1859.
J. W. Croker, *Letters, Diaries and Memoirs*, 1884.
N. W. Senior, *Conversations with M. Thiers, M. Guizot and other eminent Persons*, 1878.

C. GENERAL HISTORIES

P. Thureau-Dangin, *Histoire de la Monarchie de Juillet*, 1889.
S. Charléty, *La Monarchie de Juillet*, 1921.
G. Weill, *La France sous la Monarchie Constitutionnelle*, 1912.
G. Weill, *L'Eveil des Nationalités et le Mouvement Liberal* (1815–48).
J. Lucas-Dubreton, *La Restauration et la Monarchie de Juillet*, 1926.
E. Fournière, *Le Règne de Louis-Philippe*, 1905.

Duvergier de Hauranne, *Histoire du Gouvernement Parlementaire en France de 1814 à 1848* (1857–72).
J. P. T. Bury, *France 1814-1940*, 1949.
D. W. Brogan, *The French Nation*, 1957.
E. L. Woodward, *French Revolutions*, 1934.
P. E. Charvet, *France*, 1954.
M. D. R. Leys, *Between Two Empires*, 1955.

D. SPECIAL STUDIES

G. Lenôtre, *Les Fils de Philippe Égalité pendant la Terreur*, 1907.
R. Rémond, *La Droite en France de 1815 à Nos Jours*, 1948.
R. Burnand, *La Vie Quotidienne en France en 1830*, 1943.
G. Girard, *Les Trois Glorieuses*, 1929.
P. Bastid, *Les Institutions Politiques de la Monarchie Parlementaire Française*, 1954.
C. Morazé, *La France Bourgeoise*, 1947.
C. de Montalivet, *Le Roi Louis-Philippe. Liste Civile* (1851).
J. Lucas-Dubreton, *Louis-Philippe et la Machine Infernale*, 1951.
A. Guérard, *French Civilization in the Nineteenth Century*, 1914.
A. A. Cuvillier-Fleury, *Etudes et Portraits*, 2 vols., 1865, 1868.
R. Priouret, *La République des Députés*, 1959.
Gaston-Martin, *La Révolution de 1848*, 1948.
G. Rudé, *The Crowd in the French Revolution*, 1959.
J. M. Thompson, *Leaders of the French Revolution*, 1929.
J. Plamenatz, *The Revolutionary Movement in France 1815-71*, 1950.
J. L. Talmon, *Political Messianism – The Romantic Phase*, 1960.
J. Holland Rose and A. M. Broadley, *Dumouriez and the Defence of England*, 1908.
A. H. Jomini, *Histoire Critique et Militaire des Guerres de la Révolution*, 1840.
R. W. Phipps, *The Armies of the First French Republic*, 1929.
P. Spencer, *Politics of Belief in Nineteenth Century France*, 1944.
D. O. Evans, *Social Romanticism in France 1830-48*, 1951.
E. Starkie, *Petrus Borel*, 1944.
P. Campbell, *French Electoral Systems and Elections 1789-1907*, 1948.
I. Collins, *The Government and the Newspaper Press in France 1814-81*, 1958.
E. L. Woodward, *Three Studies in European Conservatism*, 1929.

Sir Charles Webster, *The Foreign Policy of Palmerston*, especially Vol. II, 1951.

J. Duhamel, *Louis-Philippe et la Première Entente Cordiale*, 1951.

J. R. Hall, *England and the Orléans Monarchy*, 1912.

E. J. Parry, *The Spanish Marriages 1841-6*, 1936.

Sir C. Petrie, *The Spanish Royal House*, 1958.

ed. C. Moulin, *Le Livre du Centenaire*, 1948.

Index

Abd-el-Kadr, 276, 277, 295

Aberdeen, George Hamilton Gordon, Earl, 279, 289, 291, 292, 296, 298–9, 332

Adélaïde, Princess of Orléans, 34, 53, 54, 75, 77, 82, 88, 93, 94, 116, 134, 142; gives adherence to July Revolution; 148; and Périer, 193; caricatured in press, 204; death, 312

Affre, Denis, Archbishop of Paris, 309

Aiguillon, Duc d', 42

Albert, Duke of Saxe-Coburg-Gotha, Prince Consort of England, 291, 297

Alembert, Jean le Rond d', 28, 34, 35

Alexander I, Czar, 122, 129

Algeria, 140, 277–8, 279, 312

Amis du Peuple, Les, 162, 165, 181, 183, 197

Angoulême, Louis-Antoine de Bourbon, Duc d', 122, 123

Angoulême, Marie-Thérèse, Duchesse d', 110, 145, 149–50, 156

Antwerp, siege of, 215

Arago, François, 209, 236, 260

Argenson, Marc-Rene de Voyer d', 217

Argout, Comte Antoine-Maurice d', 144, 145, 193

Artois, Charles-Phillipe, Comte d' (later Charles X). See Charles X

Atthalin, General, 124, 133, 140, 177, 204

Auber, Daniel, 178, 291

Augereau, Pierre, Marshal of France, 101

Aumale, Henri, Duc d' (son of Louis-Philippe), 80, 134, 135, 205, 236, 276, 277, 280, 289, 312, 332

Austria, campaign against, 58, 60–1, 62–5, 70–2; Dumouriez and, 79, 80, 81, 82; and the Vatican, 202; Talleyrand and, 238; Duc d'Orléans' marriage project, 240, 241; and the Eastern Question, 263

Avaray, Comte d', 98

Avenir, L', 169–70, 185

Bagehot, Walter, 315

Bailly, Jean-Sylvain, 28, 49, 91

Ball, Sir Alexander, 115

Balzac, Honoré de, 198, 248, 270

Banquet campaign, 266, 310, 313–14, 316

Banzori, Marianne, 92–3

Barbès, Armand, 165, 227, 228, 256

Barère de Vieuzac, Bertrand de, 42

Barnave, Antoine Pierre, 42, 52, 91

Barras, Paul, Vicomte de, 99

Barrot, Odilon, support for Orléans solution, 149; as prefect of the Seine, 175, 183; and anti-clerical outburst, 189, 190; in opposition, 206, 209, 239, 249, 250, 251, 287, 288, 305; and banquet campaign, 311, 314, 316; and Guizot's resignation, 320

Baudoin, —, Louis-Philippe's valet 82, 88, 89, 96, 101

C.K.— Y*

Baylen, surrender at, 114
Bazard, Saint-Amand, 163
Beauharnais, Alexandre, Vicomte de, 60
Beaujolais, Louis-Charles, Comte de, 37, 67, 76, 87, 99, 111, 112
Beaulieu, Jean-Pierre de, General, 60
Beaumarchais, Pierre-Augustin de, 99
Belgium, Dumouriez appeals to, 70; conquest of, 72; disaffection in, 79; and Holland, 177; declared independent, 178; non-intervention by the Powers, 179; crown offered to Nemours, 180; France and, 201–2, 203; attacked by Holland, 203, 211; Dutch capitulation, 215; final settlement, 252; Customs Union proposed by Guizot, 288
Belgrave Square, London, 292, 293
Belle-Chasse, Mme de Genlis at, 34–5, 37–40, 42; circle at, 54
Bentinck, Lord William, 121, 122
Béranger, Pierre de, 149, 286
Bernard, Martin, 256
Bernardin de Saint-Pierre, Jacques, 35
Berri, Charles, Duc de, 126, 135, 189
Berri, Marie-Caroline, Duchesse de, 136, 140, 150, 207, 210, 213
Berryer, Pierre-Antoine, 166, 196, 241, 251, 266, 280
Berthier, Louis-Alexandre, Marshal, 60, 61, 128
Beurnonville, Pierre, Comte (later Marquis) de, 81, 82, 122n., 136
Bignon, Louis, 175
Biron, Armand-Louis, Duc de, 42, 60, 61, 77, 91
Blacas d'Aulps, Comte de, 126
Blanc, Louis, 158, 163, 222n., 266, 274, 306, 307, 311, 315, 317
Blanqui, Auguste, 165, 181, 227, 247, 251

Boireau, Victor, 230, 231–2, 238n.
Bonaparte, Lucien, 220
Bonapartism, 166, 195
Bordeaux, Henri, Duc de (and Comte de Chambord), 135, 150, 156, 166, 207, 291, 292, 333
Borel, Joseph-Petrus, 163, 186, 214n.
Bourbon, Louis-Henri, Duc de, 205
Bourbon-Penthièvre, Duc de. See Penthièvre, Duc de
Bourges, Michel de, 199, 227, 228
Bourmont, Louis-Auguste de, 139
Bresson, Charles, Comte, 224, 300, 310
Breteuil, Louis-Auguste, Baron de, 48
Brienne, Loménie de. See Loménie de Brienne
Brighton, 31
Brissot, Jacques-Pierre, 42, 45, 58, 73, 91
Broglie, Achille-Charles, 136, 148, 149, 160; minister of education, 167, 173, 174; forms ministry, 212; resignation, 223; new ministry, 225; introduces September Laws, 235; resignation, 238
Broglie, Victor-François de, Marshal, 48
Broval, Chevalier de, 106, 117–18, 134
Brunnow, Philip, Baron, 258, 263
Brunswick, Karl William Ferdinand, Duke of, 62, 63, 65
Buffon, Georges-Louis, Comte de, 28, 34
Buffon, Mme de, 34, 36, 49, 50, 67, 76, 77
Bugeaud de la Piconnerie, Thomas-Robert, Marshal, 217–18, 220, 276, 295, 296, 322, 323, 324, 326
Bulwer, Sir Henry, 265, 267, 299, 300
Burke, Edmund, 103, 242

Buonarotti, Filippo, 165, 227
Buzot, —, 75, 76, 91

Cabet, Étienne, 163, 306
Cabre, Sabatier de, Abbé, 44
Cadiz, Francisco d'Assiz, Duke of, 298, 300, 301
Calonne, Charles-Alexandre de, 41, 44
Camus, Armand-Gaston, 79–80, 81
Candide, 30
Canning, George, 115
Caradoc, Col., 156, 157
Carlo-republicanism, 292
Carlos, Don (1st), 225–6, 241
Carlyle, Thomas, 51, 66n.
Carmontelle, Louis, 19
Carnereiro, Don Mariano, 118
Carnot, Lazare-Nicolas, 73, 82, 130
Carrel, Nicolas-Armand, 139, 142, 166–7, 185, 195, 217, 219, 236
Casimir-Périer. *See* Périer, Casimir-Pierre
Cass, Lewis, General, 271
Castelot, A. de, 37, 337–9
Catholicism, and July Monarchy, 168–70, 309
Cavaignac, Godefroy, 148, 157, 158, 165, 181, 199, 217, 219, 228, 231
Chambord, Comte de. *See* Bordeaux, Duc de.
Chambre Introuvable, 131
Changarnier, Nicolas, 277
Charette de la Contrie, François-Athanase, 97
Charivari, 214, 229, 236
Charles IV, King of Spain, 114
Charles X, King of France (Comte d'Artois), 97; Louis-Philippe and, 104, 126–7, 135; dynastic rigidity, 111; holds Lieutenant-Generalcy, 122, 124; last months of his reign, 139, 140–41, 144–5;

abdication, 155–6; begins last exile, 156
Charles, Archduke, 79, 240, 241
Charles Albert, King of Sardinia, 303
Chartres, Ferdinand-Louis-Charles, Duc de. *See* Orléans, Duc de
Chartres, Louis-Philippe-Joseph, Duc de. *See* Orléans, Duc de
Chateaubriand, Francois Rene, Vicomte de, 125, 136, 151, 166, 286, 292
Chiappini, Marie-Stella, 337–40
Choderlos de Laclos, Pierre-Ambroise. *See* Laclos
Choiseul-Praslin, Duc de, 310
Claremont, 297, 330–31, 332
Clarence, William, Duke of. *See* William IV
Clarke, Henri-Jacques, Marshal, 128
Clausel, General, 276
Clémentine, Princesse d'Orléans, 134, 275, 290, 329
Clerfayt, Count von, 63, 71
Cobban, A., 46
Cobden, Richard, 310
Coburg, General, 79, 80, 81
Cochrane, Sir Thomas, 102
Collingwood, Cuthbert, Admiral, 112, 114
Collins, Irene, 237
Committee of Public Safety, 73
Comte, Auguste, 163, 227
Condorcet, Marie-Jean, Marquis de, 78n.
Considérant, Victor, 163
Constant, Benjamin, 116, 125, 149, 151
Constitutionnel, Le, 167
Conti, Louise-Henriette, Princesse de, 94
Convention, the, 67, 73, 74, 80, 87
Cormenin, Louis-Marie, Vicomte de, 206, 228, 249, 259

Cousin, Victor, 168
Crémieux, Adolphe, 324, 325
Cristina, Queen of Spain, 289, 299, 300
Cuba, Louis-Philippe in, 102
Cubières, —, 309
Custine, Adam, Comte de, 70

D'Alembert, Jean le Rond. *See* Alembert
Dalrymple, Sir Hew, 114
Damrémont, General, 277
Danton, Georges-Jacques, 42, 49, 54n., 68–70, 74, 78, 80
Daumesnil, General, 184
Daumier, Honore, 204, 220
David, Jacques-Louis, 35
Davout, Louis-Nicolas, Marshal (later Prince d'Eckmühl), 61, 82, 125, 310
Dawes, Sophie, 135, 205, 206
Debuisson, —, 80, 81
Deffand, Marie, Marquise du, 34
Delavigne, Casimir, 186
Delessert, —, 317, 318
Démocratie Pacifique, La, 316
Desforest, General, 72, 79n.
Desmoulins, Camille, 42, 48
Diderot, Denis, 34
Directory, the, 97, 99, 100
Disraeli, Benjamin, 241, 331
Doctrinaires, 173, 185, 189, 225, 238, 249
Droit d'interpellation, established, 160
Drouet d'Erlon, Jean-Baptiste, Comte, 125
Duborg, —, 144, 152
Duchâtel, Charles-Marie, Comte, 287, 305, 308, 314, 317, 319, 324
Ducrest, César, 37
Ducrest, Marquis, 33
Dufaure, Armand, 282
Dumas, Alexandre, 143, 248

Dumouriez, Charles-François, General, as minister of foreign affairs, 58–9; in command of Army of the North, 61, 62; conducts campaign checking Brunswick, 63, 65, 70; defeats Austrians at Jemappes, 71–2; opposes extension of the war, 73–4; disagreement with the Convention, 79; defeated at Neerwinden, 79; accused of treachery, 79–80; confers with Mack von Leiberich, 80; proposes armistice, 81; ordered to Paris, 81; arrests Beurnonville, 81, 82; proclamation against Jacobins, 81; deserts to Austrians, 83; belief in Louis-Philippe, 88, 97; meeting with Louis-Philippe at Hambourg, 95–6; in England, 104, 120; in old age, 138
Dundonald, Earl of (Sir Thomas Cochrane), 102
Dupetit-Thouars, A., 295
Dupin, André-Marie, agent for Louis-Philippe, 133, 134; minister without portfolio, 174; describes situation in Paris in 1830, 181; president of Chamber of Deputies, 214; heads the third party, 223; refuses premiership, 239
Dupont de l'Etang, Pierre-Antoine, Comte de, 114
Dupont de l'Eure, Jacques-Charles, 175, 183, 185, 188
Duvergier de Hauranne, Prosper, 251, 314

Eastern Question, the, 215–16, 257–9, 263–5, 267
Economist, the, 197n.
Edinburgh Review, 183n.

Émile, 35

England, Louis-Philippe in, 103, 104, 106–11, 130, 131, 133–4, 330–5; Louis XVIII in, 110. *See also* Great Britain

Enfantin, Prosper, 163

Espartero, Baldomero, 289

Espremesnil, Duval d', 44

Eton, 297

Faure, Jules, 227

February Revolution, 315–26

Ferdinand IV, King of Naples, 112, 117, 121

Fieschi, Joseph, 172, 230-2, 236n., 238

Fitzclarence, Adolphus, Lord, 290

Flahaut, Comtesse de, 95

Flaubert, Gustave, 198, 270, 311n.

Flocon, Ferdinand, 307, 311

Fontaine, Pierre, 273

Forth, Nathaniel Parker, 37

Fouché, Joseph, Duke of Otranto, 125, 130

Fouquier-Tinville, Antoine-Quentin, 16, 91

Fourier, Charles, 163

Fox, Charles James, 32, 51, 110, 242

France, La, 236, 280

Franchise, extension of, 198, 260–1, 282, 308

Françoise d'Orléans, 34

Frederick William II, King of Prussia, 56, 62

Frederick William III, King of Prussia, 177

Frederick William IV, King of Prussia, 303

Garnier-Pagès, Étienne, 251, 253, 280

Gazette de France, 210

Genlis, Charles-Alexis, Comte de (later Marquis de Sillery), 27, 28, 34, 42, 87, 90

Genlis, Stéphanie-Félicité Ducrest de Saint-Aubin, Comtesse de, 25; at the Palais-Royal, 27, 28–9; early life and marriage, 27; character, 27–8; and the Duc de Chartres, 28–9, 34; consolidates her position, 33; calls on Voltaire, 34; governess to children of Philippe-Égalité, 34–5, 51–2; her philosophy of education, 35–6, 38–40; and Laclos, 46; education of Louis-Philippe, 51–2; Marie-Adélaïde demands dismissal, 53; in England, 54, 75; returns to France, 75; at Tournai, 76; leaves Dumouriez, 82; in Switzerland, 88; claims on Louis-Philippe for her services, 92; repudiation of Orléans, 99; meets Marie-Amélie, 125; death, 138n.

George III, King of England, 105

George IV (Prince Regent), 134

Gérard, Etienne-Maurice, Marshal, 175, 203, 215, 223, 324, 325

Germany, 302, 303

Girardin, Émile, de, 324

Girondins, 57, 58, 59, 73, 74, 75, 87, 90

Gluck, C. W., 28

Gouvion de Saint-Cyr, Marquis de. *See* Saint-Cyr

Great Britain, France declares war on, 74; Louis-Philippe's views of policy of, 119; recognizes July Monarchy, 178, 180; and Belgium, 179, 203, 215; and Eastern Question, 216, 257–9, 263, 264, 265, 267, 268; de Broglie and, 223; and Portugal, 226; Talleyrand and, 238; improved relations with France, 279; and Spanish Marriage question, 289–91, 298, 299–301

Gregory XVI, Pope, 168, 170, 202
Grenville, William, Lord, 105, 110
Greville, Charles, 173, 188n., 196,
    216n., 248, 292, 301, 302, 334
Guizot, François-Pierre, 125; and
    Louis-Philippe, 136, 171; sup-
    ports Orléans solution, 149; lack
    of flexibility, 164; minister of the
    interior, 173; as historian and
    statesman, 173-4; and popular
    insurrections, 182; and Polignac
    trial, 183; in opposition, 188,
    196; minister of education, 212,
    214, 215, 218; admiration for
    English political parties, 223;
    rift with Thiers, 224; refuses co-
    operation with Molé, 242; in
    coalition against Molé, 251, 252,
    253, 254; ambassador in London,
    259, 260, 263; in Soult's Cabinet,
    269; his political ideas, 269-70;
    and Algeria, 278; rejects reform
    proposals, 282, 283; and elections
    of 1842, 283; and Aberdeen, 291;
    and the Legitimists, 292-3; Louis-
    Philippe and, 294; disclaims
    annexation of Marquesas Islands,
    295; and Spanish marriage ques-
    tion, 298-9, 300-1; Louis-
    Philippe's view of, 304; and
    universal suffrage, 308; resigna-
    tion, 320; escapes, 324

Hardie, Keir, 136
Hardenberg, Karl Augustus von,
    Prince, 126
Hébert, Jacques-René, 59, 73
Hélène, Princess of Mecklenburg-
    Schwerin, 247, 284, 287, 325,
    333
Henri, Duc de Bordeaux (Henri V).
    See Bordeaux, Duc de
Hérault de Séchelles, Marie-Jean, 28

Holland, and Belgium, 177, 203, 211,
    215, 252
Hugo, Victor, 248, 269, 272
Humann, —, 212, 238

Ibrahim Pasha, 257, 267
Isabella II, Queen of Spain, 289, 300,
    302
Italy, 186, 302, 303

Jacobin Club, 52, 80, 81
Jacobins, 53, 55, 58, 75, 76
Jacqueminot, General, 317, 318, 319
Jarnac, —, 300, 301
Jemappes, battle of, 71-2
Joinville, François, Duc de, 134, 261,
    275, 276, 286, 291, 296, 304, 332
Jongh, Eselina de, 280
Jost, —, 89-90, 92, 93
Jourdan, Jean-Baptiste, Comte, 61
Journal des Débats, 247
Journal du Peuple, 280-1
July Monarchy, ideological hostility
    to, 162-8; Catholics and, 168-70;
    differences among supporters, 171;
    ridicule of, 172; Powers recog-
    nize, 178-9; anti-clerical riots,
    189-90; Périer's ministry, 192-5;
    social unrest, 197-9, 208-9; civil
    list under, 206; press campaign
    against, 204-5; de Broglie's
    ministry, 212-15; disorders of
    1834, 218-220, 222; limitations
    on freedom, 218-19; Rue Trans-
    nonain incident, 220; arrest of
    ringleaders of Société des Droits
    de l'Homme, 222; resignation of
    de Broglie, 223; ministerial
    crises, 223-4; new ministry under
    de Broglie, 225; uncertainty
    about constitutional functions,
    225; trial of April conspirators,
    226-9; September Laws, 235-6;

fall of de Broglie, 238; Thiers' ministry, 239–41; Comte Mole's ministry, 241–3, 247, 249–50; coalition fights elections, 253–4; Soult's ministry, 256–7; new Thiers ministry, 260–2; Soult's new cabinet, 269; Soult-Guizot ministry, 279–81, 287–8; reform proposals, 281–2; difficulties after July, 1846, 305–10; scandals under, 309–10

July Revolution, 141–52
Jullien, Mme, 58

Keat, Admiral, 119
Kellerman, François-Christophe, Marshal, 62, 63, 65, 66
Kent, Edward Augustus, Duke of, 102, 105, 115, 120, 134, 138

Laclos, Pierre-Ambroise Choderlos de, 43, 45–6, 47, 49, 50, 54, 55, 63, 87, 91
Lacordaire, Henri, 168–9, 170
Lafarge, Marie, 279
Lafayette, Marie-Joseph, Marquis de, 41, 49, 50, 59, commands an army against Austria, 61, 62; goes over to enemy; 83; in July Revolution, 139, 143, 144, 148, 151, 152; and the National Guard, 159, 172, 181, 187; replaced as commander of National Guard, 188; and Poland, 202, 203; death, 222
Laffitte, Jacques, 136; finances Le National, 139; partisan of Louis-Philippe, 143, 147, 149; minister without portfolio, 175; his ministry, 184–5, 189, 190, 193; in opposition, 195, 208, 209, 214
La Harpe, Jean-Francois de, 34

Lamarque, General, 177, 194, 201n., 208
Lamartine, Alphonse de, 27, 221, 236, 253, 259, 261, 282, 288, 307, 310, 314, 325, 328
Lamoricière, Louis, General, 248, 277, 323, 324
Lamballe, Marie-Thérèse, Princesse de, 67
Lamballe, Prince de, 21
Lamennais, Felicite de, Abbé, 168, 169, 170, 227
Lamoignon, Chrétien François de, 45
Laski, H., 170
Lebrun, —, 39
Ladru-Rollin, Alexandre, 227, 280, 311, 317
Legitimists, 166, 189, 195, 206, 236, 247, 250, 251, 254, 292, 333
Leopold I, King of the Belgians, 134, 180, 203, 267, 272
Leopold II, Emperor of Austria, 56
Leopold, Prince of Saxe-Coburg, 289, 298, 299, 300
Leroux, Pierre, 163, 227
Liancourt, Duc de, 42, 43
Liverpool, Robert, 2nd Earl, 119
Lobau, Georges, Comte de, 188, 199, 209, 232
Lodi, battle of, 60
Loménie de Brienne, Étienne, 44
Lothringer, Abbé, 91
Louis, Baron, 174, 193, 212
Louis, XIV, King of France, 16, 17
Louis XV, King of France, 17, 19, 20, 21, 23, 25, 30
Louis XVI, King of France, 15, 30, 31, 54, 59, 75, 77–8
Louis XVIII, King of France, and Louis-Philippe, 97, 98, 104, 105, 109, 110, 118, 123, 132, 134; acceptance of Constitution, 122; enters Paris, 123; and Napoleon's

landing at Cannes, 126; flees to
Ghent, 128; second Restoration,
130
Louise, Queen of the Belgians, 120,
134, 211, 275, 284, 290, 291, 297,
301
Louis-Napoleon, Emperor of France.
See Napoleon III
Louis-Philippe, King of the French,
birth, 29, 337-40; education, 35,
37, 38, 39-40, 51-2; created Duc
de Chartres, 37; and Mme Genlis, 41, 51, 76, 88, 91, 92; joins
Jacobin Club, 52; his diary, 53-4;
takes up Army command, 55;
garrison life, 56; commands
troops in Valenciennes, 57; on his
morals, 60; serves under Duc de
Biron, 60; in Army of North,
60-1; heroism at Quiévrain, 61;
in Army of the Centre, 62; promoted lieutenant-general, 62;
Valmy campaign 65-6; interview
with Danton, 68-70; at Jemappes,
71-2; in Belgian campaign, 72; at
Neerwinden, 79; secret meeting
with Dumouriez, 80; implicated
with Dumouriez, 81; deserts
with Dumouriez, 83; in Switzerland, 88, 89; works as schoolmaster, 89-90; develops hatred
for Jacobins, 91-2; inconsolable
at his father's death, 91; and
Marianne Banzori, 92-3; tours
Scandinavia, 96-7; advocate of
constitutional monarchy, 98; in
Philadelphia, 100; received by
Washington, 100; tours America,
101; captured by English 102; in
Cuba, 102; exile in England
begins, 102; tastes and aptitudes,
103; reconciliation with Artois
104-5; received by George III,
105; established at Twickenham,
106; visits Louis XVIII at Hartwell, 109-10; death of his
brothers, 111, 112; and Marie-
Amélie, 112-14; Spanish adventures, 114-15, 117-19; marriage
to Marie-Amélie, 117; views on
English policies, 119; domestic
life in Palermo, 120; and Sicilian
politics, 121; returns to France,
123; A.D.C. to Artois, 126;
returns to Paris after Napoleon's
landing, 127; offered command
of Army of North, 128; releases
troops from King's orders, 128;
withdraws to Twickenham, 129;
Wellington on, 129; Alex-
ander I's opinion of, 129-30;
speaks at Chamber of Peers, 131;
forced to return to exile, 131;
Louis XVIII's distrust of, 132,
134; domestic life at Twickenham, 132, 133-4; his children,
134, 276; his fortune, 134-5,
205-6; life at the Palais-Royal,
136-9; warns Charles X against
rejection of Charter, 141; *Le
National* calls for, 146; accepts
Lieutenant-Generalcy, 151; accepts Crown as King of the
French, 155; dealings with
Charles X after July 30, 155-7;
political ideas, 160, 162-4; his
religion, 168; hesitant policy of
his Government, 171-2; his
accessibility, 172; deterioration of
prestige, 173; first ministry 173-
5; and Charles X's ministers, 183,
186-7; support for Périer, 194;
indignities, 199; press campaign
against him, 204-5; and civil
list, 206; experiment in personal
government, 209-10, 212; assas-

sination attempts, 214, 232–3, 240, 244, 267, 305, 307; view of his rôle in constitutional monarchy, 225; personal conduct of foreign affairs, 225–6; Thiers' view of, 234, 235; and Thiers, 239, 267; opposes Spanish intervention, 241; urges political unity, 250; praise for Molé, 253; and Eastern Question, 257–9, 263–4, 267; political outlook, 269–70; Hugo on, 269, 272; Lewis Cass describes, 271; on death of Talleyrand, 271; his daily routine, 272–5; Vernet's portrait, 275–6; and Algeria, 277–8; and reform proposals, 281–2, 283, 312; calamity of Orléans' death, 283–5; and Anglo-French relations, 289; receives Victoria at Chateau d'Eu, 290–1; character in old age, 294, 304–5, 307; and Guizot, 294, 304; visits Windsor, 296–7; and Spanish marriage question, 298–9, 301–2; condemns banquet campaign, 313; unwillingness to use troops against rioters, 315–16; accepts Guizot's resignation, 319; at National Guard review, 323–4; abdicates, 324–5; flight to England, 328–30; at Claremont, 330–1, 332; English opinions of, 331; last meeting with Thiers, 334; last days and death, 334

Louvet de Couvrai, Jean-Baptiste, 75

Lückner, Nicolas, Marshal, 61, 63, 91

Luisa, Infanta of Spain, 298, 300

Lyon, insurrection at, 199–201; strike of 1834, 219–20; conditions at, 270

Macaulay, Thomas Babington, Lord, 33, 282

Macdonald, Jacques-Étienne, Marshal (later Duc de Tarente), 61, 72, 124, 126–7, 128, 136

Mack von Leiberich, Karl, General, 79, 80

Mahmoud II, Sultan, 215, 257

Malta, 112

Marat, Jean-Paul, 59, 74, 76

March, Comte de la, 42

Maret, Hugues, Duc de Bassano, 224

Maria Cristina, Queen of Spain. See Cristina of Spain

Marie, Duchess of Württemberg, 120, 254, 275

Marie-Adélaïde, Duchesse d'Orléans, 40–41, 53, 87, 91, 99, 101, 105, 116, 134

Marie-Amélie, Princesse de Bourbon, Queen of France, 112; her view of Louis-Philippe, 113; Talleyrand's opinion, 113; description of herself, 113; marriage to Louis-Philippe, 117; encourages Louis-Philippe's Spanish adventure, 120; received at the Tuileries, 124; meets Mme Genlis, 125; in England, 134; meeting with Thiers, 147; anxieties for Louis-Philippe's well-being, 297

Marie-Antoinette, Queen of France, 26, 31, 112

Marie-Caroline, Queen of Sicily, 112, 113, 116, 117, 121

Mallet du Pan, Jacques, 97, 105

Marmont, Auguste, Marshal (Duc de Raguse), 142, 143, 144, 145, 149–50

Marrast, Armand, 165, 236, 261, 307, 316

Mauguin, —, 160, 195, 208

Maupeou, René-Nicolas, 25

Mecklenburg-Schwerin, Hélène, Princess of (Duchesse d'Orléans), 247, 284, 287, 325, 333

Mehemet Ali, Viceroy of Egypt, 215–16, 248, 257, 258, 259, 263, 265, 267

Melbourne, William, 2nd Viscount, 193n., 264, 267

Merlin, Philippe-Antoine, Comte de, 77, 79

Metternich, Klemens, Prince, 122, 125, 126, 129, 176, 177, 179, 191, 210, 226, 240, 241, 254, 289, 303

Michelet, Jules, 307

Mignet, François-Auguste, 146

Miguel, Dom, 202

Mills, J. S., 165n.

Mirabeau, Honoré, Comte de, 42, 46, 50, 52, 59

Miranda, Francisco, 78, 79

Mode, La, 236

Molé, Louis-Mathieu, Comte, minister of foreign affairs, 173, 179; offered premiership, 224; earlier life, 241; becomes premier, 241; his policy, 242, 243, 247, 249–50; holds majority against coalition, 252, 253; resigns, 254; attempts to form new cabinet, 320, 321

Molleville, Bertrand de, 67

Montalembert, Charles, Comte de, 168, 169, 170, 185, 309, 313

Montalivet, Comte de, 74, 149, 185, 187–8, 190, 193, 206, 250, 273, 274, 319

Montesquiou, Marquise de, 88, 89, 92, 93, 95, 96

Montesson, Mme de, 25, 29

Montjoie, Gustave, Comte de, 88, 95, 106

Montpensier, Antoine, Duc de (I), birth, 34; at Belle-Chasse, 37;

Louis-Philippe and, 52, 60, 75, 76, 78; serves with Army of the North, 60, 61, 66, 70; with Army of the Alps, 87; held as hostage by the Directory, 99; exile in England, 102; ill-health, 104; death, 111

Montpensier, Antoine, Duc de (II), son of Louis-Philippe, 134, 276, 298, 299, 300

Moore, Thomas, 137

Moreau, Jean-Victor, 61

Morey, Pierre, 230–2, 238

Morning Chronicle, 135

Morocco, 295–6

Morris, Gouverneur, 54n., 95–6, 100, 104

Mortemart, Duc de, 145, 146, 149, 150

Mortier, Edouard-Adolphe, Marshal (Duc de Trévise), 61, 126, 128, 136, 224, 233, 310

Napier, Sir Charles, 266, 267

Naples, 120, 303

Napoleon I, Emperor, 52, 60, 100, 104, 112, 122, 126, 127, 261–2

Napoleon III, Emperor (Louis-Napoleon), 243, 262, 265–6, 333

National, Le, 139, 142, 146 149, 166, 217, 219, 236, 261, 267, 316

National Association, the, 194

Necker, Jacques, 41, 43, 45, 48

Neerwinden, battle of, 79, 294

Nemours, Louis, Duc de, 124, 180, 203, 275, 276, 277, 287, 326, 329

Nesselrode, Charles, Count, 176

Netherlands, French attack on, 59, 74

Ney, Michel, Prince de la Moskova, 127, 139, 183

Nice, 70

Nicholas I, Czar, 177, 240

Noailles, Louis, Vicomte de, 42

Normanby, Lord, 302, 327
Norway, Louis-Philippe visits, 96
Notables, Council of, 41

Orléans, Ferdinand-Louis-Charles, son of Louis-Philippe, birth of, 120; Austrian marriage project, 240; marriage to Hélène of Mecklenburg-Schwerin, 247; his views of the times, 269; in Vernet's portrait, 275; service abroad, 276; death, 283-5
Orléans, Françoise d', 34
Orléans, Jean-Baptiste-Gaston, Duc d', 16
Orléans, Louis (the Pious), Duc d', 17, 18
Orléans, Louis-Philippe-Joseph, Duc d' (Philippe-Égalité), at Parlement de Paris, 16, 20; birth at Saint-Cloud, 18; education and upbringing, 18-20; baptized, 19; presented to Louis XV, 19; amatory adventures, 20; marriage to Louise-Marie-Adélaïde de Bourbon-Penthièvre, 21-2; character, 24; a popular figure, 24; incurs enmity of Marie-Antoinette, 26; and Mme de Genlis, 28-9, 34; son and heir, 29; on active service, 31; sinecure command in army, 31; hedonistic life, 31; visits to England, 31-2; balloon ascent, 32; financial straits, 32-3; development of Palais-Royal, 33, becomes Duc d'Orléans, 33; entrusts sons' eduction to Mme Genlis, 35; cleavage with his wife, 40-1, 53; emerges as political figure, 44; influence of Laclos, 45-6; as deputy of the noblesse, 46, 47; Mirabeau's view of, 46, 50; his cahiers, 47; at the

States-General, 47-8; escapes to England, 50; returns to France, 52; renounces regency, 55; in Paris for final crisis of monarchy, 67; adopts name Égalité, 68; and the Mountain, 73, 74; Marat speaks in favour of, 76; testifies before the Convention, 78; votes for death of Louis XVI, 78; under surveillance, 87; imprisoned, 87; trial before Fouquier-Tinville, 91
Orléans, Louis-Philippe le Gros, Duc d', 17, 18, 20, 25, 26, 33
Orléans, Louise-Henriette de Bourbon-Conti, Duchesse d', 17
Orléans, Louise-Marie-Adélaïde de Bourbon-Penthièvre, Duchesse d'. See Marie-Adélaïde
Orléans, Philippe, Duc d', 16
Orléans, Philippe, Duc d' (Regent of France), 17
Otranto, Joseph, Duke of. See Fouché
Ottoman Empire, 215-6, 264
Oudinot, Nicolas-Charles, Marshal, 61
Ouessant, battle of, 31, 32

Pache, Jean-Nicolas, 73, 74
Paine, Thomas, 103
Palafox y Melzi, Jose de, Duke of Saragossa, 114
Palais-Royal, development of, 33
Palermo, Louis-Philippe at, 116, 117, 120-1, 122
Palmerston, Henry Temple, Viscount, 116, 179-80, 203, 226, 257, 258, 263, 264, 265, 267, 268, 285, 300, 301, 302, 303
Paris, population of, 161; conditions in eighteen-thirties, 164, 270; cholera epidemic, 206-7; unrest in, 208-9

Paris, Louis-Philippe, Comte de, 284, 285, 325
Paris Commune, 73
Parti de résistance, 171, 173, 191, 212, 239, 267
Parti du mouvement, 171, 191
Pasquier, Étienne-Denis, Duc de, 187, 227, 228
Peel, Sir Robert, 289, 295, 333
Penthièvre, Jean-Marie de Bourbon, Duc de, 20, 31, 32, 87, 290
Penthièvre, Louise-Marie-Adelaïde de Bourbon. See Marie-Adélaïde, Duchesse d'Orléans
Pépin, Théodore, 232-3, 238
Pecqueur, Constantin, 163
Périer, Casimir Pierre (Casimir-Périer), 136, 143, 144, 145; support of Orléans solution, 149; social policy, 164; minister without portfolio, 174; prime minister, 191-2; character and ideas, 192-3; his administration, 193-5, 196; and social unrest, 197, 199, 200-1; foreign policy, 201-3; and civil list, 206; end of his ministry, 206; death from cholera, 207
Pétion, Jérôme, 42, 43, 47, 54, 75, 76, 91
Philipon, Charles, 204, 270
Pillnitz, Declaration of, 56
Pitt, William (the Younger), 105
Pius IX, Pope, 303
Pococke, George, 133
Poland, 169, 186, 202-3, 240, 279
Polignac, Jules de, Prince, 139, 141, 143, 183, 187
Political banquets. See Banquet campaign
Pomare, Queen of Tahiti, 295
Pons-Saint-Maurice, Comte de, 19
Portland Place, London, 31

Portugal, France and, 202; succession problem, 226; Dom Miguel eliminated, 226
Priouret, Roger, 151, 160
Pritchard, George, 295, 296
Proudhon, Pierre-Joseph, 306-7
Prussia, French campaign against, 61, 62-5; negotiations with, 70; accepts situation in France, 179; and Belgium, 179; and the Eastern Question, 263
Puyraveau, Audry de, 143, 144, 217, 228

Quélen, Mgr. de, Archbishop of Paris, 167
Quinet, Edgar, 176n.
Quinette, —, 130

Railways, in 1840, 161, 283n.
Raspail, François, 165, 217, 227 229
Rawdon, Lady Charlotte, 111
Recouly, Raymond, 92
Réformateur, Le, 228, 236
Réforme, La, 307, 313, 316
Reichenau, Louis-Philippe at, 89-90, 92-3
Rémusat, François, Comte de, 142, 268
Restoration, the, 122-3; second, 130
Richelieu, Armand, Duc de, 131
Richmond, Louis-Philippe at, 106, 332
Rigny, Admiral de, 224
Robespierre, Maximilien, 42, 43, 74
Rochambeau, Jean-Baptiste, Comte de, 59
Rohan Chabot, Vicomte de, 121, 130, 133
Roll, Baron de, 97
Roussin, Admiral, 216
Rousseau, Jean-Jacques, 28, 30, 36, 38, 51, 78

Rouzet de Folmont, Comte de, 105–6, 116, 124
Royer-Collard, Pierre, 173, 236, 252
Rumigny, General, 218, 329
Russell, Lord John, 331
Russia, and France, 122, 176–7, 179, 238; and Turkey, 216, 257–8, 259, 263, 264

Saint Cyr, Laurent de Gouvion, Marquis de, 127
St. Leonards, 332, 333, 334
Saint-Simon, Claude-Henri, Comte de, 162, 163
Saint-Vincent, Robert de, 15
Sainte-Beuve, Charles-Augustin, 38n., 310
Sand, Georges, 199n.
Savoy, 70
Say, Jean-Baptiste, 161
Scheffer, Ary, 145, 147, 269
Sébastiani, Horace, 151, 174; foreign minister, 185, 186, 193, 203
Sébastiani, Tiburce, 318
Second Republic, proclamation of, 328
Secret societies, 165, 217, 218, 280
Sercey, Henriette de, 37
Servan, —, 68
Seville, Duke of, 298, 300, 301n.
Shaftesbury, Earl of, 136
Sheridan, R. B., 32, 75
Sicily, 112, 117, 120–1
Siècle, Le, 317
Sieyès, Emmanuel-Joseph, 42, 47
Sillery, Charles-Alexis, Marquis de. See Genlis, Comte de
Société des Droits de l'Homme, 165, 217, 218, 219, 220, 222
Société des Saisons, 251, 256
Soult, Nicolas-Jean de Dieu (Duke of Dalmatia), 118, 185, 187, 200, 209, 212, 223, 254–5; forms

ministry, 256; foreign policy, 257, 258, 259; new ministry, 269; retired with rank of Marshal-General, 312
Spain, France declares war on, 74; Marie-Adélaïde exiled in, 101, 105; Louis-Philippe refused persion to land in, 105; Louis-Philippe's political adventures in, 114–15, 117–18; problem of succession, 225–6, 241; French policy towards, 240, 243; marriage question, 289-91, 298–302
Spectator, 331
States-General, 47
Stendhal (Henri Beyle), 152n., 270
Stowe, 109
Straits Convention, 279
Switzerland, Louis-Philippe in, 88–90, 92–4; liberal movement, 302
Syms, Nancy (La belle Paméla), 37, 42, 54, 75, 76
Syria, 215, 257, 259, 263, 264, 265, 267

Tahiti, 295
Talleyrand, Charles-Maurice de, Prince, 27, 28, 42, 95, 99n.; on Marie-Amélie, 113; approach to Duc d'Orléans, 126; and July Revolution, 144, 148, 151; ambassador to London, 178–9, 180, 193; and partition of Belgium, 202, 203; last diplomatic coup, 226
Tarente, Duc de. See Macdonald, Jacques-Étienne
Temps, Le, 198
Teste, Jean-Baptiste, 309
Thiers, Louis-Adolphe, founds Le National, 139; presses Orléanist solution at Neuilly, 147–8; support of new regime, 157; theory

of monarchy, 160; and anti-clerical riots, 189; his oratory, 192, 196, 212; minister of the interior, 212-13, 214, 215; anti-republicanism, 217; his view of Louis-Philippe, 234, 235; prime minister, 239; his policy in office, 239-41; in opposition, 242, 243, 250, 251, 252, 253, 254; engineers overthrow of Soult's government, 259; forms new ministry, 260; and the Eastern Question, 264, 265, 267; resignation, 268; Louis-Philippe on, 271-2; supports reforms, 282; opposition to Guizot, 302, 305; and political banquets, 310, 311; refuses co-operation with Molé, 320; summoned to form ministry, 321; attempts to form new cabinet, 322; last meeting with Louis-Philippe, 334

Times, The, 183n., 273, 333

Tocqueville, Alexis de, 165n., 266, 276, 313

Toynbee, Arnold, 147n.

Treilhard, Jean-Baptiste, Comte, 77, 79

Trélat, Ulysse, 165, 217, 228

Tribune, La, 217, 218, 220, 228, 261

Tristan, Flora, 164

Turgot, Robert-Jacques, 30, 41

Turkey, 215-16, 257, 264, 267

Tuscany, 303

Twickenham, Louis-Philippe at, 103, 106, 121, 129, 130, 132, 133, 332

United Provinces, 74, 78

United States of America, recognized by France, 30; Louis-Philippe resides in, 100-2; French dispute with, 223, 225

Utopian theorists, 306-7

Valence, Comte de, 42, 55, 65, 79, 80, 83, 136

Valmy, campaign of, 62-6

Vernet, Horace, 275

Vergennes, Charles-Gravier, Comte de, 30

Vergniaud, Pierre, 91

Versailles, restoration of, 248

Victoria, Queen of England, 290-1, 292, 296, 297, 298, 299, 301, 303, 331

Vienna, Congress of, 126, 130

Vigée-Lebrun, Marie-Anne, 107

Villèle, Jean, Comte, 132, 134, 137, 173

Vitrolles, —, 122, 144, 145

Voltaire, François-Marie-Arouet de, 34, 198

Wages, in eighteen-thirties, 164, 200

Wales, Prince of, 31, 105, 110

Warsaw, 203

Washington, George, 100, 101

Waterloo, 130

Watson, Richard, Bishop of Llandaff, 107

Wellesley, Henry, 119

Wellington, Arthur Wellesley, Duke of, 114, 122, 126, 129, 130, 178, 188, 191, 296

Wesley, John, 38n.

William IV, King of England (Duke of Clarence), 105, 216n.

Windsor, Louis-Philippe visits, 296-7

Wyndham, Mrs., 37